TOWER OF SECRETS

TOWER OF SECRETS

A Real Life Spy Thriller

Victor Sheymov

NAVAL INSTITUTE PRESS
Annapolis, Maryland

Library of Congress Cataloging-in-Publication Data
Sheymov, Victor, 1946–
    Tower of secrets : a real life spy thriller / Victor Sheymov.
        p.   cm.
    ISBN 1-55750-764-3 (alk. paper)
    1. Soviet Union. Komitet gosudarstvennoĭ bezopasnosti.
2. Sheymov, Victor, 1946– . 3. Intelligence officers—Soviet Union—Biography.
I. Title.
HV8225.S46   1993
327.12'092—dc20
[B]   93-11386

Printed in the United States of America on acid-free paper ∞

9 8 7 6 5 4 3 2

First printing

To my wife, Olga

This book presents a true description of issues and events. However, for a variety of reasons, some names, times, places, and minor operational details have been altered.

Contents

Introduction

AS A PROFESSIONAL, I find that the way intelligence is portrayed in books and the movies is often grossly distorted. Along with most other professionals, I believe that our mission has little to do with reckless car chases and wild shoot-outs. Intelligence ends with the first shot fired. Real intelligence much more resembles a fascinating chess game, much complicated by the fact that not all the figures and their positions are known to the players. So in this book I have tried to show how the world of intelligence actually works. While I wrote the book for the general reader, I expect that professional intelligence officers may find some of the information in it useful, particularly where it complements their own knowledge and experience.

The first part of this book was written in 1988, two years before my existence was revealed. However, the decision to publish the whole story came much later, when the events described could be told publicly. This may seem like a long delay, but in fact most of the information is new to the general public, and indeed to many in the intelligence community as well. It is quite usual for intelligence matters to enter the public domain at least twenty years after the actual events took place. I should also note that no intelligence agency has had the right to review the manuscript, which makes this book absolutely uncensored. By the same token, I am morally obligated to limit the discussion to the boundaries which would assure that it would not have an adverse impact on the interests of the national security of the United States.

A natural question, particularly in light of the fast-moving political and social events in Eastern Europe and the former Soviet Union, is whether the events that took place more than a decade ago still bear relevance today and especially tomorrow. In my view, the answer is clearly yes. The common notion that Communism is dead badly needs clarification. The important point here is the definition of Communism. It cannot be viewed simply as a political movement. Communism is not only an ideology, it is also a mentality, a mind-set that is still alive and well. Historians will study the phenomenon of Communism and its impact on the human race—that at the very least it took dozens of millions of lives around the world—for generations to come. But now, perhaps, is too early for that. Too many participants of the so-called Cold War—which sometimes took rather hot turns—are still living, and many of them have a vested interest in having the full truth remain unknown. My point here is that for some time to come the West will be dealing with those who were brought up within the communist system and are still driven by a communist mentality. Therefore, it is imperative to understand those people, who for at least three generations were raised in an atmosphere of hatred to the West, if they are to be helped to understand democratic values and to join Western civilization. So for me this book is a logical extension of the mission I gave myself when I and my family defected in 1980. I have attempted to expose the communist mentality as it operated in the KGB, the dedicated instrument of communist power.

The KGB is a most sophisticated, deviously intelligent organization, and far more dangerous than the bunch of brutal thugs often presented to the general public. The massively multilayered complexity of the KGB is mind-boggling. Few people, even within the KGB, know enough to truly comprehend it. Despite the general perception of Soviet incompetence, it should be remembered that the Soviets drew on a culture that produced a long succession of great mathematicians and chess grand masters. The fact is that whenever the Soviets established a major priority, they usually achieved extraordinary results. Soviet space, nuclear, laser, and eavesdropping technologies are just a few examples. The operation of the KGB was considered a major priority, so the resources of the huge country were at its total disposal, and the KGB made full use of them. As a result, the KGB is probably the most deliberately and carefully created large organization in the world. All the parts of the KGB I describe are still in place. The KGB may have been renamed, but no one has been fired in the name of reform. Not for the first time, the KGB is in a "data collection" mode. Still a million strong, it has no real budget (it is, in fact, a major profit center), and cost is no object. It is a classic example of management by objective.

After much thought, I decided to write this book as a third-person account. For me it is a natural form of expression. One of the characteristics of intelligence is that one develops the habit of viewing oneself from aside, to ensure objectivity of judgment. That habit becomes second nature, and I believe events are seen more clearly from this vantage point. Besides, in this introduction I have almost exhausted my reserve of *I*s.

For the reader's reference, a list of the KGB units pertinent to the events described here is presented in the appendix at the end of the book.

Acknowledgments

I WISH TO EXPRESS MY DEEPEST GRATITUDE specifically to those men and women of the United States Central Intelligence Agency who had the expertise to design and the skill to execute this spectacularly successful exfiltration operation, decisively defeating such a formidable opponent, the KGB.

I was very fortunate to have the vast talents and experience of my editors, Roger Jellinek and Eden-Lee Murray, contributing to this book. Roger Jellinek has also been most effective as my agent.

I would like to express my wholehearted thanks to the Naval Institute Press for a great team effort in publishing this book. In particular, I would like to thank Press Director Vice Admiral Robert Dunn, USN (Ret.), Senior Editor Anthony Chiffolo, and Publicist Susan Artigiani for their outstanding contributions. I would also like to thank Tom Epley, whose enthusiasm and expertise rallied support behind this project.

Part I

THE KEEP

CHAPTER

1

SPRING 1979.

The door lock clicked softly. Victor hesitated for an instant by the elevator, long enough to hear its lumbering progress far below. He turned abruptly and raced down the eighteen flights of stairs. He was late, as always.

The bus stop was just across the street. Considering what most Muscovite commuters had to contend with, he felt himself lucky to be able to get to work in less than forty-five minutes.

The location of his apartment was enviable: near the Moscow Ring Road, and next to a large park. A pleasant setting. It was on the top floor of a new building, one of several in a complex. The buildings were only nine stories tall, so by Moscow standards the area on that edge of the park was relatively uncrowded. However, the park was quite a magnet for those who lived in the surrounding district, and on weekends people came from as far as ten bus stops away. There weren't many stores around, but there was little or nothing to buy in suburban shops anyway. Theaters and concert halls were inconveniently far, but Victor was finding less and less time for that anyway.

And he certainly couldn't stop now to enjoy the beautiful late-spring morning. He sprinted across the street and managed to scramble onto the departing bus, barely winded even after the stairs and the dash for his ride. At thirty-three, he was in good shape.

His stop was midway between the two terminals of Route #165, Metro stops Kaluzshskaya and Yugo-Zapadnaya—both of them commuter destinations. Getting on the bus was generally not a problem, and this morning was no exception. He squeezed gently between a well-padded lady holding a huge Puma sports bag and a snoozy middle-aged man with a lusty whiff of last night's party on his breath. Victor even managed to unfold a newspaper for the ride—*Pravda*, the Central Committee paper, of course. It was necessary, essential even, for him to be up on the latest news even before entering his office. Or rather, to be aware of the nuances in the latest interpretation of the news.

How did that story go? A new prison inmate is asked why he's in jail.

"For not reading the morning paper," comes the response.

"What?"

"All I did was walk into my office one morning. The Party Organization Secretary came in, looked at the Politburo portraits on the wall, and asked sternly why I hadn't removed the picture of the stupid one. I asked, 'Which one is that?' I hadn't read the paper yet. And here I am."

The punch line barely concealed the warning. Victor opened his paper. He skimmed the first page and then the last. *Pravda* usually consisted of six pages. On the front page was the major political news, editorials on important political campaigns, and Decrees of the Party Central Committee. While many of those in any position of power regarded *Pravda* as boring, for anyone connected to the realm of power it was a must. It actually contained a great deal of information—if one knew how to read between the lines. Although articles were written in the officialese developed during the post-Revolution period, in every article there lurked a subtle Aesopian guide to the Party's latest position on the issues of the day. The paper provided clues for the correct trimming of one's political weather vane, to align it safely with the treacherous winds of the Party line.

The last page contained regular and sports news as well as miscellaneous tidbits worthy of *Pravda*'s attention. Nothing was included by chance, so Victor had to pay attention.

The bus came to its stop at the Belyayevo Metro station, the point of origin for Victor's twenty-five-minute train ride. It was still possible to find a seat on the train at this station. Those down the line had to commute the hard way, jammed in and standing up. But as it was common courtesy in Moscow public transport to give up one's seat to the elderly, the handicapped, and women, in that order, Victor didn't even bother to sit. Instead, he took a comfortable stance in a corner. He unfurled his newspaper again and began a closer perusal. Nothing new this morning. The inside pages really were boring. The train was absolutely packed by the time it pulled into the Kuznetsky Most station, at the center of the capital, where a thick stream of white-collar commuters poured from each of the sliding doors.

Like ants the crowd separated into several smaller streams, and Victor flowed along with the largest one. His brisk three-minute walk via a short-cut took him through three consecutive inner courtyards into Dzerzhinsky Street, so narrow that he could see only the granite wall of the first two floors of the building opposite. He crossed to an oak door with a permanently curtained window. A small sign indicated, "Entrance 3."

Once he'd shown his pass to a security guard in military uniform, Victor went through another door into a small, dark lobby where a crowd was waiting for the elevators. Exercise first thing in the morning helped wake him up. He loped up six flights of a dark, very unfriendly stairway that wound around the elevator shaft, pushed open a heavy oak door, and strode about a hundred feet along the fourth-floor corridor to another, more formal, and lighter stairway across the lobby from Entrance 4.

Victor walked quickly up the remaining seven flights. The door had a plate with only a number on it. All the doors in the building, except the bathrooms marked simply "M" and "W," had only three-digit numbers on them. The first digit indicated the floor, the other two meant nothing in particular.

Victor approached the one numbered 728 and began to work the electronic combination lock: 7 and 3 punched together. Hold 7, release 3, then punch 2. The lock released. Victor pushed the door open and entered another corridor with five doors down each side. His was the second door on the right. It was unmarked. He opened it and entered. Victor looked up at the pair of large clocks on the wall. It was 6:07 A.M. Greenwich Mean Time, 9:07 A.M. in Moscow. KGB Major Victor Sheymov was ready for another day's work.

The space was distinctly uninspiring. It was a large office, some five hundred square feet. The twelve-foot ceiling did little to improve the impression of coldness. Apart from the two clocks, there was nothing on the dirty bluish-grey walls except the standard portrait of Lenin and a coatrack by the door—a board with a row of hooks. White, semitransparent curtains were permanently drawn across the large, oak-trimmed windows—a security measure to prevent other KGB officers whose windows faced into the inner courtyard from seeing into this top-secret place. The only furniture consisted of four old, heavily scuffed wooden desks, four free-standing safes, and several chairs. There was no trace of any attempt to make the room feel hospitable.

"Hi, Michael!" Victor greeted the KGB officer with whom he shared the office. "What's up?"

Mikhail "Michael" Zubov was quite a character—one would even be tempted to say caricature because of the first impression he made. The most startling of Michael's features were his teeth. His well-formed lips could not conceal the lower front teeth that stuck straight forward in a most challenging way. The corresponding upper teeth were a little less assertive, but one tooth on either side was missing. Although he was almost completely bald, he wore unusually long, blond sideburns—scraggly parentheses bracketing the odd features in between. These small, furry reefs seemed to take on a life of their own, giving him an air of perpetual absentmindedness. Belying his appearance, however, was a mind like a steel trap. Nothing escaped Michael, and he remembered everything. Most people thought of Victor as energetic. But in comparison with Michael, Victor was practically catatonic. Barely five foot nine, Michael's plumpish body didn't so much move as bounce like a pressurized rubber ball.

Michael had an even greater claim to fame. Victor had friends everywhere, but he was a loner compared with Michael, who was constantly wheeling and dealing. He was always helping somebody, and somebody was always helping him. If you couldn't get something in Moscow, Michael was the guy to ask. He might not know where to get it himself, but he would certainly know somebody who did. He was the quintessential favors broker. Yet neither greed nor power was his motive. He was driven by compassion, competition, and above all curiosity. He traded at par, not for profit.

The instant Victor's foot crossed the threshold, Michael bounced out of his chair, flashing Victor a grotesque smile. He chirped, "Morning, Victor. Boss was looking for you. I think it's Iran." His natural enthusiasm made it sound like news of an unexpected pay raise.

"Boss" was the nickname for Colonel Alexey Leontyevich Bosik, First Deputy to the Chief of Directorate A of the Eighth Chief Directorate, or Eighth CD.

"Thanks. Urgent, as always?"

"You bet."

Victor went quickly to work on opening his safe. It was not a simple procedure. Very few people had his type of lock, even within the Eighth CD. First, he examined the seal, a plasticine disk imprinted with his personal seal, covering the crack between the door and the frame. Most people think of safes as strongboxes to protect valuables. For the KGB, however, a safe reflected their attitude about every security measure: while protecting the contents, by far the most important function of the KGB's security devices was to clearly register any attempt to break in, successful or not.

The seal had not been tampered with. Victor pulled a chain from his pocket and slid a special key from a thin steel sleeve. This double-flanged key was in itself an extraordinarily sophisticated piece of technology, fashioned in a way that made it impossible to copy, with delicate notches less than 0.02 inches thick. Victor looked at the key carefully. Few people had ever seen such a key. Fewer yet knew that a small imperfection at the top of an otherwise symmetrical key was not a production fluke but an indicator. Inserted the wrong way up, the key would get stuck. Irretrievably. The whole lock would then have to be changed. A very expensive proposition, but a small price to pay for the extra security. Victor inserted the key into the keyhole of the prominent outer lock.

Next, he dialed his personal six-digit combination. This number was changed at least twice a year. Only after that could he turn the key gently to open the outer lock, which then opened a gatelike shield, revealing the inner keyhole. Using yet another, larger key, Victor at last was able to swing open the heavy door of the safe. The whole procedure took less than thirty seconds. After working hours, the office space itself was secured by a system that set off an alarm if the air was even slightly disturbed. The cleaning woman was directly supervised by the duty officer.

Realistically, the only possible threat to his safe was from someone within the KGB. An outsider might perceive the redundancy of these security measures as paranoia. In fact, they were a routine expression of the KGB's priorities. For security was paramount for the KGB. Defense was the key to offense. The worst case was assumed in virtually every situation. Absolutely no one was to be trusted. No expense or resource was spared to assure the most perfect security possible. For Victor this was by now a natural mind-set—quite as important as the existence of any real or imagined intruders.

Victor found the file he was looking for and scanned the most recent materials on Teheran quickly, updating himself on the newest twist in the bizarre crisis.

The Politburo and the KGB had become obsessed with the situation in Iran. The Iranian revolution had come as a total surprise. No one had taken the Ayatollah Khomeini seriously when he was living in exile in Paris. Of course, like every other major intelligence service, the KGB had compiled a thick file on him. But beyond the fundamentalist Muslim slogans his political program had been a total question mark. The KGB figured him at best as a political lightweight and a junior partner in any future Iranian power structure. Besides, the KGB was so sure of the Shah's hold on power and the effectiveness of his formidable SAVAK secret police that any threat to his rule seemed unrealistic, certainly in the short run. In the long run the military seemed to be the only potential alternative power base. But a pro-Soviet military coup was unlikely because most of the Iranian officers were closely tied to the United States through training and other forms of cooperation.

The first reaction to the revolution was an attempt to use it for Soviet interests. But frantic efforts to get reliable information had only resulted in highly controversial tidbits, from which no conclusions could be drawn. However, at least the emphatically anti-American trend of the events was encouraging. The Politburo could not imagine that anyone who was anti-American could also be anti-Soviet. As a result, even more frantic efforts were made to establish friendly relations with the mullahs. Perceiving the cool reception as a bargaining tactic, the Soviet representatives just kept raising offers of future cooperation between the "people's Iran" and the "people's Soviet Union." Slowly euphoria turned into astonishment, then outright bafflement. Finally, Soviet intelligence concluded that the Ayatollah Khomeini was neither simply a "king for a day" nor even a shrewd bargainer looking for a good price for strategic cooperation with the Soviet Union. He was now seen as a madman, a hostile force to be reckoned with.

At the same time there was deepening concern about the Soviet embassy. Many recalled the reason for the Shah's conciliatory gift to the Russian Emperor, the famous "Shah" Diamond. It was his apology for the raid on the Russian embassy one hundred forty years ago in Teheran. Everyone in the embassy had been slaughtered, including the Ambassador, the famous Russian author Griboyedov.

As luck would have it, the KGB was right in the middle of upgrading the embassy's communications and facilities. The most secret part of the embassy had just been refurbished, and new equipment was still pouring in. If there was a raid, the Iranians might be able to seize control of the KGB's files and equipment. A nightmare scenario.

The situation could suddenly require the immediate destruction of these files and equipment. Most people don't appreciate how much time it takes to burn just a single book. However, if the system was destroyed, its restoration would require tremendous time and effort—time during which communications with the KGB station would be crippled. And worse, a capture of the cipher equipment would jeopardize the security of the whole KGB communications network around the world.

The responsibility for cipher security, and the decision about what to do in this situation, lay with the Eighth Chief Directorate. It was Victor's task to assess the problem and lay out the options.

The latest report said nothing unexpected. Nothing encouraging either. Victor had not liked the whole thing from the very beginning. He had felt strongly that the Teheran situation was too unstable, and that the cipher-communications system should not have been upgraded in the first place—if anything, it should have been systematically scaled down. The odds were lousy. Victor himself was extremely vulnerable. He stood a good chance of being made the scapegoat—or at the very least being positioned squarely in the middle of the mess.

He picked up the phone and called Boss.

"Come up," was the command, which actually meant down. "I need you right away."

Victor gathered his papers, put them in his safe, and locked the inner lock. As long as he was in the building the outer door could remain open. He took the stairs down the two floors to Boss's office.

Victor found Boss on the phone, as usual. Covering the mouthpiece with his hand, Boss said, "Ah, good morning, Victor. Have a seat. This won't take a minute."

"Good morning, Alexey Leontyevich."

Victor noted that his chief had greeted him first. Always a good sign. Another one was that he had called him "Victor." Office etiquette for direct address was tricky. Every Russian has three names: the last, the first, and the second. The last is always the father's family name. The second name is the patronymic, the final suffix indicating gender: "ovich" for a male and "ovna" for a female. Calling a person by the last name would be considered either very formal, as in "Comrade Sheymov," or rude, "Sheymov." Military style, as in "Major Sheymov," would be viewed as uncivilized by the rest of the country and is never used in the KGB. They are, of course, highly civilized people. The formal and respectful address is a combination of the first and the second names, as in "Victor Ivanovich." Used by a superior, it underlines the subordination. Friends use first names. In Victor's office, the manner in which a chief chose to address a subordinate was a good barometer either of his mood or of the current status of the subordinate being addressed. So the "Victor" was encouraging. Most situations were more ambiguous, and it was common practice to avoid using names altogether.

Five minutes passed, and Boss was still on the phone. Victor knew Boss's penchant for using the phone as an implement of psychological torture. He would often keep a subordinate sitting in front of him for an interminable time—often talking on two phones at once—only to then ask why the unfortunate man's work wasn't finished on time. The charge was usually accurate, which added insult to injury. Even though Victor hated this manner, he waited quietly, watching the man from whom he had learned so much.

Colonel Bosik, First Deputy Directorate Chief of the Eighth CD, was a rising star of the KGB and was expected to be promoted to general at any time. His mind was uncommonly sharp, and he was capable of quickly grasping the core of a problem without missing the fine details—one of the qualities that made his subordinates most uncomfortable. His appetite for work was voracious, and he was indefatigable, capable of processing quantities of information with high speed. Undaunted by even the most convoluted problems, his ingenuity and resourcefulness were legendary. He was never at a loss for a solution. A slight, well-proportioned man of five-three, he was like quicksilver, the personification of perpetual motion. He had straight, jet-black hair, and while his features might have been called simian in a less-animated face, there was an attractive intensity to his mournful black eyes. A compelling, charismatic figure.

However, Victor had mixed feelings about Bosik. His style was brash— too rough for Victor's taste. And he had a not-altogether-admirable talent for making people forget the often legitimate complaints they brought in to him. He had a facility for getting away with murder. In short, Victor did not trust Boss. But then, distrust was a standard commodity in the "snake pit," as the younger officers only half-jokingly referred to the Directorate.

As Victor waited, Boss's high-pitched voice drilled the presence at the other end of the telephone. Victor noted that Boss's huge, varnished dark wood desk, piled high with folders, papers, documents, and cables, was the only one in the Directorate more cluttered than his own. Abruptly, the voice stopped. Click, and silence.

Boss raised his eyes. There was an instant of "What are you doing here?" in his glance as he shifted mental gears. Recognition followed swiftly. "Are you current on Warsaw?"

Warsaw? Victor cursed Michael. Absolutely nothing to do with Iran. Now it was Victor who had to shift gears. He answered, "I know Smirnov was recently sent there to make a deal with Ambassador Karlov. Everything seemed to go as planned."

Boss's face darkened. Instantly Victor knew what was coming. Smirnov had screwed up, and Victor was going to have to go in and mop up the mess.

"Right, Ambassador Karlov." Boss's tone indicated his opinion of the man. "Know him?"

"Only by reputation. Never met."

"Well, he's a real son of a bitch. Take a look at this." Bosik threw a sheet of paper across the desk.

It was a cable from the KGB representative in Poland, on the standard red KGB letterhead used for cables from abroad.

COMMITTEE OF STATE SECURITY USSR
CIPHER TELEGRAM

TOP SECRET
COPY #1

FROM: WARSAW
COPY # 1 BOSIK
COPY # 2 ARCHIVE

DELTOV:

WE HAVE SUBMITTED THE PLANS FOR THE PROJECT "CASE," WHICH YOU SENT US WITH THE LATEST POUCH TO THE AMBASSADOR FOR HIS APPROVAL. THE AMBASSADOR REFUSED TO SIGN THE DOCUMENTS, EMPHASIZING THAT THEY HAD NOTHING IN COMMON WITH WHAT HE HAD DISCUSSED WITH COMRADE SMIRNOV. HE ALSO EXPRESSED HIS FIRM OPINION THAT THE PROJECT HAS TO BE POSTPONED FOR THE FORESEEABLE FUTURE.

CONSIDERING THE AMBASSADOR'S CLEARLY NEGATIVE ATTITUDE TOWARD THE PROJECT IT IS RECOMMENDED THAT THE DIFFICULTY BE RESOLVED AT THE CENTER. MEANWHILE, THE ISSUE WILL NOT BE RAISED WITH THE AMBASSADOR UNTIL FURTHER INSTRUCTIONS ARE RECEIVED.

KURITSYN

Deltov was Bosik's code name.

There was silence as Victor placed the cable back on Boss's desk. A tough one, for several reasons. He cleared his throat and said, noncommittally, "I see." Victor could easily imagine what had happened. Smirnov had been sent to Warsaw to see the Ambassador to get his OK for the upgrade project. The Ambassador had been hostile, as usual, and Smirnov had backed off and had never really told him what he was asking for. Smirnov came back and reported that everything was fine, hoping the Ambassador would simply comply with the formal written request. Typical for many in a bureaucracy. So when the formal plans were presented to the Ambassador, he must have been furious, and no doubt he was now thoroughly enjoying his righteous indignation at the expense of the KGB. A real mess, and potentially a considerable embarrassment for the Eighth CD's Chief. And no less for Bosik. Victor awaited his orders.

Boss picked up immediately: "You understand, of course, if we tried to solve it from here, it would take a year. So, you're to go to Warsaw and settle this matter on the spot, once and for all."

Victor started to protest, thinking of how this assignment could only exacerbate the existing tension between himself and his nominal boss, Section Chief Lieutenant Colonel Smirnov.

Boss interrupted with an impatient wave. "I know, you want to give me ten reasons why this is not the solution, and ten more why somebody else should go. But no. Get yourself ready as soon as possible, and drop by here tomorrow with your plan."

That was it. End of discussion. Victor left.

Although he was officially a Senior Officer of Section 3, Third Department of Directorate A, Eighth CD, Victor's real job was as Bosik's principal troubleshooter. Formally subordinate to Smirnov, the Section Chief, Victor also sometimes worked on assignments for Colonel Koryakov, the Third Department's Chief. The situation was awkward. Victor's receiving orders directly from Bosik did not make either Koryakov nor Smirnov his best friends. Especially given that they usually had only the foggiest notion about what Victor was up to.

An additionally aggravating factor was that Smirnov, over fifty and not especially bright, was on his way out, and Victor, one of the youngest senior officers, was clearly on a fast track. Smirnov was one of the "old guard," intensely jealous of every one of his subordinates. Anything new or "hot" disturbed him, and he defended against it. Getting things done was not one of his priorities. His seniority meant a lot to him. Smirnov identified completely with the system—but he had no illusions. His sense of service was reinforced by a quirk of security policy. In order to restrict the number of officers with access to cipher-security matters, the people in the Eighth CD were specifically exempted from the conventional retirement rule. By the same logic, those with access to ciphers were considered to be at risk, on more active service than other KGB officers, and they received a 20-percent premium above their normal pay. This was worth far more than the pay differential of higher rank. As a result, there were numerous officers like Smirnov in the Eighth CD, inner pensioners drawing relatively high pay. There was little incentive for them to retire.

Victor's being sent to Warsaw to fix Smirnov's latest foul-up was bound to create more hostility than ever.

Working with Koryakov was much smoother. He was bright, one of the new, intelligent breed, not in the least threatened by younger officers. He and Victor generally saw eye to eye on professional matters. One of the paradoxes of Victor's position was that while Bosik and Koryakov cordially detested each other, they both liked having Victor working for them.

Before heading back to his office, Victor had to quiet the grumbling in his head over his ticklish Warsaw task to gear himself up for dealing with the Directorate's Secretariat, which, besides performing standard functions like typing and distributing mail, served as Cerberus—the gatekeeper of all of Directorate A's files. The Secretariat was not a particularly popular outfit, but nobody, absolutely nobody in the organization could do without it. The execution and completion of every KGB officer's work was completely dependent on the ladies of the Secretariat. They typed every document, they registered them, and they trafficked them. They sent and received all mail. They booked vacations. They worked very hard.

If the Secretariat's systems were to break down, the Directorate itself would grind to a ponderous halt. Victor was reminded of the story of the tiger who ran away from the zoo and somehow slipped into a large and successful research institute. Annoyed at the interruption in his meal service, the tiger started quietly snatching the employees. His preferred entrées were the Ph.Ds. He served himself in this manner for about a month, and nobody took any notice. Then the tiger made a grave error. He ate a cleaning lady as an hors d'oeuvre. Her disappearance was immediately discovered, and a grand search was mounted. The tiger was caught and shot. The same principle applied to the Directorate. The highest-ranking, most indispensable officer could leave on a mission, take a vacation, fall ill, or otherwise disappear, yet the ranks would quickly close and the office equilibrium would return to normal. However, if a lady from the Secretariat was absent for a couple of hours, the whole out-fit deteriorated into a madhouse, work backed up, everyone got nasty, and chaos ensued.

There was another critical function of the Secretariat: it served as a major rumor mill. Anyone could become grist for the constantly turning stones of Secretariat gossip. Nothing was sacrosanct, and once seized upon, an unfortunate victim rarely emerged with reputation intact. It was the kind of attention to be avoided at all costs. However, if one had at least started out on good terms with the ladies, one's chances of escaping unscathed were slightly higher.

Victor was on good terms with the ladies of the Secretariat. He saw to that. He was one of the more popular officers with this group, and some-how his work was always ready on time.

This morning he entered their room and stopped at the counter with his standard "Hi, everybody, and how are my favorite ladies this morning?"

Several voices answered. The lady in charge said, "Hi, Victor. What's up?"

"You tell me what's up. What could I know, holed up in my lair, slaving away. You know all about us, the nameless, unsung heroes of the Great Soviet Society." Victor was laying it on thick. He needed to bend a rule.

"Now you listen to me, Nameless Hero, I have a pound of mail for you. I've called you for two days now, and for two days you've had no time to pick it up. Let's see some work go back to that lair of yours." She was one of the no-nonsense ladies.

The KGB rule was that classified mail had to be signed for personally. For the officers of Victor's Directorate, all mail was classified. Everyone tried to put off receiving his mail as long as possible because accountabil-ity for time spent and action taken on a particular problem began only after the relevant documents had been signed for. The same lady insisting that Victor accept and sign for his backlog of mail was also the one he would have to ask for the files he needed.

"Hey, I'm sorry. I'll pick it up later today, I promise, but right now I need everything you have on Warsaw. It's urgent." As charm was clearly not going to work with Miss Efficiency, Victor tried to impress her by insinuating the dark importance of his mission.

"Hah, urgent. Sure. No mail, no files!" came the retort, unmoved. There was no room for negotiation.

Victor sighed, "OK, you win. I'll take it." He signed for a dozen docu-ments, all directed specifically to him, and received two bulging files relat-ing to Warsaw. He picked up the pile and retreated to his office.

Victor looked through the unwelcome mail and dumped it unceremoniously into the safe.

He started reading the material on Warsaw.

Michael got off the phone and asked, "So, what's up with Teheran?"

After such a bum steer from Michael, Victor was not particularly well disposed to his office mate. With a straight face he said, "Actually, it was Mogadishu. You're slipping, sport."

"What?!"

"Capital of Somalia. How to mount a full-scale security defense against supersophisticated eavesdropping by the local service."

For a split second Michael was completely at a loss. He rarely missed by that far. Then he understood. "Give me a break. I thought it had to be Teheran."

"Why?" Victor asked dryly.

"Don't know. Everyone's crazy about Teheran these days. And I know you've been messing around with it." Michael looked at Victor with his impish baby-blue eyes, then innocently batted his sparse blond lashes. Victor laughed in spite of himself. It was impossible to hold anything against Michael.

Over the next two hours the Warsaw picture became clear. Apparently, in recent years the KGB had accumulated evidence that the Polish Security Service was working against it. Not in the way they worked against the West, but definitely in a less than "friendly" manner. The situation was aggravated by the fact that the Poles were clever at this.

In principle, the KGB and the Polish service were supposed to cooperate on interception. Indeed, the KGB "cooperated" with every Warsaw Pact country—which meant tokens of information and a little technical assistance, and in return their service was completely at the disposal of the KGB. However, the Poles had not been content to play by these rules. They knew they were good at what they did, so they demanded reciprocal rights to intercepted intelligence. The Poles knew perfectly well that the KGB was not about to share these intercepts. In fact, intercept information was so highly valued that it was transmitted directly to the Politburo, bypassing all regular KGB information channels. It was not going to be shared with the Poles, no matter what they offered in exchange. Now the issue was becoming very sensitive, not least because the Polish demands seemed quite reasonable. So the KGB backed off, and the Poles continued to operate relatively independently.

Then the Poles gradually began to develop a similar modus operandi in their clandestine activities. KGB assets in the Polish Service reported that they were certain that the Poles had begun to withhold some of the information they were gathering. The Poles even made a rather naive attempt to modify the cipher keys for their machines, all supplied courtesy of the KGB. The KGB easily figured out what they had done and pretended it hadn't happened. But the KGB was especially outraged when the Poles were caught red-handed trying to intercept information from a sensitive military enterprise in Moscow. To monitor the emanations from the building's main power line, they had rigged a car with electronic equipment and antennas, parked it directly under the power line, and removed the diplomatic license plates. The security people had caught the Poles at the scene as they were sitting there siphoning off information. Because there was no clear reason why the Poles needed the information they were gathering, the KGB suspected that an opportunist Polish element had been acting for some third party. The KGB was startled to find out that that was not the case—which meant that the operation was an expression of deliberate policy. In addition to these increasingly provocative challenges, there had also been a few reported instances of Polish service surveillance on KGB officers in Poland. So while on the surface political relations between the two countries looked good, there was an intensifying chill. The KGB, therefore, decided to upgrade the security of their cipher communications on the Moscow-Warsaw line. Maximum security.

The telephone rang, shattering Victor's concentration.

"Victor, hi." Valentin. "Ready for lunch?"

"Sure. Drop by." The Warsaw file disappeared into the safe.

Captain Valentin Yegorov was one of Victor's closest friends in the snake pit. They had worked together in different parts of Directorate A for several years. Both men were enthusiastic sportsmen—Victor had been a sprinter and was still rock climbing once in a while, and Valentin was a crack cross-country skier. They held similar views on many issues, some of which they'd had to fight to defend. Valentin's father's position on the Central Committee—he was in charge of a major Soviet industry—placed his family in the top circle of the government elite. There was a strange dynamic operating between Valentin and his family. It was fashionable among the children of the elite to be cynical about Soviet life and to affect Western dress and culture. But Valentin took his nonconformity further than most dared. He insisted that he despised his father and the Party hierarchy he was a part of. Because of his father's position, his unusually vocal criticism was only winked at. He got away with more than most would dare to express, and Victor suspected his friend of being more than a little spoiled, playing both ends against the middle. He found this trait irritating, but he also worried where it might lead Valentin.

The two friends had very different styles: Valentin was shy, intellectual, whereas Victor was a gregarious operator. Yet where Victor's instinct was to stop and think a problem through, analyzing a situation completely before taking action, Valentin was passionately impulsive. Jump first and take the consequences.

As Valentin entered Victor's office he asked, "The Prison or the Border?" These were the nicknames for two of the Center's dining rooms. A third one was reserved for the Department Chiefs and up. The Prison's name came directly from its location. When the KGB Center prison was removed from the building, the premises were converted into a restaurant. The Border earned its name because it was located in Dom 1 near the offices of the Border Guards Chief Directorate.

"Prison, it's faster."

"When are you going to slow down?"

Victor smiled at Valentin's familiar scold, "You know how Boss puts it: 'You'll have time to rest in the coffin, with the white slippers on,'" a reference to the old Russian tradition of burying people in white cloth slippers.

Wryly conceding, Valentin patted Victor's back lightly and said, "Let's go."

En route to the restaurant, Valentin asked, "So, what's up?" Valentin was not in the loop Victor worked in, but he'd been around long enough to be part of the grapevine. Technically, any discussion of sensitive matters was a violation, but by unspoken custom it was tolerated between good friends within the Directorate.

"We've got trouble in Warsaw, and I think I'm going to have a problem with N. M." Smirnov's initials.

"Why? You don't really report to him, do you?"

"Well, officially, he is my Section Chief, and you know his ego. Not long ago he went to Warsaw to make a deal with the Ambassador on the reconstruction of the *referentura*. Everyone assumed they'd reached an agreement. Now, the ambassador has reneged. So now we've got a real mess on our hands. Boss wants me to go in and clean it up. It looks like I've got to fix what N. M. failed to do."

Valentin smiled. "Boss really knows how to divide and conquer, I'll say that for him. Does Smirnov know what's going on?"

"No."

"Who's the Ambassador?"

"Karlov."

"Damn! I don't envy you." Then Valentin grinned, and Victor braced himself for the inevitable needle. "Well, don't worry, Victor, all you have to do is live up to your reputation as an expert on impossible assignments."

"Easy for you to say. With each of these stunts the odds for a fiasco are getting shorter and shorter."

"How much space do we need for our toys there?"

"Oh, about half of one wing of the embassy."

"God, what can you offer Karlov in exchange?"

Victor shrugged. "Nothing."

Valentin rolled his eyes. "Have fun."

"What about you? Still playing rebel?"

Valentin looked at him sharply. "What do you mean?"

"OK, just keep a lid on it. Don't do anything I wouldn't do."

"Maybe, maybe not."

At lunch in the institutional cafeteria the two friends chatted about their kids. Both of them had bright, inquisitive children, so there was no lack of latest tricks to tell about. Finally, as they finished the meal, Valentin asked, "So, when do you have to leave?"

"According to Boss, yesterday's too late, as always. I suppose in the next couple of days." And they trekked back along the windowless corridors to their respective offices. Even after all these years Victor found the building disorienting. Those who had witnessed the Revolution remembered it as the notorious Lubyanka. Forming one side of Dzerzhinsky Square, it occupied a whole city block. An old Soviet joke goes that the Lubyanka is by far the tallest structure in Moscow because from it one can easily see Siberia. But the KGB's Moscow Center was not in fact a single, square, nine-story monolith. It was composed of two connected L-shaped buildings known as Dom 1 and Dom 2. The west and south sides constituted Dom 1, built before the Revolution; Stalin later added the other two sides. The floor levels of the two buildings didn't quite line up, and there were only two passages connecting the buildings, one on the fourth floor and one on the seventh. It was all extremely inconvenient. Victor once grumbled about the building to a friend who happened to be a dissident. The retort was swift and bitter: "Don't complain. That place is a lot less convenient for us mortals who don't work there."

One of the most peculiar structural features was the way in which the main buildings linked up with a nine-story tower set in the large inner courtyard. For some reason, the floors of the tower were built between the floors of Dom 2, so that one always had to go up or down a flight of stairs to get to a particular floor in the tower. There was no direct passage from the tower to Dom 1.

This tower was the most secure precinct of the entire KGB—its castle keep. Known as the "Appendix" or "Tower," its offices harbored Directorate A of the Eighth Chief Directorate, specifically, the Headquarters of Directorate A, which was in charge of the KGB's global communications system. Victor's outfit.

The base of the tower consisted of the great Hall of Columns. This cavernous space, two stories high, was lined with huge, dark, marble columns and was reserved for formal occasions of the KGB. Directorate A occupied the rest of the building, with a communications center on the topmost floor. A few antennas on the roof provided communications between the Appendix and the KGB outposts through powerful radio stations like "L'vovka," near the L'vovskaya railroad station outside Moscow.

Victor spent the rest of the day in reading the Warsaw files, as well as responding to the cables from various KGB stations abroad on the matters that he supervised. Just past six, the phone rang. It was Olga. Instantly his mood lifted. She'd always had that effect on him.

"Hi. Are you staying late tonight?" She was a Section Chief in the Polytechnical Museum, one block away.

Victor thought for a second. He knew he should stay longer to make a real dent in the homework he needed to do on Warsaw, but he felt a sudden pang of guilt about staying late too often, working odd hours, traveling abroad alone. Guilt and regret for not spending enough time with his beautiful wife.

He decided. "No, not tonight. Are you through?" He already knew the answer.

"How wonderful! Yes, of course I'm through. Let's just go out tonight."

"OK. Fine, give me fifteen minutes. I'll meet you at your building entrance."

Having placed the documents in his safe, Victor went through the meticulous full-lock-up procedure and reset his personal seal. Then he picked up the special KGB secure phone labeled "OC"—Operational Communications—and dialed a number in the Sixth Department of Directorate C, Eighth CD. Directorate C, along with the Eighth CD Headquarters, was located across town, in the Fili district of Moscow.

"Gorin."

A hard and fast KGB rule: Every officer answers his civilian phone with "Hello." The secure phone, however, is answered with the officer's last name only.

"Hi, Anatoly. Sheymov." Anatoly Gorin was an expert in technical security, one of the best. He was responsible for inspecting a large number of the cipher facilities both within the country as well as abroad. He and Victor were good friends.

"Hi, Victor. I presume your two-bit organization needs our help? What can I do you for?"

"Say, what are you doing at your desk so late? The workday for people who don't need their brains on the job ended fifteen minutes ago. Something happened to your watch?" It was a well-established fact that Anatoly's branch of the KGB had a marked inclination for ending the workday strictly on time.

"Then I'd better hang up and go home, hadn't I?" They both laughed.

"Anatoly, how're you doing?"

"Oh, the same. Writing up the damned report on the last trip. And you?"

"Not bad, but I've got a bit of a crunch here. I need to see you guys first thing in the morning."

"Can you get here by nine?"

"It's for you to say."

"Then I'll see you here at nine tomorrow. If your brain works that early."

CHAPTER

IT SEEMED TO VICTOR that the best things in his life always occurred at the worst possible time. His corollary to Murphy's Law.

Victor was twenty-six in August 1973, with the energy of youth on top of the natural arrogance of a born Muscovite. He was also a scion of the establishment: his mother a prominent doctor and his father an important military scientist. With this pedigree in addition to his own job with the KGB, Victor would have been expected to stick to a communist apparatchik crowd. Not so. He had scores of friends in the least likely places. True, he attended parties given by the children of the highest-ranking government officials and Central Committee members, accepted by them as "one of us." He was just as welcome, however, at the gatherings of dissidents and was on equally good terms with many of Moscow's professional criminals. Victor could—and did—say with confidence that The Big Moscow was his place, and he knew the city like the inside of his pocket.

That fateful late-August morning found Victor desperately ill. The only cause he could think of for the waves of nausea, the blurred vision, shaking hands, and watery knees was some kind of toxic reaction, food poisoning perhaps. No flu or virus he'd ever encountered had produced such violent physical symptoms. A darker explanation was remotely possible, but he had been too sick to think it through clearly.

He'd decided to try distracting himself from his misery with a routine task—taking his clothes to the dry cleaners. He was so weak that it was almost more than he could manage to push the clutch in and coordinate it with the gear change. He stopped the car near the cleaners, parked, wiped the sweat off his face, took a deep breath, and somehow got himself and the clothes out of the car.

Although it was still very early, there was already the inevitable line. He took his place at the end, behind a slim brunette reading a book. He stared dully at her back. As she turned a page, she shifted slightly, and he caught sight of her profile. She was exquisite! In spite of his wretched condition, Victor was stunned. The proverbial bolt of lightning. Everything he had been preoccupied with—his father in the hospital, his own acute illness—all faded away. There She was. He was mesmerized.

Victor had never had a problem meeting women. As his mother's flamboyant younger brother Anatoly had taught him long ago: "Just watch the girl carefully. Try and figure out what she's thinking about. Then casually but confidently, move a little closer and make a friendly remark on that subject. The rest will take care of itself." Simple enough, Uncle's approach had always worked for Victor, but now, when it really mattered, he couldn't even choke out a "Hello."

While not in favor of it, Victor could understand sex at first sight, but he certainly did not believe in love at first sight. Not till now.

Most Moscow lines are frustratingly slow and would have given Victor ample time to gather his wits and plan an approach. This line, however, was moving like an escalator. Victor studied the graceful figure in front of him. "I can't risk a brush-off," he calculated. "I've got to get her address. Then we'll see." He listened closely to catch the address she gave the attendant. Her voice was beautifully modulated. Instantly, Victor discerned the almost-imperceptible trace of an accent that betrayed provincial roots. He was touched by the shy politeness in her exchange with the attendant, a dead giveaway. This girl was no Muscovite. Although clearly anxious to get her cleaning done as quickly as possible, she was unwilling to risk discourtesy. To Victor she seemed irresistibly vulnerable, and he could hardly refrain from stepping in and managing the transaction for her. When she left, it took all of his willpower not to run after her. Victor dropped off his clothes and returned to his car.

He looked in the rearview mirror. "Christ, I belong in a coffin." His face was a pale blue, with dark greenish-blue circles under his eyes. Not a trace of the healthy Crimean tan he had acquired on his recent vacation. He was doubly glad he hadn't approached the girl. Still, the excitement he'd felt just from seeing her had energized him. Time to go check on his father's condition. He drove across town to the hospital, cursing the bad timing of the miracle that had just befallen him.

By the time Victor entered the nondescript reception hall of the Central Military Hospital, however, the surge of energy had subsided. He barely noticed the dull leather sofas and chairs, empty and slumped against the walls like disheartened patients. He was focused on the fact that his mother was not in the lobby. He was sure she'd be inside already. Doctor Sheymov was a well-known and highly respected physician, specializing in post–heart attack recovery. She practiced in one of Moscow's privileged clinics and consequently had entrée into almost any Soviet hospital. In addition, she had served in front-line hospitals during World War II, and now a number of her friends from that time were on the staff of this hospital. His eyes fell on a large notice that sternly informed him that no visitors were allowed inside without special dispensation for a specifically designated day. He also knew that permission was limited to visiting recovering patients. Victor fit none of these criteria, and apparently no one else did either. Even his KGB ID would get him no farther. In fact, the ID would probably make things worse, given the traditional animosity between the military and the KGB. Victor did have a military ID to use for cover when necessary, but as this was a hospital for the top military leadership of the country, nobody was likely to be impressed by an army lieutenant's trying to throw his weight around.

He mentally ran through his options: charm his way in; intimidate; bribe. In his present condition, the last seemed the simplest. He went back to his car, took a box of chocolates from the supply he kept for such occasions, added a ten-ruble note, and walked into the Senior Administrative Nurse's office. A few minutes later he emerged wearing a visitor's white hospital gown, equipped with a pass and directions. It took him about ten minutes to find his mother outside an operating room.

"Hello, Mama," he kissed her. He saw the effort she was making to keep from crying. "How is it?"

"It's very serious, Victor. An emergency operation. A substantial part of the gall bladder has been damaged. They're trying to cut the dead portions out, but the deterioration is progressing very quickly. Other organs have been affected, but we don't know how badly yet."

"Who's doing the operation?"

"An old friend of mine, Dr. Nekrasov. You've met him a couple of times. I'm not sure if you remember him, but he's one of the best. If anyone can save Father, he can."

"What are the chances?" Victor was angry at himself for asking, but he had to know.

His mother's eyes brimmed with unshed tears and her lips trembled as she struggled for composure. "Ten percent." She paused. "At best." Then she looked away from him, out the window. She took a deep breath and turned toward him again, all business. Dr. Sheymov was back.

"Darling, you look terrible. You're sick. Go round for observation immediately and let them run tests on you." The tone of voice was her no-nonsense one. No room for negotiations. "I have enough good friends here to arrange for your care. Right now."

"No, Mama, I'm really all right. Don't worry."

"I don't remember asking your opinion. I just stated that you are sick. If you are not going to be reasonable, I'll have you locked up in a hospital for a month. You know I can. Don't you tell me you feel absolutely fine. I have eyes. And at this moment I am not your 'Mama,' I'm a doctor."

"OK, OK, you win, Doctor. I'll have the tests performed, but not here and not now. I'd be better off at the KGB hospital—you know how things are between the military and our kindergarten," he teased. "I'll go. I promise I will." She gave a shadow of a smile.

After a pause, she said, "Still, I can't figure out what could have caused such a drastic reaction."

"I've been thinking it through myself. I know we both ate the same fish—you know, Father's vobla—and at the same time, too. As soon as I began to feel sick I flushed my stomach thoroughly, just in case. I asked if he felt ill, but he said no."

"No, the reason for the difference in reaction times is that your metabolism is much faster than average, even for your age group. Father's reaction would naturally be much slower. What bothers me is that ordinary food poisoning doesn't affect the system this way. Besides, we all ate that fish last week. Something just doesn't make sense."

Victor didn't respond. He did not yet wish to discuss his darker theory with her. He still had a lot to think through.

The door of the operating room opened and the surgeon emerged. Dr. Nekrasov shook Victor's hand. "You're quite grown up now, young man. The last time I saw you . . . when was it . . . ? Yes, 1961. Christ, your mother and I are getting old!"

"No, just riper." She cut the pleasantries short, anxious to hear results.

"Fair enough," he chuckled. "All right, we're damn lucky so far. Ivan is incredibly strong, thank God. The operation couldn't have gone better. With a little more luck he'll be back on his feet and functioning normally in a month. Now, let me explain specifically what we may expect over the next twenty-four hours. They'll be critical."

As they began talking the jargon shared by doctors all over the world, Victor moved a little apart from them and watched as the doors to the operating room swung open. His father was wheeled out. Victor, his mother, and the surgeon accompanied the unconscious form to the ward. By then, the consultation was completed. Victor and his mother thanked Dr. Nekrasov and left the hospital. They headed for the senior Sheymovs' home near Metro Academicheskaya.

Victor had no intention of going to a doctor. But to mollify his mother, he called the Central KGB Clinic and requested that a doctor be dispatched to his parents' address for a house call. Augusta was delighted. She hadn't quite believed his quick surrender in the hospital.

When the KGB doctor appeared at the door, Victor used all his charm, or what was left of it, to separate his mother from the doctor and to make sure that his illness would not be taken too seriously. The last thing he wanted to do was waste time with irrelevant testing. If he hadn't died by now, it meant he was out of the woods. All he wanted was sick leave from his job for a few days. His request was easily granted, with the proviso that he'd submit to the barrage of tests if he didn't feel better in twenty-four hours. Everyone was happy, although his mother eyed him suspiciously.

Victor left the apartment immediately after the doctor. He needed to make a phone call that he didn't want his mother to overhear. He went to the nearest pay phone and dialed his friend in the police crime lab.

"Somov."

"Hi, Peter. It's Victor Sheymov."

"Victor! How can this humble mortal possibly help one of our friendly brothers-in-arms?"

"No, wait, Peter. This one's personal."

"Oh, then I'm all yours."

"Peter, I've got to see you. Now."

"OK, I'll be through in half an hour. Say, 6:30 at the corner of Arbat and the Garden Ring."

"Fine. See you there."

Victor was waiting when his friend arrived.

"Victor, you look like shit! Let's have a drink."

"Sorry, I can't. Some other time."

"What's up?" They were walking toward a bench.

"I need two favors. One: don't ask any questions. Two: study this stuff quietly and tell me what you make of it." Victor handed him a small plastic bag. Peter looked inside and saw some scraps of dried fish. He looked at Victor and shook his head.

"OK, old man, I don't know what you're up to, but I guess I'd better get back to the lab and start checking right away. It might take several days, you know. Is that OK with you?"

"I hope so."

"Any chance this will become official?" Victor heard the hidden question—Peter was trying to figure out how to play it at the lab: keep it strictly off the books, or leave a loophole open. He was looking to cover himself. Just in case.

"There's always a chance, but I doubt it. You can reach me here." Victor gave him his parents' number.

Peter left, and Victor sat alone on the boulevard bench. It was the first quiet moment he'd had to collect his thoughts. The first one, at least, when he'd felt well enough to be capable of clear, concentrated thought. He set himself the task of methodically making sense of the sequence of events.

Sunday afternoon, a little over twenty-four hours ago, Victor had been enjoying a quiet visit in the country, alone with his father.

Ivan Sheymov loved the outdoors. His dacha was in a dense forest about forty miles from Moscow. One could get there by train, but that meant a four-mile walk from the station through the forest. The best way was by car. Since very few people owned cars, visitors were rare, and Ivan liked it that way. He loathed crowds. The dacha was in a compound established for the top officers of the Strategic Missile Forces and their families. Everyone there knew one another. Victor found compound life boring and only made the trek when Ivan was there. He cherished time spent with his father, just the two of them hiking or talking together in the woods. That was exactly how they spent that particular Sunday afternoon. Victor even noticed specifically how robust and healthy Ivan was looking—his strong shoulders unstooped by his sixty years, his clear blue eyes as direct as ever. His broad face, deeply etched by lines of character, bore witness to a life of discipline. His father had called him on Friday afternoon and invited him out for a "bachelor weekend." Victor had had another commitment but promised to join him on Sunday.

Late Sunday afternoon, when they returned from a long trek, Ivan announced, "Now, I've a treat for you. I dried some vobla earlier this summer. Everyone thought it was finished up last weekend when the whole gang was out here, but I saved a couple. I must confess, I felt guilty hoarding them, but now I'm delighted I did. So. We'll enjoy them together." He knew that Victor relished this traditional Russian snack—dried fish, salted and sometimes smoked—a perfect snack with beer. Ivan went to the attic and returned triumphantly with the two eight-inch fish.

As they sat quietly together, drinking beer and eating vobla on the veranda, father and son watched as the colors of the setting sun poured through the surrounding trees. Victor's thoughts drifted back to other occasions he'd spent alone with his father. There'd not been so many during Victor's boyhood, but such times had had a powerful impact on him. So powerful, in fact, that in Victor's memories of growing up his father was always right there beside him. The truth was that Ivan's job had devoured his time, and he was by nature a workaholic. And yet their relationship was so close that Victor felt Ivan's presence even when he was not physically nearby. Their bond was a source of strength for Victor. Without seeming to control or manipulate, Ivan had so encouraged his son's sense of freedom that Victor had always felt his decisions were his own. Only much later did he realize how unobtrusively but firmly he had been guided by his father.

A sudden wave of pain and nausea interrupted Victor's reverie, rudely jerking him back into the present. His first thought was that the vobla must have gone bad. It would have been hard to detect the taint through the salt and the strong smoky flavor. He asked his father if he felt anything odd, but Ivan said no, he was fine. Still, Victor was worried. Food poisoning was nothing to fool with. Not wanting to make his father feel guilty, Victor left the veranda as casually as he could. His doctor mother had taught him well. He swallowed close to a quart of water and then made himself vomit. He repeated the procedure. And again. Little relief. Could it be some kind of flu? He returned to the veranda, white-faced and shaking. Ivan brewed him some tea, which was no help either. At last, Ivan insisted that Victor go to the hospital, a suggestion that he categorically refused, out of obstinate pride and bravado. At twenty-six, he'd live forever. Hospitals were for weak mortals.

In the end, Ivan gave in and drove Victor home.

Victor went straight to bed and collapsed in a dizzy, nauseated heap, mercifully losing consciousness as the room whirled.

Then sometime after midnight, early Monday morning, a hundred hellish bells jangled, jerking Victor out of a nightmare-plagued slumber. His mother was on the phone, asking, "Darling, are you all right?"

Weakly mumbling his lie, Victor answered, "Of course. Why?"

"Father is in the hospital. Food poisoning."

"How bad?"

"We don't know yet." Her voice faltered, then she continued, "He's quite strong, knock on wood. What did you two eat yesterday?"

"Father's vobla."

"I'm going to the hospital now. I'll call you as soon as I know anything. Are you going to work tomorrow?"

"No, tomorrow is my last day of vacation." Vacation rules were rigid. If the thirtieth day fell on a Monday, so be it. He looked blearily at the clock. Half past midnight. "I mean, today."

Victor tried to gather his wits. He figured he must have slept for about three hours, and he felt worse than before. He found it impossible to concentrate. He made tea—a simple task to bring him into focus. The walls and the furniture continued to spin. He was worried about Ivan. Could it have been the vobla? But the others had eaten it only last week. . . .

A dim recollection began to nag him. Slowly, a conversation he'd had earlier that day at the dacha swam up through the miasma into his conscious brain. The neighbor's wife had mentioned that she'd seen his sister's husband, Yefim, enter Ivan's dacha last Thursday evening. "He only stayed about half an hour," she said, "and then he walked the four miles to the rail station in the dark. Can you imagine?" Victor had thought it odd at the time, but then, Yefim was odd. He had dismissed it. In light of what was happening to him and his father, however, the incident began to take on sinister implications. Then, through the haze of nausea, Victor remembered another piece of pertinent information: Yefim was an undergraduate student at the KGB Higher School, the KGB's own university. He had recently been boasting about a course he was taking in highly sophisticated methods of poisoning, and about how he was spending a lot of time in the lab and the morgues. A horrible suspicion exploded in Victor's head.

Riding a rush of adrenaline, he called a friend. By this time it was one in the morning.

"Alexey, I need a ride to my father's dacha. Right now."

"OK, twenty minutes." Victor's close friends never said no, and they never asked questions. And vice versa.

As Alexey was en route, Victor took a piece of notepaper and scrawled the following: "Elephant, if you get to read this note, I'll be dead. Take out Yefim Goncharov, my brother-in-law. And don't make it easy for the bastard. Good-bye. Your friend, Victor."

He put the note into an envelope and wrote, "Elephant" on it, along with a phone number.

In the car, Victor told Alexey that he'd left his car at the summer house. Alexey didn't buy it: "Sure, of course! Somehow you just happened to forget your car forty miles from Moscow, and you need it at 1:30 in the morning. Right. Looks like a bit more is riding on this little expedition. By the way, has anyone told you you look like a ghost?"

"Hide this for me." Victor gave him the envelope. "It's very unlikely, but if I die, I want you to call this guy, meet him, and give him this for me. Tell him you were a good friend of mine."

"'Elephant'? Hah! Another one of those criminal chums of yours?"

"He's OK. Rough childhood. Some bad luck, that's all."

"So. I gather you're not going to tell me what the hell's going on?"

"Not yet, Alexey. I'm not even sure myself."

"You never change. Do as you want. Just don't forget to invite me to your funeral." A gentle reproach, but Alexey pressed no further.

Victor smiled wanly, grateful for such a friend. "You know you have a standing invitation."

It was half past two when they arrived at the summer house. Victor forced himself out of the car and groped his way into the kitchen. Searching through the garbage pail, he found what he was looking for: the remnants of the vobla. He put a few morsels into a plastic bag, carefully leaving the rest in the trash. He chose to follow Alexey back in his own car. By this point, however, Victor's adrenaline was spent, and he could hardly drive. He even had trouble seeing Alexey's taillights ahead of him. At long last, when they arrived at Victor's apartment building, Alexey parked his friend's car for him.

"Thanks a lot."

Alexey dismissed it. "You know where to find me." A moment's hesitation. "For God's sake, be careful. Don't pull any crazy stunts."

"You're getting old."

Alexey just shook his head and left.

Victor went into his apartment. He automatically checked the hall clock—4 A.M. He stumbled into bed and then slipped into an uneasy doze. When he woke it was nearly seven. What next? He tried to clear his head. He shuddered at the thought of what might have happened, then again tried to focus on what to do next. Both he and his father were alive. If they'd been poisoned, and the poison had worked properly, they would both have been dead by now. At any rate, it was too late for an antidote— even if there was one. So there was no need to sound an alarm.

His mother was with his father in the hospital. He figured he'd not be much use there, and she would probably have taken one look at her green-faced son and hospitalized him on the spot. No, he had to be free to watch for Yefim's trap. That was when he decided he needed to perform some simple activity to distract himself from how he felt. His glance fell on the overflowing hamper of dirty clothes. The cleaners.

Revived to a certain extent by his decision, he took a long shower, dressed again, picked up the clothes, and left the apartment. He gave the elevator doors one look, then opted for the stairs. The descent seemed to take forever, but anything was better than that crypt.

As Victor sat on the bench, he took a deep breath. He'd succeeded in recapping the disastrous sequence of events leading up to the cleaners. More to the point, up to the girl at the cleaners. He was torn between excitement and guilt at being able to feel elated in the midst of a serious family crisis. As usual, his personal demon was at work. "My God! Just a week earlier or a week later, meeting her would have been so much easier to manage. Still—it doesn't matter what else is going on. I'm going to meet her, and that's that." There was nothing more he could do for Ivan at the moment, so having made peace with his conscience, he turned his attention to Her.

He reconstructed the events at the cleaners. What did he know? He knew she wasn't from Moscow—perhaps she was only visiting someone? He had recognized the address she had given—a huge apartment building on Leninsky Prospect—but he had not caught her name, so he could not find her through the local official records. The only sure thing would be to intercept her at the dry cleaners. Victor clearly recalled that she'd asked how quickly her order could be ready. That meant that she needed it as soon as possible and would be likely to pick it up right at the time they'd told her. The attendant had said "twenty-four hours." That was it. Victor would be there for the pickup, so to speak. A harsher thought intruded: "Circumstances permitting." He headed back to his parents' place.

There, he found his mother mechanically tidying the three modest, book-filled rooms of their apartment, occupying herself with mindless household chores—her way of handling emotional stress. She made small talk, chattering lightly about this and that during supper. At last, she fell silent, her plate untouched. She could not carry on the game without Victor's support, and he was unable to squeeze a word out of himself. As the silence stretched between them she broke into tears. Victor was at a total loss. What could he possibly say to make her feel better when her husband's life was in jeopardy—the man she'd loved for more than forty years, for whom she would have readily given her own life? It shook him to see her break down.

Finally, he appealed to her professionalism. "Mama, you're a doctor, and Father needs you now. You cannot afford to be weak."

She shuddered, drew in a deep breath, and wiped the tears away. Her years of training and discipline did not fail her. She was calm in two minutes. "I'm sorry, darling, of course you're right." She thought for a moment and then continued: "The crisis should come somewhere around four—maybe six this morning. I must be there with him. I might be of some help as a doctor. I know him better than anyone else."

Victor said, "I'll go with you."

She saw that there was no way to stop him.

"All right, but you must promise to stay calm, no matter what happens."

"Yes, Mama, I promise." To her, he was still a boy.

"Now, at least go to bed for the next two hours. We'll both need rest for later."

Victor felt an overwhelming weariness and realized that he was still very weak. Dr. Mama was right after all. Sleep was probably the best medicine for him now.

When they arrived at the hospital, she was absolutely calm and poised. All business. She was ushered inside immediately. Victor, however, was stopped in the reception room and told to wait. The hospital night staff was hostile. When he protested, he was promised coldly, "It will only be a few minutes. Wait here. Someone will come for you." No one did.

He selected one of the leather armchairs and settled in for the duration. His thoughts turned toward the man in the hospital bed who was fighting for his life. If in fact this was the end, what was the sum total of Ivan Sheymov's life? What were the forces that had shaped it and how had he, in turn, shaped Victor's life?

Colonel Ivan Sheymov had lost both of his parents during the Civil War that followed the 1917 Revolution. Homeless, a vagrant at age eight, he barely survived the famine that ravaged Samara—the large Russian city on the Volga River where his family had lived. And died. He headed for southern Russia, where the famine was not so severe, jumping trains from town to town and hiding in boxcars in between.

Upon arriving in Taganrog he was put into an orphanage. It was hardly a gentle sanctuary, with a high mortality rate, but it beat starvation. Because its government subsidy was very small, the orphanage required that all the boys work. The comrade caretakers were notorious for stealing from the orphanage, so the orphans found ways to protect their own interests, and a gang mentality developed. The boys turned to crime as a way of making money on the sly, out of reach of their "bene-factors." Ivan never joined them in these activities. His strong-willed inde-pendence and sense of honor gave him the strength to resist the peer pressure. Yet they were his peers, and he respected their need to survive and their right to choose how to go about it. He walked this fine line— often a dangerous one—throughout his almost ten years in the orphanage.

Ivan was saved by his avid natural curiosity and omnivorous mind. He studied whenever and whatever he could. It was probably this hunger for knowledge, along with his sense of honor and responsibility, that kept him from becoming a career criminal like most of the other orphanage boys. He also had a dream: to become a scientist. Even though he had to work full-time all the way through, he managed to graduate from high school and get into college, where he majored in aircraft design. After graduat-ing, Ivan figured it would be a good idea to get his mandatory three years of military service out of the way, even though as a potential graduate stu-dent he was entitled to a deferral. Given the usual bureaucratic confusion, he would probably never have actually been called up. But that wasn't his way. He played it straight, not caring for the uncertainty. He would sim-ply put his service behind him and then concentrate on science.

What Ivan didn't know was that once someone was in the Soviet mili-tary, the Minister of Defense had the power to retain him for twenty-five years. The only reason the Minister needed to give was that one was "of value to the State," and the subject was closed. That was precisely what had happened at the end of Ivan's three years. He was sent to the Mili-tary Engineering Academy. His only alternative would have been to remain in the Army as a petty officer.

His graduation coincided with World War II. He was sent to the front lines, became a lieutenant colonel at the age of twenty-nine, and finished the war in Austria, a thirty-two-year-old colonel in a major general's post. The general's star meant little to him, however, as he still had his heart stubbornly set on becoming a scientist. Again, he requested retirement. Again, retirement was denied. His country needed him, he was told. He was sent to another military academy for advanced studies and assigned to Marshall Nedelin, the first Commander of the Strategic Missile Forces. So Ivan remained a military officer, and yet was also at last the scientist he'd dreamed of becoming.

Actually, Victor had never known much about his father's work. Though there was little that could not be discussed in the Sheymov fam-ily, one topic was absolutely taboo—any mention of Ivan's job. His work was top secret, and he never spoke about it. Once, as a teenager, Victor had asked his father, "Why don't you ever tell us anything about what you do? I mean, what about things that aren't secret? Everything I know about what you do I've learned from other people, your friends and their children. It's embarrassing not to know what my own father does."

"There's nothing embarrassing about it for me," came the reply, "and it shouldn't be for you. It's much more embarrassing for those who do talk. But that's their problem, not mine. I'm a soldier, and my orders are not to discuss anything even remotely related to my job. Period."

Victor had been silent, knowing perfectly well that Ivan was not just a soldier, and he was hurt to think that his father couldn't trust him. As if Ivan could read his thoughts, he'd continued, "I trust you and Mother implicitly, you know that. But if anything were to go wrong and you two were to be," he hesitated, "questioned, I would want you to be able to answer honestly that you knew nothing about what I do. That would be your only hope."

Then, at last, Victor had understood the reason behind the taboo. He had gone on to ask, "And what about hope for you?"

Ivan had simply shrugged. "My prime concern is for your safety."

"Father, are you talking about what happened under Stalin?"

"I am."

"But that couldn't happen again, could it?"

"Who can say, Victor? All we know is that it happened once—and not all that long ago. You can never predict the future."

That had been the end of the discussion. Victor had come away with new respect and appreciation for his father's resolve. The taboo prevailed.

Victor's meandering memories of his father carried him into a light, dream-filled doze, broken by his mother's gently shaking him awake around 5:30. She'd come with good news: the crisis was over. Ivan's strength had held, and he'd pulled through. They hugged each other, and Victor could feel his mother trembling with relief and fatigue. Victor drove her home, then returned to his own apartment.

He had to get ready for another pivotal moment. He had already determined the precise hour for Operation Dry Cleaners. Setting his alarm for 8:30, he allowed himself a quick catnap. He wanted to be on his toes.

Victor's plan to meet the Girl was meticulously calculated. He was counting on the line at the dry cleaners to be typically long, a sure bet. He arrived ahead of the twenty-four-hour deadline and found just what he'd expected—at least a thirty-minute wait. He took his place at the end of the line. His intention was to take advantage of the Muscovite game of place-saving. A person gets in line, then asks the person behind him to hold his place while he goes off to run another errand, or perhaps wait in yet another line for something else. He then returns in time to reclaim his place in the first line, that much closer to the goal, two errands accomplished instead of one. Line-jumping is a very practical sport in a city where queuing is a way of life.

Halfway through the line, Victor asked his rear neighbor to save his place, and then he went back to the end of the line. He wanted to be sure he had a place open in the middle of that line, while he waited for Her. Absolutely no one in Moscow can resist an offer to jump ahead in a line.

He repeated this maneuver for a half-hour, keeping steady, surreptitious watch on the entrance. At last, there She was—with a girlfriend. Victor was sorry she was not alone, but he reasoned to himself, "What the hell, better than a boyfriend!" He decided to make his move immediately. He ambled casually toward the end of the line. He didn't want the people behind him on line to overhear the conversation. His plan mustn't be spoiled by a squabble. The interception point was perfect, about ten feet ahead of the end of the line. Victor almost passed her, stopped in his tracks, and turned toward her, in an exaggerated double take. He caught the girl's eyes and held them as he went through the motions of someone recognizing a face and trying to remember why it was familiar. His charade was flawless. From innocent puzzlement he shifted into delighted discovery and recognition. Then he spoke: "Hello. I remember now, we were comrades-in-suffering in this line yesterday. I was just behind you."

Both girls looked at him. She was genuinely puzzled as she studied his face with her beautiful, chestnut eyes. Victor thought he had never seen a girl as exquisitely lovely. His heart soared as recognition lit her face. She smiled: "Yes, I think so. Well, now we have the pleasure of the same entertainment."

Victor looked at the two of them and knew it was time for the "bright idea" to strike him.

"You know, the way I was raised, I can't stand to see one beautiful girl suffer. When I see two such lovely ones languishing at the end of a line, it's absolutely unbearable. Why don't you both join me, up there toward the middle?"

The Girl looked at him for a moment, her eyes revealing the smile that her lips suppressed. She knew his game. She knew that he knew his offer was irresistible. Politely, with a slight hesitation, she demurred, "It's very kind of you, of course, but I'm not sure it's appropriate."

Of course, Victor's arsenal included cruder ripostes, but he knew they wouldn't fly. Instead, he responded, "Oh, but I insist. I'm sure you have much better ways to spend your time than standing in line." He was tempted to say "we" but decided not to push his luck.

The girls looked at each other and then at him. She breathed a charming sigh of capitulation and said, "All right, thank you very much."

When they slid into Victor's place in line, the little old lady who had saved his place broadcast her protest in a loud and plaintive voice: "I don't remember seeing these two young ladies here before, and I've been in this line the whole time." Others in the line, with nothing else to do, began to peer around, eager for any diversion.

Victor knew that the slightest hesitation on his part would dash everything. "Well, my goodness!" he replied, just as loudly, with a great flourish for the benefit of his audience and his guests, "Then you have missed the most attractive part of this line. Do yourself a favor, buy a monocle." His message was clear. The onlookers laughed, the babushka subsided, laughing in spite of herself, and the incident was over.

The three of them chatted casually, and as his heart pounded, Victor kept thinking, "Don't push, be cool, don't ask their names—yet." As they neared the counter, and possibly the end of the encounter, Victor tried to gauge his next step. If he accompanied them on public transportation, he might get no closer than her stop, and besides, it would be difficult to have a personal conversation on a train or bus. No. To find out her address for sure, he would have to offer them a lift home in his car. This led to a troubling thought. Very few people in the Soviet Union owned cars, and certainly not many young men of twenty-six. All too often he'd seen girls go after men not for themselves but for their cars, their apartments, or other material considerations. He didn't want that to be the case with this lovely girl. He had to know that she'd choose him for himself, not his privileged position. As these calculations raced through Victor's mind, he was bantering with the girls.

The Girl collected her package and completed the transaction. Victor asked about his laundry and, just as he'd planned, was told it wasn't ready. The girls responded to this news with moans of sympathy, launching on a chorus of commiseration about time wasted in Moscow lines. At last, in high spirits, the three of them left the cleaners.

Once on the street, Victor said, "By the way, my name is Victor."

"Olga," they both replied simultaneously. They all laughed. There was a well-known superstition that it was good luck to be between two people with the same name. The person in between gets to make a wish. Victor made his.

"So, make your wish," said Olga Number Two, the friend.

"I already have."

"Then tell us what it is," Olga Number Two pressed.

"Of course he mustn't, Olga!" She came to his rescue. "It wouldn't come true if he did."

"Well, I can guess what it is." Olga Number Two looked Victor straight in the eye and smiled provocatively.

"I'll bet you can," answered Victor, deliberately ambiguous. Her boldness irritated him. She was certainly attractive, but all in the front window. Too aggressively self-assured for his taste. Pushy. She made Olga Number One even lovelier by comparison. Victor decided to throw caution to the winds.

"You know, I just can't stand by and watch while you lug that heavy bag onto a public bus. I'd suffer terribly." He spoke directly to Olga Number One. "Luckily for me, I've got a car here. It seems that the perfect solution would be for me to offer you a ride home."

Olga Number One looked at him. Again, he saw a flash of humor playing in her eyes. "You certainly must suffer a lot if you worry about every attractive woman you see. You must have all sorts of other problems because of them, too. You have my sympathy." He laughed, and she continued: "Thank you very much, it's very kind of you. But I live nearby, not far to lug my heavy bag, as you say. And, of course, I really don't want to take up your time."

Victor found her combination of spirit and vulnerability irresistible. "Not at all. As a matter of fact, I have absolutely nothing to do this morning." A lie. "I must admit, I rarely have spare time, but to tell the truth, I'd rather take a drive to a beautiful place, like Lenin Hills, for instance, in the company of two lovely ladies, than anything else I might have planned to do." Then he looked straight at Olga Number Two. "Ah, but then, I don't wish to impose." That was true.

And right on cue, Olga Number Two came to the rescue. "What a wonderful idea! Come on, Olga, I know you don't have anything better to do, let's go." And she jumped into Victor's car—the front seat, of course.

Number Two was exactly the type he had worried about. Not so, Olga Number One. He cheered inwardly. He picked up the laundry bag, which was in fact quite heavy, and threw it into the car. Then he bowed and with an elaborate flourish extended his hand and helped her into the back seat. So far, so good.

All three of them had a great time getting to know one another, talking and laughing. It was an interesting triangle. Olga Number Two had clearly set her cap for Victor, who in turn was more smitten than ever with "his" Olga. During the course of their excursion, he learned that his first impressions had been quite accurate. She had been raised by her grandparents in Samara—coincidentally the town of his father's family. Victor's carefully casual questions disclosed an intriguing profile: her family represented the best of the provincial intellectual elite; there had been fine artists scattered throughout the family for five generations; she was the only girl of her generation in the family clan and had been fiercely protected by her seven male cousins; she'd been well educated in the classics; she'd received seven years of piano training, five years of ballet, and four of *Characternye* dance; she was as comfortable on a formal stage as in a family concert; she'd been offered a place in a professional ballet company, but her family had forbidden her to join, insisting instead on a technical education that would guarantee her a more stable future. She'd gone to an engineering university in Moscow, where she'd learned a lot about fast-paced, competitive urban living, but even after five years she still was not at ease in the city. Victor somehow managed to pursue his purposeful interrogation of both Olgas without indicating his preference. The difference was that he eagerly filed all information coming from the back seat and barely heard the voice in front.

Three hours after leaving the cleaners, Victor pulled up to their apartment building. Both Olgas thanked him and invited him to call. He took both their numbers and assured them that he would.

Happier than he could ever remember being, Victor drove straight to the hospital. His father was very weak but conscious and recovering. He spent time with him, then drove his mother home.

Later, the phone rang. It was Peter Somov, working late. He asked Victor to meet him on his way home near the Taganka Theater.

Peter looked grim. His expression confirmed Victor's worst suspicions. "I've found something interesting. Our standard test showed simply that the fish had spoiled and certainly could have caused food poisoning. But because it's for you, I went a little further, and sure enough, a surprise. That poison did not come from the fish."

"Are you sure?"

"Absolutely. Someone wanted it to look like food poisoning, but it wasn't. There's absolutely no doubt that poison was injected into the fish. Need the technical particulars?"

"No, too complicated for me. You've given me what I needed. Thanks, Peter."

"Victor, I'm a friend of yours. For God's sake, give me at least a hint of what this is all about. What's the body count so far?"

Victor looked at him. He owed his friend that much. "Body count is zero, thank God. I still need one more piece of proof to be 100 percent certain, but it looks like my beloved brother-in-law has just tried to kill my father and me."

"Christ! You and your father are damn lucky, you know that? The fact that you're still walking around is a miracle." He continued excitedly, "How did the son of a bitch get hold of the stuff? I can assure you, there's no way to buy it or cook it up in a kitchen. The only folks with access to it are in your outfit."

"You've got it. He's an undergraduate student at the KGB Higher School. Probably stole it from the lab. He's been bragging that he's studying the finer points of poisoning as part of his education."

Peter was shocked. "What's his motive?"

"Start with the fact that the guy's a shit. Came from the boonies to Moscow, wants to stay here. No trace of moral restraints, a sociopath, if you ask me, and this little stunt confirms it. He was counting on my father to advance his career. He didn't take the trouble to find out that Father never plays that game—as a matter of fact, he's never even helped me. He distrusted Yefim to the extent that he even refused him an official share in the apartment, and that really cooled their relations. I guess Yefim figured that with Father out of the way, my mother would relent and allow him and Helena the official share. The fact that I nearly bought it as well was purely accidental. Yefim had no way of knowing I'd be out with Father that weekend."

Victor knew this would answer Peter's question about motive. As far as Victor was concerned, Yefim represented the worst of the KGB. He'd been an informer in the Army, working for the KGB's so-called Military Counterintelligence, the universally despised Third Directorate. Sponsored by a senior KGB officer from his village, he'd managed to get a place at the KGB Higher School. Once there, like the thousands who flock to Moscow in the hopes of improving their lots, Yefim was trying to establish an official claim to residency.

As a member of the Moscow police, Peter would be all too aware of the catch-22 involved in realizing that dream. First, one must obtain a *propiska*, the residency permit from the police. In Moscow, getting that official permission was next to impossible. There was a desperate shortage of available living space. It was not at all uncommon for entire extended families to share one apartment and consider themselves fortunate. To get a permit, Yefim needed a job in Moscow. To get a job in Moscow, however, one must be a resident of Moscow. Yefim had two choices: either land a high-ranking job with a special KGB residence quota in Moscow, or marry a Muscovite, in which case he'd be allowed to share his spouse's residence. As the first option was unlikely for a man of Yefim's limited talents, he chose the second. Victor's sister, Helena, was to be Yefim's ticket to Moscow residency. When that scheme didn't pan out, he'd simply decided to take matters into his own hands.

Peter pressed further, "Why don't you just report this whole thing to the police?"

"Go public? Are you mad? It would destroy the family. You know how these things go. Too much embarrassment for my folks. And the rumors. . . . No. That's out of the question."

"OK, then in that case, please don't tell me what you're going to do, but if you should need something, ah, let me say, effective, it can be arranged. Indirectly, of course."

Victor smiled. "Peter, you're the best. But first, that's not my style. Second, I still don't have indisputable proof. And third, I honestly haven't decided what to do." Silence. There was nothing more to discuss.

"Peter, I owe you one."

"That's what friends are for. When you're well enough to have a drink, give me a call. By the way, my girlfriend has a terrific friend. Your type."

Victor just smiled as they parted.

The next morning, still not back to full strength, Victor drove to the dacha. No surprise: all traces of the fish had disappeared from the garbage pail. He stopped in next door. He knew his neighbor would be there. The wife of the Chief Doctor of the Strategic Missile Forces, she stayed at the compound all summer.

"Hello. I'm sorry to disturb you, but I thought I left my notebook out here, and I can't find it anywhere. I think perhaps Yefim may have picked it up? I asked him to, but then never heard back from him about it. Did you happen to see him here?"

"Victor, shame on you. That poor boy doesn't have a car, and you run him out here for a notebook! You should be nicer to him. Of course he came. I saw him myself. He was here for a short time last night. Do you know he walked all the way back to the station in the dark again? That notebook must be very important to you."

"Yes, it certainly is. Thank you very much. And I guess you're right. I'll be sure to make it up to Yefim, I promise."

There it was, crystal clear. The proof he needed. "Thank heaven he's stupid," Victor thought.

He faced a serious dilemma, nevertheless. Yefim must not go unpunished. He was a walking time bomb for the Sheymov family. Clearly he'd not balk at murder. An official criminal investigation was out of the question. Retribution had to come from Victor, privately, but he could not kill his sister's husband. He needed a subtle but effective solution.

Victor phoned Elephant. He was a powerful criminal boss whose gang specialized mostly in burglaries of small stores and warehouses. He was usually elusive and inaccessible, but for friends Elephant was always available. Victor went to see him.

Elephant's reputation in criminal circles was almost mythical. Had fate been kinder to him in childhood, he probably would have become a powerful public figure. As it was, his boyhood had schooled him as thoroughly in street-mean survival as any fine university could have honed a leader of the *apparat*. Yet he was known for his integrity and fairness. To his gang, Elephant was God. He'd earned their devotion the hard way. They knew he'd never let them down. Elephant and his men lived by strictly observed rules and values, the code of the street. Victor had grown up in the same neighborhood and had been privy to its system of favors, obligations, and punishments. As a boy, Victor had played with the children of criminals, though he did not join in their criminal activities—there was no reason to, and he was his father's son. However, in any turf war he'd stood with them. Elephant was five years older than Victor and was already one of the rulers of the street. Even now, they did occasional favors for each other. Victor could get his car serviced quickly and at a reasonable price. Elephant sometimes needed connections.

On this occasion Victor entered the older district where his parents had once lived in a huge, new apartment block assigned to military officers. He drove down the street past this bastion of military might and after only a quarter of a mile found himself in a neighborhood where even the police would not venture at night. Elephant's territory. Victor parked at the entrance of a shabby two-story loft building. He entered. Elephant was waiting for him.

They shook hands and patted each other on the back.

"Hi, Elephant. How's it going?"

"Hi, Victor, it's been a while."

"I know—too long. Elephant, I need a favor."

"I figured. By the way, has anyone mentioned that you look like shit? What happened?"

"A little prick got the idea that the best way to insinuate himself into a Moscow address was to poison my father and me." Victor saw Elephant start. "Don't worry, Father's all right now. Recovering."

"So name this prick." Victor saw that Elephant had already buried whoever had threatened Ivan.

"Hold on. Believe me, I wish I could kill the little bastard myself, but that's out of the question. He's Helena's husband."

"Damn. I didn't even know she was married. So, what do you want me to do?"

"I need some muscle for a little reeducation exercise."

"No problem. I owe you." Victor had by chance been present when the police had been giving some guys on the street a hard time. He had recognized one of Elephant's men and noticed that he was quietly trying to ditch a switchblade. If he had been caught with the knife, possession alone would have been enough to put him in jail for a couple of years. Victor had brushed by the man, and the switchblade had disappeared.

"Just give me two or three of your boys, and I'll handle it."

"They're yours. Name the place and time."

Victor dialed Helena's number. In the course of their conversation, he established that Yefim was in the main KGB School building on Leningradsky Prospect and would be going straight home at 4:30. Perfect. Victor knew a quiet alley he would have to pass by. Elephant refused to stay behind. Victor, Elephant, and two of his men left for the alley at half past three.

"Remember, don't kill him," Victor instructed. "Just shake him up a bit and bring him to me for a little talk."

Near the alley they found an empty boiler room in the basement of a large apartment building. They didn't have to wait for long. Victor spotted Yefim, pointed him out to the boys, and disappeared inside.

The boys snatched Yefim quickly and quietly. In no time all of them were together in the makeshift tribunal room. Victor praised Elephant for a smooth job. He shrugged. Business as usual. His boys were pros.

Victor looked at Yefim. Yefim's widely set, washed-out, lashless eyes flickered with animal fear. Normally, these ugly eyes were blank and expressionless beneath his Neanderthal forehead. His long, narrow nose lent a cruelty to his face, and the thatch of unkempt, dirty, blond hair added a slovenly cast to his appearance. Five foot nine and stocky, he looked much smaller as he tried to disappear into his uniform.

There was silence. The only sound was Yefim's shallow, rasping breath. Victor could see that Elephant was seething and touched his arm to calm him.

Yefim lost control and wailed, "I ain't done nothing! What you gonna do to me?" His terror erased all traces of his recently acquired grammar.

Victor felt his own anger flare at Yefim's whining. "Not to worry. I just wanted to treat you to some of Father's vobla. I know how much you love it, and I saved some specially for you." Victor took a small plastic bag out of his pocket.

Yefim's face turned ashen. He nearly collapsed at the sight of the poisoned fish. His lips trembled as he shrieked, "No!"

"You are a fool," said Victor coldly, keeping his own feelings in check. "You were stupid enough to try to mess with me and my family. I hope you are at least smart enough to realize that you are about to die."

"No, please! Victor, please don't kill me. Whatever you want, it's yours, I'll do anything . . . ," he trailed off, incoherent with fear.

Yefim's cowardice in front of Elephant and his men embarrassed Victor. "I don't want to dirty my hands with you, you little piece of shit."

Elephant couldn't bear any more. "Let me finish him; it'll be much simpler."

Victor did not acknowledge him, bearing down instead directly on Yefim, face to face. "Here's the deal: I'll let you go now"—a moan of relief from Yefim, overridden by Victor—"but if ever my father, mother, sister, or I die, you will be dead quickly. I guarantee it. And it won't be an easy death."

Yefim stammered in dismay, "But, your parents . . . they're old, they'll die anyway. . . ."

Victor continued, "Well then, that's your bad luck, isn't it? But I'm not finished. My friends here are much less generous than I am. The only reason you're still alive is because I asked them to spare you. If you step out of line again just once, or if you even piss me off, for whatever reason, I will waive my request. Now, that's all."

"Thank you, thank you. I promise you'll have no trouble from me. No trouble, ever. I promise," he whined, although as he looked at Victor he could not hide the hatred on his face.

Victor took a half-liter bottle of vodka from a small bag and gave it to Yefim. "Drink it. All of it. Now," he ordered.

Elephant nearly burst, "What? Not only are you going to let this miserable coward walk out of here, but you're going to waste vodka on him as well?!"

Victor just nodded and continued to watch Yefim, who didn't dare argue. He finished off the bottle quickly. In half an hour, while the four of them chatted and swapped dirty jokes, Yefim was ready to pass out, dead drunk. Victor told Elephant's men to take him home and make sure that the neighbors witnessed his condition. As they left bearing the semiconscious Yefim, Victor turned to Elephant and answered his question. "It's just extra insurance. If he's stupid enough to report the incident, it will be dismissed as the DTs. Just another drunk hallucinating."

Elephant only nodded. "Remember me to your father."

The incident was over, and they went their separate ways.

Never failing to be unpredictable, Helena came to her parents several months later and announced, "There's something you should know. I am divorcing Yefim." Nobody asked for reasons. The family's reaction was one of relief.

CHAPTER

AS WAS AGREED THE DAY BEFORE, Victor's morning commute took him into the Fili district on the western outskirts of Moscow. By about 9 A.M. he'd arrived at the "Aquarium," the nickname given to the cheap-looking steel-and-glass building containing Directorate C of the Eighth CD. In fact, the Aquarium also housed the Headquarters of the entire Eighth CD. Its Chief, General Nikolai Nikolaievich Andreyev, had his main office there. He also operated out of another office, in the Appendix, next door to Boss. Directorate A was the only part of the Eighth to operate from the Appendix.

The Aquarium was an unremarkable three-winged building, indistinguishable from hundreds of other post–Stalin-era office buildings. It stood in the middle of a large, undeveloped piece of land. Most people assumed it was some sort of scientific research institute—which, in a way, it was.

The undeveloped lot was in fact a controlled zone, which ensured the detection of anyone attempting to intercept the electromagnetic signatures of the activities taking place inside. The building itself was surrounded by a tall concrete fence, topped by high-voltage barbed wire that was invisible from the outside. There were armed, uniformed KGB guards on the inside of the wall. For the curious there was also a mousetrap. Outside the fence the parking lot for the officers of the Eighth CD was temptingly unguarded. Anybody could enter and park there. At least so it appeared. In fact, the lot was monitored around the clock, and every officer's license plate was known. Once a Bulgarian diplomat had parked his car there. He'd been visiting someone in the neighborhood and was delighted to find the perfect parking place, cleared of snow. Poor man. Within fifteen minutes his car had been towed away and virtually disassembled in the search for interception equipment. He was then given a very hard time about his reasons for being there. Nothing was found, of course.

The Bulgarian was luckier than the Western diplomat who, apparently trying to be cute, parked his car in an open KGB parking lot next to Dom 2. Within twenty minutes a military truck was on the scene, followed by a tow truck. The military truck "accidentally" smashed into the car, diplomatic license plate notwithstanding, and the damaged car was immediately hitched up and towed away. When it came to dealing with potential eavesdroppers, the KGB defense was ruthless.

This morning Victor passed through the security checkpoints at both the gate and the entrance into the building. His business was with the two departments responsible for the security aspects of all Soviet cipher-communications facilities, the First and the Sixth. The Sixth was his first stop. It was more pertinent to Victor's mission. This department was responsible for the technical-security inspections of cipher-communications facilities in every Soviet embassy. In addition to inspecting and ensuring the technical security of the systems already in place, the scientists of the Sixth Department were constantly working on developing improved technologies for the prevention of interception.

At the Sixth he found Anatoly, along with Nikolai Leskov and Eugene Kolsky—all top experts in their field—in the cipher-intercept laboratory. In this lab KGB scientists simulated all known methods of interception and then devised appropriate countermeasures.

"Good morning, guys. You must have quite a problem here if they've got all three of you on it together." Victor grinned and waited for the predictable explosion. He knew that they were working on research requested by his own people, who had yet again infuriated the Sixth Department. Victor had spoken truly; the problem was not a simple one. The people in the Eighth CD knew that regular light bulbs were absolutely unacceptable in sensitive areas. They could easily be transformed into unintentional bugs, particularly when attacked using the electromagnetic-flooding method of interception. So in sensitive areas fluorescent lamps were absolutely mandatory. Bosik's people suspected that some types of starters for the fluorescent lights also posed a security threat, so they had ordered the research people to classify the different types of starters as "secure" or "nonsecure." A tough task, and as always the order was "urgent." Because Victor had been in the loop, he was a fair target for the men's irritation.

"Hah, Victor. If we've got a problem, it's thanks to you guys and that Boss of yours. You've perfected the technique of turning your headaches into ours. In a rotten capitalist system you'd be heroes for giving us work, but not here, my friend. Have you ever heard that one idiot can ask more questions than a dozen wise men can answer?" Eugene was a curmudgeon, rude to friends and colleagues even under the best of circumstances. Now, tired and overworked, he was close to the edge. He stormed on, "Just take your last letter . . ."

Anatoly laid a hand on his arm to quiet him as Victor interrupted, unruffled, "OK, but who got you the trip to a rotten capitalist place called New York, and let you stay there for months so you could buy a car?"

This reminder only irritated Eugene further, but before he could retort, Nikolai intervened. "All right, that's enough. Time out. Sorry, Victor, he's just frustrated. We all are. You guys have given us a small problem that so far even our three heads together haven't been able to crack. We're all a little testy."

There were no hard feelings. All four men were on great terms personally and respected one another professionally. Otherwise the conversation would have been chillingly polite.

"So, stranger, what's brought you to the wilderness?" asked Anatoly.

"I need all you've got on Warsaw."

"Put that in writing!" shot back Eugene with a melodramatic grimace.

"I'd be happy to, only I need the answer in less than a year."

"What specifically do you need, Victor?" asked Nikolai, the peacemaker.

"I need all the technical-security derogatory on the embassy's cipher facilities, and I've only got a couple of hours."

"Christ! Are you saying you're going to try and get away with shutting the place down?"

"No. I just need the goods on the place. The more, the better."

Nikolai spoke for all of them, "OK, we'll drop everything and dig the stuff up. Are you going on to the First?" That was the First Department of Directorate C, Eighth CD.

"Yes."

"Come back when you've finished with them."

Dealing with the First Department was far simpler. Its people performed the general inspections for compliance with security regulations. A list of the Warsaw embassy's *referentura* violations was easy to compile: things like the destruction of cables and cipher materials a day or two later than required, diplomats' writing out the full text of cables in their working notebooks, use of real names instead of code names, sloppy placement of personal seals, and such. These were the standard, petty violations found in any embassy, but they would serve Victor's purposes.

When he returned to the Sixth Department, Victor found that the guys had done a miraculous job on Warsaw, considering the limited time they'd had. Victor was now armed with an amazingly long list of security violations in the Warsaw embassy, sins that had persisted despite the demands for rectification made by Eighth CD KGB inspectors. He had what he'd come for, and he knew exactly what to do with it.

On the train ride back to the office, Victor reflected on his morning's harvest. To begin with, he knew perfectly well that really serious security violations did not exist in Soviet embassies. The "violations" cited in the stack of reports now in his briefcase were for the most part petty technical infractions, insignificant in the larger scheme of practical security. Just like every other ambassador, Vladimir Karlov did his best to get clean security reports from the inspectors. He treated them well and saw to it that they were generously entertained. If all else failed, he'd negotiate to get as many violations as possible removed from the list. However, properly arranged, the information could be used to build a formidable case, and the Ambassador could still quite easily be made to appear as if he were not only deliberately covering up dangerous breaches but also actively jeopardizing the embassy's security. In Stalin's day that would have been more than enough to get him shot. "It's just a question of presentation," Victor mused.

Ironically, it was Victor's unregistered and unreported possession of this top-secret list that constituted a vastly more serious breach of security. As ever, Victor observed wryly, the enforcers of the law were themselves above the law.

By the end of the day he'd completed his preparations. Victor had a clear grasp of the situation and a plan. He leaned back in his chair and mulled over his own position.

He definitely did not want to go to Warsaw. As far as he was concerned, the problem was being solved at the wrong level; the embassy's cooperation for installing the new equipment should have been secured at the highest levels of the KGB and the Ministry for Foreign Affairs, the MFA. Not only was it inappropriate to use a troubleshooter like Victor to solve the problem, but his solution was going to be extremely risky—and he was the only one who was going to bear the risk. A ready-made scapegoat. The worst-case scenario did not look good: failure would mean certain demotion and probably spending the rest of his twenty-five-year career in some rural Russian backwater. An attempt to blackmail a Member of the Central Committee would not be taken lightly.

Victor went down to see Boss. Boss was in good spirits and smiled expectantly as Victor entered his office. "So, Warsaw. Any bright ideas?"

"Nothing pleasant."

"We are not here for 'pleasant.' Come on, I'm smart enough to realize you're not happy about this assignment. I wouldn't even have to be smart to see that. But your happiness is irrelevant." A gentle scold, but his face had darkened.

"Well, I agree that we should treat the Warsaw problem seriously. We need to ensure good protection there."

"No kidding? You really think so?" Boss needled. "Well, Victor, I forgot to tell you the decision's already been made, whether you agree or not. The only question is how to execute it." Boss paused, waiting for Victor's response.

Victor was quiet.

"Well," Bosik prompted, "what's your plan?"

Victor took a breath and began. "What can I offer the ambassador? I need some chips to play with."

Now Boss was all business. "There's nothing I can think of, that's the problem."

"Then my only option is to bluff. We don't really want all-out war with the MFA, and we don't want to take this as far as Andropov and Gromyko, do we?"

"No, of course not. But you need ammunition, even for a bluff. So far, I don't see what you could use."

"The embassy's accumulated a lot of violations. A lot of petty stuff, but properly organized, it could be made to look significant. I think we might, how can I put it, impress the Ambassador."

Boss paused, looking Victor straight in the eye. "I hope you understand the implications of what you are proposing." Like Victor, Bosik had also carefully avoided the word "blackmail."

"It's the only solution I can see."

Boss was silent for a moment as he considered the angles. Victor couldn't read his reaction. Then a sharp intake of breath, a decision: "You think you can pull it off? Karlov is one hell of an opponent." It was a go.

"Do I have a choice?"

Boss called Andreyev over the Kremlevka, the top-security government phone, and briefed him. Victor couldn't hear Andreyev's side, but he didn't need to. He knew what the answer would be.

Boss hung up. "OK, go get him. But, of course, you understand that neither Andreyev nor I know what you are up to. As far as we are concerned, you're going there simply to clear up a misunderstanding. It's all very friendly."

Once again, Victor was to walk the wire without a net. "I understand."

"Victor, the Leadership values you for missions like this because you deliver, but I don't want to lose you over a stupid ambassador. Be careful."

"Right."

"Now, send the necessary cables and go."

"I'll need a couple of days to clear my desk. Besides, I'll need to cable for an appointment to see Karlov. I don't even know if he's in Warsaw."

"No, Victor. Show up unannounced, or you'll never get an audience. This SOB knows his way around. Clear your desk when you get back."

"We could ask the KGB rep if Karlov's there."

"No, you can't trust those guys. They have to live with the MFA over there. They make their deals with the ambassadors; that's where their bread's buttered. If Karlov's not there, no big deal. Just cool your heels for a couple of days."

"You're the boss."

"By the way, classify your cables Flash, and we'll get Andreyev to sign them. You'll need all the clout you can get."

"Very good. I'll send the cables tomorrow afternoon and leave the morning after." Victor bargained for at least one day.

"You're incorrigible!" Boss growled, then conceded, "OK, that much you win. Now get going."

Back in his office, Victor opened his safe and took out the cable letterheads. He wrote the cables quickly. Now he was ready, but he couldn't set anything in motion until tomorrow. He wanted to keep his trip secret as long as possible. He put the cables back in the safe and reached for a stack of files. The telephone rang. It was the Directorate's Party Secretary.

"Victor, have you got a minute?" Polite as always.

"For you, always." He closed the safe; he knew there'd be no escaping this one.

Victor was the Deputy Secretary of the Department's Party Organization. He hadn't asked for the job. He'd been appointed by the Directorate's Leadership because a Party position was a prerequisite for future career advancement. It was an irritating job, mostly ideological busywork, and time-consuming. The Party Secretary was a senior officer who had run out of career opportunities and was headed for retirement. He was sensitive about his position and about the obvious skepticism of the younger officers on the rise. His job was technically full-time, and he liked to play at being overworked. He had become increasingly annoyed with Victor's unavailability because of his urgent job assignments and frequent trips. The comrade didn't dare express his displeasure, but Victor knew all too well that he had to watch his back. The Secretary would certainly fume when he heard that Victor was going on yet another trip.

"Comrade Grimov is with me now," the Secretary explained. "He needs to discuss a sensitive matter. Unfortunately, I'm awfully busy now. Could you meet with him?"

Victor always tried to duck these assignments, but because of his upcoming absence he thought it politic to be available now. "Who is he?"

"One of our officers. A clerk. You've probably met him."

"OK. I'll see him in the Committee meeting room in fifteen minutes."

Victor knew exactly what was coming: someone reporting on a peer. Victor had been raised to despise tattling. To legitimize it with the official euphemism of "keeping the Party pure" only made it worse. After this type of interview he always felt as if he needed a shower. He locked his safe and went to see the squealer, to deal with the matter in his own, far-from-conventional way.

Outside the Committee meeting room he met the type he had expected: a nondescript middle-aged man, a lower-level civil servant with the colorless kind of face and persona that are eminently forgettable. They greeted each other and entered the meeting room. There stood the mandatory conference table. Solemn portraits of the Politburo Members stared down at them from the wall.

At thirty-three, Victor was usually considerably younger than most supplicants. To compensate for the disadvantage, he had to conduct these interviews quite formally. He knew that he had to take control right from the start.

"Well, Comrade Grimov, how can we be of service?" Victor looked the man straight in the eye. The Great Inquisitor.

The man was clearly ill at ease. He couldn't meet Victor's gaze. He clasped and unclasped his hands. He was the picture of unctuous servility. When Victor addressed him directly, he seemed to lose what little nerve he had, like a green actor struck with stage fright. He stammered, barely audible, "I, ah, I just wanted to, uh, report something. I, well, I thought it was, well, important, otherwise, of course, I would not have wanted to take up your time." The last phrase tumbled out in a rush.

Victor's tone was paternal. "Of course not, but you must not worry. We always have time for important matters. That is the nature of our Party work." He set his trap with a velvet voice. "Come now, Comrade Grimov. What is it you wish to tell me?" His pen was poised above his notepad to prove his interest in Grimov's cause.

Grimov relaxed a bit, his voice growing stronger with the importance of his mission. "Well, you know, Victor Ivanovich, I think I have, uh, discovered some, shall we say, improprieties in the lifestyle of a co-worker . . ."

He paused for some sign of encouragement from Victor, who complied, "Yes? His name?"

"Suvorov." Victor wrote it down, and Grimov continued, "Yes, Comrade Suvorov, uh, seems to be, well, I mean, it looks like he is, well, you know, fooling around . . ." He paused for effect, then added confidentially, "And I know with whom." Victor was silent, taking notes. Grimov pushed on, fairly bristling with righteous indignation for the benefit of his sympathetic audience. "Quite by accident, you understand, I saw him, not once but several times, with the same girl. I saw him entering her apartment, and well, you know, he does live in a different part of town. Well, when Suvorov was with her in there, I took it upon myself to call his wife, and I asked to speak to him. She said he was at work! There." He waited for Victor's response, but none was forthcoming.

Silence as the pen scribbled notes, then paused, waiting for more.

Grimov took the cue, "Well, that's about all, for now, I mean. Of course, if you want me to, I could go ahead and find out more. If you like I could . . ."

Victor had been looking at his notes, and interrupted, "All right, now let me see. You said, 'I think I have discovered.' Which one is it? You think or you have discovered?" The paternal tone was gone.

"Excuse me . . . ?" The question caught Grimov by surprise.

"First of all, Comrade Grimov, I must commend you on your vigilance and your determination to keep our proud KGB free of any impropriety." He slowed his delivery for emphasis: "I can assure you that we will take care of all who commit misdeeds."

As Victor stressed "all," Grimov grew uneasy, his confidence dwindling. Victor continued, "I assume you understand the seriousness of your accusation. I am prepared to launch a full inquiry into the matter, but first I need two things: a formal complaint and indisputable proof. Without them I cannot proceed officially. Now. Does Suvorov complain?" It was hard to keep a straight face.

Grimov looked confused. "Why should he complain?"

"It doesn't matter why. Does he complain?"

"No."

"All right." Victor made a note. "Does his wife complain?"

"Oh, well, you see, she probably doesn't know. How could she complain?"

Victor feigned irritation, "'I think.' 'Probably.' Can't you give a straight answer, Comrade Grimov?"

"Well then, uh, no, she does not complain."

"Thank you." More notes. "Does the girl complain?"

"No."

Duly noted. "Fine. Now, are you complaining, officially?"

"Oh, well . . . I'm not really sure. Uh, you see, Victor Ivanovich . . ."

Victor cut him off, "Oh, of course, I see. You want the Party Committee to take the responsibility for your unsubstantiated accusation, is that it?"

"No, no! Victor Ivanovich, you misunderstood me . . ."

"I misunderstood?"

Grimov was quaking. "No, wait, I mean I did not put it properly."

"That is certainly a possibility. So. Put it properly."

There was a long, tense pause from Grimov. Finally he said in a very small voice, "I think I may not have understood the complexity of the situation." He wanted out.

"That's all right. It's what we're here for, to help you understand." The paternal tone returned. "Now, we can go two ways: either we make this meeting official, in which case you must present indisputable evidence and put your complaint on record; or I can do you a favor and forget that this meeting took place. If you come up with concrete evidence and wish to take official responsibility, then come back to me and we'll start over again."

"I'd be thankful if you would do that."

Victor looked at him quizzically. "Which?"

"Uh, forget this matter, I mean."

The meeting was over. When Grimov reached the door, Victor fired the final shot. "Oh, by the way, what is your job situation in relation to Suvorov's?"

"We're peers."

"Ah. And aren't you both contenders for the position of Deputy Group Leader?"

"Oh, well, I don't really know . . . there are some rumors, but . . ."

"Yes or no?"

"Yes." He almost swallowed the word.

"Be careful, Comrade Grimov. Somebody might misinterpret your intentions."

"Thank you, Victor Ivanovich, thank you." Perspiration beaded Grimov's forehead. He scurried out the door.

Victor had seen the last of Comrade Grimov.

The next morning Victor went over to Personnel, a building on the corner of Dzerzhinsky Street and the Garden Ring, to pick up his Warsaw Pact passport. This passport appeared to be a perfectly ordinary one, but the KGB Border Guards and Polish Security Service agents would instantly recognize it as belonging to a special KGB officer. A Deputy Foreign Minister signed regular Soviet passports. In the KGB, a number of different signatures might be used for KGB passports used in Warsaw Pact countries—except for Yugoslavia and Romania. The Chiefs of the First, Second, and Eighth CDs could sign passports for their people. Victor's passport was signed by Andreyev. The Border Guards and the Poles would also note that a canceled entry visa for East Germany immediately preceded the entry visa for Poland—issued by the KGB, of course, not by Poland. This sign of sensitive status assured Victor instant cooperation. Personnel booked his flight on Aeroflot, which for security reasons was the only airline he was permitted to fly. He arranged to pick up his ticket that evening.

Back in his office, Victor opened his safe, took out the cables, and checked them again. The first was on KGB letterhead and was addressed to the Warsaw KGB Representative.

In accordance with standard security protocol, Victor used code names, both for individuals and for official bodies like the Central Committee, which was referred to as "the Instance." An exception was Kuritsyn, because he was the official KGB Representative. It was not uncommon, however, to use real names for cables to the Communist Bloc countries.

The KGB had an elaborate system of code names. For instance, "Orlov" in quotes indicated a Soviet Illegal operating abroad. "Comrade Murray" meant a foreign "friend," such as an official in a local Communist party. A foreign first name in quotes, like "Roger," meant a local agent. A foreign surname, like "Murray," in quotes indicated a mole.

A regular KGB officer was referred to in all communications as "Comrade" plus a Russian surname, as in "Comrade Yermakov"—Victor Sheymov's code name. In foreign postings all KGB officers were supposed to address one another by their code names whenever they were working inside the KGB station. This practice had its comic aspects. For instance, a junior officer might feel uncomfortable interacting with a considerably senior officer on a single-name basis. It would feel awkward, if not outright insubordinate. Yet he couldn't risk violating the code-name regulations. Very often the solution was simply to dispense with names altogether.

This complicated system had been established over many years. For some reason one of the first decisions Kryuchkov made when he became Chief of the First CD was to completely reform it. The stroke of a pen changed the formal identity of every KGB officer, agent, and "friend." Instant confusion. The ensuing massive resistance sabotaged the implementation of the new system. The old one could not easily be restored. As a result, confusions were frequent, from the top down.

However, Victor thought wryly, from a security point of view there was something to be said for Kryuchkov's approach: the opposition must have been every bit as confused by the results as was the KGB itself. He reviewed the cables.

<u>FLASH</u>

TOP SECRET

KURITSYN:

UNDER THE AUTHORITY OF THE INSTANCE, OUR SERVICE REPRESENTATIVE COMRADE YERMAKOV WILL BE GOING TO WARSAW TO DISCUSS THE EMBASSY SECURITY PROBLEMS WITH THE AMBASSADOR. PLEASE PROVIDE THE HIGHEST-LEVEL SECURITY MEASURES FOR COMRADE YERMAKOV, AND EXTEND HIM YOUR FULL COOPERATION.

COMRADE YERMAKOV HAS TOP-LEVEL SECURITY CLEARANCE AND HAS AUTHORIZED ACCESS TO ANY PREMISES OF THE EMBASSY, REFERENTURA, AND RESIDENTURA.

HE WILL BE ARRIVING WARSAW ON TOMORROW MORNING'S AEROFLOT FLIGHT.

ARTEMOV

Artemov was Andreyev's code name.

Since this was Victor's first trip to Warsaw, and his code name wasn't on record at the Station there, it had to be sent, but it had to be done by a separate cable. For security reasons, this so-called "tail" had to be processed with a different kind of cipher. Thus if one of the cables somehow got into enemy hands, there would be only a partial breach of security.

A third telegram had to be sent, in accordance with the standard operating procedure, this time to the Ministry of Foreign Affairs. In this case, code names were not used. Victor was one of the very few KGB officers to have an MFA cipher telegram letterhead notepad. He read:

<u>FLASH</u>

TOP SECRET

SOVIET AMBASSADOR:

IN ACCORDANCE WITH THE DECISION OF THE CENTRAL COMMITTEE OF THE COMMUNIST PARTY, AND UNDER THE AUTHORITY FROM THE CENTRAL COMMITTEE, REPRESENTATIVE OF THE CLOSE NEIGHBORS COMRADE SHEYMOV VICTOR IVANOVICH WILL BE GOING TO WARSAW TO DISCUSS URGENT SECURITY PROBLEMS WITH THE AMBASSADOR, COMRADE KARLOV.

COMRADE SHEYMOV HAS THE HIGHEST SECURITY CLEARANCE AND IS AUTHORIZED TO ENTER ANY PREMISES OF THE EMBASSY. HIS SECURITY WILL BE PROVIDED BY THE CLOSE NEIGHBORS. DURING HIS STAY IN WARSAW HE MUST RESIDE ON EMBASSY PREMISES. PLEASE MAKE ALL NECESSARY ARRANGEMENTS.

YOUR COOPERATION IN THIS MATTER WILL BE APPRECIATED.

ZEMSKOV

Zemskov was a Deputy Foreign Minister. "Close Neighbors" meant the KGB. The arbitrary presentation of this visit as a *fait accompli* was sure to irritate the MFA, but they'd have to comply. The cable would be automatically signed by the Deputy Minister of Foreign Affairs and sent under his name to the embassy through MFA channels.

Victor locked his safe and, cables in hand, waved to Michael. "Back in a minute."

He sent them off. All set.

Victor spent the rest of the day in taking care of routine business and putting the major projects he was juggling on hold. There was the usual backlog of phone calls. He had to move on the endless stream of requests from all over the world for changes in cipher-security procedures. They all claimed that some peculiar local condition made fulfillment of this or that security measure a practical impossibility. "Can we place the cipher machine ten centimeters from the wall instead of thirty centimeters?" "Our Residence is very small. The cipher clerk can't go into town with his wife. The guy's virtually in jail here. Can we make an exception for him?" These requests were a real pain in the neck. Everyone out there wanted variances to save their butts. Nobody in the Center wanted to give them for the same valid reason. And there was no such thing as a simple request. Even in a case where an exception was clearly feasible, Victor still had to get a dozen approval signatures from every conceivable department. Whenever possible the Center's response was "Hell, no!" It was less complicated that way.

There were also the never-ending requests for communications and security equipment. The suppliers were always way behind their deadlines, despite sworn promises to their "buddy," Victor.

Worst of all were those odd requests that Boss or Koryakov didn't know what to do with. They simply dumped them on Victor, with a scribbled order in the margin: "Research and report." "Coordinate with everyone concerned." Or simply, "Take care of this."

Victor knew the first rule of bureaucracy: "Don't rush to carry out an order. The next one could contradict it." He had learned to operate according to the logical derivative of that rule: Every paper given to you to work on should be seasoned in a safe. Chances are that no action will be needed at all. If the issue doesn't go away by itself, at least you'll know more about it, so your decision will be based on a better-educated guess.

The next morning he went to Sheremetyevo International Airport. Alone. Maybe it was superstition, but he never let Olga see him off on a mission. She'd be waiting at the airport when he returned, though.

After one glance at his special passport, the Customs officer waved him through. Boarding and takeoff were routine, and by midmorning Victor was well on his way to Warsaw. He relaxed in his seat and began his final mental preparation for the adventure ahead.

CHAPTER

VICTOR WASTED NO TIME in using the number Olga had given him. As he dialed the phone, he prayed the *coup de foudre* had struck her as well. She answered.

By the end of three weeks, they were spending all of their spare time together. Rather, all of Victor's spare time. Having just graduated from the University, Olga had a grace period to find a job—thanks to her family's academic contacts she was not subject to arbitrary placement by the State. Instead, she was one of the few who had the privilege of "free distribution"—the right to find a job on her own, and she was looking around. And Victor, usually the last to leave work at night, now shot out of his office each day at the first possible chance. They couldn't get enough of each other. Victor had to endure a little friendly teasing at the office, but he'd paid his dues, and no one could accuse him of not working hard enough.

During his student years, he'd been involved in a disastrous first marriage, and he was now understandably gun-shy. He had avoided getting involved in anything beyond casual affairs, in which he had called the shots.

His family's social standing, along with his own privileged lifestyle, made him a target for Moscow "wanna-be's." He'd grown accustomed to having girls chase him. The pattern was predictable. First an attraction, a flirtation, dates, perhaps the beginning of an affair, and then the girl would start inquiring about the possibility of marriage, usually right after she learned just how well off he was. He was not surprised, just disappointed to be pursued only for his job, his car, and his apartment. As a result, he kept his guard up and his heart to himself.

Not now, not with Olga. She was totally unlike anyone he'd ever met. She showed little or no interest in material things and seemed unimpressed by Victor's standard of living. She clearly loved Victor for himself. He plunged headlong into the most intense relationship of his life. He had never wanted to be so close to anyone before.

Instead of being threatened or overwhelmed by his passionate curiosity, little by little she revealed herself to him. She let him know that her "secret hobby"—sketching—went well beyond being a hobby. As a girl, fine arts had been her passion—not surprising with five generations of artists in her blood. Discouraged by her family for practical reasons, she'd taken her talent "underground," continuing to draw only for her own pleasure. Up to now, she'd never shown her work to anyone. When she allowed Victor to see some of her sketches, he was impressed and urged her to take up her art again in earnest.

A favorite pastime of theirs was taking long day trips by car. Victor knew the countryside around Moscow as well as he knew the city itself. He loved showing Olga his favorite drives, vistas, and picnic spots. One of their delights was Abramtsevo, a favored haunt of artists since the time when it belonged to Mamontov, a famous Russian patron of art. In autumn Abramtsevo was beautiful beyond description.

On one of these excursions, toward the end of their idyllic first three weeks together, Olga announced, "Victor, the Universiada, the International Student Olympics, starts next week—did you know?"

"Yes. Sure." Victor had professional reasons for knowing. The KGB regarded the Universiada as a major occasion for games of their own, using the event for bringing some agents home and for getting some moles to come to the Center in person. And the KGB could also observe the many foreign agents who were sure to accompany the groups of visiting athletes. It was also an admirable recruiting opportunity.

"Well, I am going to get to help with it."

A warning light flashed. "Oh, really? You never mentioned it. What will you be doing?"

She shrugged, "I'm not sure yet. When I was still at the University they asked us to help out. I volunteered." She misunderstood his concern and teased him: "Oh, I'll still have time for you, I promise. It's only for two weeks."

Victor paused. This was the down side of his job. He chose his words carefully.

"Do you remember when you asked me where I worked, and I told you I was a scientist?"

"Yes . . . ?"

"Well, I didn't actually complete my answer." Victor paused, reluctant to take the next step. "You see, I really was a scientist once, and not a bad one at that. I worked for a space research group." He could stall no longer. "Now, I'm an officer in the KGB."

Olga was quiet. Victor watched her face carefully. He knew all too well that most people associated the KGB with the Red Terror and Stalin's purges. He didn't want her to jump to the wrong conclusion. He added quickly, "I can assure you, I have nothing to do with internal affairs. My work is only with activities abroad."

"I see."

Silence. The sky was falling.

"I'm sorry I didn't tell you earlier, but I couldn't. As a matter of fact, I shouldn't be telling you this much now, but I love you, and I think we've reached a point where you must make a decision. I wouldn't blame you if you backed away."

She looked at him. He still didn't know her well enough to read her expression.

Finally, she broke the silence. "Victor, what do you think I am? Do you think I would back away from you because of what you do? I am in love with you, not your job. I trust you, no matter what it is you do."

Relief surged through Victor. He said simply, "I am grateful for your trust."

"Love is always blind," laughed Olga. "Otherwise it's not love, right?"

Victor hesitated. He had never let himself approach anything blindly. Until now.

She touched his face gently. "You're still worried? What else is there that I shouldn't know?"

"I'm afraid I can't tell you exactly what it is I do, but I must tell you that it is extremely sensitive. Top secret. What I'm trying to say is that there are restrictions on what I can do and who I can meet."

"Do these restrictions apply to your women?" Her eyes danced as she teased him.

"I'm afraid so." He was serious.

"Aha, I see! You are allowed to consort with only the best?" She was irrepressible. How he adored her.

He laughed, "No, just the most tight-lipped."

"In what sense?"

"You guess."

They both laughed at that. Then, still giggling, unwilling to take him seriously, Olga asked, "You don't mean that you have to report our relationship?"

"I don't need to. They already know about it." That stopped her.

"But how? Victor, are you saying that they spy on you?"

"It's called surveillance."

"Is that because they don't trust you?"

"Oh no, of course they trust me." He shrugged. "To the extent that they can trust anybody." He quickly reassured her. "It's actually for my own protection."

"Protection from what?"

"You see, I'm quite an attractive target. . . ."

"I already know that."

"Thank you, but what I was going to say is that the information I have access to makes me valuable to foreign intelligence. So the purpose of the restrictions is to protect me from them." Then he laughed, "And, perhaps from myself."

In the middle of one of their scenic detours, they stopped at Izba—one of Victor's favorite countryside restaurants—for lunch. Izba was a log house, in the old style of Russian inns. There weren't many of them left.

The food was authentic old Russian fare—a reminder of the days when there were plenty of fish in the rivers and suckling pig was not about to be listed in the Red Book of Endangered Species. A time when pickling was commonplace—necessary, even, to preserve the overflow of produce. It was a world far removed from the present food lines, shortages, and hoarding.

After they were seated, Victor continued the conversation.

"It's important that you understand about the restrictions, Olga, because they will affect what you yourself can and cannot do, as well." Despite her assurances, he wanted her to be absolutely clear on this issue. "For example, I can't travel abroad unless I'm on official business. I can never be a tourist. I can't have contact with a foreigner, directly or indirectly."

"What is indirect contact?"

"If a relative or close friend of mine is in touch with a foreigner."

"Like me?"

Victor smiled, "I think you qualify as a close friend."

"Now I see why you frowned when I told you about my job with the Universiada. But can't I do it? I promised them, and besides, it would be so exciting to play a part in the event. Oh, Victor, please?"

Victor fell silent. He was on tricky ground. If he said yes, an official report would be made, and the consequences could be most unpleasant. He'd probably be told in a "friendly" way that it could happen to anyone—nothing to worry about. However, a stiff lecture on vigilance would follow, with a gentle but firm order to cease and desist. If he obeyed the order, he'd lose Olga. But if he defied it, his career might well be finished, and he could easily wind up in a dead-end busywork job until his happy retirement twenty-some years hence. On the other hand, if he said no to Olga now, he'd be infringing on her freedom. He didn't have the moral right to do that. Suddenly, he was annoyed with a system that could set them both up with such a dilemma, and his reaction startled him. Never before had it crossed his mind to question security regulations. He'd certainly never imagined the possibility of deliberately violating them. He was surprised to realize that his feelings for Olga had led him to this critical juncture. He weighed the options and their consequences carefully and concluded that regardless of the risk, he simply could not penalize Olga for loving him. It was a dangerous decision. For both of them.

"All right. Let's see if we can get around the wretched rules."

She laughed delightedly, unaware of the significance of the risk he was taking for her, and leaned across the table to kiss him.

"Now, here's what we can try. You'll probably be assigned as a hostess to one of the visiting delegations. Accept the position, but make sure you don't talk to anyone from the delegation without the KGB guy at your side."

"How will I know which one he is?"

"You can't miss him. He'll be the one person who seems to serve no useful purpose, and he'll be the most obtrusively stupid one there." They both laughed. He continued, "Don't worry about identifying him. He'll probably be introduced at your briefing. As the games get under way, I expect he'll tell you to get friendly with someone in the delegation. That will be because he thinks that person is an undercover intelligence officer or a target for recruitment. Just play dumb and innocent. He'll get frustrated and let you alone. In the meantime, I won't report anything about this 'indirect contact.' Let's see how it goes. The most important part is this: you must promise to tell me everything that happens, no matter how insignificant it seems to you. I'll advise you on how to proceed."

"I promise."

Of course, the KGB surveillance would see what was going on. He was betting on the "no effective contact" card. This was, after all, a controlled environment. However, it was important to ensure that a minor problem did not develop into a major one, where serious action would have to be taken as a matter of routine. Anyway, morally he felt he didn't have a choice.

Olga was subdued for the rest of the meal. Troubled. Finally she spoke. "What does it feel like? I mean, isn't it awful to know you're being watched day-in, day-out?"

"Oh, well, it's not like that, Olga. It's not all the time, just periodically." He tried to think of a way to change the subject. In the light of his decision, he didn't want to dwell on the thought of surveillance at the moment.

But she wouldn't let it drop. "It sounds terrible. What kind of job is worth living in a fishbowl?"

"My darling, like it or not, in this country everyone's in some kind of a fishbowl. The only difference is that access to my fishbowl is extremely limited."

She was stunned. "Victor, are you telling me that ordinary people like me are spied on?"

"It's not spying, Olga, it's just simple surveillance. . . ."

"Is there anyone not being spied on?"

He shrugged, giving up on semantics. A rose was, after all, a rose. "Only those so insignificant that nobody cares about them one way or the other."

"How horrible!" She covered her face with her hands.

She was so naive, so untouched by the world. It was a strange experience for Victor to see the things he took for granted—surveillance, security, and complex restrictions—through her innocent eyes.

"Welcome to the real world, Olga," he said gently. "I'm sorry I'm the one who had to make the introduction."

Suddenly, she lifted her face from her hands, her eyes wide with yet another shocking thought, "Do they watch us when we are making love?"

Victor had to smile. "No, only when we are not, which means they don't see much of us."

She laughed, and he continued, "But seriously, you mustn't worry about that. It's not the sort of thing they're concerned with. They check on me from time to time, and they are unobtrusive. It's simply a fact of life."

The black cloud passed on, for the moment, and they teased each other about evading surveillance by round-the-clock lovemaking. Although Victor was relieved, he was certain the subject would come up again.

Later in the week, Olga attended an orientation meeting at the University for those who were going to work on the Student Olympics. It was quite formal, and the fifty volunteers in Olga's group sat looking somewhat lost in the cavernous main auditorium as they waited for the three men seated at the red-draped table up on the stage to begin. Olga recognized only one of them, the Deputy Dean, the man who controlled student activities. Literally. His job was to know everything about each student, and much of his intelligence came from the informers who permeated the student body. It was well known that, in keeping with the tradition of the position, he was on very good terms with both the KGB and the University's powerful Personnel Department. In fact, most Deputy Deans were awarded their positions after serving as KGB informers. They often determined the placement of students after graduation. The Deputy Dean was the faculty member the students feared most of all.

As Olga watched, the Deputy Dean rose and approached the podium. The most distinguishing thing about him was that he was completely nondescript. He gave a short introductory speech on what an honor it was to be entrusted with the responsibility of working at the games.

Later that evening, when Olga related the gist of his speech to Victor, she said, "Victor, you'd have thought he was prepping us for an international summit meeting the way he harped on how important these games are to the country. For heaven's sake! They're student games—not even the real Olympics!"

Victor nodded, then said, "I know it may seem ridiculously exaggerated to you, but the Party views the Student Olympics as an important event because they offer a chance to advance the country's image in the world. In a way it really is a kind of summit because it draws the international media. So everything must go smoothly. There can't be any embarrassments."

"But Victor, wait till you hear the rest!" Victor was quite certain that he already had, if not with Olga's particular spin on it.

She continued, "So, he introduced the next speaker." There was a mischievous twinkle in her eyes. Her sense of play delighted him, and he looked forward to her performance.

She stood behind an upright chair, her mock podium, and set the scene.

"OK, Victor, this guy was in his late twenties, me-ti-cu-lous-ly groomed." She struck a pose worthy of Pushkin's Onegin and continued. "Every inch the successful young bureaucrat—I mean he was the epitome of an up-and-coming Party apparatchik. He must have his hair done at least twice a week." She dropped the pose for an instant, giggling at her recollection of the young fop. Then she went right back into character.

"So. Now he steps up to the podium with great dignity." Olga fixed Victor with a Significant Look, drew a deep breath, and continued, "Now he begins to speak like the Practiced Reader of Official Speeches." Here she changed down into a very deep and mellifluously fruity voice, pretending to address a large gathering.

"'Comrades, I salute you. I am honored to be speaking to you today on behalf of the Moscow Komsomol Committee. As you all know, this event is especially significant in today's extremely complicated international environment. The enemies of our great country are becoming increasingly sophisticated in their campaign of disinformation. You all know as well as I that the agents of international imperialism would like nothing better than to see Moscow fail as the host of these games. While this poses a tremendous challenge, it also gives us a great opportunity to succeed in the eyes of the world.'"

Victor laughed heartily as she burlesqued the functionary's style. Given Olga's delivery, standard Party rhetoric was hilarious. And absurdly predictable.

"'The struggle to spread Communism has shifted to the ideological front.'" Fierce face now. "'The enemies of Communism delight in finding what they think are flaws in our system.'" Here she became positively evangelical—a fervent fop. Victor was helpless with laughter. "'Your task is to prevent such misinterpretation.

"'Let me give you an example: you are all aware of the fact that most families in our country share apartments with other families. If the capitalist visitors discover this, they will try to tell you that in their countries every family has its own apartment. Now we all know that is absolutely untrue, but you have no way of proving that. The only solution is not to let them make the discovery in the first place. If they do, despite your efforts, simply tell them that most of the families here have their own apartments, and those who don't will soon. End of the question.

"'Another example: The enemy capitalists will no doubt tell you that in their countries a common worker can buy a car. Again, a lie, but again, no way for you to prove that. Do not provoke an argument, simply tell them that our public transportation is so good that our citizens do not need to squander their money on cars. Of course, the capitalists will be provided with special transportation. As far as they are concerned, it is our standard public transportation.

"'They will try to flash a lot of spending money. Do not be fooled. Their imperialist masters supply them with money to show off in front of the Soviet people. They want you to believe that the standard of living is higher under the capitalist system of exploitation. This is not true, and we all know it.'"

Olga took a breath and, dropping out of character for a moment, said: "Victor, it was such a silly speech. At least it certainly seemed so to me."

"I'm sure it did. But he was playing the game. He wasn't speaking for the benefit of you and your group; he was speaking for the record, to qualify for promotion. As for the Party instructions he delivered, well, for some reason a lot of people at the top believe that by covering up and denying our shortcomings we'll be able to recruit more believers in the Communist goals. Personally, I can't agree with that approach, but so what? Those are the rules of the game, and everyone has to play by them. Or be out."

Olga was momentarily sobered by Victor's serious tone. Then, unwilling to leave the charade unfinished, she shook her head gaily and snapped back into character. "'I can assure you that one of the main reasons they are bringing these games here is to try and corrupt you, to make you believe that material advantages outweigh ideological commitments. Never forget their ultimate goal is the defeat of Communism and the conquest of our Motherland. With this in mind, let me warn you of one other grave problem we anticipate: there is bound to be a good deal of espionage activity on the part of the corrupt agencies of imperialist Western intelligence. To address this issue, I would like to introduce Comrade Arkady, representing the KGB, the Iron Guard of our Soviet State. Before I yield my place, however, permit me to speak for the Moscow Komsomol and express our heartfelt conviction that each of you will meet this challenge successfully. We trust that you will make us proud that you bear the title of Member of the Lenin Komsomol. Thank you.' Then he nods graciously to the polite applause that follows and sits down."

Victor began to provide the polite applause, but Olga stopped him with a dramatic gesture. Ominously she said, "Then the third speaker rose.

"This man was roughly the same age as the Komsomol representative, and I mean roughly. Any similarity between the two ended with age. This guy was tastelessly dressed and crude. Victor, he looked like he slept in his clothes—all the time. Where the last guy had been like refined oil, this one was like sand in the machinery! Just listen: I give you your colleague, an officer of the KGB."

Victor acknowledged the needle with an exaggerated wince. He was, in fact, quite offended at being tarred with the same brush, but it was too complicated to try to explain. At least for now.

As he watched, her body completely transformed itself from the posture of a dandy to that of a Neanderthal. Victor knew already that her voice would be commensurately loud and aggressive.

"'Hello, Comrades.'" It was something between a roar and a grunt. Victor smiled, instantly recognizing the type. "'You have been entrusted to work with the Canadian delegation, and you will be reporting directly to me. I hope the importance of this work is clear to you. Canada is a member of NATO—one of our principal enemies.'"

Without knowing it, Olga had hit a nerve. It would have been easier with Bulgarians or Hungarians or athletes from some other Bloc country.

Olga continued, unaware of his concern. It was a tribute to her skill as a mimic that she soon had Victor laughing again. "'The Canadians aided those traitors in the White Army who opposed the Revolution and gave them shelter when they were driven out. Canada has been a major center of anticommunist activities ever since.

"'The first thing we want from you is absolute discipline. We will not tolerate any deviation from instructions. While your orders will not be complicated, we expect them to be executed precisely as given. Remember, we at the KGB know how to deal with smartbutts who think they can play games with us.

"'Your job is to entertain these people as guests, but you must never forget that they are our enemies. Even those who are not spies have been so indoctrinated with anticommunist propaganda that they will only be able to see what they've been told to see. Don't let your hospitality carry you away. These people must travel in groups, and only to assigned destinations. If you are accompanying a group, make sure that nobody disappears or goes off on his own. I warn you, it will be your responsibility to keep the group together. Some will try to sneak off at the first opportunity to do their dirty spying business, and I assure you, you will be held accountable.

"'They are clever. Be alert at all times. Accepting gifts or money is, of course, out of the question. You must report everything to us. We watch everything. Whatever we don't know, we find out.'" Olga finished with an emphatic grunt, then collapsed in a giggling heap. Wiping her eyes, she finished the scene, "And then he told us we'd get our specific assignments from him tomorrow morning. He asked for questions. No questions. He sat down. No applause. The Deputy Dean stood up, thanked the speakers, and declared the meeting over."

Victor stood, laughing and applauding. But in a tiny corner of his mind the warning light was blinking. Play this very carefully.

At the end of the first day of the Olympics, Olga met Victor. She laughed, "You were absolutely right last week! The KGB guy you said would be there was our friend Arkady, and he's just as stupid and obtrusive as you said he'd be. Not only that, but he has already asked me to 'charm' a Canadian named Glen."

Victor suddenly realized that his "no effective contact" rationalization would not bear much scrutiny. "Who is Glen, and how did you handle the request?" he questioned Olga.

"My assignment is with the Canadian delegation, and Glen is the assistant coach of their volleyball team. I suppose Arkady thinks he's the spy. Anyway, I did what you advised and pretended not to understand what Arkady was asking me to do. He had to spell it out and ask me to sleep with Glen. Well, I put on such a show of outrage, Victor, you'd have been proud of me. I said I was shocked that the KGB could possibly encourage anything as immoral as sleeping with a foreigner. I said I'd have to check with my uncle in the Central Committee." She was laughing helplessly, remembering Arkady's face at the remark.

"Do you have an uncle in the Central Committee?"

The question dampened Olga's glee. "No, of course not, I was just bluffing, but isn't it funny?"

"Olga, this is very serious; there's no room for jokes with someone like Arkady. Believe me, I know the type. Never bluff unless you have to, and then be extremely careful." Victor could well imagine what this detail might add to a hostile interpretation of his "indirect contact."

"But, Victor, he backed right off and said that it was a misunderstanding. He said what he meant was that I should chat with Glen, informally, and then report the conversations back to him."

"Good."

"Then, I led Arkady to Glen and introduced them. I started talking nonstop. Arkady was stunned, and Glen must think I'm the most garrulous and stupid KGB agent in Moscow. Neither of them knew what to do, so they just stood and listened to me blab. They were quite relieved when I finally let them go. I'm sure Glen will stay as far away from me as he can."

"You've done well, but you must be careful. You should know that Arkady is just a decoy whose job is to make Glen, or whoever the under-cover agent is, let his guard down and grow careless. The KGB guys you don't see are smarter. This is nothing to fool with, Olga. Do you under-stand?" Victor was referring to a standard KGB practice. There would most certainly be a highly professional KGB surveillance team ready and waiting to work "from the shade" if needed. She nodded, subdued by the intensity of his reaction.

Despite Olga's fictitious uncle, it became clear over the next few days that Arkady had not in fact given up on the idea of using her charm and beauty to work on Glen. From what he heard from Olga, Victor read Glen as a first-class professional who was willing to lay low and play along. Victor wanted Olga to stay out of this game. If the KGB was not going to leave her alone, help would have to come from the Opposition. So Victor asked her to clarify things with Glen.

The next day, as Olga escorted the team to a match, riding the spe-cially designated bus, Glen slid into the seat next to hers and said, "I don't know much about Russian social customs, but it strikes me as a little odd that your friend Arkady doesn't seem to mind if I invite you out for a drink or dinner. In fact, he has encouraged me." He smiled, "So, would you like to join me tonight?" Olga was learning fast. She knew enough by now to understand that this was an indirect way of finding out if she was working with the KGB. Of course, he'd know that only those affiliated with the KGB would be allowed to consort with foreigners. If she agreed to go with him, he'd have his answer.

Looking him steadily in the eye, so that there'd be no misunderstand-ing, she smiled and said, "You know, you'll be gone soon, but I live here. With Arkady and his friends around, the last thing I'm looking for is com-plications. Also, I have a boyfriend whom I love very much. I don't think drinks or dinner would be a good idea. But thank you all the same. And good luck with your match today." The message was delivered sweetly, but it was clear: "I don't work for the KGB, and I don't play around."

Glen understood. "OK. Thanks," he said quietly.

During the next two weeks, Victor worried that Olga might miss some-thing important and be more vulnerable than she realized. He was frus-trated at having to keep his distance and desperately wanted to take a closer look at the situation for himself. He even went as far as setting up a plan to shadow Olga on an outing to the Moscow Circus—special enter-tainment arranged for the Canadian delegation. He weighed the pros and cons of his scheme carefully and in the end abandoned the idea. If anything untoward did happen, and he got involved—which he was bound to do if Olga was in any danger—there'd be hell to pay. His position was precarious enough already.

Later, as he listened to her account of the outing, his judgment was vindicated. "And then I got such a scare, Victor! After the circus, Arkady and I escorted the Canadians back to the University on foot—it's just a short walk—and Glen was telling me about circuses in Canada. We were comparing styles and individual acts. I guess we were walking more slowly than the others because we began to fall behind. One of the guys from the team—Michel—dropped back to see if we were OK, and he got into the circus act with us. He was so funny! Victor, he almost had us weeping with laughter! Then Glen stopped to light a cigarette—isn't it odd that a coach smokes—and couldn't get a match lit because of the wind. Michel started to describe his favorite clown act from his home-town circus and had me in stitches. I didn't even notice that we'd started walking again. I turned around to see if Glen had finally lit his cigarette, and he wasn't there! Victor, my heart stopped! Michel took one look at my face and said, 'What's the matter? He hasn't run away from you. Didn't you see him pass us to get a light from someone up ahead?' Oh, Victor, thank God! For a moment I thought I was in very hot water. Then we went back to circuses and laughed all the way to the University. So, you see? No problems. You didn't need to worry."

Victor just smiled, thinking, "A clean break of his surveillance—neat job. Christ, I'm glad I wasn't there." His initial sympathy for the assistant coach who didn't seem to know all that much about volleyball was instantly transformed into professional appreciation.

Needless to say, Victor and Olga were immensely relieved when the Universiada was over. But it would be another three weeks before Victor could feel confident that there had been no damaging fallout.

CHAPTER

THE AEROFLOT TU LANDED on schedule at Warsaw airport. The passengers were herded into a bus and driven to the run-down Customs building. Ordinary Soviet travelers dreaded running this Polish gauntlet, which could not have been more irritatingly inefficient and time-consuming. Not a problem for Victor. Automatically, he scanned the small crowd. He was sure he'd be able to spot the chief of Embassy Security. He always could. This time proved no exception. There he stood, a smartly dressed man in his mid-thirties, slightly apart from and behind the others. He'd be personally responsible for Victor's security as long as he was in Warsaw. Their eyes met, and they advanced toward each other. The other man spoke first. "Comrade Sheymov?"

"Yes."

"Titov. Valery. I'm the Security Officer of the embassy. Welcome to Warsaw." They shook hands.

"Victor. Glad to meet you."

Valery guided Victor toward the head of the line at Passport Control. Abruptly, he snatched Victor's passport with one hand, leaned over the counter under the nose of the Polish passport-control officer, picked up the official entry stamp, flicked open the passport, and stamped it. The Polish officer looked rather embarrassed. Not that he questioned Valery's authority. He was just dismayed by the unceremonious manner with which Valery exercised it. The Pole accepted the stamp back from Valery with a curt nod.

They walked out to Valery's Soviet Lada, chatting about the weather and the deplorably shabby condition of the airport.

Victor was warily polite—he knew his visit was not welcome. But Valery was a type Victor could relate to. He was flamboyant and boyishly good-looking with quick, confident movements. His style suggested he'd be at home anywhere. He certainly seemed so in Warsaw. Streetwise and slightly defiant, Valery was a man whom in office slang they'd call a "hooligan," someone who doesn't hesitate to break the rules to get the job done. Victor knew a player when he saw one, and as they got acquainted, he found they had much in common. Both Muscovites, they had grown up in the same type of neighborhood: rough, with a strong criminal element and gangs that lived by a strict code of street honor. Those who survived this school could recognize a fellow alumnus anywhere. By the time they were halfway to the embassy, they were friends.

Valery went out of his way to be helpful and briefed Victor: "Kuritsyn is furious with you guys. He was fit to be tied yesterday when he was notified by the Center about your arrival and ordered to help, without having been consulted. I don't know what your plans are, but you don't have too many friends around here, even at the Station. And by the way, the Ambassador flew off to Moscow yesterday. You'd better watch your step on whatever red carpet they roll out for you."

"Come on, you know how they do things in the Capital City. Let's just say I didn't volunteer for this job. And that's an understatement."

"In that case, you have my sympathy."

"We'll find a way to manage, I'm sure."

Once inside the embassy grounds, Valery pulled the car up to the main entrance and ordered a guard to take Victor's suitcase to his quarters.

They entered the embassy building and took the elevator to the top floor. There was only one door in the hall. Valery pushed a secret button hidden under the nearest windowsill. The door opened, and they entered the KGB Station. Because it was a Warsaw Pact station, there were in fact two KGB teams here. One was more or less visible, run by the KGB Representative, ostensibly for friendly liaison purposes only, and operating with the Polish service against third parties. The KGB Representative even had an office in the Polish service's headquarters. The second team, however, was strictly undercover, run by a Resident, who reported to the Representative. This team had no official contact with the Polish service. In fact, as far as they were concerned, the Poles were no less an enemy than the service of any Western country. The Bloc services were aware of this KGB practice and bitterly resented it. Not openly, however.

"Kuritsyn is waiting for you now. Don't forget, he's boiling. I wouldn't unpack anything until after your meeting."

They threaded their way past a number of strained hellos and approached the Representative's office. Valery presented Victor to the secretary in the outer office, who then immediately opened the general's door. Valery stage-whispered, "Good luck." Victor entered to find General Kuritsyn sitting at his desk.

They had not met before. The man before him was stocky, grey-haired, in his mid-sixties. His bulky, ill-fitting suit and stale, wrinkled shirt were indicative of the rude style with which he ruled his little kingdom. But Victor was not about to underestimate him. He had heard that this man's career in the KGB had been legendary.

The two men sized each other up. Victor chose the most courteous form of address and spoke first: "Good afternoon, Nikolai Pavlovich."

Kuritsyn rose, and Victor approached him. They shook hands over the desk.

"Hello. I wish I could say, 'Welcome,' but . . . ," he shrugged. Not a happy man. "Take a seat, Comrade Sheymov."

Victor sat in the chair facing the desk.

After several moments of tense silence, Kuritsyn began to speak in a quiet, fatherly voice. Victor was not fooled by the tone. Not from this veteran shark.

"I must be getting too old for this job, Comrade Sheymov."

Victor wondered where this unusual opening gambit would lead.

Kuritsyn continued, "Yes, I think so. You see, you look very young to me, a much younger man than your paper credentials would have led me to believe." He sighed and shook his head slowly, as if in dismay. "And that, I suppose, is a sign of age."

Victor tried levity to ease the tension. "Well, they say the disadvantage of youth disappears with time."

Kuritsyn ignored the joke and went on in the same paternal voice. "I had hoped those in the Center, those making the decisions, were older and, perhaps, wiser."

Another provocative pause. When Victor did not rise to the bait, Kuritsyn exploded, "What the hell's going on? Do you understand why I am here? What it is I do? Well, let me make it clear for you." He stood up and leaned over his desk toward Victor. He punctuated his points with his fists on the surface, scattering the papers piled there. "I am here in Poland as the Representative of the KGB. I represent the KGB to the Poles. I represent the KGB to the Ambassador. I represent the KGB to anyone else we come across in this wretched country. Me. Period. Do I make myself clear?"

Victor was silent, letting Kuritsyn vent his spleen.

The tirade continued, at a slightly lower pitch. "I have problems enough with the goddamn Poles, and I have my hands full with this Ambassador, who resists anything our people do. These problems are not our controllables. But this business of yours has to be our controllable. And I damn well intend to control it. Myself. As a matter of fact, I was just about to phone Andreyev and insist that he recall you. I even thought of calling Deputy Chairman Tsvigun. Then I decided to wait and talk to you first. So. Would you be kind enough to explain to this old man why you are trying to go around me?"

Victor paused as Kuritsyn sat back down. Then in a respectful, reasonable tone, he began his own gambit. Kuritsyn needed to be mollified before he could be persuaded to cooperate. And this man was no fool. "Nikolai Pavlovich, I believe I need to clarify my position. First of all, I don't make this kind of decision."

"Really?" snorted Kuritsyn sarcastically. "Then who does?"

"As I'm sure you know, all cipher-security matters are the prerogative of the Leadership of the Eighth CD." Victor was making sure the issue stayed on his own turf. "Our problem is that there is strong pressure from the Central Committee to improve the technical-security situation immediately."

Kuritsyn shrugged. "'Pressure' can always be created, and then used as leverage. No, Comrade Sheymov, I won't swallow that line."

"Unfortunately, that's not so in this instance. The Central Committee is adamant. Of course, we'd prefer to have more time. Frankly, we aren't prepared to move as fast as they want us to, even if we do get the green light from the Ambassador."

Kuritsyn was unimpressed. Victor decided to change his tack to a more personal appeal. He'd be risking Kuritsyn's contempt, but he had a hunch that vulnerability might work with this man where hardball wouldn't. "Nikolai Pavlovich, I don't think I put my position clearly enough. I am between a rock and a hard place. If I cannot convince you and the Ambassador here and now, I'll get a black eye for having failed. Even if I succeed with this mission and get what I'm asking for, I will still get a black eye later for failing to get the job done on time, no matter how much help I get from you. Now do you see?"

Kuritsyn narrowed his eyes and peered at Victor shrewdly as he considered this new angle. Victor hung there, out on his limb, waiting. Would it be the boot or the hand?

At last, Kuritsyn made his decision and shrugged. "Sounds familiar. I've been there myself."

He thought a moment longer, then continued in a friendlier voice, the paternal tone replaced by one of fraternity. "All right, Victor Ivanovich, tell me in plain language exactly what we are up against, and start at the beginning."

With the first squall of the storm over, they both relaxed in their chairs, and Victor began to explain. "As you know, despite significant advances in international intercept technology, there have been no major changes in any of our embassies' cipher-security measures for many years. Nobody wanted to fix what wasn't broken. However, not long ago there was a complete review of the communication-security systems. Our conclusion was that the standards for protecting our cipher communications and our secure conversations against possible interception were not as high as they needed to be. After the Central Committee read the report, heads rolled at the Eighth CD, and the command came from the Central Committee in no uncertain terms: 'Fix the problem, at any cost. Overnight.' In order to keep the matter quiet, only a handful of people could be involved. The sheer volume of work involved is enormous. Having an unlimited budget helps, of course, but we desperately need more people. We can't have them because of the sensitivity of the situation. Catch-22. So, in a few words, that's where we stand."

Kuritsyn was dubious. "You're being melodramatic?"

"Not at all."

"But you are talking in vague generalities, and I don't like it. If you want me to be your ally, or at least to be neutral, you've got to convince me with specifics."

This was Kuritsyn's ploy for gleaning information he was not supposed to have access to. And he was using the vulnerability of Victor's position for leverage. Victor could easily have outmaneuvered him, but in this situation it presented an opportunity for the perfect barter. He knew that KGB officers like Kuritsyn were completely in the dark about Eighth CD affairs and curious to learn anything they could. Victor figured that he could feed him a few convincing details without giving away anything really sensitive. He decided to try.

First, the set up:

"All right, Nikolai Pavlovich," Victor conceded. "But we'll have to take a walk."

"What?"

"I'm sorry, but you have no rooms secure enough for this conversation."

"If you are saying what I think you are saying, you are really starting to piss me off. Are you telling me that every conversation that has taken place in this room could have been intercepted?"

Victor shrugged.

Kuritsyn sputtered, incredulous, "Either you're crazy, or someone must be shot for gross negligence, or incompetence, or both!"

Victor dangled his bait: "As far as I know, this embassy does not have secure conversation rooms because it's in a Warsaw Pact country. We are supposedly among friends. I leave it to you to judge how far you can trust these 'friends,' but from a technical standpoint this place is not secure. If we are to speak of things which I should not even be discussing in the first place, I have to play it safe. I can't afford a misjudgment. Now, would you like to take that walk?"

Kuritsyn reached for his intercom, hesitating for an instant as he glared distrustfully at it before pressing the button. He barked, "Tell Valery to bring his car to the front door." Then he stood slowly and motioned Victor to the door. He seemed reluctant to say anything else in his office.

As they walked to the elevator, he spoke in a gruff whisper. "My car has a Polish Security Service driver. We're going to the Lazienkovwski Park nearby in Valery's car instead."

The ride took all of thirty seconds. Victor reflected briefly how it seemed that all generals hated to walk, and this one certainly could have used the exercise. Once inside the park, Kuritsyn ordered Valery to remain at a distance and keep his eyes open. Then he and Victor ambled past the famous statue of Frederik Chopin and sat on a bench. The general said impatiently, "Well?"

Victor began his performance. He drew a deep breath, to underline his plunge into forbidden territory, and began, "The rapid advance in intercept technology over the last several years has alarmed us. . . ."

"So you've already said. Get to the point."

"Hear me out, Nikolai Pavlovich. I presume that your primary interest lies in what specifically has to be done in response to these advances, rather than in the details of the technology. Am I correct?"

"You are."

"Well, since the protection of cipher communications is a priority for both of us, that's what I'll focus on. Agreed?"

Kuritsyn nodded. "Proceed."

Victor lowered his voice. Kuritsyn hunched down, listening intently. "The cipher machine we use is close to fifteen years old. From a cryptographic point of view, it's still effective. However, its plain text can be intercepted right as it's being typed. Of course, you have to have the proper equipment and technical know-how. But the most troublesome aspect is that the intercept equipment can be operated from quite a distance, certainly from outside the embassy buildings."

"And can the Poles do that?"

"We don't know exactly. But we do know that they've become very active and that they're fairly effective—generally. And we have no idea what level of operational capability the Americans have here, how close they can get to us. I'd appreciate any input on that. Later, of course."

"Are you telling me that we don't know whether or not our cipher communications are being read by the opposition?"

"I would rather say that there is a slim chance that technically they can be read. And that's a chance we cannot allow."

"Go on." Riveted, Kuritsyn was going to press for all he could get.

"When this problem was discovered a while ago, we took immediate measures. The 'quick fix' was a metal-mesh cage that would encase the cipher clerk and machine. Its effectiveness was limited, but it was only intended as a stopgap. It covered us while we developed the new cipher-security system. This new system emits a much weaker signal and is enclosed entirely in steel for complete shielding. In addition, there are electromagnetic-noise generators inside the enclosure. By themselves these could prevent interception even if they weren't enclosed."

"So, does this new system provide absolute security?" Kuritsyn demanded.

"So far as absolute security is possible, yes." Victor paused for effect, then carefully approached the crux of the matter. "There is one major drawback, however, and here's our problem. The upgrade takes a lot of room. The complete cipher-communications system requires three enclosures, one apiece for the KGB, the GRU or Military Intelligence, and the MFA. And then yet another room is needed in the basement for the motor generators."

"What do you need those for?"

"Weak but readable signals can still be picked up through the power supply line. To block such leaks, the new cipher-communications system has its own motor generator, whose motor is powered directly from the city's power line. This extra step is sufficient to mask the signal pulses. We refer to these as 'dirty' and 'clean' power supplies."

"You seem to have gone to great lengths to cover all the bases."

"For a good cause, wouldn't you say?"

Kuritsyn, sensing they were reaching the bottom line, grew noncommittal. "So what is it you are asking for now, specifically?"

"Space, Nikolai Pavlovich. Space. If you include the working rooms for each of the cipher clerks, it adds up to a lot of space. And that's what I need from the Ambassador."

"You've got some fight on your hands. As you know, space is extremely scarce in any embassy, and ours is no exception," Kuritsyn warned, beginning to position himself for solving the problem.

Victor sensed he'd turned the corner. "I know. But there's still one more critical point we have to consider," Victor said, drawing his new ally into the task. "We have to manufacture all materials ourselves, every item right down to the last nail—and we have to have absolute control of their transit. That's where you come in. It will be your responsibility to guarantee complete security for the delivery and storage."

"How much 'material' are we talking about?"

"About twenty tons."

"My God, you must be crazy! Come back to earth. How can anybody do that?"

Victor had anticipated Kuritsyn's reaction and was ready with reassurance. "Actually, here it will be easy. In Washington and New York it was far more difficult. In this case we'll simply send a couple of sealed trucks as diplomatic mail. All you have to do is meet them at the border with two diplomatic cars, bracket the trucks with the two cars, and escort them to the embassy."

"Young man, you've seen too many spy movies! If I tried that, I'd be the laughingstock of the entire intelligence community." No intelligence officer needed that kind of fame.

"I think that would be preferable to having one side laughing quietly for years."

"Are you seriously implying that equipment can be bugged while it is inside a moving truck?"

Victor shrugged. "I am."

"Come on."

"It not only can be done, it has been done." Victor's tone made it clear that that was as much as he would say.

Kuritsyn was amazed and desperately curious to know exactly how the rabbit had been slipped into the hat, but he understood that he was to ask no further questions.

Having established his authority, Victor took the opportunity to score an extra point with the general. He wanted his full commitment. Lowering his voice, Victor said, "A while ago the Japanese changed the cipher equipment in their Moscow embassy. Our guys didn't know until the last minute how it would be transported. They had only a few hours' notice that the sealed diplomatic truck, complete with diplomatic courier, would enter the Soviet Union from Finland through Vyborg, near Leningrad, and proceed nonstop to Moscow. Four hundred miles. Unfortunately for them, the Japanese didn't watch their tail, and our guys bugged the equipment en route. The bugs are still good, by the way, and probably will be for another ten years."

Kuritsyn was excited. He didn't seem to notice that Victor still hadn't told him how it had been done. For the first time since their meeting his face reflected admiration.

"Great job! The poor Japanese seem to have outstandingly bad luck with their communications." Kuritsyn was obviously referring to the famous code-breaking operation in World War II, which enabled the Americans to read the Japanese cipher telegrams at the same time as the Japanese. "Was this just one spectacular shot, or is it a pattern with your boys?" He was pressing his luck.

"Sorry, Nikolai Pavlovich, I'd rather talk about something else. I shouldn't have told you that story in the first place. It's just a question of discipline."

"Yes, of course, of course. But it sounds impossible . . ."

"As far as we're concerned, nothing can be considered impossible." The rebuke was gentle but unmistakable.

Kuritsyn was quiet. Now was the time to lighten up. "Let me give you a less sensitive example of how we do the impossible." The general brightened at the prospect of another tidbit. "In 1974, when Brezhnev was going to Washington for a big summit meeting, the KGB was humming like a beehive—more like a madhouse, actually. I was sitting in my office, doing my work, and quietly enjoying the fact that the presummit craziness didn't touch me directly. Suddenly, a friend of mine from the Politburo Communications Group popped in. Naturally, under the circumstances, he looked as if he were about to jump out of his skin. His voice was tense and strained as he pleaded, 'Victor, you've got to help me.'

"I said, 'Sure. How?'

" 'Do you know where I can get ten tons of scrap metal?'

"I was sure he was joking, so I looked closely at him, waiting for the telltale smile. No smile, just naked desperation. So I told him, 'Look, take a break, walk around a little, relax, and then, if you still think you need it, go to the junk yard.' I thought he was going to cry.

" 'Look, I'm serious. I need it in legit military-type crates—you know, like the ones we carry our equipment in.'

"I asked him what on earth he could possibly need such a thing for.

" 'Victor, you won't believe this. When Nixon came here for a visit, do you remember he brought about twelve tons of communications equipment with him? Some idiot reported it to Brezhnev. Now Brezhnev's given the order to top that. At the very least to bring the same amount to Washington! Now, we've got half a ton of actual equipment, and I managed to get a ton and a half of scrap metal. So we are ten tons short of the target.'

"I reminded him that the Americans had been bringing something else for their embassy and had simply taken advantage of the occasion.

" 'Sure, but who cares? He's given the order, and that's the end of it.'

"Now, I knew the system well enough to realize that under the circumstances it would be much easier just to carry out the order than to get someone to try and change Brezhnev's mind. So I said I'd do it, but only under one condition—I was an experienced bureaucrat by then.

" 'Name it!' He was desperate, so he'd have agreed to almost anything.

"I told him that when he got back he'd have to get rid of the junk himself. He was only too happy to agree.

"Well, I got on the phone, and by the end of the day I'd arranged for ten tons of scrap metal from all over Moscow to be packed in standard military crates and delivered RUSH to the KGB warehouse, where they awaited pickup by a special plane. The whole shipment traveled successfully to the U.S. And back."

Kuritsyn got a good chuckle out of the story, but he was not about to surrender unconditionally. He grew serious.

"So far, everything you've discussed has concerned communications with the outside. What about protecting conversations within the embassy?"

Victor tried to sidestep the question. "Secure rooms for conversation are not our forte at Eighth CD. That's more for the First CD, Directorate OT." Victor was referring to the Operational Technical Support Directorate.

"Yes, of course, I know. But I also know that the two fields have similarities, and you guys are much more sophisticated." True enough.

"Well, Nikolai Pavlovich, you put me in a difficult position. I can only answer that one off the record, and even then, remember, these are just my personal opinions."

Kuritsyn leaned forward eagerly, "It's a deal."

"Conversations are much easier to intercept than cipher communications. The embassy's conversation rooms here are not much good. Oh, and please, never try to use the radio to conceal conversations in a room. It's a complete fallacy. It simply doesn't work."

"And how about those clear plastic cubes, used in the West?"

"Those clear plastic cubes are either a product of total incompetence or somebody's idea of a good practical joke. They actually do more harm than good. It's almost as if they were designed to broadcast what they're supposed to be protecting."

"Are you serious?"

"Yes. The irony is that you're better off without them than with them. Actually, the only truly safe place for a top-secret chat is right inside our new cipher-machine enclosure."

"That would be fine, Victor, but the trouble is that, apart from the cipher clerks, I'm the only one permitted to enter the cipher area. So who would I have to talk to?"

Victor should have realized that making off-the-cuff suggestions would sooner or later have led him to say something stupid. Of course, nobody was allowed in those rooms. The general was alert, and Victor needed an out. "I mean you'd have to get extra cipher enclosures to use as secure conversation rooms."

"Can the OT Directorate do that?"

"Yes, if they use our specs."

"All right, then I'll request them."

"Please, but do it after I'm gone."

"OK."

Good luck. Victor didn't mention that the Eighth CD would not give out its specifications to anyone.

They fell silent.

Suddenly Kuritsyn blurted, "Why Poland?"

"We have taken care of the places that were in worse shape. Poland was next on the list."

"Why wasn't I briefed on this problem?"

This was what had been eating at the general. Moscow was concerned about a security problem on his turf. He was being kept in the dark. He'd crossed Moscow Center once. That was almost certainly why he had ended up in Warsaw. He must be wondering if Victor was the bearer of more bad tidings. Victor chose his words carefully.

"Well, you haven't been to Moscow for a while, and the Leadership wants this to look routine, to keep as low a profile as possible. They find it embarrassing that we've been vulnerable for such a long time. And, of course, we want to keep the opposition in the dark about the upgrade as long as possible."

"I don't find that answer satisfactory."

"Well, then, your question is beyond my salary." Instantly Victor regretted his wisecrack. Not only was it tactless, it was untrue. His pay was that of a major general in the military and higher than that of most civilian executives.

Fortunately, no offense was taken. "Angling for a raise?" joked the general.

"I could tolerate one."

They both laughed at that, then Kuritsyn grew quiet.

"Victor, what you've told me makes the pieces of the puzzle fit." He toyed with his watch. "I made a few inquiries about you this morning. You have a good reputation as an expert, and people seem to be convinced that you know what you're doing. Tell you what. The Ambassador will be in Moscow for at least a week. We'll make your time here as pleasant as we can, and when he returns, I'll help you handle him. In return, you'll help us. You forget you're working for the Eighth CD for the moment and let us make use of your expertise on some of our problems here. Unofficially. Also, I would like you to give me, personally, an absolutely unvarnished report on the danger of interceptions here, along with your recommendations. And I don't mean the crap you guys load your official reports with. I mean real solutions. Do we have a deal?"

"Well, I'm not really a technical expert. I don't do this kind of stuff anymore."

"Who are you, then?"

Victor thought for a second, then answered wryly, "A jack-of-all-trades, rapidly turning into a goddamn politician."

The general laughed, "Aren't we all?" Then he said sternly, "Actually, you don't have a choice. That is, if you want my support and, consequently, a chance with the Ambassador."

Victor had to hand it to him, this was an experienced operator. He had Victor right where he wanted him and had extracted the maximum he could hope for in the circumstances. But then, thought Victor, the reverse was also true. "Deal," agreed Victor.

"And don't forget, I still don't like the way your chiefs treated me. This is the second rotten hand they've dealt me."

They returned to the car. Kuritsyn said to Valery, "Make sure Comrade Sheymov has everything he needs. You are personally responsible for his security and for his having a good time here. Whenever he wants to go to town, you will take him. No substitutes. Clear?"

"Yes. Will do."

At the embassy Kuritsyn let them go with a gesture and went on up to his office.

In the corridor Valery asked, "What did you do to the old man? I thought he would have kicked you back to Moscow."

Victor shrugged. "He's one smart, tough cookie. I guess I'll just have to slave for you guys a while."

"Welcome aboard. For now. Let me show you where you're staying. It seems you're the guest of honor. You'll have the only available apartment on the premises. It's not too bad."

In fact, the accommodations were astonishing. Victor's familiarity with the top secrets of the Soviet State precluded his staying anywhere outside the embassy compound, and he had been given the embassy's guest suite. It consisted of eight large rooms and was identical in plan to the ambassador's, which was located directly below, taking up the entire third floor of the right wing. Two rooms were bedrooms, and the other six were drawing rooms. Every one was crowded with beautiful antique furniture, none of which matched. There was collector-quality crystal everywhere and fine oil paintings on the walls. The magnificent parquet floor had been polished to a mirror finish and was overlaid with rare Oriental rugs. A guest had the choice of two concert-size Steinway grands. Numerous gilt-edged mirrors added to the overall impression of grandeur. Still, Victor couldn't shake the feeling that he was in the plunder-stuffed lair of a mighty pirate.

Ironically, the top brass who were qualified to stay in the guest suite were unlikely to entertain more than a half-dozen people at a time and, aside from sleeping, would probably spend very little time there. As far as Victor could tell, the main purpose of the apartment was to stroke the ego of the occupant. Victor enjoyed elegance, but he found this jumble of grandiose opulence profoundly oppressive.

He walked over to one of the magnificent pianos, cautiously opened the lid, and plunked a few keys. It was hopelessly out of tune.

CHAPTER

SEVERAL DAYS LATER VICTOR was still waiting for the Ambassador to return from Moscow, and he became all too familiar with the embassy on Belwederska Street. The grim, greyish yellow building stood by itself in the compound. It had the obligatory pillars across its massive main facade and two symmetrical wings, identically ugly. Several years back, the entire building had been painted a cheery bright ocher to lighten its pall. This effort had not been a smashing success, and evidence of the lack of quality control in the paint used was literally flaking off the walls. It didn't help to have the elegant palace of the Polish Minister of Defense General Jaruzelski next door, and that of the Prime Minister just across the street. Victor, who appreciated fine architecture, found his eyes carefully studying the asphalt driveway every time he approached this monstrosity.

Gloomy memorials from the Stalinist era, these buildings symbolized an unimaginable power: anyone who looked on them was, supposedly, forced to confront his own vulnerability, his relative insignificance. Yet Victor had to admit that for the chosen few the sight of these grandiose tombs reinforced their sense that they had a personal stake in the Party's power over hundreds of millions of ordinary people. Reflected glory that it was, it was still heady stuff for those with an appetite for it. Nevertheless, Victor reflected, there was no security for those at the top. They could not inherit their stake, nor own it, nor pass it on. It took hard work and good luck along with some questionable qualities to stay there, and the risks involved were considerable. As Victor understood all too well, the margin for political error was nonexistent, and the potential cost of a misstep devastating.

In his present limbo Victor had time to play and replay his own situation. He knew that no one seriously challenged the need to upgrade the security for the cipher communications. It was only the latest round in the eternally escalating spiral of offense and defense. Nor was his mission to the Ambassador simply an attempt to resolve a squabble about space. The KGB's leadership was flexing its muscles. The embassy was technically the MFA's turf. The players had let the game get out of hand. The strategy he had chosen made Victor the wild card.

And he was quite aware that the fruits of victory were not in proportion to the penalty of defeat. If he succeeded, he'd return to the Center, having not fallen out of favor, and be allowed to keep going, ever hostage to the future. And to the next stunt. If he failed, he was dispensable. Bosik had warned him in no uncertain terms: end of the line.

Bosik was mad at the delay. He called Victor every other day on the military, secure-HF telephone to ask questions concerning the other projects Victor had had to drop in his rush to leave for Warsaw. The rush Bosik himself had insisted on.

Meanwhile, Victor's idle presence in Warsaw presented an opportunity that the station was determined to exploit. Although Victor was now too senior for nuts-and-bolts technical fieldwork, his background had given him a solid command of technical matters, and he was kept busy as a consultant. He put an end to the Station typists' habit of keeping the office windows open all day—just above the spot where the Polish Service agents were allowed to park. He recommended that the case officers going to clandestine meetings unplug the antennas from their car radios. He also spent time in evaluating ways to eavesdrop on the embassy, and ways to counter such measures. Fortunately, while planning his strategy for dealing with the Ambassador, he'd done a good deal of homework on the security problems of this building. He had his splendid list from his friends in the Aquarium.

Every Soviet embassy has three protected areas: the KGB "*residentura*"—or station; the GRU military-intelligence *residentura*; and a "*referentura*," or chancery. The KGB is in charge of the security for all three. The first two areas would be considered very secure by anybody's standards—anybody, that is, except the KGB. Even though they usually are equipped with secure rooms for conversations, with eavesdropping-detection devices, and with sophisticated security systems, the KGB still does not consider them secure enough. No classified materials are allowed to be kept in the *residenturas*. Classified materials can be brought in for work during the day but are certainly never to be stored there overnight, or even left unattended for a moment.

The only area that meets the stringent KGB standards for security is the *referentura*. Its walls are of reinforced concrete, and the single entrance is protected by a steel vault door, at least eight inches thick. This door is then masked by another "cover" door, which makes the entrance to the *referentura* indistinguishable from any other door in the embassy. Neither of the two doors has a key lock. The vault door has a typical vault dead-bolt lock with still another dead-bolt lock used only at night. Both can be operated only from inside. The *referentura* is manned around the clock by a guard who sits inside, right next to the door. In the vault door a peephole allows the guard to observe the space between the vault and the cover doors. The cover door has only one lock—an electric one, remotely controlled. Outside the cover door there is a hidden doorbell. Anybody going into the *referentura* has to know its location. After a visitor rings the bell, there is a standard electric-lock buzz, which means that the *referentura* guard inside has pushed the button in response to the bell and has opened the electric lock of the cover door. The visitor then opens the cover door and steps inside the uncomfortably tight space between the two doors, where a powerful electric bulb shines directly in his face. The guard looking through the peephole is required to personally recognize the visitor as one on the list of those cleared to enter. Then the guard waits until the cover door is securely closed—which is confirmed when the red indicator light in front of him goes off. Only then can he open the vault door to allow the visitor in. Then that door is closed and dead-bolted again. There are no exceptions to this procedure.

The security of the KGB *referentura* does not stop there. The *referentura* itself is divided by a partition into two major parts: "outer" and "inner." This partition is sometimes called a "lifestyle partition" because in any foreign posting those who are allowed into the inner part of the *referentura* are forbidden to go into town alone. Nor are they allowed to visit the town with their own wives—a measure to deter defections. The standard joke is that one is allowed to defect only with somebody else's wife. The rebuttal is, who in his right mind would want to defect with his own?

The outer part of the *referentura* consists of a number of rooms: the soundproof rooms for sensitive conversations, and other rooms for reading. These rooms are divided up between the KGB, GRU, and MFA. Those diplomats cleared for classified information, the cipher clerks, and the guards are allowed into this outer part of the *referentura*.

Within the inner part of the *referentura*, each of the three organizations has a separate room for its own cipher clerks, as well as an enclosure for its own cipher equipment. There is also a "safe" room—yet another vault with a door similar to the vault door at the entrance of the outer part of the *referentura*. There is one difference, though: an outside lock. This vault contains the safes of the KGB, GRU, and MFA.

Only the cipher clerks, the local heads of the three organizations—the KGB Resident, the GRU Resident, the Ambassador—and visiting officers of the Eighth CD are allowed into this inner part. Ironically, the Security Officer of the embassy and the Technical Security Officer, who is responsible for sweeping the embassy for bugs, are not cleared for the inner part of the *referentura*, even though they are both officers of the KGB.

Victor had a field day confirming the items on the menu the Aquarium provided, and added a few dishes himself for good measure.

Valery assisted Victor as best he could. He showed him around the embassy building and the compound. He took him into town and showed him the tourist spots in Warsaw, such as they were. Most of the city had been destroyed in World War II, and the subsequent rebuilding made Moscow look very attractive by comparison. On their second tour of the city Victor asked Valery, "Did you see those guys on our tail?"

"Oh, sure." Valery shrugged. "They're pretty good, too, don't you think? Not the best in the world, of course, but smarter than you'd expect, right?"

"Yes, but what the hell's going on? This is the second time I've come into town, and it's the second time we've had surveillance. In Warsaw? Come on, this is outrageous."

"Well, it may seem ridiculous, but they do it to us from time to time. They don't trust us and suspect we're working against them. In a way, they are right. But we have a very good relationship with them, personal as well as operational. What concerns me is that you seem to be the main attraction."

He paused. When Victor didn't respond, he shrugged, "Oh, never mind. They're just trying to figure out what the hell you're up to here. Don't worry. If my hunch is right, they'll make a move pretty soon."

Valery parked the car, and the two of them began to stroll down Marshalkovska Street. Suddenly, a man walking toward them broke into an enormous smile, opened his arms wide, and yelled, "Valery! My friend! So nice to see you again. How are you?"

Valery responded in kind. The scene was broadly played: two old friends meeting unexpectedly after a long separation. They patted each other, eyes shining. They did not seem to have enough meaningful words to express their feelings. Victor stood aside, quietly watching.

At last, the newcomer blinked. "Well, I see you're here with a friend. Why don't you introduce us? We mustn't seem to be rude." His Russian was good, hardly a trace of the Polish-Ukrainian accent.

Valery played along. "Oh yes, of course, you're right. Forgive me, this is my friend, Victor. Victor, this is Zdenek, the shining star of our friends, the Polish Service."

Now Victor joined the game, and he and Zdenek expressed the highest pleasure at meeting each other. Then Valery said, "Victor is only here on a short visit."

Zdenek's energy was boundless. "But that's wonderful! We must welcome him immediately, then. Let's go celebrate somewhere now. Oh! I know just the place, too! We must go to the hard-currency restaurant. You know I have friends there, and the girls . . ." He paused and winked, "Well, they are very friendly. No man can resist, eh? Let's go this minute!"

Victor could hardly keep a straight face. The gambit was so crude. "Well, I can't tell you how much I appreciate your generous invitation, and believe me, I hate to be a wet rag, but, alas, I do have another engagement." He checked his watch. "In fact, Valery, we'd better be getting back."

Zdenek was crestfallen, then rebounded instantly. "What a pity . . . But then we'll set a date right now for another day, yes?" He was not going to give up easily.

Valery intervened, "Oh, absolutely. Victor, I know your dance card's pretty full, do you have your program with you?"

Victor pulled a long face, "I'm afraid I don't."

"Well, I'll tell you what. Why don't we check our schedules first thing tomorrow morning, and I'll call Zdenek to set it up."

Zdenek had run out of options. He threw his arms open in a good-natured shrug and pumped up his smile. "Wonderful! I'm really looking forward to it."

Valery and Victor kept straight faces until they were safely inside the car and under way. Then they exploded into gales of laughter. Valery had tears in his eyes. "I knew it, didn't I tell you?"

Still laughing himself, Victor asked, "Are they always that clumsy?"

"No, but with you they had no choice. You don't go to the Diplomatic

Corps receptions, you know. How else could they make contact with you?"

"By the way, just out of curiosity, when was the last time you two saw each other?"

"Yesterday." Another good laugh.

Valery said, "They must be really curious about you. I just wonder what they do know . . ." Valery was watching Victor, then changed the subject abruptly. "By the way, speaking of your busy schedule, my wife and I would like to invite you to have dinner with us tonight."

"It will be my pleasure."

That evening, Victor very much enjoyed the company of Valery, his lively wife, and a massively handsome—fortunately charming—Great Dane named King. After the meal, Valery's wife retired. Valery poured brandy for himself and Victor—none for King—and the three of them settled into chairs.

Valery toasted Victor with his snifter, "So, Victor. How are you finding your stay in Poland?"

Victor returned the salutation. "Quite agreeable, so far, thanks to you. But I must confess things are a bit different from what I'd expected."

"Really? In what sense?"

"It's more the people than the city that have surprised me."

"How so?"

Victor thought a minute. "Well, I had no idea the Poles were so poor, and I haven't seen very many signs of any changes for the better. It looks like the whole country's sliding downhill."

"You're absolutely right, things are getting worse. They're only just able to survive, and then only by a kind of semilegal smuggling. You see, they're legally allowed to go abroad as tourists four times a year, and they take full advantage. The Poles are the best traders in the Warsaw Pact. They do their homework, and they know the prices of consumer goods in other countries like we know hockey scores. You've seen the black market: anything can be bought—it's simply a question of price. The luckiest are those who get help from relatives in the West."

"But this kind of trading doesn't seem to help them prosper. Overall, where do you think they are headed?"

"Just as you said, downhill."

Victor digested this. "You know, I've also been surprised by their obvious hatred of us. Of course, I'm aware that none of our satellite brethren are especially friendly toward us, except, perhaps, the Bulgarians. But take Czechoslovakia, for instance. They're not that friendly an ally either, but the individual Czechs are not as openly hostile as I've found the Poles. This feels personal. Everywhere we've been so far, the moment we've been recognized as Russians, people have turned sullen. They look at us the way they must have eyed the Nazis."

"Oh, they hate us all right. If they're presented with the slightest chance to kick our butts, you'd better believe they'll take it. And they're no cowards either. Don't forget, they didn't hesitate to attack German tanks with their cavalry at the start of World War II."

"I imagine Polish morale got a real boost when their cardinal was elected Pope."

"If John Paul were to give the call, every Pole would be in the streets, fighting our tanks with whatever he has. Then our choice would be either to kill all of them or get the hell out. As a matter of fact, he's our biggest headache."

"Realistically, is there anything we can do about it?"

"We have two options. We can eliminate the Pope—which I think would be a grave mistake. The Poles would revolt immediately, and there'd be massive casualties on both sides. The other option, the one I think is our only hope, is to support General Jaruzelski, the Minister of Defense. He's tough as nails, he's Polish, and he knows how to deal with them. Besides, he doesn't have to be persuaded. He knows all too well where his bread's buttered. If we go, he'll be hanged in no time flat for his collaboration. Pretty good incentive for him."

"Do you think Moscow understands?"

"Not really. They certainly don't have any idea how deeply rooted the problem is."

"Perhaps the reports from Warsaw are too optimistic?"

"Sure, but Moscow could read between the lines if they wanted to. Naturally, they hope the problem will go away, and when that isn't happening, they pretend to take action by giving us general orders to get things back to normal. The fact is, they just don't have a clue what to do."

"Do you? I mean, the Station."

"No."

"Well, based on what I've seen so far, this doesn't look like a terrific place to be."

"Jesus, no! Especially considering the pay! In most postings abroad you can easily buy a car after a couple of years, right?"

"Sure."

"Not here. Forget about the car, you can't even buy a decent stereo.

Oh, there are plenty of them available on the black market, but they're expensive as hell. Our friendly Polish traders like to tease us that way."

"Well, in Moscow you can buy a lot in the Beriozka store, with foreign currency."

"Hah! We can only exchange zlotys for the striped certificates, but most of the best things in Beriozka are not available for the striped certificates. Remember, this is a Warsaw Pact country, and the worst one at that."

Victor realized this was a sore spot. Valery helped himself to more brandy and poured some for Victor. "All my friends, not to mention my family, think Poland means 'abroad.' Hell, it certainly does not. Add my wife's friends and relatives. Everyone wants a present. You know as well as I do how everyone looks at you when you're posted abroad, like you're a millionaire. Let me tell you: I spend a third of my pay on gifts, and still everybody thinks I'm either selfish or cheap. In my other postings abroad I spent only 5 percent of my pay on presents, and I was like Santa Claus."

Victor took a moment to savor the brandy, and looked for a way to change the subject. "That's rough. . . . By the way, how did you manage to wind up here? You're too young to be stuck in this preretirement backwater."

Valery shot Victor a dark look. "I got burned. Twice." It was the first time he'd been anything but forthcoming.

Victor's curiosity was piqued, both for his new friend as well as for himself. What kind of error or misstep could sideline someone like Valery? "What happened?"

"Well, the first time was in India, when we messed around with that damned nuclear gadget in the Himalayas. The Indians PNGed me in a hurry. You know what *persona non grata* does to your career."

"Well, surely they could use someone like you somewhere else . . . ?"

"Oh, sure. Until I got burned again, in Switzerland."

"How?"

Valery cleared his throat uncomfortably and took a large swallow of brandy. "I was accompanying a delegation of scientists to an international meeting. And I got friendly with one of the leading scientists in our delegation."

"Did he have any idea who you were?"

"Oh, no. They all fell for the setup and suspected another one of our guys who'd been deliberately given a very thin cover. They assumed he was the only one of us. You know the scenario."

Victor nodded.

"Well, that son-of-a-bitch scientist was one smart bastard. I had absolutely no advance indication. Nothing at all. I personally searched his luggage. No memorabilia, no unpublished articles, none of the typical shit that tips you off. Well, all of a sudden, in the center of Geneva, while just the two of us were driving around, he gets out of the car and says, 'Valery, you are a very nice guy. I don't want to make trouble for you. If they ask, just tell them you know nothing—that I went shopping alone. I'm going to the Swiss police. I'm defecting. Good-bye, Valery.'"

A KGB security operative's nightmare. Victor asked, "What did you do?"

"I said good-bye, wished him well, and hit him in the head as hard as I could with the only thing I had in my hand—my camera."

"With people all around?"

"Sure. I knocked him out and shoved him into the car. I shouted, 'This man is sick! He needs a doctor!' Then I jumped in the car and raced to the Soviet Mission. The rest was easy."

"What happened to the scientist?"

"Nothing out of the ordinary. That bastard's doing his fifteen years' hard labor. But look what happened to me."

"So . . . ?"

"Our wise leadership accused me of lacking vigilance and professionalism. See, I was supposed to spot warning signs beforehand and take necessary measures before things came to a crisis. I didn't even get reimbursed for my camera, which was completely smashed—my personal camera. All they said was that I was lucky I'd hit him hard enough to keep him from getting away. Otherwise it would have been much the worse for me. Can you imagine?"

"The guy must have been working on something top-secret—that always makes them crazy."

"No, not at all. He was just an ordinary lab rat. He didn't even have the lowest Access Three clearance!" Valery poured himself another splash of brandy and toasted the powers-that-be. "Anyway, that was a long answer to your question, and it's how I ended up in Warsaw."

Valery's story sickened Victor. Valery's handling of the situation had been as far from the purpose of intelligence, as Victor understood it, as one could get. In fact, it was a shocking throwback to the crude violence of the KGB under Stalin—a style that Victor had naively assumed was no longer acceptable. He prided himself on the finesse and skill his work required. Furthermore, it horrified him that a seemingly decent guy like Valery felt no remorse whatsoever for his brutality. *He's even proud of his ingenious solution. He actually sees the would-be defector as the villain and himself as the victim!*

Victor had never seen the point of putting innocent civilians under surveillance in the first place. It had to be costly and unproductive. Indeed, he'd never understood why civilians were not simply permitted to leave the country if they wanted to. Obviously, anyone with access to State secrets had to be restricted—that was a reasonable quid pro quo in wartime—but the image of the bleeding and unconscious scientist brought a dangerous thought to mind: *There's only a small step from an act like that to shooting women and children for ideological unfitness!*

Victor was shaken. He wanted to get outside, alone, for some fresh air and a chance to clear his head. His self-control prevailed, however, and he tried to offer token words of comfort. "Well, that's tough. But surely you can work your way back to where you belong . . . ?" This sounded hollow, even to him.

Valery gently reproved him. "Well, but you know that's not possible. In this business, once you're down, you never get up. I'm getting used to it." He shrugged philosophically. The two men finished their brandies in awkward silence.

Afterward, Valery drove Victor back to the embassy.

Later, as he prepared for bed, Victor looked at himself in the ornate mirror above the marble mantelpiece in the absurdly pretentious chamber. He was still deeply troubled by Valery's story, by the fact that Valery clearly felt he was an innocent victim, wronged by the organization they both served. Now it was more difficult than before to avoid thinking of the system itself, of its purpose.

Valery worked in Directorate K, First CD, a particularly controversial outfit. One part of K was perfectly respectable; indeed, it had one of the toughest assignments in the First CD: to penetrate other countries' intelligence, counterintelligence, police, and other services. The other part of K, larger, more visible, and much more active, took care of the so-called "security work," which was feared and despised by many within the KGB Intelligence. Directorate K was responsible for preventing defections abroad. The security officers in the Soviet embassies around the world, along with other officers of Directorate K, carried out this mission. Their job was to recruit informers among Soviet citizens stationed abroad, to poke into all aspects of everybody's private life, reporting who slept with whom and how, and so on. K also had a vast cadre of officers who traveled with virtually every Soviet group that went abroad: scientific delegations, like the one Valery had accompanied; sports teams; any kind of artistic troupe. These officers were unscrupulous. Victor recalled how by chance he'd come across a series of cables from Directorate K discussing a proposal to break Rudolf Nureyev's legs in retaliation for some mildly anti-Soviet remarks he had made during his exile in England. The third part of Directorate K's responsibility was its work against Russian émigré communities in the West: discrediting them with the host governments, recruiting agents, setting up internal squabbles, and so on.

Victor instinctively loathed this kind of barbaric modus operandi. Always before he'd managed to close his eyes to it, telling himself it was none of his business—that such brutality had to be an aberration of some "extremists" in the leadership. Then he stayed as far away from it as he could. Now, however, Valery's story forced him to confront the unsavory truth about Directorate K. However despised by some in the organization it might be, it was nevertheless an integral part of the KGB, and it was carrying out the explicit policies of the Central Committee.

What was even more puzzling for Victor was that Valery seemed to be a nice guy—a good family man and a conscientious friend. How could he be so detached from the immorality of his act? He didn't strike Victor as a psychopath. There was only one logical conclusion. *That behavior was a conditioned response—something that he has been systematically programmed for. If that's the case, then there must be something wrong with the program—and the system that produced it.*

At the moment when this thought occurred to Victor, a circuit-breaker cut the subversive current. *Warning! If you think too much, you'll go crazy. You'll lose focus, lose your edge. Concentrate on your own job, don't tell others how to do theirs.* This was the refrain in KGB Major Sheymov's brain as he put his head onto the pillow and drifted off to sleep.

The next morning Victor met General Kuritsyn in a corridor. "Good morning, Nikolai Pavlovich."

"Good morning, Victor." Kuritsyn was in a good mood. He slapped Victor on the back. "Come on into my office. Let's chat."

When they were settled in the comfortable leather armchairs, Kuritsyn asked cheerfully, "Well, what's up?"

"Nothing in particular. I'm still waiting for our beloved ambassador to get his butt back here to work."

Kuritsyn shrugged, rolled his eyes sympathetically, and changed the subject. "Listen, Victor. I've heard good things about you from our guys. They are delighted at the chance to pick your brain. Your field of cipher-communications security is so different. Everyone knows it's the lode from which the richest intelligence is mined. If you get something there on your enemy, you're a real hero, and after all, that's what we're all shooting for.

But, in order to get something, you need to know what you're looking for. The trouble is, we don't. You guys are so secretive. You tell us, 'Give us whatever you've got, and we'll see what we can make of it.' Fine. We send you what we get, and then we never hear back from you. No feedback. It's extremely frustrating."

As with all KGB stations, the Warsaw KGB Station's staff never got enough feedback from Moscow. They had no idea how the Center evaluated and responded to the information they sent "home," especially concerning sensitive technical matters. The routine year-end evaluations issued by the Center were very general, often formulaic clichés. Sometimes, for security reasons, they were even deliberately misleading. Receiving technical information on cipher communications from the field often put the Center in a tricky spot. On the one hand, showing a lack of interest would in effect be an admission that Moscow already had the information. On the other hand, a strong reaction to the information was tantamount to admitting that it had not been known. For the Center, either case was undesirable. Consequently, the Center was routinely noncommittal in its reactions.

Victor offered professional sympathy: "Of course it is, Nikolai Pavlovich. The trouble is that the defense—the security of our own cipher communications—and the offense—breaking into somebody's cipher communications—are too closely related. You see, by telling you what we need for penetrating the opposition's security, I would also have to tell you quite a bit about our own. I'd have to give away the store to keep you posted. That's why we play so close to the vest. It's a fundamental problem, not capriciousness on our part."

Victor felt he needed to sweeten this dose of reality. "The good news is that I can probably give your guys a better idea of what the Center is after, and give you a few pointers on what your people should be on the lookout for."

"We'll be thankful for whatever you can share with us. We recognize your problem."

Kuritsyn paused. Something else was bothering him. He studied Victor, then asked, "What about our facilities for secure conversations here? I know you've been sniffing around. What do you think?"

"That's a tough one. I don't know if anybody is listening to you, but I do know that if anyone reasonably good went to a bit of trouble, it wouldn't be too difficult. It's just a question of whether it would be worth the effort. Technically, it's not a big deal."

"You're sure?"

"Absolutely. We are talking off the record, of course."

"Of course. So, what do we do?"

"As I've already said, get an extra cipher enclosure for a secure-conversations room. But meanwhile, let me give you my personal opinion: theoretically, it's possible to create an acoustical fortress around the embassy, but even then somebody would probably find a way to penetrate it. Theoretically. As you know, the only airport that is totally secure is the one that's closed. The same principle applies here."

Kuritsyn shrugged, "A realistic approach. Go on."

"I would suggest splitting the communication of important issues. Use different ways of transmitting information."

"For example?"

"OK, suppose you're talking to a case officer, discussing a meeting that's to take place with an agent. Verbalize some of the details, but write the time and place on a piece of paper. Don't speak that information. Use paper for 'insertions.' Simple. But it works. Unfortunately, it's not used often enough."

"That's because it's a pain in the ass."

"Yes, that's precisely the problem. Inconvenience. But security always involves inconvenience, doesn't it? By the way, the Achilles heel of even the most sophisticated security system is the human factor. More often than not, incompetence or carelessness is at the source of a security breach."

Victor saw Kuritsyn start to bristle and quickly continued, "Look, it's a given that the weakest link in any security chain is always a human being because people can become accustomed to anything. They get used to the importance of their work and inured to the danger involved. After things become routine, they make mistakes. Careless, silly ones. Sometimes those silly mistakes cost them their careers—sometimes their lives."

Kuritsyn was clearly not pleased at the possible implied association between himself and incompetence. Victor moved quickly to repair the damage, mindful that the Representative could still screw up his mission with the Ambassador. He knew Kuritsyn could not resist a good war story. "Occasionally, there are happy endings. With luck, human error can sometimes be fixed. I can tell you an incident that took place in the KGB Technical Directorate. One of the KGB's star illegals recruited a guard at a NATO center—the night guard of a vault with top-secret NATO documents. Following the illegal's instructions, the guard made an imprint of the key to the vault. The imprint was sent back to the Center. As usual, the first copy of the key—the 'signal' duplicate—was made of a very soft alloy, mainly tin. Then two steel copies were produced. One of the copies was sent to the illegal, who gave it to the guard.

"On his next night shift, the guard tried to open the vault. To his horror, as soon as he inserted the key and started to turn it, it bent badly. Not only did it not open the vault, he couldn't get it back out of the keyhole. Someone at the Center had goofed and sent back the 'signal' copy instead of a steel one. Nobody knows how the guard finally managed to get the key out, but he did. He was understandably upset and confronted the illegal and accused him of deliberately trying to set him up. It's anyone's guess how the illegal managed to calm him down and persuade him to try again. On the second attempt—with the proper key—he was able to open the vault. Since it contained a great many documents, the guard was instructed to photograph the shelves of documents, then close the vault without disturbing anything. The photograph was sent to the Center and analyzed by the experts to determine a sequence of priorities. Then it was sent back to the illegal as a guide. The illegal and his agent 'milked' that vault for years."

It worked. "That was quite a lecture on common sense, young man, but I must say, coming from you in this context, it does make one think."

"Yes, that's what it boils down to, isn't it? When you're a rookie, you speak in truisms and common sense. It's all you know. As you gain experience in the field, you talk in very sophisticated terms. When you really know your stuff, you find yourself paying attention to the basics and common sense again. Don't you find that true in the operational field as well?"

"Yes, I suppose you're right," Kuritsyn conceded.

The telephone rang. Still slightly out of sorts, Kuritsyn snatched it off the receiver and aimed his irritation at the mouthpiece. "I told you we were not to be interrupted!" He listened for a moment, then relented. "OK, let him in."

Embassy Counselor Solovyev entered. Tall, balding, smooth as anyone can be and always elegantly dressed, he prided himself on his previous posting in Paris. He never missed a chance to mention it, for he was ashamed of this one. The end of the line for him.

Counselor Solovyev was the Resident, in charge of the undercover KGB Station. He was reporting to Kuritsyn, who was openly identified to the Polish service as the KGB Representative.

Kuritsyn asked curtly, "Now what?"

"It's about the Pope." Solovyev shot a sidelong glance toward Victor, questioning his presence.

"Forget it. This guy knows more than we'll ever imagine. Oh, by the way, Victor, is it true that you can see any cipher telegram in the Center, regardless of what department it concerns?"

"It is. Yes."

"Christ! I really have to guard you closely! If anyone were to snatch you out from under us, I'd be on the wrong side of a firing squad."

The general turned back to Solovyev. "So?"

"The Center wants all the information we have on the Pope. Urgent."

"We've already sent that to them. Twice."

"No, they mean all of it. All personal acquaintances and any derogatory on them. Anything that could get us close to him. Physically. They've also prohibited us from opening new inquiries. No footprints. What do we do?"

Suddenly, there was silence in the room. The three men looked at one another. All knew perfectly well that in KGB jargon the phrase "getting physically close" meant only one thing: assassination. The Pope. Victor felt lightheaded as he watched the two *residentura* bosses calculate the possible political consequences of a murder that would shake the world.

Solovyev placed the cable carefully on the desk. Kuritsyn hesitated for a split second before picking it up. Long enough for Victor to catch sight of a security breach typical in Communist Bloc countries: instead of the code name Sviridov, the signature read "Andropov." The silence continued as Kuritsyn studied the crucial message.

At last, Kuritsyn exploded. "Idiots! This is political suicide. Not just political, either. If we take the Pope out, our days here are numbered. Even if we tried to hold on, we'd have to wipe out the Poles—every last one would die for him. This is likely to start something I'm scared even to think about! Yes, a while ago we could have pulled off the quiet liquidation of a cardinal and gotten away with it, but not now. It's just too late."

Victor was appalled that the Politburo would authorize such a course of action. He knew that the Politburo had to approve every liquidation abroad—which often meant the Head of State made the final decision. The KGB Chairman did not have such power. Kuritsyn's response also shocked Victor. This was the first time he had ever heard criticism of a top-level decision from such a highly ranked KGB officer.

The general paused, shaking his head incredulously. Then he made his decision and turned to the colonel: "Do as they say. Dig into the files. Do it yourself; don't involve anyone else. As they said, no footprints, especially not yours or mine."

"We don't have much, I know that. May I make a few very discreet inquiries?"

"Absolutely not. The results could be disastrous. No footprints. Period."

"Done." Solovyev disappeared.

The general was lost in thought, far from Victor's concerns. Conflicting emotions played across his face, until finally, like a fulminating volcano he exploded anew: "Damn fools! I hope they know what they're doing, otherwise they're hanging us out to dry." Clearly he needed to vent his anger to someone. He focused on Victor. "You mentioned bureaucracy the other day. Do you want a perfect example of the irrelevant stupidity of our very own bureaucracy?"

"Sure."

"It was well known that the Polish cardinals were never really close to the top echelon of Vatican insiders. So, when the second-ranking Polish cardinal was elected Pope John Paul II, everyone was astonished. I certainly was. Guess what kind of telegram I received?"

Victor shrugged, "Some scolding from the Center for not having received any indication from you of the outcome of the election?"

"Oh no, worse. 'How could you have possibly allowed a cardinal from the socialist country of Poland to be installed as the Pope? Signed: Andropov.'"

"What did you answer?"

"Well, I know how to play the game. My answer was, 'We had no indication here of the outcome of the election. Since the event in question took place in Italy, it seems to us that this question would be more appropriately posed to the Rome *residentura*.'"

Despite the cloud left by the colonel's visit and Victor's lingering uncertainty at criticism of the Leadership, he could not contain his laughter. "Brilliant. What happened next?"

"The Center cabled the Rome *residentura*. Their answer was: 'As the Rome *residentura* concerns itself primarily with Italian affairs, we are not properly prepared or equipped to effectively cover events in the Vatican, which is, of course, a separate state. None of the information from our sources indicates that the Italian government was involved in a conspiracy to install a Polish Cardinal as Pope. However, if the Center wishes us to expand our activities to effectively include the Vatican State, the *residentura* will fully support the move. Of course, considering the complexity of such a move, we would require a substantial increase in station personnel and budget. Regarding your direct inquiry: it seems logical to question the Warsaw station, as the new Pope is a Polish national.'"

Now both men laughed, and Kuritsyn finished, "And that's why nothing gets done."

Victor asked, "I know it's not my business, but why don't we just leave him alone?"

"Out of the question. He's just too damn dangerous. You can't imagine his power here. We could lose the whole damn country overnight, not to mention our international standing and credibility. He's our greatest headache now, and we've really got to do something about him. I'm glad it's not my decision. All I have to do is provide some background information. The rest is up to the Center." Kuritsyn had used exactly the same rationale as Valery, clearly indicating to Victor that this was the Station's collective assessment.

The meeting was over, but it haunted Victor long after he left. This was the second time in two days that the acts of his organization had morally outraged him. The most disturbing aspect was that only people who held nothing sacred, or at least immoral, could conceive and condone such clearly criminal activities. These were not deeds perpetrated by loose cannons acting randomly. He was so shaken that it was difficult to concentrate on the tasks at hand. He knew that he would never forget those two conversations.

The next morning Kuritsyn's secretary called Victor to tell him that the Ambassador was arriving that afternoon and that the general wanted to see him immediately.

Victor proceeded to Kuritsyn's office.

"It's your turn, Victor. We'll take care of your business now, as promised. I'll help you, but you must understand that I have to live here with him, and I don't want one more chip on his shoulder. He's too damn vindictive."

"I understand, Nikolai Pavlovich."

"Good. Then my recommendation is that we play 'good guy-bad guy.'"

Victor smiled. "Let me guess: I'm the heavy, right?"

The general laughed, "That's it. Let me be the good guy for a change."

Victor could anticipate what came next.

"Now, I'll tell him you're a cut-glass bastard, and that he's got to handle you with kid gloves. I'll slip him some rumors from my quarters. This will set you up with some clout."

"So far, so good."

"Now, tell me, what have you got up your sleeve?"

"Oh, nothing, really," Victor hedged.

"Too bad. OK, then you play it cool, and I'll advise him to give you what you want, just to get rid of you. Remember, we're not on good terms with you."

Victor left the general's office. On his way out, he asked Kuritsyn's secretary to make an appointment for him with the Ambassador about urgent business.

After lunch, he received a message from the Ambassador's secretary, a young male attaché, requesting that Victor drop by his office. Victor quickly complied and upon entering the Ambassador's reception room came face-to-face with the attaché. He was a type Victor recognized instantly—neat, fastidiously dressed, with an air of chilly politeness designed to intimidate—every inch the up-and-coming Komsomol leader. It flashed through Victor's mind that Kryuchkov had been Ambassador Andropov's secretary in Hungary during the uprising in 1956.

The secretary's opening volley absolutely confirmed Victor's intuition. "Greetings, Comrade Sheymov. I understand you have been here for a few days already. Unfortunately, my busy schedule did not permit me the pleasure of making your acquaintance until now." He spoke slowly, in a silky, condescending tone.

Bullshit. You've nothing to do, and still you're busy. And the pleasure is that we didn't get acquainted. Then he replied, as casually as the secretary had been formal, "Hello."

"Now, Comrade Sheymov, I understand that you have requested an audience with Vladimir Yakovlevich, our ambassador . . . ?"

"Yes."

"Well, what is it you wish to discuss with Vladimir Yakovlevich?"

Victor was not about to be screened by an attaché. He spoke quietly in a voice of ice. "I requested an audience with the Ambassador, not with you. Are you saying that you have asked me to come here only for me to tell you what I plan to discuss with the Ambassador?"

The secretary blinked. "Well, Comrade Sheymov, no offense was meant, of course, but Vladimir Yakovlevich is a very busy man. A very strict man as well. He wishes me to be aware of the matters that are brought to his attention. He distinctly ordered me to brief him on such issues," he stumbled for an instant, "uh, before he grants the audience."

The man was bluffing. Screening was the rule only for the "clean" diplomats. It did not apply to KGB visitors. Victor knew that, and he knew the attaché knew he knew it. He continued in the same frosty tone. "The Ambassador received a telegram from the Deputy Minister on this matter. And as far as your being informed about my business with Vladimir Yakovlevich, let him brief you, should he think it necessary."

The secretary drew what was left of his dignity around him. "The Ambassador will arrive within the hour. I think you can expect an audience sometime tomorrow morning." All traces of the patronizing tone had vanished.

"I haven't the slightest interest in what you think. When you have ascertained the time of our meeting, communicate it to General Kuritsyn's secretary. In advance." He turned on his heel and left the stunned attaché.

In the hall, Victor remembered his father had said to him once, "You know, you have a real knack for making enemies. If you just knew when to keep your mouth shut, life might be much easier for you." Victor shrugged at the memory.

That evening, Kuritsyn's secretary telephoned Victor in his suite. "Victor, your appointment with the Ambassador is set for ten tomorrow morning. General Kuritsyn is seeing him now."

"Thank you."

Victor made a point of entering the Ambassador's reception room at precisely 9:59 A.M. He walked up to the attaché, who was seated at his desk, writing, and stood quietly. He knew the secretary had heard him come in. Deliberately, the secretary laid his pen down and slowly lifted his head. Victor looked him straight in the eye and waited. The secretary had no choice but to speak first. "Hello, Comrade Sheymov."

"Hello."

Without an invitation, Victor settled himself comfortably into a large leather armchair. He was certain the Ambassador would keep him waiting—a standard bureaucratic tactic of intimidation—so he made himself at home. He could just imagine Vladimir Yakovlevich sitting in his own comfortable chair on the other side of the closed office door, twirling his thumbs and trying to figure out the purpose of Victor's mission. He reckoned the Ambassador wouldn't make him wait longer than about fifteen minutes, just in case. It would have been easy just to sit and enjoy the lavishly furnished room, for there was certainly plenty to look at, but Victor preferred to give the impression of not wasting time. He opened his briefcase and removed some meaningless papers that he pretended to study intently for the "extra" quarter of an hour. It was an act, of course. He knew what he needed to know by heart.

After a short while, the intercom on the secretary's desk buzzed. Victor checked his watch: 10:15. Here goes.

The secretary rose and walked over to the Ambassador's office door and opened it, poking his head inside. There was a brief, murmured exchange, after which he turned back to Victor and indicated that he should enter. Victor carefully replaced his papers in the briefcase, rose, and crossed to the secretary, who was still standing in the doorway. As Victor passed through the door, he turned and very deliberately closed it in the man's face.

The office was cavernous. Victor took what felt like an endless walk across the room toward the monumental, antique, leather-topped desk, where the Ambassador was seated. Victor's first impression of Vladimir Yakovlevich, former First Secretary of the Komsomol, Member of the Central Committee of the CPSU, was that of a caricature: a little man with a large, round face stuck on top of a white shirt collar. His body looked too puny to support the outsized head. It seemed as if the neck wasn't even trying. Victor recalled the reports of some rather grotesque sex scandals the Ambassador had been involved in. Thinning strands of dark hair were combed straight back, and he had deep-set, beady little drab-green eyes and a fixed, disagreeably snakelike expression. Victor noticed that his jacket was on. *A good sign. He's nervous.*

Victor spoke first, as he approached the desk.

"Hello, Vladimir Yakovlevich."

"Hello, Comrade Sheymov. Have a seat." He had not risen to greet Victor, and there was no hand extended.

Bad sign. He'll try to bully me.

Victor sat in the armchair that had been placed for him. There was a long pause, during which he continued to study the face above the desk, a face that he knew belonged to one of the most disliked officials at the top of the Soviet hierarchy. As the Ambassador's strange eyes drilled into him, Victor deliberately did not drop his own but matched him stare for stare.

At last, the Ambassador broke the silence. "Well, I have been informed that you have an important, urgent matter to discuss. I am listening."

"I am here to discuss the matter of improving the security of our cipher communications. By a Decision of the Central Committee, the service I represent has been assigned to implement all necessary measures. As a part of a worldwide operation to further improve security, the communications system of your embassy needs to be upgraded. My purpose here is to coordinate with you all the steps that will be necessary to carry out this Decision."

"Some time ago, a man named Smirnov came to discuss this matter. He's your subordinate?"

The Ambassador was testing the waters, trying to pinpoint Victor's status. Victor knew all too well that if he let on that Smirnov outranked him, that would be the end of the audience, not to mention the mission. On the other hand, he could not afford to risk lying to a Member of the Central Committee. He sidestepped the question. "I know him."

Irritated by Victor's evasive maneuver, the Ambassador shifted gears. "Let me be direct. The communications system is your problem. Yours, not mine. Period. If you have come here expecting me to work for you or your service, you have miscalculated. You have your own resources. Use them. I don't care what you do or how you do it, as long as you don't even try to get me working for you. Is that perfectly clear, Comrade Sheymov?"

Victor's smile was disarmingly polite, and he said cheerfully, "Well, in that case, it seems we have everything in order. You're quite correct, we have our own resources, and we most certainly would never expect a Soviet Ambassador to do our job for us. We understand that you have much more important matters on your hands. We will manage everything. All we are asking of the embassy is a little patience with the day-to-day housekeeping inconveniences bound to occur as we carry out our improvements. Oh, yes, and a bit of space to put the new system in."

The Ambassador's eyes narrowed as he tensed, instantly suspicious. "What do you mean by 'a bit of space?'"

"Oh, not much, really. Just the third floor of the left wing. I trust that won't be a problem for you?"

The Ambassador blew up, furious both at the preposterousness of the request and at having been outmaneuvered. "What?! A whole wing? Don't you realize how scarce space is in any embassy? Absolutely not. It's out of the question."

Victor listened quietly to the anticipated outburst, then to the grandfather clock across the room ticking the seconds of silence following the explosion. After a long pause he said carefully, "Well, in that case, you put me in a difficult position, Vladimir Yakovlevich. You understand, of course, that I am not here arranging things on my own. I am not even here on behalf of the KGB. It is the decision of the Central Committee . . ."

"Don't you presume to tell me how Decisions are made," he interrupted furiously, "I'm a Member of the CC myself, don't ever forget that. I know how you guys put together idiotic reports, push them through the CC staff, where, I assure you, nobody reads them, and then you wave them as a flag to get whatever you want. Well, that little game is not going to work here."

Here's where the real negotiations begin, thought Victor. "I can assure you, Vladimir Yakovlevich, that that is not the case here. The Politburo is fully aware of the critical importance of this issue, and they have demanded that we accomplish the complete restructuring of the system in the shortest possible time."

There was a flicker in the Ambassador's eyes that told Victor he'd hit home. "Are you saying that we have a major problem and that somebody is reading our cipher telegrams?"

"No, of course not. This is just a routine measure necessitated by recent technological advances. Our ciphers are still the safest in the world."

Karlov tried to corner Victor. "Exactly who in the Politburo has been informed on this matter?"

"Brezhnev, Andropov, Kosygin, Gromyko. I'm afraid I don't know of any others."

The Ambassador was infuriated by Victor's having one-upped him. "If you are bluffing, it will cost you your job before the day is over, I promise you."

Victor was silent.

Karlov decided to play hardball. "If this matter is so important, tell me why I should even discuss it with a kid like you?"

First mistake. He prepared to plant his boot in the Ambassador's butt. "I'm afraid the choice of personnel responsible for these matters is our Leadership's prerogative, not mine."

The Ambassador recoiled as if he'd been struck. His next mistake was inevitable. "I am a Member of the CC, and nobody even mentioned this matter to me last week when I was in Moscow. In the unlikely event that you are telling the truth, why don't you just have Brezhnev call me."

Idiot! He doesn't even know he should have said "Gromyko." He paused slightly, as if retreating, and then responded in a humble voice. "I'm afraid that could pose a bit of a problem, Vladimir Yakovlevich. You see, I cannot imagine anyone just walking into Leonid Ilyich's office to ask for the use of a few rooms in Warsaw. No, the way the system is set up, we'd need to show some precedent to support our appeal against your objection." Victor played his ace. "In other words, if you want to object officially to granting us the space needed to accommodate the new cipher-security system that the Central Committee has ordered, then we will be obliged to compile a report, which can then be presented to Leonid Ilyich as the basis for considering your objection." Pause. "Of course, in order to establish strong precedent, this report will be as complete as possible and will necessarily include all security violations, past and present, which have gone uncorrected at your personal request, a list that has already been prepared. Then and only then could we bring the matter to Leonid Ilyich's attention."

That's where the real bluff was. The Ambassador could focus on the *fait accompli* of the list. On the other hand, he might ask to see it. Any excuse for refusing to give it to him would seriously weaken Victor's position, and showing it to him would decrease his chances for success and vastly increase the risk of his blackmail gambit. Once the Ambassador saw the list he'd be able to judge it for what it was. So, deceit would be added to blackmail. Victor knew that he was at the breaking point. His fall-back position was to say that he did not have the list on him, but he happened to remember it quite well. A lousy one.

But as he watched, it looked as if he'd bet correctly. The blood drained from the Ambassador's face as he grasped the meaning of Victor's words. He shrieked, "What?! Are you trying to blackmail me, a Member of the Central Committee?"

Butter wouldn't have melted in Victor's mouth. "Oh, no! What a suggestion, Vladimir Yakovlevich. How could I? No, I have simply outlined how we can go about fulfilling your wish to have Leonid Ilyich call you on this matter. Furthermore, to tell you the truth"—the standard preface to a lie—"the procedure I've just explained very nearly took place after your unfortunate misunderstanding with Smirnov. I personally insisted on coming here to try and find a less dramatic solution."

The color was coming back to the Ambassador's face. However, a flicker of an expression told Victor that the Ambassador knew he'd lost. Now he was asking for a face-saving gesture to prepare for an honorable retreat. He reached for the secure military telephone—the HF—saying, "All right, never mind. I'll call Leonid Ilyich myself. I have other issues to discuss with him as well."

Victor knew perfectly well the man was bluffing. *Bullshit. Even Gromyko wouldn't take that call, and you know it better than I.* He topped the Ambassador's bluff, "By all means. And I'd appreciate it if you'd mention my name."

The Ambassador had hit a dead end. He searched for an out and looked over at the grandfather clock. "Ah, no, I'm sure he'd be in a meeting now. I'll call him at home this evening. As well as Gromyko. I do that from time to time, you know."

Victor nodded. *Right. Gromyko doesn't have the HF phone at home, and you don't even know it.*

At last, the Ambassador surrendered. "All right, Comrade Sheymov. I'll tell you what. Unless Leonid Ilyich indicates to the contrary, you'll get what you want. Give me whatever papers need to be signed. You'll have them back tomorrow morning."

As Victor rose, his demeanor gave no indication of the tremendous relief and rush of elation he felt. "Well, Vladimir Yakovlevich, I thank you for your cooperation, and for your support of our efforts. Good-bye."

The Ambassador did not answer. Victor walked the distance back across the room to the door he'd closed earlier and reopened it. The attaché was standing close by and looked as if he'd just moved very quickly. Victor glared at him, then continued to walk on as the young man entered the inner office. Victor hesitated on his way out long enough to hear the Ambassador say, "Now I understand why the general warned me to be careful with that bastard." Satisfied, Victor smiled to himself. He'd managed another high-wire crossing. Terra firma felt good.

Back in the general's office, Victor said simply, "It's over, and we won."

"Good for you. How did it go?"

"Tough. You know him better than I do—you can imagine the scene. He thought he'd scare me by saying he was going to call Brezhnev."

The general laughed. "He does that to me all the time. I'm waiting for the day when he threatens to call God."

On his way out, Victor asked the general's secretary to book him on the next day's Aeroflot flight to Moscow.

Sure enough, the next morning the signed documents from the Ambassador were delivered to Victor in his suite. All he had left to do now was pack. Then the general's secretary phoned. "Victor, your plane leaves in three hours. And the general wants to see you for a moment."

The general met him, saying, "I know we said our good-byes last night, but something's just come up. The head of our friends in the Polish Service just called to ask if we have any officers flying to Moscow today. They need to get a parcel to their liaison there. It's unusual, I know, but you're the only officer flying today."

"They've really tried to get to me here, haven't they. I'm sure it's a ruse to talk to me—try and figure out who I am and what I was up to here."

"I expect you're right, but by refusing we'd only attract more attention. Besides, it is a personal request from the head of the service. Would you like me to order somebody to meet you in Moscow?"

"No, thanks, I'll handle it."

"One more thing, Victor. It seems to me that there's no sense in making a big deal out of the Poles' interest in you." That translated into "don't bring it up in the Center because if you do, it would imply that you made some sort of mistake and attracted attention." The general would then be stuck with an inquiry, as it might very well have been his mistake in the first place.

"Of course. I'm sure it's not worth any attention."

"Well then, have a good flight. And thanks for all your tips."

"Thank you for your help, Nikolai Pavlovich."

They shook hands, and Victor left. He went to call Boss to get his OK for accepting the parcel. The response was, "Sure. No problem"—as expected.

Valery escorted Victor to the airport, and the first person both of them saw at the departure gate was Zdenek, smiling beatifically. There were two heavy-set Poles behind him, one of whom was holding a small parcel.

At the gate, Victor was given the parcel. He asked Zdenek, "Is it all right if I drop this off to your man tomorrow?"

"Oh, don't worry. He'll meet you at the gate in Moscow."

Ah, It's not over. Not yet.

They said their good-byes, and Victor was off.

When he disembarked at the Sheremetyevo Airport, he immediately spotted the Moscow Representative of the Polish Service waiting for him at the gate, accompanied by the standard backup heavy. The guy was smooth, disarmingly considerate, offering Victor a ride home, determined that his offer should not be refused. It cost Victor ten minutes and his temper to get rid of him.

He deliberately spoke very loudly and did not stop moving as he went through the formalities. No need for any surveillance to report on this contact.

At last, the mission was behind him. He was happy to hug Olga, grab a cab, and head for home.

CHAPTER

7

THE NEXT MORNING VICTOR slipped right back into his routine. As always after being away, Victor's visual perception of familiar places heightened, and he found himself noticing details about the building that he'd soon take for granted again. This time he found himself acutely aware of the walls. He'd never liked the colors, and now he was particularly irritated by the dingy bluefish-grey band of color that started at the baseboard and ended six feet from the floor. The once-harsh white of the upper walls and ceiling had faded to a dingy grey. The slick shine of the paint left a disagreeable impression of wetness.

As he passed the floor-repair team, Victor chuckled to himself. It was practically an institution. The parquet floors throughout the building were of a soft, low-grade pine and were constantly wearing out. For some reason the workers didn't take out the worn squares and replace them. Instead, they simply kept adding layers of the same shoddy material, perpetually circulating through the building. One local joke was that in fifty years the shop would have to be closed because there'd be no space left between the floor and ceiling. The implication was that the days of the Communist Party's power were likewise numbered.

Victor quickly dropped that train of thought and headed to Boss's office to report. He found Boss seated at his desk, behind the usual mountain of paper. As Victor entered, Boss looked up, scowling. He growled,

"Hello, stranger."

Victor wondered, "What's up now?" and replied in a neutral tone, "Morning."

"Everything came out all right?"

"We got what we were after. We can start the construction any time."

"Good. How did it go?"

"As expected."

So far the exchange had been very cool and perfunctory. Not quite the enthusiastic response to a successful mission one would have expected from Bosik. Victor waited warily to see what was coming next.

It was a short wait. Boss straightened up in his chair, folded his hands on the desk, and looked at him, black eyes flashing. "I've got just one question: How the hell did you manage to waste so much time? Will you explain that? Why didn't you check the Ambassador's schedule before you left? That way you could have been done in two days instead of almost two weeks. You've got too much work to do here to take time out for a little vacation." He'd started in a quiet measured voice and worked his way up to a shout.

Victor couldn't believe his ears. He was so angry that for an instant he forgot to breathe. After all, he'd tried to convince Boss it would be more efficient to check the Ambassador's schedule first. He controlled his anger, steadied his breathing, and reflected that he probably should have anticipated the criticism. It was typical of the snake pit. Boss was always jammed with work, and he'd probably forgotten. Still, Victor couldn't quite conceal his irritation. He said, very slowly and quietly, "Well, that seems to be our style, doesn't it? We crack the eggs first and then start looking for a pan."

Boss looked at Victor incredulously for a moment. Victor met his eyes evenly. Then Boss burst into laughter. "That's a good one!" It was Victor's turn to be startled. Typical Boss response—absolutely unexpected. Almost any other chief would have put Victor on the blacklist for his insubordination.

Finally, Boss wiped his eyes and said, "Come on, there's no reason to get mad. I recall now it was I who told you to go first and check later. Right?"

"Right."

"OK. I'm sorry. You have to understand, though, my backlog is considerably larger than yours. So smooth your feathers and don't be a goddamn prima donna.

"Sorry."

"OK. By the way, where's your subordination, dammit?"

That was it. The incident was over, the air was cleared, and Boss was his old self.

"Good job, anyway. Thanks. Andreyev is happy, and asked me to tell you that. Now, get back to work. I reckon your mailbox is full."

Victor left.

Boss had been right. Victor had to sign for several pounds of paper at the Secretariat. For the rest of the day he was up to his neck in paperwork.

Some of the work involved the problems the Directorate's suppliers were having with deliveries. Victor was called on as the designated troubleshooter, and told to do whatever it took to get the job done. Victor had dealt with industry before, during his time in a military research institute. He'd learned a few valuable pointers back then, and developed the skill later. The most important one was the law of the network. All the orders and all the decisions in the world weren't worth much unless they were backed up by networking. Any manager could always find an excuse for not delivering according to plan. Most often, they'd claim that the suppliers had caused a delay or failure. As Victor had found out the hard way, with so many suppliers, any attempt to find the party responsible was a waste of time and energy. It was far more productive to go directly to the head of an enterprise and find out what it would take to get the order fulfilled. This might mean finding a good job for someone's relative, sending someone to a high-paying position abroad, or simply procuring something from another country that was unobtainable at home.

Sometimes it was necessary to activate the "5-percent rule." This was a powerful incentive directly related to the peculiar accounting system of the Soviet Union. In the case of an especially important project, the Central Committee could give an enterprise the right to transfer up to 5 percent of the amount budgeted for the project directly to the payroll account as a financial incentive for the participants. In reality, this meant getting the 5 percent in cash from the bank. Considering the vastly inflated numbers in the general accounting for a project (calculated with funds that didn't actually exist), that 5 percent would double—or in some cases, triple—the salaries of the participants. As Victor built his network, however, he rarely needed to invoke the 5-percent rule.

Victor worked into the evening. He found the after-hours the best time to work. Most of the building was empty and quiet, and it was easier to concentrate. As he continued digging himself out, his friend Nikita dropped by.

"Hi. Time to stop."

"Hi." Victor looked at his watch. Already seven. "You're right." The stack of papers in his "out" tray indicated a productive day.

Nikita leaned against the office wall under the two clocks and folded his arms as he watched Victor start to close up shop. He said, "So you pulled off another of your stunts in Warsaw?"

"Yes." Looking up at his friend, he smiled and added, "It got a little dicey, too."

Nikita shifted weight and asked, "You know the best thing about advice?"

Victor was still loading papers into his safe. "I think it depends on the advice."

"No, I mean any advice."

"Then, no. I don't." He gave Nikita his full attention, unsure what to expect.

"It's that you don't have to follow it."

They both laughed, and Victor relaxed. "That, I like."

"Now, having said that," Nikita continued, "why don't you keep your feet on the ground for a change? If you don't, I can guarantee you're going to break your neck on one of these stunts. Some son of a bitch is going to make sure of it."

Victor shrugged. A lecture after all. "That may be, but it's more fun this way."

Nikita wasn't going to stop there. "Look, you are 'widely known in a very narrow circle'—maybe too widely by now. Do you get my point? What bothers me is that every time out you're set up as the perfect scapegoat."

"Oh, come on, you know the rules of the game as well as I do. If you win, it's your chief's win. Lose, and it's your loss—the chief had no idea what you were up to. Total deniability. If you accept the assignment and do as you're told, it's your own risk. But if you refuse to take it, you're in deep shit and probably out of the game altogether. Great choice."

"Sure, sure, but that's true for anyone on the move in a bureaucracy. What I'm saying is you're excessive, Victor. You go way beyond all reasonable bounds."

Again, Victor shrugged. "And just what's the standard for reasonable bounds?"

Nikita ignored the question. "And you're a compulsive competitor—which just makes it worse. The sure way to get you to do something is to label it impossible. Listen, all I'm really trying to tell you is, just be careful. OK?"

Nikita had gone a considerable step further on his behalf than most of his peers would dream of doing. It wouldn't have surprised Victor if some even looked forward to his taking a spectacular fall. He was grateful for Nikita's intentions, even if he didn't plan to take his advice. "Thanks. And don't worry, I'll be careful."

"The hell you will. That's OK, it's your ass. And please don't think I worry about you. I just don't want to feel guilty later on for not having warned you." Nikita covered his retreat with mock irritation. There was a long pause, and he changed the subject. "You probably think I only came to lecture you . . . ?"

"No, actually I thought you came to get me the hell out of here."

"You're right. But that's only half my mission. Let's get the hell out of here and go have a drink."

"Sorry, but I can't. My folks are coming for dinner tonight, so I'd better go home." He thought for a moment. "You know, we haven't gotten together for a while. Tomorrow's Friday—why don't you and Marina drop by? Maybe Oleg and Artem can come too, along with their better halves."

"That's a great idea. We'll get the ladies to organize the operation."

"Sure. They won't screw it up the way we usually do."

Victor completed the ritual at his safe, and the two friends headed out of the Tower for home.

Oleg and Artem both worked with Victor and Nikita in the Eighth CD, and all four men were good friends. They were in the same cohort of KGB officers and shared many semi-official views in the office. Their similar ages, backgrounds, and outlooks drew the four of them together in the snake pit.

Olga was delighted to arrange the party, keeping the phone lines busy Friday morning in the pleasant frenzy of last-minute party plans. By lunchtime the four men had been fully briefed by their respective spouses. Their instructions were as precise as any they might receive for a mission.

Around 7:30 the three couples arrived at the Sheymovs' place. There was no ice to be broken. All eight knew one another well enough to dive in as if they'd visited just the day before, and their get-togethers were always lively. Kidding and laughing were the way they communicated.

This evening, Victor was on the receiving end of most of the teasing. He was a little too tired to fight fire with fire, and he paid dearly for his passivity. His friends were merciless. And hilarious. Part of Victor's Party job was to conduct Party meetings. Artem, a gifted mimic, scored high with his burlesque of Victor's most recent speech. He'd had to deliver a homily on morality to young KGB officers. Artem had them all laughing uncontrollably. Then, having extracted all he could from his outrageous imperson- ation of Victor, he said, "Come on, you, Party Official, the guys want fun, they want girls. And there you are telling them they must be celibate because the next girl they sleep with just might be a CIA agent . . . ?" Of course, he knew, as they all did, that Victor's text had been pure Party line.

Victor looked for a neat way to escape the assault. "You want to hear the latest story on this very subject?

"It seems this young guy was about to be accepted as a candidate for Party membership. Standard scene: big room, official red tablecloth, three- man committee, political portraits on the wall—and lots of pressure. The poor guy's nervous, hasn't slept, looks like hell, and they've kept him wait- ing in the hall for forty minutes. Finally he's invited in. He sits nervously on the single chair in the middle of the room, wringing his hands. And then the crucifixion begins. The committee drills him with all the standard questions.

"Finally, when the guy's half dead, the personal part. The question, asked accusingly: 'Do you smoke?'

"He answers guiltily, 'Well, everyone does, so do I.'

" 'Not good!' comes the response, 'Comrade Lenin did not. Would you quit if the Party tells you to?'

" 'Yes, I would.'

"Next question: 'Do you drink?'

" 'Well, everyone does, so do I.'

" 'That's bad! Comrade Lenin did not. Would you quit if the Party tells you to?'

" 'Yes, I would.'

" 'Good.' Next question: 'Do you screw girls?'

" 'Well, everyone else does, so do I.'

" 'That's really bad! Comrade Lenin did not. Would you quit if the Party tells you to?'

"Tiniest hesitation, then, 'Yes, I would.'

" 'All right, good. Now, the final question: Would you sacrifice your life for the Communist cause?'

"The guy thinks to himself, 'No smoking, no drinking, and no girls? Who the hell needs a life like that?' And then he answers, 'Of course I would.' "

And they all exploded in laughter.

Around eleven, the ladies retired to another room to share the latest Moscow gossip. As the men smoked and savored cognac, the conversation shifted inevitably to the office.

Nikita reminded them about shooting practice on Monday morning at the country firing range.

Artem reacted angrily, "Shit, you're right. Christ Almighty, it takes an hour and a half to get there. This is the fifth or sixth time, and what the hell do we need it for? We've always used the Center's firing range. Five minutes' walk from the office door. Why on earth do we have to use the country range?"

Nikita volunteered, "Because the Center's firing range is not fit for machine guns, that's why."

Artem was still upset, "So tell me why we need machine-gun training, along with all the rest of the street-fighting shit we're getting? Our weapon's always been a pistol."

Victor said, "It's a firm order from the very top. New line on training. Get completely trained—just in case."

Artem was adamant. "In case of what . . . ?"

Victor said, "It's none of our business. 'The less you know, the better you sleep,' remember?"

Oleg chimed in, "Come on, Victor. Seriously, what's up?"

Victor shrugged. "Wake up, will you? This has been going on for quite a while now. Haven't you noticed that the Party has redefined our official primary mission?"

"What do you mean?" Oleg was a good man, but a bit slower than the others. His forte was his terrierlike pursuit of a subject.

Victor explained, "I mean that from the time of Khrushchev's reforms, our ideological-fitness program started with the credo, 'You are first of all members of the Communist Party, and secondarily are you KGB officers. Communist justice is what you are defending.' Right?"

"Yes." Oleg was on the trail.

"Well, only recently it's been changed to: 'First and foremost you are KGB officers, and your primary responsibility is the precise execution of your commander's orders.'"

Oleg's face registered the fact that the penny had at last dropped. The other two men just nodded. For them it was not a revelation.

"Come to think of it, you're right. I just assumed some busybody was getting uptight about office discipline."

Victor said, "Think about it, Oleg. What's going on at the top? I mean at the very top?" There was no answer. He wondered how his colleague could be blind to what was taking place under his very nose. He continued, "Look, Brezhnev is ill. Very ill."

Artem was the first to get the full implication. "Are you saying that

Andropov may be planning to grab power himself?" Instantly, it was clear from each man's body language that the same unspoken word had flashed through their minds. Coup. However, it was too dangerous to pronounce. They were friends—but one never knew.

Victor reacted with mock horror, "God forbid! I couldn't even have thought about it, let alone saying it." Then with a sly smile he added, "What I mean to say is that perhaps he's anticipating that somebody else might be thinking about it. And he intends to prevent it."

Yuri Vladimirovich Andropov, the ambitious Chairman of the KGB, had started his career in the Komsomol. One of Victor's older friends vividly recalled the young Andropov as a high-level Komsomol functionary who had headed one of the "propaganda trains" that crossed the country with an appeal from the Komsomol for Red Army volunteers. The campaign's theme was, "Our Communist Motherland is in danger. You have an obligation to defend it." All functionaries on the train had been exempted from military service—one of the major incentives for joining the team.

Andropov had looked really impressive. He had worn the full military uniform, though because he was not actually in the military he couldn't wear any military insignia. But he more than made up for that lack with a gun in a huge, tan leather holster slung on his hip.

Andropov had served as a party functionary in World War II, engaging in stormy activities in quiet places. Having thus survived the war, he was sent to Hungary as Ambassador. There he distinguished himself in the eyes of the Politburo in two ways. First, somewhat unconventionally for an Ambassador, he managed to suppress the revolution in 1956. Second, he personally beheaded the uprising. He invited the Hungarian Prime Minister Imre Nagy to the Soviet embassy. Nagy knew that he was risking his life by accepting the invitation, but he nevertheless did so, counting on Andropov's official status as Soviet Ambassador and his guarantees of personal safety.

The meeting was short, since Andropov's only goal was to get Nagy into Soviet hands. Imre Nagy was arrested in the Soviet embassy, whisked away, and executed.

Artem was stunned. There was silence for a long minute as they all took thoughtful sips of their cognac.

Then Nikita spoke. "Actually, a lot of things are pointing that way. There have been a lot of officers from the Border Guards hanging around the Center, have you noticed?" General nods of affirmation. "Well, have you also noticed that many of them sport pilot's wings?"

Again, Oleg needed to catch up. "Yeah, but so what . . . ?"

"Come on, think!" Artem lacked Victor's and Nikita's patience. "Up to now, the Border Guards never had aviation. Now, all of a sudden here they are in Moscow, and they're pilots! Victor, you have a better vantage point than we do—what the hell are they doing here?"

"Training at the Border Guards School in Babushkino. As I understand it, around a hundred of them are always here on rotation. The same thing is true for the officers of the tank units as well. Contrary to popular belief, there are still other armored units in the Border Guards, although they never gave the Kantemirov armored division stationed near Moscow back to the KGB after Khrushchev. These officers are being rotated in to receive their training in the same school."

Oleg conceded, "OK, I guess it certainly looks like something's brewing. But I still don't understand what it's got to do with us in the Eighth. We're not exactly a fighting unit."

Nikita said, "I think it must be because we're the most reliable group. We all have high security clearances. We're the most trusted people in the whole KGB. They must have figured we'd be the most loyal."

Oleg digested this thought. Then, his eyes grew wide with another realization. He looked at the other three who, for once, had to catch up with him. Then the same thought occurred to Nikita and Artem. The three guests looked at their host. Victor understood instantly and laughed, "Don't worry, I've taken care of all the gadgets they've put in."

There was a collective sigh of relief. Then Oleg said, "I still don't understand why they bug our apartments. It just doesn't make sense."

Nikita added, "It's a joke, really: they know we can get around whatever they plant, and still they do it. Why?"

Artem was quick to answer, bravado replacing anxiety. "I suppose they know we know too much about it. But the damn bureaucrats have to report that they have covered all the bases, to show they have a record of what we're whispering. Surely they know that it's insane to suspect us of disloyalty."

"And we all know that if they wanted to bug us properly they'd have neither the time nor the wherewithal to accomplish anything else," Nikita granted. "So, the silliness continues."

Victor took up the explanation. "Obviously, we're all subject to the same random surveillance. Besides, the whole department in the Second

CD exists purely for our security. Can you imagine that—that the only reason for the existence of that department is to ensure the security of Directorate A? I guess those guys have to do something to justify their salaries." And in fact they did, well beyond placing clumsy bugs.

By this time, the ladies had chewed over all the worthwhile Moscow news. Olga had told them about an exhibition of Ilya Glazunov's paintings she'd just seen. Glazunov was a semiprohibited artist. Olga was still elated by the experience, and the other women listened enviously. Never mind that she had had to stand in line in the cold rain for three hours to get in. Energized by her coup, they stormed the room and ended all shop talk by turning the music up loud. The group partied until well past two in the morning.

On Monday morning Victor received two urgent telegrams from Teheran. The situation was becoming increasingly unstable. The events unfolding there were clearly jeopardizing the embassy's security. The decision on what to do with its most sensitive part, the referentura, had to be made quickly. Victor immediately began analyzing the options.

One: ignore the turbulence, hope for the best, and continue work to implement the new security-upgrade measures, just like in the Warsaw embassy. Two: order all work stopped and wait to see which direction the current crisis would take. Three: order the immediate destruction of all sensitive papers, ciphers, materials, and equipment.

The third option—destruction—would require a lot of time, much more than most people appreciate. First, it takes a full thirty minutes to burn a single book, that is, if one doesn't separate the pages. In an emergency ambush, no one would take the time to separate pages. If books and papers were burned continuously, the furnace would quickly overheat. Any further burning would be impossible until it had cooled down. The furnaces in the Teheran embassy were old and certainly could not withstand even a few hours of continuous emergency burning.

The situation with the cipher equipment was much worse. Tests had shown that the destruction of just one machine took at least eight man-hours. The KGB had learned that lesson the hard way. Victor had in mind the famous experiment conducted after the coup against Allende in Chile. In preparation for evacuating the Soviet embassy, all sensitive documents had been burned. The cipher machine also had to be destroyed. After removing the two separate security cases, it took two hours to disassemble the 50-pound electromechanical machine. Then, with a steel hammer expressly provided for the purpose, one man spent twelve hours smashing every single piece, deforming them all beyond recognition.

The debris was put in a bag and flown to Moscow. Because it had been rumored that the runway was mined, they even brought in an expert military pilot to fly the plane out with a dangerously short takeoff. The debris was given to the Eighth CD's intercept people, and they were to figure out what the bits of metal might be. That group was chosen so that they would not be familiar with that particular machine. In a short while they had restored it, at least to the point at which they could specify precisely how to manufacture an operating duplicate of the original.

Between the MFA, KGB, and GRU, the Teheran embassy had six old cipher machines and four new ones, not to mention numerous other gadgets of a very sensitive nature, and a ton of top-secret papers, many bound into books. If the embassy was attacked, no one could tell where all the materials would wind up. Victor knew that the decision to destroy everything would have to be made considerably in advance of an emergency. He'd have to estimate very carefully how much time was needed for complete destruction. An error in judgment in either direction would be excruciatingly costly.

All of these factors were flashing through Victor's mind as he tried to establish as clear and complete a picture as possible of what was going on in Iran, based on the conflicting, somewhat confusing information in the two telegrams he had just received.

The phone interrupted his train of thought. Boss. Victor was sure he was calling about Teheran, and he didn't feel ready to discuss it.

Without preamble, Boss said, "Look, here's what's just come up: Andreyev called me from East Germany and said that the Herr Direktor of the East German Service, Mielke, is worried about his cipher communications. He's asking for assistance."

"But we're already supplying them with the machines and the ciphers. What else does he want?"

"Andreyev feels that Mielke has somehow sniffed out the fact that we're up to something with the cipher security. I have no idea how. He's probably only got a very general sense that there's been an upgrade. As you know, this stuff is so secret and tightly guarded that even very few Members of the Central Committee have any idea what we're doing."

"Does Andreyev want us to investigate?"

"Perhaps later. For now, he's chosen to give Mielke a birthday present—at least he says it's his birthday—the secure enclosure for a cipher machine."

This really caught Victor by surprise, "What?!"

Boss chuckled. "Don't worry, it will be our special gift model, the one that's been stripped of all the protection."

"Well, he's the chief."

"Right. And he wants it delivered today. You are to make sure that everything is in order."

Victor was furious. He was being instructed to drop the critical situation in Teheran just to mess around with a stupid birthday gesture. Remembering Boss's crack about his "subordination," however, Victor said cautiously, "With all due respect, I must remind you that I am currently working on the Teheran situation—on your orders. We have to make the decision quickly, and it's a big one. I respectfully submit that the matter of this birthday present perhaps could be handled by some kid in the supply section."

"Andreyev does not want any slipups. He specifically requested you. That's how it is." End of argument. "Now, the military airplane is on its way to Sheremetyevo. The car and driver are waiting for you. Go to our warehouse in Sheremetyevo, make triple sure that the damn thing is stripped of all—and I mean all—protection, that it gets loaded onto the plane and is on its way to Berlin today."

"Should I accompany it personally?" Victor couldn't keep the sarcasm out of his voice.

Boss didn't seem to notice it. "No, just make sure that plane takes off."

Thank God for that, at least.

On his way to the car, Victor did a slow burn. Making this empty gesture to Mielke couldn't conceivably be equated with the crisis in Iran. Yet in the face of Andreyev's whim not even Bosik was willing to question the priorities. Nikita's warning came to mind. It was Victor who would be the scapegoat if things went sour in Teheran.

He was usually polite with his drivers, but this time he barked, "Sheremetyevo. Step on it." The car had just accelerated, when Victor cried, "Stop at once, over there." He pointed ahead across the street. The driver braked hard, crossed the oncoming traffic, and stopped by a gift shop. Victor went in and emerged minutes later with a roll of the widest baby-pink gift-wrapping ribbon available and a pair of scissors. He jumped back in, and the car sped off to the airport.

At the Directorate's warehouse, Victor surprised the workers by ordering them to unpack the cipher enclosure, strip it of all protection, and repack its parts in their original dark-green military crates. As usual, the wood was of extremely poor quality.

He watched as the crates were loaded into the military cargo plane. Then, energized by mischievous impulse, he leaped into the cargo bay and tied pink ribbons around each of the rough crates. The bows were large and perfect. He surveyed the results with malevolent satisfaction. Victor watched the plane take off, then returned to the real work waiting for him in his office.

By midnight he had a pretty good idea of the decision he'd recommend to Boss on Teheran.

The next morning, as he was preparing to report to Boss, his secretary called: "Boss wants to see you."

A bad sign. Usually Boss called Victor himself.

He entered Boss's office and had to struggle to keep a straight face. Boss's face was as pink as the ribbon Victor had used.

"I've told you your damn sense of humor would get you in trouble, but that's your business. Now Andreyev is furious with me. I am not going to tolerate this. Do you understand?"

Victor was all innocence, "I am sorry, but I'm afraid I don't. What's the problem? What happened?"

"And now he asks, 'What happened?' Those idiotic ribbons, that's 'what happened'!"

Victor was the picture of virtue itself. "Ah, the ribbons!" And then, instantly concerned, "What about them? Mielke didn't like them? Oh no! They were the best I could find, I assure you."

"Don't play games with me. Why did you do it?"

"But I thought you said this was to be a birthday present. I just figured . . ."

"One more joke like this and I'll send you to Katmandu. Or Addis Ababa. As a cipher clerk. Is that clear?"

Oh no you won't, you need me here to get your work done. "Yes."

"That's all. Get out. I can't stand the sight of you."

"Oh, one thing. On the Teheran business . . ."

Boss cut him off, "Don't bother me. Do what you want on Teheran."

"But . . ."

"No 'buts.' Make your recommendation. It's your responsibility. Send me the cables to sign."

* * *

Victor returned to his office and drafted two cables for Teheran, one from Andreyev, and another joint cable from the KGB and MFA. The cables directed that the security upgrading and modernizing be put on hold; that all nonessential materials be destroyed; that all cables and correspondence be put on film for rapid destruction if necessary; that all nonessential personnel be sent home; and, finally, that the embassy begin active preparations for the coming emergency.

CHAPTER

THE NEXT DAY A SECRETARY from the Personnel Department called Victor to remind him officiously that he still had not turned in his Warsaw Pact passport.

"Sorry, can I do it next week? There's no rush, is there?"

"Victor, don't give me that. I don't need to give you a lecture on the regulations."

Victor sighed: "OK, on my way."

Between Mielke's birthday present and the crisis in Iran, he'd completely forgotten about the damn rule: any passport for travel abroad had to be returned to the Personnel Department in person, immediately upon completion of the trip. He set off for Personnel, two blocks away on Dzerzhinsky Street.

On his way back, he noticed a familiar figure clad in the uniform of an Air Force colonel. The man was walking slightly ahead of Victor on the other side of the street.

Victor crossed and quickly closed the distance between them. He tapped on the epauletted shoulder and asked belligerently, "Hey! You gotta match?"

The colonel turned sharply, ready for a confrontation. Instantly his expression changed into a broad grin. "Victor! You son of a bitch! How great to see you."

"So, how've you been, Vladimir?" Victor gasped, recovering from his friend's exuberant bear hug.

"Good, very good. And you?"

"Just fine."

Colonel Vladimir Zotov, Ph.D., was one of the leading scientists in Space Warfare. He looked wonderful—healthy and as energetic as ever.

"What are you doing right now, Victor? Can we go have a drink?"

"I'd love that, but first I've got to go back to the office for a couple of hours. After that, I'm a free man."

"Great! I've finished my business here, but I still need to shop for a few things. Wife's wish list, you know. We don't have the stuff in Bolshevo that you guys have here in the capital. So, why don't we meet in two hours' time. Are you still in the Center building?"

"Yes. I'll meet you on the corner by the Children's World store."

Victor returned to his office. His thoughts took him back to the time he'd spent in TsNII-50, where he'd begun his first career.

When Victor graduated from high school, he entered Bauman Technical University, commonly referred to as Bauman Institute, the oldest, most prestigious technical university in Russia, founded in 1837. Its list of alumni was impressive—the vast majority of the industrial leaders of Russia and, subsequently, the Soviet Union had graduated from Bauman. Famous for its demanding six-year curriculum, it was equally infamous for its arbitrarily harsh treatment of students, treatment that bordered on psychological torture. Bauman Institute's 60-percent dropout rate was an honored tradition. Given the stringent entrance examinations and the hostile environment the students faced upon acceptance, it was easy to understand why those who did manage to graduate were well prepared to survive anywhere.

Bauman's regime was rigid. Victor's days were filled with classes. There were no electives. Victor was required to study every kind of basic technology, for Bauman graduates were trained to become the essential expediters and coordinators of the Soviet military-industrial complex. From Bauman, everyone went to war. In fact, as a security measure, almost no Bauman student was permitted to travel abroad.

Victor fulfilled his requirements with little thought for the future. His real energies were dedicated to partying and sports. He became a serious sprinter and broke the school's 100-meter record. After three years, however, he resolved to buckle down and focus on academics. The Deputy Dean was extremely displeased at the prospect of losing one of Bauman's public-relations assets. He accused Victor of compromising the interests of the University and promised to get him expelled. The threatening tone was entirely of a piece with the school's general style. One word from the Deputy Dean and the faculty's attitude toward a student could become instantly hostile. Normally, if students received just three failing grades, they were thrown out of Bauman. The rule actually specified one fail as grounds for rejection, and it was made clear to Victor that if he dropped track that rule would be enforced literally. Nonetheless, Victor did drop track. He became one of three students in his class to win a special scholarship for the final year of study.

Victor took an interest in economics and management. His economics course focused on the advantages of the Socialist system over Capitalism. The basic premise of the class was that the "socialist conscience" of the workers would yield higher productivity than would capitalist greed. However, the management course acknowledged the need to balance the motivation of a socialistic conscience with material incentives. If too much weight was given to material incentives, there was a danger that workers would become too materialistic and would lean toward the capitalist attitude. Once that happened, no reward would ever satisfy them. They'd ask for more and more. On the other hand, without enough material incentives, the workers would work poorly. So the balance was the key. The course did not specify just where that balance was.

The management course did explain why under the Soviet accounting system a single bolt could cost several hundred rubles, especially in the factories of the military-industrial complex. But the course also made it quite clear that the allocation of cost was not really relevant. The most important measure of each enterprise's performance was its *valovoy* product, or the actual total output, because the output was what was supposed to satisfy the demand.

According to this course, the budgeting process was not important and should be viewed only as a reference. First of all, for strategic reasons, real budget numbers were kept top secret. Secondly, there was a fundamental accounting problem. There were no fewer than four different "rubles" in the country. One was the accounting ruble, the unit the enterprises used to charge one another and by which they related their activities to the budget. The second was the paper ruble, the only real ruble. In an enterprise's budget, payroll accounts were the only ones carried out in real rubles. Throughout the country payroll accounts were separated from all other accounting, so they had no bearing on the rest of the enterprise's budget. Third was the "gold ruble," which didn't actually exist. This was the accounting unit used in foreign transactions, and it was tied to the dollar by an arbitrary rate of exchange. At any rate, since those transactions were carried out in foreign currency, no harm was done by this system. Finally there was the fourth, the Comecon ruble, similar to the "gold ruble," but used in the accounting for transactions within the Comecon countries. The fact that none of the four kinds of rubles was exchangeable with the others made the budgeting process even more irrelevant. Because they all had a solid grounding in math, this concept was hard to sell to the students in Victor's class. The popular joke was that the budget didn't need to be classified information, as it was quite inaccurate enough to mislead any foreign analyst. However, the country's real budget was kept highly secret, and in any official budget most of the funds earmarked for military and intelligence purposes were directly allocated to ministries with innocent names like Ministry of General Machine-Building, which actually stood for ICBM manufacturing.

Toward the end of his days at Bauman, Victor came face to face with the realities of life after university: it was time to launch his career, or more accurately, have one launched for him. University graduates in the Soviet Union didn't choose their jobs. The University Placement Committee dictated where they went, and the range of available placements varied wildly from excellent to disastrous. The same was true of starting salaries.

In theory, the primary consideration in placing graduates was supposed to be the demands of the economy—where young specialists were needed—along with the student's "overall performance," which in effect meant his or her participation in political activities, such as Komsomol work. Academic distinction was strictly secondary.

That was the theory. In practice, landing a decent job was a wild scramble. As graduation neared, everyone—family, friends, and other connections—was called on to pull any available string that might set up a personalized request from within a sought-after workplace.

In most universities, the geographic location of a job was the critical factor. Not so for Bauman Institute's graduates, who were practically assured of a job in Moscow. But even for them, there was a considerable range in the quality of jobs available. So they too took part in the frenzied search for connections and strings.

As Victor surveyed his university career, he was forced to admit that in terms of his Komsomol work, his position wasn't great. In fact, his political track record was probably going to be a hindrance. His family's connections were quite another story. One phone call from Ivan Sheymov would have been enough to place Victor in a top spot. To Victor's intense disappointment, however, that call would never take place. Victor tried, very tactfully, to broach the subject to his father and was met with a terse, forbidding "No!"

Victor argued, playing every possible angle. "But, Father, that's the way everyone else is doing it. Everyone. That's how the system works now. Don't you realize you're handicapping me by refusing to help?"

"Victor, as I have told you before, I am not responsible for how others conduct themselves. If everyone else becomes a thief, that's still not enough to convince me to become one. The subject is closed, and I do not wish to return to it again." That was Ivan Sheymov. Not a chance with him. Then he added the stinger, "By the way, if I find out that you have asked any of my friends to help you, I will make certain you regret it."

There went Victor's back-up scheme. He had pretty much anticipated Ivan's reaction to his request for direct influence. He had indeed planned to turn to his father's powerful friends, many of whom had watched Victor grow up and would have been all too happy to help.

So, with no strings to pull and an absence of positive political references, Victor's only hope was his academic record. Not a wonderful prospect. To his grateful astonishment, he was assigned to TsNII-50, Scientific Research Institute #50 of the Ministry of Defense—a dream placement. He never did discover whether he'd been chosen as a result of his performance, or whether his last name had played a role after all. But in any case, Victor was happy with his fate.

TsNII-50 was the elite of the Soviet military research centers. It belonged to GUCOS, the Chief Department of Space Affairs, a newly independent body of the Soviet Strategic Rocket Forces. GUCOS had been put in charge of everything connected with space warfare and as a result controlled the entire Soviet space program. It was responsible for the direction and coordination of all Soviet space research, as well as the testing and acceptance of space weapons by the military. A job there meant being at the very heart of the Soviet space program.

The only minor drawback to the job was the location of the Institute. It was a fifteen-minute bus ride from the Bolshevo railroad station, which was roughly a thirty-minute train ride from Yaroslavsky Station in Moscow, in turn a twenty-minute Metro ride from home. Victor's daily round-trip commute was about three hours, but the job was well worth it.

He was placed in the Second Directorate of the huge outfit. The Spacecraft Directorate. The First Department of the Directorate was

Guidance Systems, and Victor was first placed there as a researcher. He was excited by everything around him. Every task was a real scientific challenge, never mind the glamour of the enterprise.

To his surprise, Victor's first assignment did not involve guidance systems of spacecraft per se. It was much more peculiar. His first reaction was to question whether the assignment was a practical joke at the expense of a rookie. When he was persuaded that the conundrum was genuine, however, he eagerly accepted the challenge.

The problem was that a spacecraft's spy camera had to take into account the relative motions of the earth and the spacecraft. The spacecraft itself moved at about eight kilometers per second, and the camera had to take this into account as it followed the movement of the earth's surface. Victor's problem was twofold: First, even the best Soviet film was too slow; and second, the best Soviet sensors were not accurate enough to measure the relative speeds precisely. In other words, the problem was how to provide a guidance system that could follow a moving target with an accuracy greater than the system itself could measure. Catch-22.

The crazy problem required an unorthodox solution. The technological limitations were the givens. Victor decided to apply a statistical processing of numerous measurements, and he succeeded in coming up with an algorithm that provided a high probability of getting a clear shot.

One of Victor's sponsors was a brilliant scientist in Air Force uniform— Major Vladimir Zotov. In addition to his scientific achievements, he was also renowned for his wildly imaginative sense of humor and for his legendary practical jokes. One of them nearly got him demoted.

The Institute's compound was heavily guarded. All along the perimeter of the solid wood and barbed-wire fence were machine-gun towers, manned around the clock. Every building entrance and even some of the floor entrances were heavily guarded, with soldiers checking the passes of everyone coming and going. One could go by the same guard fifty times a day and still be required to show him a pass every time.

The soldiers guarding the compound were a special breed. All of them were drafted from the Muslim central-Asian republics. They were reputed to be dedicated and ruthless, very much of the shoot-first-ask-questions-later school. There was serious question among the scientists about whether the guards would even bother to ask. Or if they could. These soldiers spoke very little Russian and had no local attachments other than to their unit and commander. No conceivable conflict of loyalty. They were used to guard many of the strategic locations. The idea was probably borrowed from the Egyptians and their Mamelukes. The Soviets modified the idea slightly, however, and never promoted these soldiers.

It's said that when the idea of discipline was introduced to the military, the fliers were off flying somewhere and missed the meeting. The scientists must have been elsewhere as well, perhaps at a convention. Vladimir Zotov was both a scientist and an Air Force officer—a combination that aggravated his hostility to discipline. Irritated by the pass rule and the presence of the guards in general, he began to observe them closely and concluded that they really weren't so effective as they appeared. In the presence of a dozen friends—scientists all—he proposed an experiment in the form of a bet. He would change the photograph on his pass to a shot of his golden retriever, Lucky, and use it for one whole day. The guards, he hypothesized, wouldn't notice.

His bet was readily taken up, and his colleagues agreed to a code of silence. Zotov did exactly what he said he'd do. He must have showed that pass to a dozen guards on at least thirty occasions, and not one of them stopped or questioned him. He won a ruble from each of his colleagues and immense satisfaction. The next day, however, when the story broke, he was called in to see the Chief of the Institute, General Melnikov himself. Nobody ever learned exactly what was said during their discussion. Vladimir returned, slightly pink, but otherwise none the worse for wear.

One day, Vladimir approached Victor and asked if he'd like to try covering his shift as duty officer in the Flight Control Center for a few days during the next space mission. He presented this job to Victor as an honor, an opportunity for experience, and a big responsibility. Victor was elated. He accepted at once, worried that he was still too inexperienced, but eager to do whatever he could to be of service to the cosmonauts. He learned later, to his chagrin, that this was in fact a nuisance job—probably the most tedious and time-consuming chore of all. Everyone was required to take a turn and tried like hell to find a substitute. Victor's naive eagerness made him a perfect target, and Vladimir hooked him easily.

A mission launch was scheduled right in the middle of Victor's initiation shift. He was terribly excited. One of his tasks was to announce the countdown over the intercom, starting three hours prior to blast-off. Victor felt very important. He started out just as he'd seen in the movies, dramatically intoning the minutes remaining, with his idea of the diction and projection of a professional announcer. Nobody had told him that everyone involved with a launch was quite aware of the time and that the updates were customarily done quietly—only as an unobtrusive reminder.

He was still in the first hour of the countdown and had just finished his fourth stentorian announcement when he saw the angry face of a general moving toward him. The general stopped in his tracks, recognizing Victor, and burst into hearty laughter. It was an old friend of his father's, who'd known Victor since he was three. He quickly got the picture. "Victor, what the hell are you doing here?"

"Filling in."

The general then explained the protocol to the red-faced rookie, finishing with, "Don't feel bad; everyone has to get broken in." They had a short, pleasant chat, and then he left Victor. The rest of the updates were sotto voce.

Someone told Victor later that after his first announcement, people had looked up from their work in surprise. As the second one was similarly overdone, people had looked at one another and giggled. Bigger laughter after the third, and as the fourth one thundered over the intercom, the general had said, "I've got to see for myself who this idiot on P/A duty is!"

After four months and a few other humbling incidents, Victor was accepted into the brotherhood of the scientists. His reward for successfully completing the assignment on the guidance system of the spy camera was permission to start work on his dissertation. He was also transferred to the Second Department, Spacecraft Weapons, where he was to work on the weapons' guidance systems.

The mission of this department was threefold: to provide advanced research on spacecraft weapons—i.e., weapons fired from spacecraft in space; to formulate the orders to the manufacturers; and to supervise the design, testing, and production of spacecraft weaponry. By definition this work required extensive interaction with all the major participants of the entire Soviet space program. From a purely scientific standpoint, it was a job Victor found fascinating, challenging, and satisfying. The only problem was time. There never seemed to be enough.

The institute had a support system consisting of one of the most powerful modern computer centers in the country and two libraries. The "open library" contained an excellent collection of worldwide technical publications. The updating was so efficient that American periodicals were on the shelves just a few days after publication. The "closed library" housed probably the largest collection of technical intelligence in the world. It was the pride of both the KGB and the GRU. Victor was amazed by the extent of information available on the Americans. Everything they were up to was spelled out in detail.

Victor started out by studying everything that had already been done in his new field. In the case of space weaponry, the history was short. Soviet development of spacecraft weapons had begun in the early sixties with a handful of projects, but by 1969, when Victor first got involved, the field was very much in business.

Victor was quite surprised that he could find no indication that the Americans were also developing space weapons, with the obvious exception of ICBMs. During a meeting with the Department Chief, Victor raised the concern that perhaps the Americans were more advanced in the field than the Soviets were aware of. The answer was short and clear: "We know everything they are up to. They have not even seriously considered space warfare yet."

Victor realized he was entering a political minefield, but he couldn't resist the temptation to ask—tactfully, of course—whether the Institute's work was not perhaps incompatible with the ongoing talks between the two governments about prohibiting, or at the very least limiting, space weapons. The answer was quite definite: "Our business is to develop, test, and deploy the weapons. The job of the diplomats is to make sure that the Americans don't. Or at least to give us a head start. This way we will have a strategic and political advantage. Remember, they are our enemies. There's no such thing as cheating in the game of strategic international affairs. The winner is never judged, only the losers."

At first, this kind of explanation made Victor uncomfortable. Then he reasoned that those who made the policy knew their jobs better than he did. He concluded, *After all, every peasant knows what the Prime Minister should do. The trouble is that he fails to get his own work done. The best thing for me to do is to stick with my job and do it well.* And that's exactly what he did.

Victor's work presented him with an endless progression of problems to solve, each one technically challenging. One particularly tough team assignment was a missile-guidance puzzle. With traditional antiaircraft missiles, the shock waves generated by a missile's exploding anywhere near a target will destroy it. But shock waves need air to travel through, and in outer space there is no air—so no shock waves. Moreover, the density of the exploded shell fragments decreases very rapidly with the distance from the point of explosion to the target. The weight a spacecraft can carry is limited, so heavier shells could not be used.

High-powered lasers had not yet been developed, nor was there at that time a source of energy aboard the spacecraft capable of powering them. Nuclear warheads were too heavy. So the guidance system virtually had to assure a direct hit. Because of the very high angular speeds possible between two objects in space, the problem was a daunting one. It was handed to Victor. His solution would serve as his dissertation.

Among the numerous known methods of navigation there were none that could be directly applied to this problem. Soviet missile-guidance experts discussed trajectories in terms of "pursuit curves." The so-called "dog's pursuit curve" refers to the dog's habit of chasing its prey by running straight at it. The "wolf's pursuit curve" is much more efficient because the wolf aims at a point ahead of its moving prey—one of the reasons why wolves catch their prey more often than dogs. The "proportional navigation" method results in an even more effective trajectory: the missile is aimed ahead of the target, when the missile's guiding impulse is proportional to the target's angular speed. This approach was still inadequate. The missiles available then could not carry sufficient fuel to support this type of guidance for the entire flight. Moreover, with spacecraft-based control, it was impossible to sustain the necessary pinpoint accuracy over the considerable distance the missile had to travel.

The solution was to shoot the missile from the spacecraft like a bullet, aimed at the best estimate of the point where it would intercept the target. Then, at the halfway mark, the missile would switch to the proportional navigation, controlled from the spacecraft. On the final portion of the flight the missile would switch to the infrared self-guidance. That approach fit very well with the weapon nicknamed Hedgehog, developed in the Granat program. The nickname was earned by the missile's strange appearance. Shaped like a symmetrical egg, it had "needles"—twelve dozen small, one-shot jet engines used for guidance. The missile was set spinning like a bullet for stability. Just before impact with the target the tiny, burned-out jet engines were simultaneously released from their seats. Centrifugal force would hurl them outward, but they could not travel too far from the missile because they were connected in groups with circular wires. This web of bullets would hit the target at a speed of at least twenty-five hundred feet per second. No explosive device was necessary with that speed and density. The bullet web was far more lethal than shrapnel. It was a good solution.

All in all, the job was full of similarly crazy technical problems. Victor learned that the best way to solve crazy problems is with crazy ideas. That was exactly what happened time and again. The brilliant minds at the institute generated crazy solutions. And they worked. For a scientist it was the best possible environment. Victor was happy. He worked very hard and was too absorbed to worry about anything beyond his projects.

There was one notable interruption in the otherwise steady work of

TsNII-50—an emergency inquiry from the Central Committee. According to their information, the Americans were looking into the possibility of direct television broadcasts to the Soviet Union—something along the lines of Voice of America. For the first time Victor and his peers could recall, the Central Committee truly seemed to be running scared. Brezhnev was purported to have said, "If they pull this off, all our propaganda efforts will be worthless."

The Institute received top-priority orders: figure out technical countermeasures. It was hinted that the Central Committee would be pleased with a TV equivalent of the jamming used against foreign radio broadcasts. Everyone dropped every other project and worked at an insane pace for several weeks, frantically trying to solve the problem. The conclusion was discouraging. A satellite-based television transmitter creates a cone of potential reception, with a huge footprint on the surface of the earth. Receiving antennas on the ground need only a very narrow angle to avoid any kind of jamming. Detection of the receivers would be a huge task in itself. There were thousands of people in the U.S.S.R. technically capable of making and setting up antennas. To jam the broadcasts effectively, the Soviets would have to position a satellite very close to the American source, one that would have the same coinciding footprint. However, if the American source moved, the Soviet source would have to move with it. Besides, there were on-board energy limitations. This would require developing an entirely new satellite system dedicated solely to the purpose. The space-warfare chiefs had to report that "as a practical matter there is nothing we can do to counter such broadcasts, short of shooting down the communication satellites, and that is the job of the Anti-ICBM Defense branch of the Ministry of Defense."

Their report prompted the Central Committee to conclude that the only hope lay with diplomacy and political maneuvering. These tactics were successfully implemented with the very effective help of the KGB's Active Measures, a coordinated effort of numerous subversive measures to influence foreign governments and the public to think favorably about the Soviet Union. The American TV-broadcast satellite never got off the ground.

By 1971, Victor's dissertation work was advancing well. Most of the theoretical problems had been solved. The two systems he'd helped develop had been successfully tested on the ground. The main body of his dissertation was close to completion. Then the clouds began to gather. In fact, the problem went back to the time when Victor had joined the Institute—he'd just not been aware of it. Behind his back, his detractors were saying that he could not have gotten so far in his work without the scientific help of his father.

The gossip was unfair—not to mention untrue. The first time he heard it Victor felt the very breath knocked out of him. He was vulnerable to the story because it sounded so plausible. Ivan certainly had the knowledge and experience to help him, but Victor had worked like a horse to accomplish what he'd done—on his own. Besides, business discussions were taboo at home. Anyone who knew Ivan Sheymov would have known that.

When he first learned about the rumors, Victor went to Vladimir, who tried to calm his friend and protégé: "Come on, you know about the assholes who spread this kind of dirt do it because they're incapable of doing the kind of work you do. It's just plain envy. There's nothing you can do about it. You're a good scientist, Victor. You have the respect of those who matter. Ignore the rest." These were helpful words, but Victor's pride had been deeply wounded.

Victor was torn between his desire to defend his father and his outrage at the impugning of his own professional integrity.

Dismayed, Victor agonized over the situation for several weeks, then went to talk to Ivan. He said simply, "I'm going to quit."

His father responded bluntly, "It's your decision. But if you're making this choice to protect me, you're making a mistake. I'm not afraid of gossips. I'm above them. Of course, such cheating is common practice. That's why people can believe such a rumor. The irony is that if I had actually helped you, nobody would probably dare accuse me of it."

Victor paused, then said gently, "I know that, Father. But it's not only your reputation at stake here—it's mine as well."

"Victor, there's one more thing for you to consider. Your dissertation is almost finished. Do you realize that because of its sensitivity it must stay at the Institute? You won't be allowed to take it with you. If you quit, you'll have to forfeit it."

"I know."

It had been a critical passage.

The following week at a party at his parents', Victor mentioned that he was going to look for another job. One woman asked what kind of work he had in mind. "Something exciting," he joked. One of his father's old friends took him aside and said, "I think I can help you, Victor. I have a friend who's high in the intelligence branch of the KGB. I think something there would give you all the excitement you can handle."

The idea of working with the KGB had never occurred to Victor. He knew his father despised the organization. "Dirty job, dirty people," he'd remarked more than once. Now, suddenly, the idea appealed to Victor. There could certainly be no conceivable accusation about his father's pulling strings for him there.

"You're right, it might be very interesting. . . ."

"I'll call you tomorrow after I talk to the guy."

The next day it was all set. Victor was told to go to the KGB's Personnel Department for an interview. His parents were not at all happy.

"It's the intelligence division. It has nothing to do with the purges," Victor brushed his mother's careful argument aside. Ivan confided later to Victor that he had felt so strongly about the KGB that he had even seriously considered pulling a few quiet strings to prevent Victor's going there. But he had concluded that if it was not right to intercede on Victor's behalf for any position, then it was hardly fair to intervene against him.

And so Victor had embarked on his new career.

In his office, Victor put away his memories of TsNII-50, finished off his remaining work, called Olga to tell her he'd be late, and left to meet Vladimir at the corner as planned. Unfortunately, the Berlin, an excellent restaurant nearby—formerly the Savoy—was off-limits to them both. It was probably the best restaurant in Moscow, but they belonged to the most sensitive part of the Soviet Inner Ward, the category of people who traffic with State secrets at the highest level. Foreigners frequented the Berlin, and thus it was at the top of the Inner Ward's official taboo list. Vladimir suggested the Prague instead. It was a decent restaurant on Arbat, famous for its cake of the same name. Victor agreed. This place was very close to the main tourist district but, for some mysterious reason, not very popular with foreigners. It was one of the favorite watering holes for the most highly paid members of the Inner Ward. Those in the know could easily spot top Inner Ward members there virtually every night: military men in highly sensitive positions like Strategic Forces Chief of Staff Marshal Tolubko; GURVO, the ICBM Chief Directorate, Chief General Smirnitsky; army industry leaders like ICBM designers Korolev and Chelomey; GUCOS Chief General Karas; or top scientists from the spookier areas of chemical and biological weaponry. This restaurant was also the favorite hangout of the cosmonauts, Yuri Gagarin and German Titov in particular. Victor and Vladimir grabbed a cab and in fifteen minutes were seated at a table at the Prague.

When they'd gotten settled, Vladimir resumed their earlier conversation: "So, you're not in the science business anymore?"

"Not really." Victor put him off gently. He had the advantage because he knew exactly what Vladimir was involved in. The reverse was not true. The rules were clear: Victor could not hint to a living soul outside of work that he had anything to do with ciphers, especially KGB ciphers, and certainly not those used for communications abroad. On the other hand, he liked and respected Vladimir and did not wish to offend him with a lie or a cheap shot of mystery.

"Well, it's a pity. I'd much rather see you as a scientist. That KGB spy crap is not for you. Your brain is too good for that. By the way, if you ever want back in, I can help."

"Thanks, but there's no way back from the KGB. Only up or down."

"That's what I thought. Sorry."

"You guys aren't so holy either. I heard that story about the famous reunion of the Soyuz and Apollo astronauts at the space control center. Just the other side of the wall your colleagues were busy developing weapons to shoot the Americans down."

"So it goes." Vladimir shrugged sheepishly.

"Anyway, don't get me wrong, Vladimir. I'm quite happy where I am, doing what I do. It's a lot of fun. And believe it or not, sometimes I really do get to use my brain. Today's KGB is not just a bunch of bullies running around shooting guns, the way it may have been twenty years ago."

"Yeah," he responded dubiously. Neither military men nor scientists liked the KGB, and Vladimir was both.

After a minute of uncomfortable silence, Victor tried to lighten things up. "Let me tell you a true story. This happened just a little while ago. Two of our guys went to sweep one of our embassy buildings. Routine debugging mission. Usually one of the two guys would have been fairly senior, but for some reason, this time both were green. As you might expect, they were eager for something sensational, heroic even. You know, one of those missions that comes along once every ten years that they could brag about for the next twenty."

Vladimir interjected, "We were all young once. I seem to recall a few of your own stunts." Both smiled.

"True enough. Anyway, everything was routine with the sweep, which by the way took place about a week before the October Revolution State reception. The last places left to check were some offices on the second floor. Suddenly, one of them found a hollow cavity under the floor of a closet. I bet their hearts were racing. They followed procedural instructions to the letter, didn't speak to each other, just gestured. Together they lifted the loose piece of flooring that had been placed over the cavity, and there it was! A huge nut that didn't seem to be holding anything in place. They were going to be heroes! They didn't want to tell anyone else about what they'd found or ask for advice. One of them ran for a wrench—probably from the embassy's garage. When he returned, the two of them managed to loosen the huge nut and unscrew it. At which point the humongous crystal chandelier it had been holding crashed to the parquet floor in the main ballroom below."

Vladimir burst into such a sudden loud roar of laughter that the waiter raced over to their table to ask nervously if they needed help.

Their convivial mood restored, Vladimir asked, "Come on, Victor, you must have made that up."

"No. True story, I swear."

"That's incredible."

"Well, that's the way real life is, sometimes."

"Look, Victor, don't get me wrong. I don't question the need for intelligence. We've benefited from it many times—when we shot down the U-2, for one."

"The U-2?"

"Yes, I was directly involved as a weapons specialist for the Air Force and assigned to the project."

"Never knew you'd done that. So, what's the story?"

"Well, it seems that during the May Day parade in Red Square, Nikita Khrushchev was standing on the Mausoleum in the parade lineup as usual. What wasn't usual was the figure everyone noticed behind the lineup moving toward Khrushchev. He saw the man too. Apparently, he forgot to turn off the microphone in front of him—the one that was to broadcast his greetings to the crowd assembled for the parade. The mike picked up Khrushchev's voice, loud and clear: 'Well, did you shoot it down?' The question reverberated throughout Red Square and all over the country as well, on TV and radio. Nobody had a clue what he was talking about. At the time, in the confusion of the festivities, nobody took much notice. In subsequent TV reruns, that incident was edited out.

"What Khrushchev had been referring to was the U-2, piloted by Gary Powers. Khrushchev had been absolutely furious about the American U-2 forays over Soviet territory. They were not only a political embarrassment, they also jeopardized his strategic ICBM game by disclosing the real strengths and weaknesses of the Soviet strategic posture. He ordered the flights stopped by any possible means. Khrushchev's assessment, which later proved correct, was that if one U-2 was shot down, the trespassing would halt. But given the Soviet technology at the time, shooting down a U-2 was exceedingly difficult.

"However—and this will interest you—we had one important thing going for us: we knew the exact flight plan of every U-2 invading Soviet airspace several days in advance.

"That's pretty good."

"Yes, but it still wasn't enough to bring a plane down. So an elite squadron of top pilots was assembled. Their aircraft were specially enhanced for the job, but to no avail. The problem was the inaccuracy of the ground guidance given to the pilots. Even when this was preset for a convenient point on the U-2's flight path, by the time they could see the U-2, the pilots found they were out of missile firing range. To close in on the target, they needed a booster. But the booster could only be turned on at a low altitude, so by the time they had dived down to where they could turn the booster on, the U-2 was long gone. They couldn't go up initially with the booster on because of the fuel restrictions. So the hunt dragged on and became routine. The operating logic was that according to the law of probabilities, sooner or later a U-2 would run out of luck. If we hadn't had access to the flight plans, it would have taken nothing short of a technological breakthrough to shoot down the U-2. Meanwhile, Khrushchev was furious and insisted that a U-2 be shot down immediately. And, as it happened, there was a breakthrough—of sorts.

"There were very few ground-to-air missiles at the time; and their ground radars weren't good enough to guide a missile to the high-flying U-2. However, it was reckoned that a ground-to-air missile could hit the plane if the plane either flew directly over the missile's ground radar, or if the plane banked and exposed more of its surface, making it easier for the radar to guide the missile. The breakthrough apparently came from intelligence."

"What kind of breakthrough?"

"We figured that the Soviet source leaking the flight information not only knew the flight plans but was also able to influence them. On this occasion the source fixed things so that one of the flights, scheduled for a major Soviet holiday, required the pilot to fly within reach of the ground-to-air missiles and execute a turn—banking left at precisely the necessary point. A perfect setup. Khrushchev had been anxiously awaiting the news of the outcome during the May Day parade."

"Amazing."

"The hunt wasn't a 100-percent success, however, either as a result of the usual policy of redundancy or perhaps excessive motivation—the squadron pilots had been promised the Hero of the Soviet Union medal for shooting down a U-2. In any event, although the interceptors were ordered to disperse just before the U-2 reached the missile site, one plane continued the pursuit. It wasn't clear if his radio malfunctioned or if the pilot, intent on being a hero, had simply ignored the recall order. His plane was shot down by the first missile, while the second one got the U-2. As you know, firing two missiles is standard operating procedure."

"They were pretty lucky," Victor commented. "It sounds as though the Americans had had their chance. Those Soviet military pilots' radio communications must have been scrambled, of course. I'd guess what we would call their crypto-resistance must have been pretty low—no more than an hour. The Americans should have been able to descramble their code within that time. I think that a routine security measure, a thorough analysis of the squadron's communications after each flight, would have revealed that the pilots hunting the U-2s were the same bunch each time, regardless of the flight path. That would have tipped off the Americans that their flight plans were being leaked. From there, it would not have been too difficult to plug the leak. Obviously, they didn't make use of their opportunity, though, and Gary Powers was shot down. Quite a failure. But a nice May Day present for Nikita."

Vladimir looked at Victor intently, finally getting a sense of his friend's area of operations.

They then turned to catching up on mutual friends and rivals.

Over dessert, Victor asked, "Well, how're things going in my former domain?"

"Not bad. Your guidance system is working. We're in the flight-testing phase now. Your dissertation was successfully defended by the creep you know so well. He's a respected scientist now, an authority on the class of guidance systems that was your specialty." Vladimir paused, as if he wanted to stop there. Then he changed his mind and added, "Shit, I can't stand it. That guy, that whole story makes me sick to my stomach."

"Vladimir, it's OK. It's history. Forget it. I'm just glad the damn thing works."

"Yes, and it works very well. You should be proud of it."

"I imagine you're about to have a breakthrough with the power lasers. Must be fun to work on."

"You bet. We're working day and night on that one. Push, push, as always."

Dinner ended pleasantly over coffee and brandy. Then, given that Vladimir still had to go all the way back to Bolshevo, they parted amicably, and went their separate ways.

CHAPTER

FOR A FEW DAYS things were relatively quiet. Victor was able to catch up on overdue reports and settle into an almost sane working rhythm. He knew the lull would be temporary. There was no such thing as routine troubleshooting.

The very next crisis sprang unexpectedly from a quarter that had almost gotten Victor into hot water before. Although the problem had never been officially assigned to Victor, he nonetheless felt responsible for the consequences.

Just as he was surveying his much-diminished pile of papers with satisfaction, a copy of a cable arrived, distributed to him as a matter of routine. The cable said that a KGB clerk had died in a secure cipher-machine enclosure in a Soviet embassy in Africa. What was unusual was that the cause of death was not stated. Instinctively, Victor knew that what he'd feared for a long time had come to pass.

Back in 1975, when Victor had first gotten involved with the technical security for cipher communications, he'd been surprised to learn that the medical aspect of the field had been completely ignored. He was amazed that no one had made the slightest attempt to determine and evaluate the influence of the high-intensity electromagnetic emanations on the human body over time. Not even the short-term effects had been studied at all. This was odd because it had been clearly established from research performed in other—nonsecret—areas that high-intensity microwaves could cause leukemia and were suspected of causing other forms of cancer as well.

This oversight was particularly reprehensible, considering the methods used to intercept foreign embassies' cipher communications. In one method, for instance, the KGB "flooded" an embassy with intensive high-frequency electromagnetic waves, to induce and receive a response from any telltale electric circuit operating there. That was based on the simple fact that every electric circuit responds readily on its resonance frequency to electromagnetic waves of the same frequency—emanating its own signal. And this signal would be modulated and thus would carry information that is very interesting to the interceptor, such as a conversation, or the typing of a typewriter, or the operation of a cipher machine. The signal could then be easily demodulated by a receiver.

Victor remembered all too well his conversation on the subject with a high-level officer of the Sixteenth Directorate—the unit responsible for intercepting foreign cipher communications.

"We don't know for sure that any danger exists, do we? And after all, these are foreigners. Who cares about their health? The more of them that die, the better off we are."

At the time, Victor was not about to openly criticize the Party's urgent mandate for intercept intelligence at any cost. It was clearly understood that there could be no restrictions. There was a war on, and every war has its casualties. Naturally. But he was troubled about the effects on innocent embassy personnel: the diplomats, the staff, their wives and children. "Not my territory," he rationalized.

However, he did remember asking, "But there are a lot of Soviet people living and working nearby. What about them? Not to mention our own guys who work with the equipment."

The pat response: "Look, millions of our people died for the Communist cause during the revolution and World War II. Not contras and capitalists, but our people—communists. They sacrificed their lives for our cause without hesitation. Should we hesitate now to sacrifice a few hundred lives? No, of course we must not. And anyway, we don't even know if it's a question of sacrifice at all. We just don't know, do we?"

Suddenly, Victor had found himself in a treacherous quicksand. The questions he was asking could easily set him up to be accused of unpatriotic, perhaps even anticommunist thinking. He knew that he needed to back off as smoothly as possible. He joked, "Well, I've heard that the flowers in the American embassy are dying rather quickly, and nobody knows why." Never mind the children in the embassy and in the Soviet buildings surrounding it.

The joke worked. "Not to worry, they're rich enough to change them often." Still, the conversation had ended ominously. "By the way, you're responsible for the security of our communications, right? So, get busy with your own business." The message was clear.

Victor had heeded the warning and kept a low profile on the issue, but the questions remained with him, rankling his conscience. Victor's responsibilities kept him aware of the problem, whether he liked it or not. There were three main technical aspects of cipher-communications security: the mathematical basis of the cipher; the electromagnetic "leakage"; and the acoustic "leakage." The first area was left entirely to the mathematicians, but Victor was directly concerned with the last two. He was also involved in the highly vulnerable operational aspects of security, particularly the human element.

The electromagnetic emanations of the cipher machines presented potentially the most dangerous security problem. With the right equipment these emanations could be extremely revealing. Two distinct methods were used to assure their security: electromagnetic shielding by means of a barrier, a complete enclosure, and then a further masking of the emanations by the generation of meaningless electromagnetic signals—"noise." To assure maximum security, each technique had to provide a sufficient defense in itself—the famous KGB redundancy.

The level of electromagnetic noise produced by the numerous noise generators inside the enclosure was so high that if the specially sealed door of the enclosure was accidentally opened while the noise generators were working, all the noncable TV sets within a mile would be "snowed" out. The cipher clerk inside the enclosure was continuously exposed to that level of radiation. This exposure was what continued to trouble Victor as he went on minding his own business.

During the four years since he'd first become aware of the problem, Victor noticed that those who designed the system and those in charge of it—himself included—took great care to avoid exposure to the high-intensity electromagnetic waves. But there was evidently complete official indifference to the fate of the cipher clerks and other personnel who were continuously exposed.

By 1976, he couldn't ignore the problem any longer. He felt morally responsible. He had to speak up. Finally, he decided to express his growing anxiety to Boss.

Boss was less than receptive. In fact, he was downright irritated.

"Come on, Victor. We don't know for sure what the impact from the emanations is, do we? No. It's the medical profession's job to determine that. As far as I know, there is no solid proof of any danger to human health."

He was ready to close the subject, but Victor persisted. "That's true. Of course there's no proof. How could there possibly be proof? Proper research can't be conducted because the medical profession hasn't got the slightest idea what we're up to here."

"Absolutely. And we aren't about to let them have any idea." Boss changed his tactics. "You don't seem to appreciate the critical sensitivity of this matter."

Victor disregarded the veiled warning and pressed on. "But what bothers me is that we might be slowly killing our own people. I'm also concerned with another related problem. Because of other technical-security restrictions, ventilation and heat removal in the enclosures are, to put it mildly, inadequate. The conditions inside are unbearable."

Boss was incredulous, but for the wrong reason. "'Conditions?!' Forget about 'conditions.' With the salaries these guys get they should perform well regardless of their 'conditions.'" Exasperated, he slammed the door on the discussion. "What I really don't like here is your line of thinking. Keep in mind that it could easily be interpreted as a lack of comprehension on your part about an assignment of the utmost importance entrusted to us by the Party. And a notable lack of patriotism."

A shot across the bow. Victor realized that he was in a minefield now and that he had to retreat or risk severe consequences. He had no illusions about Boss in this respect. The only feasible way out was to shift the argument into bureaucratic maneuvering.

"Yes, of course, I understand all that, but my real concern is that if something goes wrong somewhere down the road, we'll be held responsible."

"Ah, I see." Boss's tone grew friendlier. This was a concern he could appreciate. "You needn't worry about that. Between the importance of this assignment and the level of secrecy at which we are working, nobody could possibly be in a position to accuse us of anything. OK? As for the rest of your worries, as I said, I'd advise you to stay away from that line of thinking. It could be easily misunderstood. Is that clear?"

"It's clear." Once again, mind your own business.

"Right." Boss paused. "And by the way, don't even think of putting anything about what we've just discussed in writing. Ever."

Boss's other nickname—Gypsy—was well-earned. The Russian equivalent of a "horse trader," someone not to be trusted around a glass corner. If anything did in fact go wrong, there'd be no record of Victor's pre-science. This conversation would never have taken place, Boss would never have been briefed on the matter, and Victor might even find himself the scapegoat. He simply said, "Understood." And it was.

Victor was pained by the idea of putting people at risk who were igno-rant of the danger. It was not any better for those cipher clerks who did understand and still had to keep their mouths shut. Now, in 1979, upon reading the cable, Victor knew his unwelcome fears were about to be sub-stantiated. Something had to be done. The question was, what? First, he'd have to brief himself more thoroughly on the circumstances of the clerk's death.

When KGB cipher clerks were posted abroad, their files were trans-ferred to the First Chief Directorate for the duration of their assignment. So Victor turned to his classified telephone directory and looked up the name of the officer in charge of the specific KGB *residentura* in Africa. He called the guy over the OC and immediately took off to meet with him. He was sticking his neck way out, but he felt in some way obligated.

When Victor joined the KGB in 1971, all of Moscow Center was located in the main building on Dzerzhinsky Square. Following the major expan-sion in the mid-seventies, particularly of the First Chief Directorate, a new building had been built on the outskirts of Moscow—literally in a forest, near the village of Yasenevo. The very large forest domain pro-vided a vast area of controlled space. Most of the First CD had been relo-cated there. During the preparations for the move, the place had been nicknamed "The Forest" because of its location. Now it was the head-quarters of almost all KGB foreign operations. There were only four areas of KGB activities abroad which were not commanded from the For-est: the Illegals, or Soviet spies assuming false identities in other countries; the Acutely Active Measures—assassinations; interception—global eaves-dropping; and cipher communications. The first two were still under the Chief of the First CD, General Vladimir Kryuchkov, former Chief of the Secretariat to Yuri Andropov. The last two were the domain of the Eighth CD, and the Sixteenth Directorate—responsible for intercepting commu-nications. It was during the same expansion of the 1970s that the Eighth CD's Ninth Department branched out of the Eighth CD and became an independent, Sixteenth Directorate. Most of the First Department of Directorate A, Eighth CD, which provided communications for the First CD, was located in the First CD Headquarters in Yasenevo.

The KGB shuttle dropped Victor off a hundred feet from the First CD security checkpoint. As he approached it, he realized how different the air here was in comparison with that of the Moscow Central District. The leaves of the birches were just starting to break out, and he became aware of the freshness and the smell of spring in the air. The whole compound was meticulously maintained. The elegant modern, three-wing, stone-and-glass building was luxury itself. No traffic, no city noise—peace and calm. "A perfect place for scientists to work," thought Victor. The appearance of tranquility was misleading, however. Inside the building, beyond its quiet marble halls and paneled corridors, thousands of people worked with nonstop, blue-flame intensity.

Victor presented himself to the security guard. Access to the Forest was strictly controlled. It was one of the very few places where a KGB ID—even one with a collection of access stamps as complete as Victor's—was insufficient. Victor had to use his special First CD ID to get in there. Very few people outside the First CD possessed one. He entered the imposing ground-floor entrance hall. The only visible object was a disproportionately small bust of Felix Dzerzhinsky set dramatically in the center of the opposite wall. Victor paused for a moment. He was about half an hour early for his appointment. He decided to drop by the First Department of his Directorate to see some friends. The department occupied the entire wing of the second floor, near Kryuchkov's main and Andropov's auxiliary offices, and was by far the most secure area in the building. Victor opened a plain door to a hall that led to another door, which was locked. Only Eighth CD people—the cipher-communications personnel—were permitted access. Only one person from the First CD was allowed in—Kryuchkov. The rule was absolute. Even if there was a fire no one else could enter. In fact, there had been a fire a couple of years before, and the KGB's own firefighters, employed by the First CD, had not been admitted. The fire had been contained and extinguished by the cipher clerks themselves. Otherwise the whole floor of the wing would have been allowed to burn.

Victor pushed three, seven, and nine. The lock clicked. "Funny, they never change the code," Victor mused. Actually, there was little need to change it, and really no need for the lock at all. The door was manned around the clock, and the guard admitted only those people he personally recognized. The young guy at the door was too new to know Victor. Victor noticed the quick motion of his hand toward the alarm button. At that very moment one of Victor's old buddies from his training days just happened to pop out from a nearby door. The young guard's hand dropped back as the senior officer indicated that it was OK to admit the stranger. Victor and his friend shook hands warmly.

"Victor! What a surprise! You haven't honored us too often lately." Which was true—it had been more than a month since his last visit. They proceeded to Igor's office.

"Look, just let me quickly get rid of a couple of things, and we can talk."

"No, listen, Igor, I'm here to talk with the line-department people about the death of that cipher clerk. When I finish with them, we can talk. For now, just tell me briefly what you know about it."

Igor seemed a bit taken aback by Victor's brusqueness, but he answered, "I don't know much about it at all—heart attack, officially."

"So what was it unofficially?"

"All I know is that it was rumored that he'd complained about his general state of health for a while. Fatigue or something. He went to a doctor, but the doctor couldn't find anything."

"Was he healthy before the posting?"

"Of course. How else could he have gotten past our preposting physical? You know that better than I do."

"How long was he on the job in the cage there?"

"About a year and a half." There was an uneasy pause, and Victor suspected Igor had more on his mind.

"Anything else?"

"Well, actually, yes. You know the guys complain about the lack of air-conditioning in the cages. It's pretty brutal. Isn't there anything we can do to improve it? Is it really because of security? Personally, I find that hard to believe."

Victor put him off. "Look, it's complicated." He checked his watch. "Let's talk when I get back."

Victor headed off to the line department in charge of the geographic division the unfortunate cipher clerk had worked in. The Section Chief with whom he had the appointment had just returned from the same posting as the cipher clerk. He'd served as Station Chief. The interview did not yield anything particularly new or significant, except for the detail that the clerk had gradually grown very pale during his posting.

As promised, Victor returned to Igor's office to find his friend had gotten quite worked up. Igor pressed Victor, "Look, you and I have known each other for a long time. Cut the official crap and tell me honestly why you can't give our guys in those damned enclosures of yours decent, humane working conditions?"

Victor knew all too well the conditions Igor was referring to. The cipher enclosures could be as small as two meters by two meters by two meters. Depending on the ambient temperature, the interior could get up to twenty degrees hotter than the room in which they were installed. In a hot climate the clerks were, therefore, miserably uncomfortable. The cages were solid and ventilated only to the inside of the room. For security reasons, the number of cipher clerks available for duty in any one posting was deliberately limited, so the shifts could be brutally long and unrelieved—often twelve hours.

Victor felt uncomfortable in the face of Igor's attack, and guiltily aware that the problem was far worse than Igor imagined. "All right. For security reasons we cannot permit any link between the cipher enclosures and the outside. In other words, the ventilation unit for the cage can't be ducted to or fixed in any way on the outside of the building. It must hang on the enclosure itself, and so only exchanges the air and the heat with the room in which the enclosure is located. The same is true of the air-conditioning unit hanging on the enclosure—it heats the room the enclosure is installed in. Vicious cycle. Besides, to cool air in such a situation you've got to have a very good air-conditioning unit. We don't have units that good. Both Soviet-produced models are junk. And you know that for security reasons we can't risk using any foreign-manufactured equipment inside that room. If I tried to push to get around that rule, I'd probably be accused of jeopardizing security, but nothing would change. Do you see the problem?" Victor added lamely, "That's where we are."

"In a nutshell, what you're telling me is that things aren't going to get any better?"

"I'm afraid not. At least, I don't see it happening in the foreseeable future."

There was no way that he could help. Victor felt like a real bastard. He knew perfectly well that Igor did not have enough information to understand the full extent of the problem, the potential impact of the electromagnetic energy contained within the enclosure. And Victor couldn't even hint at it. There was an awkward silence as both men realized the subject could be pursued no further.

"So tell me, how are things here?" Victor asked.

Igor had taken his shot. Now he accepted the retreat Victor was giving him. He shrugged. "You know, same old shit. One of the world's best chess grand masters screwed somebody behind the curtain at the last embassy reception; world reaction to Brezhnev's latest statement; propositions on whether a certain whore should go to the German big guy on Wednesday or Thursday; how to organize public outrage in the States toward their

government's policy in Latin America; meetings with agents; defeating surveillance; requests for money from all over the place to maintain agents,
left-wing parties, anti-American demonstrations, and the Peace Movements. . . . Same old story."

"Any good news?"

"The Active Measures people seem to have derailed the neutron bomb
project nicely and for good, and we've got peacenik campaigns well
focused on the other strategic weapons we don't want the Americans to
develop."

After his chat with Igor, Victor saw a few other friends in the Department. By mid-afternoon he'd finished his rounds and harvested all the
current gossip. Victor decided not to go back to the Center, opting
instead to go home early for a change. The Forest was only a twenty-
minute ride to his apartment, and the First CD shuttle passed nearby.
He'd surprise Olga. The prospect lifted his sagging spirits.

The next morning Victor's conscience would not let him rest. He had to
try again. He knocked on Boss's door.

After a minute or two of small talk, Boss asked abruptly, "Just what the
hell do you think you're doing?"

"What do you mean?" This time Victor genuinely did not understand.

"I mean your sniffing around the Forest." Boss was extremely irritated.
"I never knew you had such an interest in the dead. I'd always thought of
you as a man whose interest lay primarily in the future."

Victor was caught off-guard. He'd expected to be the one to broach
the subject. It was a given that Boss—and others—would learn of his
investigations. That was the nature of the system. However, he hadn't
been prepared for the speed at which word of his "sniffing around" had
spread. Literally overnight.

He plunged in. "You're right. The future is precisely what I'm interested in. That's why I went there in the first place."

Boss's voice turned icy, a signal for Victor to think quickly. "Are you
thinking of being a whistle-blower? Want to be a better Catholic than the
Pope? It seems more like an attempt to sabotage our most important mission—one entrusted to us directly by the Politburo."

As Victor heard Boss parroting the line he had used almost word for
word in their last discussion of the subject, three years before, he realized
he was on extremely thin ice. The best he could do now was to save his
own skin.

He said, "I don't know who your source was, but this accusation really offends me. My purpose in investigating this matter was to try and assess if there was any danger of damaging rumors. If there was, we'd better take strong countermeasures in advance."

Boss seemed confused for an instant, perhaps even embarrassed. He looked hard at Victor, evaluating this new twist. Finally, he said, "Sorry, Victor. I should have known better. But I knew that the health aspect has been troubling you for some time, right?"

"Well, to a certain extent that's true. There's still a chance we might be killing our own people. I'm sure you wouldn't endorse that either, if we had any viable alternative." There it was, Boss's out. Victor had given his superior the opportunity to back down without losing face. Clearly appreciated, and accepted.

"You're absolutely right. If we had any alternative. But you've got to consider that even in the worst-case scenario the price is not really that high. Any one of us would give our life to save the State and the Party's top secrets. We've sworn to do that. Here we are talking about a few cipher clerks." He shifted into a more jovial mode. "Don't worry, Victor. If one dies, I'll give you another one. I promise."

Victor forced a smile and responded correctly—the methodical KGB officer: "Thanks, but the trouble is time: it takes at least two months for all the necessary paperwork to go through, not to mention getting him a visa." His only apparent concern, logistics and efficiency.

Boss approved. "You're right, there. Why don't you think of a solution? Maybe some sort of standby pool or something. Just in case."

"OK. I'll report personally. No papers." Of course not.

Victor assumed that the interview was over, and that he was back on safe ground. He stood up to make his escape, and Boss fired another shot. "Where the hell is that report on the Washington embassy business?"

"I'm working on it. It's just about complete."

"Andreyev wants it by the end of the day."

The Directorate had to approve the plans and procedures for the new Soviet embassy in Washington, from the perspective of its cipher-communications security. Boss had given Victor the task of assessing the risks of every available approach and of coming up with a final recommendation.

After several hours' of amazingly uninterrupted work, Victor finally finished it. Just in time. The phone rang. Boss.

"Aren't you ready yet?"

"I was about to call you to report."

Boss wasn't convinced. "Sure. I'm here, then. Come up."

In his office Boss said, "Well, are you ready to sign off on it?"

"Yes, with two question marks. A big one and a small one."

Victor unfolded a set of drawings and put his accompanying report on the desk. Boss briefly looked through the whole stack. He was thoroughly familiar with the subject. Then he took his reading glasses off, closed his eyes, and pressed the inner corners near his nose, in a rare gesture of fatigue. In a moment he opened his eyes again. "So, what's the bottom line?"

Victor started his summary. "Well, the site's perfect. The negotiating team obviously did a great job. Our control zone is bigger than we hoped for. The construction plans incorporate every requirement we put forward initially. The construction watch team is well trained. Our latest model of the cipher-equipment enclosure has been fully tested in Fili. The results are better than expected. Frankly, I was worried about it. We're on a new technological plateau and, as always, there can be surprises. Miraculously, production seems to be right on schedule. Obviously, for the time being, we can only install it in Washington. Other orders for it have not even been discussed yet. The only hitch with it was when Andreyev showed up at the testing and got stuck inside for half an hour. The hydraulic lock failed, and there's no backup."

Boss laughed, "I heard about that one. The 'General's Effect': If anything is likely to fail, it'll fail during the official inspection."

Victor took a breath and continued, "So, to take the small question first: there's the standard dilemma of whether to let the Americans finish the building inside or not." He was referring to the normal KGB policy of not revealing the future location of the *referentura* at the time of construction of a Soviet embassy. Usually, the opposition was not permitted to finish the secure spaces. In Washington's case two alternatives were being considered. One was to let the Americans do the finishing work—and then of course tear it all out again to take care of the bugs. The second was to have them leave the whole building unfinished. But that would be too much for a temporary Soviet work force to do. Because they were a potential giveaway, the reinforcement of the floors required for the *referentura* was always done by a Soviet work force.

Boss responded, "I'm not too happy about either alternative myself. Neither solution is guaranteed to prevent the Americans from figuring out the location of the secure areas, and then we'd have a bigger problem on our hands than we bargained for. We have to fool them somehow. More actively."

Victor thought for a moment. "How about a red herring? Like ordering the unfinished space somewhere else."

Boss responded quickly, "Good. Do that," and then he added, "If you get any more ideas on it, let me know. Now, what's the big question?"

"It's very basic. In Washington the Americans are doing the construction. Here in Moscow we'll be building their new embassy. As far as I know, there is no defense against what we are planning to do—I mean our rigging the whole place as one system with the new technology. So at this point we're betting that they can't do the same thing to us. Is that a safe bet? Can we be sure?"

"Yes. We're sure. Don't worry about that one." Victor knew that he couldn't pursue the question any further. Coming from Boss, the reassurance was solid.

"OK, then I'll have the sign-off memorandum typed up immediately. By the way, how is it that we can get away with having the high-voltage side of the embassy transformer on our territory all the time and the Americans never seem to fight for it?" He was referring to one of the essential requirements of technical security.

"The same way they have local personnel working in all their embassies, which is immeasurably more dangerous. I'd say it's insane. But apparently they don't care. Thank God. Besides, our lobbyists are obviously doing a good job. After all, those guys in the First CD have to justify their salaries somehow."

Two hours later the memorandum had been typed and attached to the drawings. Victor put his signature on the approval list. Boss signed it too, then sent it on to Andreyev. The multiple sign-off was standard KGB procedure. It provided a hierarchy of scapegoats to choose from, depending on the level of the failure.

Victor had just returned from Boss's office when Olga phoned him. "I can bet you've forgotten something, as always . . . ?"

"I can bet you're right. What's up?"

"Victor! You're picking me up at six o'clock, and we're going to a party, remember? At the Portnovs'."

"Oh yes, of course. Yes, OK, I'll pick you up at six."

"And don't worry about the wine and flowers. I took care of that."

"Thanks, I really appreciate it."

The call lifted Victor's spirits. Vasily Portnov was also a KGB officer. Victor was easily bored at parties, but he never had that problem at the Portnovs'. Their's was one of the very few homes where one was likely to find an extremely diverse crowd: scientists, artists, actors, KGB personnel, and numerous other unpredictables. He had no idea how they managed to pull it off. Whenever Olga and Victor tried to mix a widely varied assortment of friends at their parties, it never quite worked. The mutual incompatibility of many of their friends had turned several such attempts into outright disasters. Vasily and Nina Portnov apparently had some secret gift—a talent for bringing together different types without provoking a fight.

Holding wine and flowers, Victor and Olga rang the bell at the Portnovs' fashionable high-rise co-op on Kutuzovsky Prospect. Vasily opened the door, and there were warm greetings all around. Then, accompanied by both Vasily and his collie, Lada—who took quite a shine to Victor—they strolled through the large flat, greeting the other guests. Every time Olga and Victor were introduced to a new face, Lada took the opportunity to reintroduce herself to Victor, putting her paws on his shoulders and planting large, sloppy kisses on his face. Fortunately for Victor, the Sheymovs already knew most of the people there.

They paused at one circle of conversation that consisted of a celebrated writer, two actors from the Maliy Theater, and an assortment of Moscow socialites. The center of attention, however, was neither a celebrity nor a socialite. Victor and Olga had never seen him before. He was dressed in an ill-fitting suit that seemed more appropriate for the foreman of a shoe factory and looked quite out of place in this fast-lane crowd. Nonetheless, as with everyone who came to the Portnovs', he was accepted as an equal, and he was certainly holding his own. Victor and Olga quickly learned that he was probably one of the top if not the very best master craftsmen in wood inlay in the country. He was telling the story of his latest piece, a highly acclaimed portrait of Fidel Castro, to defend the position that he was not an artist, but above all a craftsman. To prove his point he cited what he felt was the high point of the piece—Fidel's eyes. Each one was composed of about five hundred pieces of wood, of different types and shades, which he insisted were absolutely necessary to give the eyes the spark of life, and as close a resemblance to the original as possible. This man had received no particular fame as a result of his work. Very few knew who had created the extraordinary portrait, presented to Castro by the complacent Soviet Ambassador. Someone asked him what he'd been paid for the portrait. The man answered proudly, as if proving his point, "Oh, I am not paid by the job. I'm no starving artist. I have a salary. Two hundred rubles a month. It took me several months to do the job."

Two hundred rubles a month was the average salary of a factory worker with two to three years' experience. Victor was appalled that someone so gifted should be so meagerly rewarded. *Christ, what exploitation—and he doesn't even know it! Some real crooks must be running his place.* He felt sorry for the man but thankful that there were still some artists—or master craftsmen—like him around.

The party flowed on: playful banter, serious polemics, eating, drinking, and dancing. At one point, well after midnight, a large group of men found themselves discussing one of the most popular topics: cars. As usual, the discussion touched on interesting places to drive, traffic problems, difficulties in getting service or spare parts. No one present had to worry about the fundamental problem of getting a car in the first place, so that was the one issue that was never even raised. Someone brought up the hottest new topic: the ubiquitous radar speed detectors that the Moscow traffic police had recently acquired. As the speed limit in the capital was 40 mph and had up to now been universally ignored, the radar detectors were proving to be a real pain in the neck. Three violation clips on your license and you could lose it. Everyone had the same question: what could be done about these detectors?

Victor suddenly got an idea. "Psychological warfare!"

"What?"

"We can use psychology. Look, Moscow traffic cops are not too smart, right? So if a rumor spreads that radar detectors are a menace to the user's health, what do you think would happen?"

His answer was the crowd's roar of approving laughter. "All the detectors will 'accidentally' break or disappear!"

Vasily took center stage. "OK, guys. For the next few weeks, if I see a traffic policeman with a radar gun, I'll pull over, on my own, approach him, and say, 'Look, Chief, I drive this road every day. I don't exceed the speed limit. So please, don't measure my speed with this thing. I value my health.'

"His response will be 'What does this detector have to do with your health?'

"And then I'll say, 'Come on, you mean you really don't know?'

" 'Know what?'

" 'Look, I'm a scientist. I know what I'm talking about here. The radiation from this device can cause significant damage to your body. The first symptom is impotence. By the way, how long have you been using it, anyway?' He'll start getting worried. Probably say three or four months, and that he hasn't felt a thing. Then I'll finish it off, 'Well, it's too soon yet, but wait a year. Even in three months your wife may start complaining.' And then I'll leave. The more the guy thinks about it, the more paranoid he'll get. Perhaps he really will slow down a bit. Ha! Psychology! Victor's right. That's the way to go. If each of us does the same, this will be the joke of the year!"

The party ended on that high note. And on the way home Victor realized that his mind had probably played a joke on him. Associative thinking. His latest preoccupation with the hazards of the high-frequency electromagnetic waves had probably triggered the idea.

A few weeks later, Victor picked up some mysterious rumors about the dangers of the radar detectors. And sure enough, all but a few detectors disappeared from the streets of Moscow. Especially after a traffic policeman tried to measure the speed of Kosygin's *Zil* limousine. He was probably just curious about how fast these high officials always traveled. When he raised the radar gun, the bodyguards took him for an assassin and shot him dead on the spot.

CHAPTER

10

"SHEYMOV, PLEASE."

"Speaking."

"Personnel. Your annual vacation: you must take it immediately or forfeit it."

Victor bridled at the peremptory tone, annoyed at the inevitable complications an unplanned break would create with his work. He tried feebly for a postponement.

"Sorry, you know the rule."

He went to Boss to relay the news and received reluctant consent. Not that Boss had any real choice—vacations were mandatory. But Boss was adept at making his subordinates feel guilty for taking what they had rightfully earned, and Victor emerged from the meeting feeling like a deserter. However, he soon found himself looking forward to a break from the snake pit. He sensed he had much to think about.

It would take a few days to sort things out and clear his desk in preparation for his thirty-day absence. Boss called to ask Victor to interview several new prospects for the Directorate before he left. "You're messing around with Personnel anyway, sorting out your vacation plans. So spare us a few minutes to chat with the boys early tomorrow."

The next morning, on his way to the official Reception Office of the KGB Center on Kuznetsky Most, it struck Victor that eight years had passed since his own entry into the KGB. It was hard to believe. He remembered his first encounter with Personnel at the beginning of his KGB career as clearly as if it had been yesterday.

In January 1971 Victor, with some solid scientific accomplishments to his name, was already a little arrogant. His attitude toward Personnel was defiant. He did not like this group as quintessential bureaucrats, and he didn't bother to conceal his attitude. Victor's first interview had been with the head of the Personnel Department—Colonel Nesterov. It was extremely unusual for one so highly placed to conduct an initial screening. The level of the interview was directly related to the clout of Victor's benefactor. Victor had found Nesterov to be a considerable cut above the standard Personnel type. He never once hinted at his power. Probably, Victor had speculated, because he was truly powerful. Much later, after Victor had learned the ropes a bit and gotten to know Nesterov better, he realized how easy it must have been for him to handle Victor.

Victor's first impression of Nesterov was of a stocky, grey-haired man with the weathered face of an old salt. He was tough without being humorless. Even friendly, which put Victor off balance. After a brief greeting, Nesterov asked bluntly, "So, what can you do?"

Victor was taken aback by what he felt was a lack of respect. He answered curtly, "I can think."

Nesterov's eyes widened in surprise for an instant, then the creases around them deepened as he suppressed a smile.

To Victor's surprise, instead of trying to put him down, Nesterov simply said, "Well then, I'm afraid you've come to the wrong place. Here our job is to do. We let others think." At the time Victor did not have the frame of reference to appreciate the accuracy of that statement. In fact, it was not so much a statement of humility as a statement of fact: the KGB was an obedient tool in the hands of the Politburo or, more precisely, in the hands of the Head of State.

Victor responded immediately, "But as history shows, doing without thinking can be harmful."

Nesterov smiled, picking up the verbal gauntlet, "Yes, but in our case it can mostly be harmful to others, not to us. That's important. When the Central Committee is doing the thinking for you, you are in pretty good shape."

Victor could feel himself rapidly losing ground in his duel of wits with this smiling man. He had no response.

Nesterov watched Victor carefully and changed tactics. "I see you are eager to lock horns with anybody. That's unusual. And it's OK," he paused, "for someone of your age. If you were ten years older, I would have kicked you out. An attitude like yours in an older man would have indicated either bitterness toward society or mental imbalance." There was a moment of silent mutual appreciation.

From there, the interview followed a more-traditional path: Victor's background, schooling, university, relatives, friends. Nesterov tried very hard to discover what Victor had been working on in TsNII-50. He approached the subject from various angles, pretending that he already knew but was interested in hearing it from Victor directly. Victor's security training served him well. At no time was he caught off guard, and he gave nothing away. He wondered whether Nesterov's interest was purely professional, testing Victor's ability to keep his mouth shut, or if he was genuinely curious. Probably both, he decided.

The interview ended on a friendly note. By way of conclusion Nesterov said, "Well, we seem to speak the same language. I think we can find common ground. You ask what kind of work we have for you. I can't answer that. You are already familiar with tight security, as a result of your experience at TsNII-50. I assure you that was nothing compared to the level of security you will find here. So, this is what we'll do: we will complete your background check, and then you will meet your future Chief for the final interview. In your case, the check will probably take about six months." He noticed Victor's dismay. "That's exceptionally fast. It usually takes at least twelve months to clear a candidate for the Directorate you are being considered for."

And that was how it had turned out. Victor was called in periodically to see the dull junior officer who was handling the technicalities of the background check. He asked a lot of seemingly silly questions, like "We could not find the graves of your father's parents. Where exactly are they buried?" Or "Ask your mother what she was doing between June and September of 1939."

In fact there was a good deal of systematic method and experience behind the questions. One way or another, almost everyone concealed biographical information—intentionally or unintentionally. It was Personnel's job to document any discrepancy and to detect any patterns of inconsistency that might be significant. The process was set in motion just after high school, when every candidate for university wrote an autobiographical essay. The exercise was repeated again twice at university. Autobiographies were periodically required at every significant step in a person's career—changes in status or job changes. Not many people thought to keep copies of their autobiographies, so discrepancies inevitably occurred and were duly noted. Indeed, it was the discrepancies that Personnel specifically looked for.

The KGB had access to all of these autobiographies. If a person was being vetted for a sensitive job, the KGB would compare the detailed personal questionnaires that were required against the series of autobiographies. Then they would compare both against the official records. They would wire the local KGB station for any and all records of political problems or other "derogatory" they might have on the candidate and his immediate family from their place of origin. They were also required to double-check all biographical details with the local Militia—records of births and deaths, jobs, residential addresses, and any moves from one domicile to another. And, of course, they checked against their own records at the Center.

In most cases this process took a year, but not because it actually involved a year's work. Elapsed time was in itself regarded as an important security measure. Practiced eyes routinely checking over the inevitable discrepancies could see patterns over time that might not be evident at first glance. A candidate trying to hide something was more likely to be successful at the beginning of the process but could grow nervous with time. Or careless. If a record was under particular scrutiny, the flow of other information might be triggered.

Candidates were not told of any discrepancies. They were given no chance to explain or correct them. If a job or promotion was denied, Personnel never cited background problems as the reason. The irony of this system was that very few people were ever totally "clean." Indeed, given the confused and turbulent history of the country, 100-percent purity of background was unlikely—even suspect.

In the end, hiring could not simply follow a formula. Detailed background check notwithstanding, it all came down to a judgment call. This left Personnel in a very powerful position.

The simple clerks assigned the respectable and selfless task of helping executives with the technicalities of appointments and promotions took on a parasitic power of their own. They used their position as gatekeepers to skillfully manipulate the decisions of their masters. Personnel was a formidable brotherhood, and its network permeated the entire system. There was absolutely no way to get around these people. The fact that they could not directly appoint anyone to a position in no way diminished their power. They could usually block a candidate's appointment if they disapproved of the choice—either by direct veto or, if their reasons for damning the person were unjustifiable, simply by stalling the process with petty technicalities—a de facto veto. They could keep saying, "No" for one stupid reason or another until the "powerful" executive made the right choice—the candidate whom Personnel had wanted all along.

By June of 1971 Victor was notified that his "basic" background check was complete. He was invited to meet his future chief. This meeting took place in the main KGB Center building. There Victor met Colonel Altov, the friend of Victor's father's friend. As Altov ushered Victor into his office on the fifth floor of the Tower, Victor was startled by how humble and low keyed he seemed. Only later, when he discovered the extent of Altov's power, did he realize the degree to which he'd been misled by this man's modest demeanor. It turned out that many others had jumped to similarly wrong conclusions. Such miscalculations proved grave indeed for Altov's enemies.

Altov started the interview by praising the friend who'd recommended Victor. Then he made a few respectful remarks about Victor's father and concluded by saying that the KGB—his directorate in particular— needed people like Victor. At long last, he told Victor that he'd be work- ing in the Eighth Chief Directorate, which was in charge of the KGB's cipher-communications systems. He was to be assigned to work with the KGB's foreign communications.

Victor was quite disappointed. Altov read his expression and asked him what was wrong. Victor tried to explain tactfully that he thought communications were somehow subordinate to the mainline work of KGB Intelligence he'd had in mind.

Altov smiled. "Most of our new recruits think that way when they first arrive. Please, forgive me, I don't wish to sound patronizing, but you have no idea what you're talking about. That's not surprising. No one outside knows what we do here, not even the regular KGB Intelligence officers. That's exactly the point, in fact. Allow me to explain." He paused as if he were really asking Victor's permission to go on. Victor nodded automati- cally, and Altov continued. "The Eighth Chief Directorate is the sanctum sanctorum of the KGB—its most secret, most tightly guarded part. We are the Keepers of the Secrets, the Trusted Ones. You probably do not realize that historically almost every major intelligence failure one way or another has been the result of a breach in communications security. Secu- rity of cipher communications is more valuable than a spy or a mole. Communications is only one part of the work we do. The interception of communications is another major part of our CD's mandate. And there are others. The KGB is a highly compartmentalized organization, perhaps the most compartmentalized in the world. Except for those at the very top—by that I mean the Chairman of the KGB, his Deputies, and their small staff—no one in the KGB knows what's going on outside of his own domain. There are exceptions, of course, when pieces of information are shared, but even then it's only on a need-to-know basis. But as the saying goes, our sum is greater than our parts. One way or another in this Directorate, we have to know everything: who is doing what to whom and where. We are directly linked to the Central Committee. We receive many of our orders straight from them. I can tell you that it is a great honor to be accepted here, in any capacity. Something to be proud of. You are being given absolute trust, the trust of the top leadership of this country—the Politburo. You'll soon see the cloak-and-dagger stuff differently than you do now."

Victor had mixed feelings. He asked about his career prospects. In the face of the young man's persistent ambivalence all traces of Altov's humble veneer vanished. "Look. We've got a lot of people here. All of them are happy just to get into this Department. Most of them retire at fifty-five with the rank of captain or major at best. Very few are selected for higher destiny. You are one of the chosen. Do you understand? We study people very carefully before we accept them. Because of your family background, as well as your own abilities, you will go very far. That is, of course, if you don't make a mess of it." He paused to let his words sink in, then continued in a friendlier manner. "I'll personally supervise your career. You'll have to learn the whole system. So, after indoctrination and initial training, you'll work your way through a variety of assignments. In a few years you will have had experience in every field. Then you will rise. Remember, I'm counting on you."

And Victor plunged in.

The transfer formalities were wrapped up in a day instead of the usual two weeks. Often when a person wanted to change jobs, the gremlins in Personnel would throw up one bureaucratic barrier after another, so that in many cases the process became so frustrating that the person trying to transfer simply gave up and stayed in his old job. In his case, however, there were no obstacles. Nobody argued with the KGB. Just three days after meeting with Altov, Victor reported for work in the main KGB building. Little did he realize how much he'd have to learn before settling into any regular position.

First, Victor was shown around the building. It usually took a couple of months for someone to become comfortable finding his way around it.

There had been numerous additions to the original structure, and the result was a bewildering labyrinth. Passages from one part of the building to another were in the most illogical and inconvenient places. There were no signs on the doors, just numbers. It was hard to tell if one was in the old part, Dom 1, or the new part, Dom 2. Each had an identical series of door numbers. There were no outside reference points because there were no windows in the poorly lit corridors. Some of the staircases led to the street entrances, others led only to the inner courtyard—a confusing place in itself.

The entire building was heavily guarded. The KGB Center's security was famous for its infallibility. It was said that a mouse couldn't get through without proper ID. Every entrance was manned by a warrant officer armed with an automatic pistol and a soldier with an AK-47 and two hand grenades. The warrant officer, his boot near the alarm button, checked IDs and saluted the senior officers—those in the position of Department Chief and higher. The soldier simply stood by on a two-by-three-foot mat, an implacable statue, his AK-47 at his shoulder. During peak hours a second warrant officer helped monitor the heavy traffic. The guards were changed every three hours to prevent errors due to fatigue. Warrant officers unobtrusively patrolled the entire building at all hours.

A couple of years after Victor arrived there was an incident that made the famous Center security the laughingstock of the whole KGB. Around lunchtime a drunk was found wandering around lost in the corridors, asking for directions to the exit. Someone got suspicious and promptly delivered him to security. Not only did he have no KGB ID, he had no ID at all. It turned out he was a peasant visiting Moscow and had not the slightest idea where he was. The poor man had simply been in the wrong place at the wrong time. Staggering along Dzerzhinsky Street at 8:45 A.M., badly hung over from a night of partying, he'd gotten caught up in the rush-hour flow of KGB employees and been swept into the building. In the crush, the guards, trained and tested constantly to spot a forged KGB ID, somehow let him slip—or reel—through. Naturally, he'd gotten lost in the building and at noon was still trying to work his way out of the Center's maze. Heads rolled over that one.

The Center was a generally depressing place. Victor noticed that like almost everyone he took a deep breath of "fresh" air upon emerging from the building at the end of the day. Ironic, given the pollution for which the Moscow Central District was notorious.

During his first days on the job Victor became intrigued by the red lights high on the wall at the turns of each corridor. They were never lit and seemed to serve no purpose. When he asked about them, the response was that they'd been used during Stalin's time, when interrogations were conducted in the building. There was an elaborate procedure for preventing the prisoners from seeing the faces of the KGB personnel. Whenever a prisoner was transferred from the Inner Prison through the corridors to the Interrogation Office, he was escorted by three guards. One stayed with the prisoner. The second walked ahead, and the third one remained behind. The lead guard turned on the red light to warn the upcoming KGB personnel in the corridor that an escorted prisoner was coming. If anyone was already in the zone or emerged from a nearby office, the prisoner's face was pushed into the wall so that he couldn't see the passing officer. When they'd cleared the corridor, the rear guard would turn the light off again. "Unnecessary measure," remarked Victor's guide, a soft-spoken veteran. "None of them would live to tell anything anyway."

Another peculiar thing Victor noticed was that many doors had keys hanging from the outside keyholes. Victor's guide explained that this tradition was also a vestige of the Stalinist past. Lavrenty Beria, the organization's Chairman at the time, was absolutely paranoid about assassination. He did not even trust his own KGB. When he walked through the corridors, he, too, was escorted by three guards—his personal bodyguards. As they progressed down the hallways the guard in front would lock all the offices in the hall with the keys hanging outside so that nobody could suddenly appear near Beria. After Beria and his second bodyguard had passed, the rear guard would unlock the doors again. Victor's guide told him a grim anecdote, "Once a secretary forgot to leave her key in the door, so it could not be locked from the outside. It was her bad luck to be leaving her office at the wrong time—right when Beria was walking by. She did not even get past the doorway. Shot on the spot. . . . Those were strict times," sighed the guide, "but that was the order back then."

Another one of Beria's security customs was particularly humiliating for KGB officers. If an officer happened to bump into a Beria procession, a sharp order would ring out: "To the wall!" The officer would have to stand with his nose pressed to the wall. With Beria's bodyguard at his side, gun in hand, the officer would have to wait until Beria had passed. The command reflected the typical gallows humor and referred to the slang expression "Putting someone to the wall," which actually meant putting someone in front of a firing squad.

Victor's new career started with an extensive course of indoctrination, as well as the initial general training given to every cohort of new officers. Nothing about ciphers yet. At this point the recruits were lectured on the overall structure and history of the KGB. They learned general security and office procedures and played out endless what-if scenarios. By the end of each day Victor felt as if his circuits were overloaded, and he was relieved when that part of the training was over. Then he was told that the real course work was about to start.

First, there was a course in security: security of ciphers, security of the premises where ciphers are located and used, and security of those who have anything to do with ciphers. Victor had thought himself accustomed to following strict security procedures from his days at TsNII-50, but as Nesterov had predicted, he was amazed by the KGB's system of defenses. Meticulously detailed, they seemed to go to absurd lengths to anticipate every conceivable contingency. Victor could hardly keep a straight face when he was told about the destruction procedure for cipher materials abroad. They had to be thoroughly burned, crushed, and then flushed down the toilet. Later he would realize that this procedure was not an example of KGB redundancy. At the time, however, he had no way of knowing that what seemed extreme was in fact absolutely necessitated by the sophistication of the techniques that had already been developed for compromising cipher security.

At last they got into ciphers. First, there was an introductory course on the basics of ciphers and their history. That was the beginning of the interesting part.

Victor learned that the practice of encoding dated back to ancient history, and he studied some of the more exotic coding methods. He also learned that modern cipher systems were based on the same fundamental principle. A message is first encoded using a code key. To this encoded message is added a random sequence of symbols, or a cipher key. At the receiving end the process is reversed: the same random sequence is subtracted from the enciphered message, which is then decoded. It is the addition of a random sequence that actually turns a code into a cipher. The random sequence is known as the "key." Keys can take many different forms, depending on the type of cipher equipment being used.

An instructor gave an example of one of the earliest techniques used for concealing a message. First, the sender had to write the message on the freshly shaven head of the messenger. Then, after his hair grew long enough to cover the message, the messenger was dispatched to his destination. Having arrived, his head was shaven again, chopped off for extra security, and delivered to the addressee on a silver platter. So, the question was whether that was a code or a cipher, since the message had been covered by the random sequence of the hair.

Victor learned that a tremendous amount of ingenuity is expended on acquiring or creating random sequences. The cipher experts looked for these random sequences in the "noise" emitted by all kinds of natural and other phenomena—so-called "white noise." They looked at everything from the chaotic roar of rush-hour street traffic to the apparently meaningless pattern of emanations from transistors in the silent mode. But "random" sequences sooner or later turn out to have a pattern. Inevitably, the computers that create the "random" sequences are sure to be outpowered by newer computers that can find a pattern in them.

The quality of the cipher is almost solely determined by the quality of the key, i.e. how truly random it is. The random cipher key sequence—the "gamma" in KGB slang—is used only once and is often called the "one-time pad." For a cipher clerk, using the same cipher key twice is an extremely serious offense.

The variety of manual ciphers made for every conceivable occasion the KGB might face surprised Victor. There was the regular manual cipher, used in the residenturas with relatively light cable traffic; the personal cipher of the station chief; the emergency cipher for the residentura to be used when other ciphers were either destroyed or compromised; the temporary cipher for use when a newly opened embassy had not yet been equipped with a secure referentura; the miniature cipher used by a communications officer accompanying the First CD's Directorate K officers working with delegations, such as the Soviet Olympics team; numerous superminiature ciphers used by the Illegals; and so on. All of those ciphers operated on the same principle and differed only in their degree of reliability and packaging. The sizes varied widely, starting with a hardcover book for the initial encoding and supplemented with a large supply of the one-time pads packaged in blocks the size of a regular chocolate bar, to the most miniaturized ones, the size of a hard candy. They could be disguised as almost anything.

At the end of this course Victor was told, "You need some hands-on experience out in the real world. You'll work as a cipher clerk for a while. After that you'll do more studying." When Victor first went to work as a cipher clerk, he thought it was fun to see how the seemingly random rows of numbers were transformed into meaningful messages. And the content of the messages was as thrilling for Victor as for any newcomer. Here was the shadowy world of espionage. Agents' code names, meetings, dead drops, intelligence reports . . . Victor felt proud to be trusted enough to take part in the game being played all over the world. He felt like an athlete chosen to represent his country on a national team—except that the stakes here were much higher. At the same time, Victor knew that the job would probably become boring over time. The mechanics of the manual-cipher procedure were quite simple, requiring only discipline, concentration, and a somewhat distorted perception of arithmetic. In cryptographic addition, eight plus three equals one, not eleven; six plus seven equals three, not thirteen. Similarly, two minus nine equals three, not minus seven, and so on. One just had to remember.

Altov kept a watchful eye on Victor and was not about to give him time to get bored. Quite soon Victor was told, "OK, you've had a glimpse of cipher work in the real world. For now, that's enough. Back to the classroom." Another course, this time electromechanical cipher machines.

A variety of these cipher machines were in use in the Soviet Union. Victor had to study all of them, with special emphasis on the top model "Apatit" used by the GRU, MFA, and KGB. This was the most secure cipher machine available—the one used for communications abroad.

Victor found these machines far more technically interesting than the manual ciphers. They were modeled on a typewriter: the text was typed in by the clerk, and the machine made an initial conversion of the text into an encoded version that was different every time, in accordance with a combination of three different types of cipher keys. The machine was set to change to a new conversion every month with one tuner, every day with a second, and every five hundred strokes of the keyboard with the third. Then the random sequence, fed into the machine by a paper tape, was added to the scrambled text. On the other end the reverse process took place. The mechanical part of the machine was extremely complicated.

After he'd studied these machines, Victor was sent to the First Department of Directorate A, which served the First CD's foreign communications. This time he worked as a cipher clerk on the major lines of KGB communications that used the electromechanical machine—Washington, New York, Bonn, London, Paris, Ottawa, etc. The job gave him much deeper insight into the KGB's work abroad. A lot of geopolitics passed under his nose, as well as many detailed technical and economic analyses of the major issues and situations. The KGB's work at those stations was far more sophisticated than at the smaller ones.

Victor's tenure there was not long. Once again, Altov sent him back to school, this time to study the computer. At that time there was only one enciphering and deciphering mainframe computer in the Soviet Union. It was manufactured by the KGB computer factory, nicknamed "Polin's Enterprise." This factory also produced computers designed to crack other countries' ciphers. The mainframe computer was Soviet state of the art at the time. It was quite large and complicated, and it took Victor longer than he expected to become comfortable with it. By the end of a few weeks, however, he was able to run it, to encipher and decipher telegrams, and to get the machine up after a breakdown within an hour. This was crucial, as there was no backup system.

As he'd come to expect, after completing the course, Victor was sent to work on a shift that used the mainframe. The group in which he found himself was composed of the elite among the communications officers. Every one of these men had a degree in engineering or science, along with a great deal of experience. Valentin was one of them. For a while they worked on the same shift, chatting during the infrequent "quiet" nights in their command post—the computer control room. After several months of twelve-hour shift work, Victor was once again recalled.

His next assignment really tested his mettle. The relocation of the First Chief Directorate to the Forest was imminent. The First Department of Directorate A, Eighth CD—the cipher communications department for the First CD—was to move there as well. The problem was that the Directorate had only one mainframe computer.

The decision was made to procure a second, upgraded computer and install it in the Forest. The new computer had been ordered a few months earlier and was now ready for installation. But for security reasons it was out of the question to allow the representatives of the manufacturing unit into the new First CD premises, let alone the Eighth CD premises there, even though some of these computer people were KGB officers. The only solution was to have personnel from the Eighth CD itself install and fine-tune the computer. This was unprecedented and, on the face of it, impossible for a second-generation mainframe.

As a result of his broad technical background and expertise, Victor was named to head "Delta-2," the team assigned to the problem. There were only four in the group, a ludicrously small number for such a daunting task. To their astonishment, they were given just one month to get the job done. In normal circumstances the project would have been assigned to a group of at least ten highly specialized manufacturer's representatives, who would have been given six months to do it. Delta-2 seemed destined for a high-profile failure.

Victor assembled his crew. Each one of them had experience with computers, but that was a very far cry from knowing how to get one up and running. The briefing was short. "OK, guys. Everyone thinks this assignment is impossible. Maybe it is. But the only way to find out is to try. It's a long shot, and the odds aren't good. My approach is simple: The only way we have a chance is to do our best. If we fail, we can at least say to ourselves, 'We did absolutely everything we could.' I want no what-ifs. No regrets."

The computer was packed into crates at the factory arrd delivered to the Forest. Being second generation, it was built with semiconductors, which are very sensitive to the environment. It, therefore, would require a very powerful air conditioner, separate from the building, and a great deal of fine-tuning after it had been assembled. The team had the wiring diagrams and not much else to go by. First, they assembled each major component and got it running. Then one by one they interfaced each component with another, then another, until finally they got the whole thing up and running, tested and tuned.

The month would have been a nightmare—if they'd had the time to sleep. They were running on adrenaline. Their hearts beat faster and their brains operated at high speed. The intensity of the work seemed to inspire their collective intuition. Of course, Victor knew that he was lucky. His team was damn good. To the total amazement of those aware of the affair, not only did the job get done, it was completed literally two hours ahead of the deadline. The guys couldn't possibly explain how they'd managed it. When it was all over, they were drunk with emotion and fatigue.

The climax of the affair, planned to coincide with the deadline, was an official visit to the Forest by the Chairman, Yuri Andropov. He arrived with a small entourage consisting of Kryuchkov, Altov, and the Section Chief. Not surprisingly, Andropov looked much older, balder, and altogether less attractive than his portraits. He seemed tired and ill. It was known at the time that his kidneys were giving him problems, which he regularly tried to cure in Kislovodsk under the complaisant and humble eye of the regional Party boss there, Mikhail Gorbachev.

The team, expecting incredulous praise, could not believe their ears when Andropov's only remark was, "Well, it looks impressive . . . but if I ever see windows this dirty again, I'll make sure it's the last time. Personally." Clearly, he knew nothing about the circumstances surrounding the birth of his new mainframe. He did not know that the team had literally not had time to let the cleaning people in.

After the official visit and inspection, an acquaintance of Victor's—a senior officer in the Directorate and a rival of Altov's—told him over a drink, "With all due personal respect, I was sincerely hoping you guys would fail. That would have exposed the poor planning and sloppy leadership. Well . . . some other time." Victor could not disagree with him. There had been no objective reason for the emergency. The rush had just been to cover up someone else's incompetence. Someone at the top.

The next day the team was given a reprimand for the dirty windows, two days off for getting the job done, and then promptly dispersed.

Victor was summoned for a meeting with Altov.

"I am pleased with your progress, Victor. You have proved that you learn fast and that you can work well under pressure. Now you know something about every area in the Department. Except for one. What do you know about the Shift Chief's position?"

"Not much, really. It's a sort of coordinating job, isn't it?"

"Yes, but it goes way beyond that. The Shift Chief has to know everything. And I mean everything. He has to know who's doing what in the KGB, especially in the First Chief Directorate—Intelligence. He has to know precisely what major operations are currently under way all over the world, in detail. He has to know where everyone in the government and KGB leadership is at any given time. His is the first in the chain of decisions concerning who gets what information."

Altov took a long pause, then continued. "As you know by now, the KGB is highly compartmentalized. Information is distributed strictly on a need-to-know basis. You're only told what you absolutely must know to execute your assignment. So, when something turns up, it's the Shift Chief who has to make the initial decision about whom to inform and how quickly they need to know. A matter can be so urgent that it needs to be reported to Brezhnev himself, instantly. A matter can be so sensitive that it needs to be readdressed—and the actual addressee of the telegram must not be given a copy. On the other hand, a matter can sound extremely urgent but in fact not be worth awakening even the line Department Chief, much less Kryuchkov or Andropov. In other words, the Shift Chief is in the hot seat. He has very little chance of becoming a hero, and an excellent chance of becoming a scapegoat."

Victor smiled. "Sounds intriguing."

The next question was not unexpected. "Well, what would you say if I proposed you for the job?"

"I would like to give it a try."

"That won't do. You don't 'try' in this spot. Either you do it or you don't. The stakes are too high there, not just for you but for me as well. If something goes wrong, if you make a mistake, I'll be held accountable." Altov took another of his famous pauses. "Traditionally, these guys are at the end of their careers—as high as they are going to get. They're all around fifty and very experienced. Because of their past postings abroad, their connections are too good. As a group they're getting to be a bit more powerful than I want. I need to move some of them around. I'd like you to be the first young one."

"Then I'll do it."

Altov replied, "Good. It will be excellent for your career. It will be very tough at first, but you'll manage. Now, by way of preparation, I want you to study something that few people in the KGB are ever allowed to learn—the KGB itself. You will be schooled on its complete structure. When you've finished that, you'll have to get up to speed on all current operations. Then, go to work. Good luck."

"Thank you."

Victor had mixed feelings about this challenge: his pride in his new position and Altov's faith in his abilities was leavened by apprehension about the reception he'd get from the other, far more senior Shift Chiefs. There was bound to be jealousy and resentment at the fact that his career was starting at the very point theirs were winding down. He was sure they'd give him a hard time.

With the exception of the general introductory courses, Victor's classes so far had consisted of three students to one instructor. This time, however, he was alone, with multiple instructors—each teaching his own specific area. Individually, none of them knew the whole structure of the KGB. Little by little, over a month in the late summer of 1974, the overall picture was pieced together in front of Victor. It was breathtaking, and he was amazed by the sheer size and astonishing diversity of the KGB system. He saw clearly that the KGB was a state within the State, fully self-sufficient, living a life of its own, answering only to the Politburo—or more precisely to the Head of State.

Even before this course Victor's knowledge of the overall system had already been far more complete than that of the average KGB officer, and even more complete than many of the officers at the Center who considerably outranked him. Now he could see that all he had learned up to that point had just been the tip of the iceberg. The comprehensive picture he was being given was generally accessible only to the Collegium of the KGB and the offices of the Chairman and his deputies. Only a handful of people outside of that rarefied circle were privy to it, and Victor was rapidly becoming one of them.

The insistence on compartmentalization meant that entire departments were hidden from ordinary officers. It was even possible for an officer in the position of Department Chief to be completely unaware of the existence of another Department in some other part of the KGB. Sometimes it seemed that there was no logic to certain parts of the structure.

But as Victor was learning, even if it was not evident at first glance, there was always an operating logic. The organizational model of the KGB was exquisitely functional.

After he'd completed his study of the overall structure of the KGB, Victor moved on to specialize in the First CD, which was KGB Intelligence. He was placed as a Deputy Shift Chief of the cipher Department, in the First Department of Directorate A, Eighth CD, which was attached to the First CD. At first, the resentment Victor had anticipated was palpable. The whole group of Shift Chiefs clearly felt their monopoly threatened by this Young Turk. Victor's boss refused to help him. Victor decided to be patient. He sidestepped confrontations, asked few questions, and kept studying the Journal.

Every order, request, or note about an item to be on the lookout for was recorded in the Journal. The Journal was full of entries like "Direct everything on operation 'Spring' to Kryuchkov"—meaning that Kryuchkov had to receive a copy of the telegram sent to the addressee. That was very different from "Direct everything on operation 'Spring' to Kryuchkov only"—which meant that only Kryuchkov could receive a copy, regardless of the addressee specified by the Station Chief. It was also different from "Notify Kryuchkov immediately"—which meant that Kryuchkov must be called wherever he was, even in the middle of the night, on the secure phone.

There was no cross-referencing in the Journal, and all the entries were written in the order in which they had been received. Some of them were changed or canceled the next day, and others stood for months. The Shift Chief had to carry most of this information in his head. The most difficult cases were those that had no reference in the Journal at all, and the Shift Chief had to make a decision based on experience and intuition.

Although rocky at first, Victor's relationship with his boss improved over time. The work load also took its toll. The Shift Chief simply couldn't do everything himself. Gradually, he allowed Victor to fill in for him, even though he knew he'd be held responsible for any decisions Victor made. He came to respect Victor's ability to get along with people even under tricky circumstances. His attitude changed, and he began to take Victor under his wing, tutoring him and facilitating his acceptance by the other Shift Chiefs. In a few months, by early 1975, Victor had been accepted as one of the Trusted and was working on his own. Later, the Shift Chief's position became that of a colonel, and that particular group of Shift Chiefs was named "Group of Referents." Because of their powerful connections and a certain mystique they were quickly nicknamed the "Black Colonels."

The Group of Referents was also responsible for the flow of information along two lines: between the Forest, the First Chief Directorate's headquarters in Yasenevo, and the Chairman of the KGB; and between the Chairman of the KGB and the Members of the Politburo.

The Forest and the Center had on-line enciphered communications for urgent cables. The second line was the critical channel, for the most important function of the Group of Referents was to provide Members of the Politburo with the KGB information dispatched by its chairman—Yuri Andropov.

Not all Eighth CD communications were high tech, and in particular the traffic between Andropov and the Politburo was not exactly set up in a sophisticated manner.

The door to the Referents' office inside the Eighth CD premises at Yasenevo was like any other door; there was nothing but a number on it. The office had two rooms. The first one had two desks facing each other, sideways to a curtained window. There were several phones, a wallboard with two dozen keys hanging from numbered hooks, and a metal chest. The adjoining wall had a dispatcher-type blackboard. The third wall had pigeonholed shelves with black folios in them. The second room also had two desks, as well as a safe, a sizable table, and a large Xerox machine—the only piece of "high tech" in the place. The only remarkable items in this office were the labels under the top two rows of pigeonholes—the names of the Moscow-based Members of the Politburo. Just last names, not the usual full names or even first initials.

Every one of the black leather folios in the pigeonholes was special, and was never used for any other purpose. They were produced by the tampering experts of Directorate B of the Eighth CD and had no outside seams. None inside, either. There was no way of knowing that a tampering indication layer was inside. A false outer flap covered a flat key and combination lock. Dialing the combination and using the key would open the folio. That gave access to a flat metal box, where the actual contents were stored. Despite all these complexities the folio looked so inconspicuous that no one on the street would pay any attention to it—if they ever saw it.

After Andropov had decided on a document's distribution list, a Referent's aide would pick it up and bring it to the office. There, all the necessary copies would be made and placed in the appropriate folios. Depending on the contents of the document, the time of day, and the location of the designated Members, the Referent would decide when and how to deliver the copies. Several cars and drivers were always on twenty-four-hour standby. Special armed couriers were also on standby in a separate room—outside the Eighth CD premises, of course. When it was time for delivery, the folio was locked. An armed courier was summoned. The officer met him just outside the Eighth CD premises and handed him the folio. The courier had to sign for it in a special journal, noting the exact time. That detail was critical, as time was of the essence. The courier put the folio into his own scuffed and nondescript briefcase and went to a waiting car. Once in the car, the courier locked the portfolio in a hidden safe, which would be reopened only at the door of the addressee's building. Of course, the cars had scrambled communications with the Center.

The cars in that car pool were equipped with special blinking signals from both the Ninth and the Seventh Directorates. Having the signals for both directorates gave the cars every available priority. Moscow traffic police are an unusual group. Some are really cops and some aren't. The Seventh Directorate of the KGB—Surveillance—had many officers working undercover as traffic police, primarily in the streets most frequently used by foreigners, as a part of its stationary surveillance system. The Ninth Directorate of the KGB—the Bodyguards—also had their officers working undercover as traffic police. They were placed in the streets frequently traveled by the Politburo Members. There was some rivalry between the Seventh and the Ninth Directorates, which, while not serious, was enough to strain cooperation and led to each challenging the other's priorities.

The Big Change, when the KGB underwent a major expansion, occurred in 1975. By autumn it was the Eighth CD's turn to be restructured and expanded. Altov called Victor in again.

"Victor, you are doing very well indeed. The Leadership is pleased with your performance. You're now one of our experienced officers—and certainly one of the best informed. It is time for you to move on. Especially now that the Directorate is expanding. I have a couple of suggestions. Number one is the position of Section Chief of Section Three of the Directorate. What would you think of that?"

That post bore serious consideration. Section Three of Directorate A was a section that was not subordinate to any Department. Its Chief reported directly to the Directorate's Chief. It handled all the KGB cipher communications with the Illegals. It also trained them in communications. The position was very attractive, offering a lot of independence. On the other hand, Victor knew that the job could very well be a dead end. Why would anyone want to move a man who knew the identities and activities of every KGB Illegal around the world? Victor felt that in the long run that job would become a trap for him. He responded carefully,

"Well, of course, I'm flattered by the offer. On the other hand, I fully appreciate the necessary restrictions involved in handling communications with all the KGB Illegals. I think I would prefer to do something else. Besides, I think that position might be a bit too quiet for me." He was wondering about the other "suggestion" Altov had in mind.

"Well, to tell you the truth, I'm not surprised. I feel the same way myself." Altov played with his letter opener for a moment, then continued. "The other vacancy I have in mind for you is in the Third Department, which is still in the process of being formed."

Victor didn't know much about this new department. He checked his response, hoping for more information.

His silence was rewarded as Altov continued, "You know its functions, don't you?"

"Vaguely."

"Well, it's not set in stone yet, but basically, it's security."

"That's what I reckoned."

"If that is your choice, you'll have to remain a Senior Officer for a while."

"I think that might suit me better."

"OK, done." Altov thought for a bit, then said suddenly, "Oh, there's one more thing I want you to know. I am moving to Directorate B for a while. Later, God willing, I'll move to the Chief Directorate, as a Deputy. I'll keep my eye on you. And one more piece of news: the CD Chief is retiring. Andreyev, from the Sixteenth, will be the new one. His buddy Bosik, also from the Sixteenth, will be your Department Chief."

That was significant information—a change in CD Chief was an event that did not come more than once in a decade. It meant a change in style, especially since the new Chief would be General Nikolai Nikolaievich Andreyev, a superstar of the Sixteenth, Interception, where he'd been famous for his outstanding results in tapping foreign cipher systems. He was personally well known and highly respected in the Politburo. As the Chief of Interception, he had reported directly to that body.

Victor just nodded in acknowledgment.

Altov rose, extended his hand, and wished Victor luck.

At the entrance of the Reception Office, Victor was jarred out of his time capsule by the guard's request for his identification. Back to work. He prepared himself mentally for the upcoming interviews.

CHAPTER

11

VICTOR CONDUCTED THE INTERVIEWS according to standard procedure, meeting with each candidate individually. He usually tried to evaluate candidates' personalities as well as their track records, but this time he was in a hurry to complete the task and get back to preparing for his vacation. These guys had already been preselected, so he could afford to focus his questions solely on their professional experience and potential.

Although questions from candidates were extremely rare, one of them actually chanced one. He blushed, cleared his throat nervously, then, stammering slightly, said, "Please, excuse me, I know this is irregular, but there's something I really need to ask. May I?"

Unusual initiative. "Go ahead."

"Well, I have a confession to make. It wouldn't be right to leave this interview without telling you that I am a very poor marksman. Is it crucial to shoot well?" He hesitated, then plunged on, further qualifying his confession. "I'm sure I could learn, but I haven't had the opportunity to shoot much up to now. Would the KGB be willing to train me? I really do want to serve my country . . . ," he trailed off, anxiously awaiting Victor's reply.

Victor smiled at his naivete. "Guns are not really what we're about. You'd learn to shoot, of course. But more out of tradition than anything else. Intelligence ends with the first shot fired. After that it's anything but intelligence. At any rate, in our line of work, if things go sour the only one you have to shoot is yourself—you know too much." Victor noted with interest that the candidate didn't seem to be scared off by this information, just disappointed.

"You mean there's no actual risk involved with this job?"

"Oh, there's always risk," said Victor. "The risk of somebody getting killed or jailed because of an error on your part. The risk of having to pay dearly for the mistakes you make. The risk of causing a political scandal—just to name a few." He was about to add that additional risk came from the knives aimed at your back in the office, and the risk of having to pay for somebody else's mistakes, but he refrained from making the joke. One had to be in for a while to appreciate that kind of gallows humor.

Victor reported the results of the interview to Koryakov, the Third Department's Chief. Victor had liked both candidates. They'd come across as intelligent and straightforward. Slightly intimidated, but so what? Everyone who comes into the KGB's Reception Office is intimidated.

Koryakov thanked him and then, as an afterthought, asked, "Incidentally, Victor, how come every time you're involved in the business of selecting rookies we're never sent straight-A students? I don't believe that's accidental."

"No, it isn't. We need highly motivated people with sharp minds and good concentration."

"That's right. So what makes you think that straight-A students aren't just that?"

"Well, it's extremely unlikely that a student can be genuinely and seriously interested in each and every subject he has to take. There are just too many widely varied courses required of him. If he manages to pull an A in all of them, that suggests his goal was simply getting As. I don't think that kind of person does well for us. Our work requires a specific kind of focus. With the possible exception of those who are geniuses, most of these A achievers would focus on furthering their careers, and not on specific problems to be solved."

"And what happens if you come across a genius?"

"Well, as I'm not qualified to supervise a genius, I wouldn't want to be accused of ruining talent."

Koryakov laughed, "Go away. Can't you do anything the way other people do it?"

Victor had laughed along with Koryakov, but the exchange stayed with him, and on his way back to his office he reflected on his own experience. He was certain his theory about focus was accurate. In his own career he may have made some wrong choices, but he'd had his biggest successes when he'd been able to channel all his energy and imagination into a single project or task. He was sure it was precisely this capability that had attracted Bosik to him in the first place.

Victor thought back to Boss's arrival at the Directorate less than four years before. Boss's characteristically disordered enthusiasm had generated such a blur of activity that the time before Boss felt like ancient history.

His last private meeting with Altov had been in the autumn of 1975 and had concluded with Victor's appointment to the Third Department. Shortly after, Boss had blown in from the Sixteenth Directorate like a tornado, preceded only by his reputation and the nicknames "Boss" and "Gypsy." His first day on the job he'd conducted more than a dozen private meetings before lunch. People emerged from these sessions shell-shocked, unprepared for the pace he set. By the end of two weeks, they'd gotten used to it. Those who'd survived. In his first two days Boss had purged 70 percent of the officers tentatively appointed to the Department. Although his approach appeared extreme, he could afford it because Andreyev had given him a blank check.

At the time no one knew that he also had a mandate from the Politburo to radically change the profile of the Directorate. Bosik was in effect assembling an assault team. This necessitated a very different kind of personality from that of the traditional methodical and disciplined Eighth CD type. Bosik wanted people who were quick and decisive, with sharper political instincts. They needed to be better educated technically for the tasks ahead. The security policy that had been used to discourage Eighth CD officers from resigning, to restrict the numbers of those who knew too much, had resulted in a glut of officers with considerably more seniority than responsibility. These officers lacked the skills now required.

Victor'd been among the first called in to see the new Chief of the new Department. After the briefest preamble, Boss went straight to the point.

"You have a pretty impressive record. I see it includes some scientific research."

"That's a past sin."

"I hope we can work together. Now, have you ever given any thought to the criteria we'd need for an in-depth, overall evaluation of the KGB's cipher-communications system? Any ideas on long-range planning for improvements in communications security?"

He'd caught Victor off guard. These issues were enormously complicated, and the cold, brusque style with which the questions were fired put him on the defensive.

"Well, not exactly. Those issues have been sitting in the back of my mind, not in front." That sounded lame, even to Victor.

Boss pounced. "Such criteria are critical to the success of our mission! They have no business being at the back of our minds—they belong directly in front. I was appalled to discover that no one has even tried to do this systematically." He paused, challenge flashing in his black eyes. "So. Your first task is to work out coherent and uniform criteria for evaluating the entire KGB communications system. You will consider the human factor as well as all technical security. You have three weeks."

Victor almost fell off his chair. He stared at Boss, trying to guess whether he was kidding or simply did not understand how outrageous his request was. It would take a good scientific department a couple of years at least to carry out the task Boss was blithely assigning Victor to complete in three weeks. This man was a loose cannon.

Victor hesitated, choosing his words carefully. "Well, the task, as you outline it, would take a substantial amount of research. Since I don't have any experience as yet in this particular line of work, I'm afraid it will take much longer than three weeks . . ."

Boss cut him off, "Don't waste time with excuses. Your record indicates you've had plenty of general background experience. I don't need a Ph.D. dissertation. Make it as detailed as time allows, but I'm most interested in the overall picture. Go and think. Think. That's what you said you do, so go and do it."

Victor was startled to hear his own words thrown back at him—words he'd naively spoken during his initial KGB interview with Nesterov years before. It was his first experience with Boss's gift for retaining detailed information. And his uncanny knack for using it.

Victor realized at once that the purpose of the task was twofold: To introduce and familiarize Boss with a system that was new to him, giving him a quick overall grasp of it. And to test Victor.

But the assignment was ludicrous. Victor was being asked to formulate a scientific study with neither sufficient time nor support to execute it properly. The danger was that the resulting study would be superficial and pretentious. Still, Victor didn't have much choice, so he decided to make the best of it, work like hell, and let the chips fall where they may.

Three weeks later he reported back to Boss. He'd produced a chart of all the system's requirements, showing how they were interrelated. At first, Boss appeared skeptical as he examined the five-by-four-foot sheet of white drawing paper, covered with squares and connecting lines.

"Looks impressive enough," he grunted. Then with a cold smile he said,

"Let's see if it makes any sense." He started studying the chart in earnest.

Little by little all traces of skepticism disappeared from his face. Victor watched as Boss became totally engrossed by the presentation, oblivious to all else.

Suddenly, he turned to Victor. "It's better than I'd expected. Leave it with me. I want to see you here tomorrow at seven. We'll talk then."

Oh brother, another early bird. Tentatively, he asked, "Seven . . . in the morning?"

"Christ, no! Evening, of course. I'm a night owl."

Thank God.

He left Boss with the chart, along with the thirty pages of explanatory notes. The Secretariat typist had not had a good time with those notes. She'd complained, "Victor, I always thought you were a rational guy: what on earth is this stuff? This is the first time in my career I haven't understood a single word of a document I've typed." Victor had developed formulas for general evaluation, taking into account the performance of components in the system, down to a rather low level. To anyone not directly concerned they might as well have been written in code.

When they met the next evening, Boss was downright friendly toward Victor. The few questions he asked in regard to the chart clearly showed that he'd understood everything perfectly. He seemed to like the fact that Victor hadn't been afraid to admit where the interpretations were debatable and that he had been up-front about not having all the answers.

Their intense in-depth discussion left Victor impressed by the quickness of Boss's mind and his total command of the vastly complex subject. Boss had immediately grasped the principle behind every single formula.

In conclusion, Boss said, "By the way, Andreyev saw your work this afternoon. And liked it." Boss continued, as if reading Victor's thoughts, "Don't worry about the few loose ends here and there. Others will continue working on the project. As I'm sure you've guessed, this was also a test for you, and you've passed. We've decided to take you onto the team. Congratulations."

As they shook hands, Victor said, "Thank you. But I don't quite understand. What team?"

"It's why you are here in the first place." Bosik smiled, pausing to heighten the impact of what he was about to say. Then he began, "As you know, over the last several years we've been trying to develop new principles in cipher-communication intercepts. Recently we've made some real breakthroughs. As a result we've had some successes against the West—

spectacular by any standard. I know your business is security, not interception, but now the time has come to upgrade our communications security, to prepare us for the time when the Americans manage to achieve our level.

"Are they close?"

"No, not yet. They're still a few years behind us. At least, as far as we can determine. But we can't guarantee that, and we cannot afford to gamble. We've already had indications that they've scored a few hits on our ciphers—which, in our view, are already vulnerable to current American expertise. So, a team is being assembled to upgrade our defenses to the next level of security. And this is where you come in."

Victor's heart raced. This was what he wanted—cutting-edge work with top people. The kind of team he'd been on at TsNII-50. "Who else is on this team?"

"Not so fast. Let me explain. This business of our new technology is extremely sensitive. Do you understand?"

Victor nodded.

"We can't afford to give the enemy the slightest inkling that we've achieved a higher technological plateau. Never mind the fact that some of the methods we use are, let's say, unconventional. If the West were to find out about them, there'd be a big stink. To put it mildly."

"What methods do you mean?"

"I mean the use of X rays and radioactive isotopes."

That struck a sensitive nerve, but all Victor could do was nod. *My God! It's bad enough to shoot high-frequency electromagnetic waves at people. Now we're going to use X rays and radioactive isotopes on them.*

"As I said," Boss continued, "we can't give the slightest indication of what we are up to. Not even to our own people—the rest of the KGB, the MFA, and so on. The task ahead of us is enormous: upgrading the security of all of the cipher communications of the KGB, the GRU, and the MFA. When we reported this necessity to the Politburo—specifically to Andropov and Brezhnev, the order came back to create a small team of crack officers—absolutely reliable people—and execute the mission very quietly. Even the Members of the Central Committee are not to be informed. Any outside help we use has to be blind. We have virtually unlimited authority, but we may use it only under extreme circumstances because it would attract attention. In the event of a confrontation, we can go directly to Andropov and Brezhnev for help. But whoever is responsible for creating that kind of high-profile confrontation will be in very hot water. So we'll be doing a lot of, let's say, unorthodox political maneuvering."

"It sounds as though we'll need time as well as luck."

"Luck's not part of the equation, and time's precisely what we don't have. I can't stress enough how urgent this matter is."

Victor slightly shook his head.

"Call it impossible, if you like, but we'll accomplish it, no matter what. Now, no more than a dozen people will ever know exactly what's taking place. Andropov has placed Andreyev in charge. Personally. I report only to Andreyev. You will report to me. Directly. There will be a few other people involved on this assignment. No one else must know what's going on. For every situation each team member will be provided with a cover story to give to colleagues who are not with the project." He was referring to the KGB's standard practice of using several levels of cover stories. Again, the redundancy.

"Understood."

"You'll be dealing with the overall policy and overall security—technical, physical, and personnel. You'll receive most of your assignments directly from me. Starting tomorrow, you'll familiarize yourself with the technical aspects of the issue. You'll have a week for preparation, then you'll get to work."

"Very well." Victor stood, assuming the briefing was over.

Boss stopped him, "Oh, one more thing. When we do accomplish our mission, we'll be heroes, and obviously your career will get a good boost. Speaking of careers, we'll need some clout. In a few weeks I'll become the First Deputy of the Directorate's Chief. You'll still report to me. You'll also need one more component to rise. A Party job. We'll make you the Deputy Secretary of the Party Organization."

Victor's heart sank. That was not his idea of a wonderful career move. He knew, of course, that to rise to the top one had to serve in a Party position, at least for a while. The position of Deputy Secretary was a perfect launching pad. But Victor was indifferent to showy titles and the elite privileges that came with them. He tried to back out gracefully.

"Well, that's a great honor. But I'm worried about two things in particular: one is that I'm probably too young for the job, and the other is that I won't have the time to do it well. I'd prefer to concentrate completely on the security assignment."

"Nonsense. What's wrong with being the youngest Deputy Secretary in the KGB? As for the time it will require, I'm sure you'll manage."

Victor tried one more escape route. "I am not sure that the Central Committee staff . . ."

Boss interrupted with an impatient wave of his hand. "Don't worry. It's been cleared with Andreyev and everybody concerned. Stop grumbling, and go home. The decision's been made."

Victor continued to be uneasy about the Party job. Even though that particular position was probably beyond the wildest dreams of most of his peers, he was profoundly ambivalent. He loved his country and certainly would not hesitate to give his life for it. But his patriotism was for Russia, not the Communist Party. It was not that he was disloyal to the Party—he sincerely admired its so-called Highest Final Goal of liberating all the less fortunate on earth. Yet he didn't feel the slightest inclination to hold a Party job. He'd seen too many worthless Party functionaries. People who could do only one thing—talk. Many of them had become Party officials because early in their lives they'd realized that they couldn't compete successfully with their peers, so their ambition led them to look for an alternate route to importance and influence. Not by creating or achieving something on their own but by talking their way up. They were parasites. As children, they'd usually gotten by as tattletales and teachers' pets, thoroughly disliked by their classmates. In the university they'd compensated for academic mediocrity with time-serving Komsomol activities. They never risked anything themselves but persuaded or "inspired" others to take on challenges instead. Of course, they were the first in line when rewards were handed out. Then there was their peculiar ability to disappear when something went wrong. Generally disliked and feared, they were a breed most decent people tried to stay clear of.

Victor was not happy with the prospect of joining the ranks of a group so disliked. The professional people among whom Victor had been brought up had no respect for them, and he feared being tarred by the same brush. But obviously he wasn't going to have any choice in the matter.

A few days later, Valentin called and suggested they meet for a drink after work. He was the last person Victor wanted to see just now. As they sat together in a café with a bottle of red wine, Valentin didn't waste any time.

"So. I heard a rumor that you're going to be our next Deputy Party Secretary."

"Yeah. I heard the same one," Victor shrugged.

"Victor!" The tone was reproachful, "This doesn't sound like you at all. What the hell's going on?"

"Oh, nothing much." Victor was extremely uncomfortable discussing the matter with his friend. "Look, Boss told me to take the job, and that's all there is to it."

Valentin was not to be put off. "Come on, Victor. You know as well as I do that a job like that doesn't come out of nowhere—especially for someone your age. You're being groomed for the top, everyone knows that. But this seems to be above and beyond the proverbial call of duty, don't you think?" He waited for some response from Victor. When none was forthcoming, an awkward silence grew between them in the midst of the noisy café. They both sipped their wine.

Finally, Valentin spoke, "Don't get me wrong. I'd rather see you in that position than some other real asshole, but I don't get the feeling that you're particularly happy about it. I also know you won't enjoy the damn job. You and I both despise the Party-functionary type. The danger is that once you're in that swamp, you'll be sucked into it. I'd like to help you. Maybe you could use some advice on how to duck the job without repercussions—I do know a bit about it."

By now they were on their second bottle of wine.

Victor could no longer control his anger. He was mad at the world, and especially angry that Valentin could read his own reservations so clearly. He snapped, "Well, I don't see anything wrong with taking the job. Some people—more to the point, some people's parents—haven't managed to duck jobs in the Central Committee."

Victor instantly regretted the remark. It was a low blow—a cruel reference to Valentin's father. Victor knew perfectly well that Valentin had nothing but contempt for his father and his Party career, and that the only reason Valentin even spoke to his father was for the sake of his mother—a kind, gentle woman. To the outside world, the image carefully projected was that of a perfectly happy family. Very few people knew the truth, and Victor was one of them, thanks to Valentin's frankness with him. As he watched the color drain from his friend's face, he loathed himself for having used Valentin's confidence to hurt him.

He tried to take it back. "I'm sorry, Valentin. I really am. I must be drunk. That was a cheap shot. What I meant was that I really don't have any choice. I have to take the job whether I like it or not, and I'm afraid that's all I can tell you. They've put me to work on a special project, and this job is a part of the package."

Valentin was too kind to hold a grudge. They'd been friends long enough for him to shrug off the thoughtless remark. He simply asked, "Do you know the difference between a human and an ape?"

Victor smiled, ready to take whatever his friend was going to dish out. "No."

"A human thinks first, and then acts. An ape acts and then thinks.

Don't be an ape, Victor."

Victor laughed, relieved. "You're right."

During all the courses that had been required, Victor had never taken communist theory seriously. It had been easy to get by because nobody else seemed to either—even those headed for Party jobs. Thanks to the vast staff of the Institute of Marxism-Leninism, quotations from the founding fathers were always readily available for any imaginable situation, both in the country and abroad. As were sound bites from the current leaders. Victor had even found it amusing. Everyone could quote from Lenin and the other icons of Communism, but few ever studied or even looked into the original works to read the quotes in context.

Victor had always approached a new subject methodically. His custom was to understand what he was talking about before attempting to discuss it. In this new Party position he was supposed to be a leader along the communist path, and yet beyond the ability to parrot a sizable catechism of standard slogans, he really didn't know much about Communism. His ignorance troubled him, however irrelevant it might be to others. The only solution was to study. Victor resolved to become thoroughly versed in both communist theory and history.

As it turned out, this particular mission would prove to be among the most difficult he'd ever undertaken, and it would have far more serious consequences than he could have possibly imagined.

CHAPTER

AFTER TYING UP MOST of the loose ends relating to his job, Victor still had to deal with several Party matters before he could start his vacation. That meant a lot of paperwork—writing reports and mandatory Party references for officers' promotions. And he had to conduct the monthly Party meeting. It was two days away, and he had yet to prepare his speech.

The phone call from Nesterov, Chief of the Personnel Department, was an annoying interruption.

"Victor, I've got a job with your name on it. I know you're going on vacation, but this shouldn't take too long. As a matter of fact, it's got to be done in the next couple of days."

"What's that?" Victor made no attempt to conceal his sigh of resignation.

"Church draft."

"Again? We went through that six months ago."

Nesterov chose to ignore Victor's lack of enthusiasm.

"Apparently, they want more people to go to the Spiritual Academy. Anyway, you know the requirements."

"All right. I'll beat the bushes again. But I seriously doubt I'll have any luck. Who the hell from our Directorate would want to go?"

"Victor, I understand your problem, but it's my problem too. If someone does go from the CD, then I'm the one who has to find a replacement for him. Believe me, your success only complicates my life, but an order is an order. Just see what you can do, OK?" That plainly meant, "Don't try too hard, but make sure you show you tried."

"Sure. I understand."

"Oh, there's one new wrinkle. They've lowered the requirements. Full Party membership is no longer necessary. Now it's enough to be a candidate for Party membership."

Experienced bureaucrat that he was, Victor couldn't wait to drive through that loophole. "That's great. Perhaps I can get the Komsomol guys involved?" he asked innocently.

Nesterov knew instantly what Victor had in mind, and even though he laughed, he nixed the maneuver, "Nope, sorry. It's too damned sensitive. The order is clear: the approach must be a joint effort—the Party and Personnel. Period. Don't try to be cute."

Victor sighed again, "OK, I'll call you in a couple of days."

"Good. By the way, where do you want to go on vacation, Yalta or Mahindjauri?"

That was a question that wouldn't be put to ordinary officers. Accommodations of any kind were scarce in the Soviet Union. Even when traveling on government business, getting a place—a bed, not a room—in any hotel was a major accomplishment. It was even worse at the recreation facilities.

There were basically two types of Soviet recreational facilities, both run by the State: resorts—"Dom Otdykha"—and "Sanatorium" or spa. The former offered bed and food, along with some more-or-less organized activities: local tours; limited sports, like ping-pong and volleyball; in the evening, movies and dancing. The Sanatoriums offered these, but they also offered an in-house medical staff, and their general service was far superior.

Originally, the Sanatoriums had been predominantly used by people in need of medical treatment. Over time, however, they evolved into the recreation facilities of the privileged. One's position in the government or Party hierarchy determined where one could go. Midlevel personnel went to the Dom Otdykha. The rank-and-file stayed home. Most of those granted reservations had to go either without their spouses—if their position was not high enough—or out of season, or both. Only a small percentage of KGB officers could take their spouses on a Sanatorium vacation.

All KGB personnel had to stagger their vacations more or less evenly throughout the year, so three quarters of them had to go off-season. Victor's position assured him an in-season vacation, job situation permitting, with Olga, and his choice of the KGB facilities. A summertime vacation was a real privilege.

One popular anecdote described a friendly Chief's scheduling a subordinate's annual vacation: "Well, Peter, do you like warm vodka?"

Peter, aghast at the thought, answers, "Heavens, no!"

The Chief continues, "And Peter, do you enjoy the company of perspiring women?"

"Of course not!"

"Good. In this case I can do you a big favor. You will take your vacation in November."

Victor didn't care for the KGB's sanatorium in Yalta, Crimea. Close to Brezhnev's dacha, it was too large and formal for his taste. "I'd prefer Mahindjauri."

"You've got it. Taking your wife?"

"Of course." Elena would remain at her school's summer dacha.

"You can pick up the papers any time."

"Thanks very much."

"OK. Don't forget to take care of that Church draft." He hung up.

The Church draft was the result of the KGB's penetration of the Soviet Orthodox Church. It had started years before, with the KGB initially recruiting agents and informants from among the Soviet clergy. The program had developed to the point at which full-time KGB officers were placed in critical Church positions immediately after graduating from the Church's university, the Spiritual Academy in historic Zagorsk, and were guaranteed an amazing career in the Church. Although all legitimate candidates for the clergy had to pass rigorous entrance exams, the KGB had its own entry quota for the Spiritual Academy.

The complication for the Party and the KGB was that the Russian Orthodox Church Outside Russia, a relatively small church established by the Holy Synod of the Russian Orthodox Church after it emigrated during the Revolution, refused to relinquish its rights as the true Orthodox Church. Its followers around the world were people with a vivid firsthand knowledge of Communism. The Soviets had worked very hard against this church ever since the Revolution, to no avail. They viewed it as a serious rival and a potentially dangerous threat to the power of the Soviet Orthodox Church, which by now was thoroughly infiltrated and dominated by the KGB. As a result, one of the major Soviet goals in Israel was to make some kind of deal with the Israelis that would permit the Soviet Union to take over all the properties of the Russian Orthodox Church in Jerusalem. The value of the real estate alone was over a half billion dollars—a lot of rubles—but the goal that far outweighed the material gain was the weakening of the Russian Orthodox Church Outside Russia.

The problem did have its unconventional aspects. Since the U.S.S.R. and Israel did not have diplomatic relations, the KGB *residentura* in Israel was located in the Soviet Church in Jerusalem. A secret room was built in the basement of the priests' house, and packed with more spy gear than even any KGB priest could need. It had a fancy secret entrance. Power for the automatic door was generated by a car battery sitting innocently on the floor of the house's entrance hall. The catch was that the wires—a car jumper cable—had to be connected to both ends of a curtain rod every time anyone wanted to open the door, then stored away again after use.

The official rationale for the infiltration of the Church was the necessity to counteract the propaganda of the contras—all those opposed to communist ideology—that permeated the Orthodox Church. Nevertheless, Victor found the program deeply troubling.

Together, Personnel and the KGB's Party Committee sought candidates for the KGB's Spiritual Academy quota from the pool of younger KGB officers. These candidates had to satisfy certain criteria:

> —They had to be members—now at least candidates for membership—of the Communist Party. Party candidacy meant the universal one-year probation period.
> —They had to volunteer for the Church duty.
> —They must be officers.
> —They had to be unmarried.

Those candidates who met these criteria had to be individually approached, and the offer was handled as a sensitive matter. If the answer was no, there was to be no further mention of it, and a rejection of the invitation would not reflect on the officer's career. As a practical matter, officers in Directorate A were unlikely candidates. Considering all the filters they had had to pass through to get into Directorate A, they rarely attained officer's rank before the age of twenty-six. By that time they were often married. Moreover, the prospects for a career in Directorate A were far superior to those offered by the Fifth Directorate—the directorate that ran the Church.

Victor, opposed on principle to the KGB's infiltration of the clergy, would see to it that nothing came out of his search for undercover "priests." No one would suspect his resistance. In the KGB, as in any bureaucracy, negativity was not the exception but the rule. It was quite difficult to push things through the system but extremely easy to block them without any danger of serious criticism. The last time he'd approached candidates, he'd presented the offer in such a way that no sane person would have even considered the job, much less have volunteered for it—and yet nobody could have accused him of sabotage. Everything had been strictly along Party lines. This time would be no different. He would interview the candidates and then submit the proper report on their refusals to Nesterov the following day. He leafed through the personnel roster and picked a handful of candidates to approach, just enough to show that he had gone through the motions.

Preparing for the monthly Party Organization meeting was a bit more time-consuming. Traditionally, he and the Secretary took turns chairing the meetings. It was Victor's turn. In addition, each of them was the main speaker at two meetings a year. Other communists in the Organization covered seven other slots, and a high-ranking official from outside the Directorate spoke at the remaining session. It also happened to be Victor's turn to speak.

Victor pulled the Party Organization's Annual Plan from his Party files. The topic of the main speech for July was "The Current International Situation." Not too bad. The speech wouldn't take long to prepare because the nature of his job kept Victor abreast of that subject. In no time at all he'd drawn up an outline for the speech. Then he looked up his notes from the Central Committee seminars for KGB Party officials. Regular attendance at these meetings was mandatory for Victor and the Party Secretary. The notes Victor had taken at these meetings—like the seminars themselves—were separated into two distinct categories. One consisted of comments on Party policy toward current issues, labeled "For Your Personal Information." The other contained instructions for answering questions about current issues from rank-and-file members of the Party. Often the two did not coincide. The trick was not to mix them up. Fortunately for Victor the gap between the FYI data and the rank-and-file material for this particular Party Organization was far less striking than for most others because this Party meeting consisted exclusively of KGB officers, who were privy to more information than most of their fellow comrades. Being in Directorate A of the Eighth CD further extended their "need to know."

Like all Party Organization meetings, this one conformed to the standard routine. Large conference room, long table covered with the red cloth, and the speaker's podium. Victor at the table, a couple of dozen men and a few women in the audience. As soon as everyone was settled, he opened the session.

"Let me start our meeting. Our agenda is as follows:

"1. The report on the current international situation.

"2. Miscellaneous.

"First of all we have to elect the presidium. Suggestions on the size of the presidium?"

Victor had handed out the "suggestions" himself on small slips of paper just prior to the meeting. In the past he'd simply told people at random what to suggest. That is, until someone had gotten confused and mixed things up by nominating the wrong person to the presidium. The Party Secretary had reprimanded Victor for his "lack of control over the meeting." Now, thanks to the slips of paper, things went more smoothly.

A voice in the audience responded: "Four people."

Victor repeated, "Suggestion to have a presidium of four people. Any other suggestions?" As no pieces of paper cued additional suggestions, there was silence. "No other suggestions. Let's vote. Who's in favor of four people in the presidium?" All present raised their hands. "Against?" No hands. "Anyone abstaining?" No hands. "The suggestion is accepted unanimously. Are there suggestions for who the four in the presidium should be?" Those holding the appropriate pieces of paper now shouted out the names written on them. One by one Victor wrote them down. Or rather, pretended to write. He already had the list: the secretary; an older man in a clerical position who'd won the "Socialist Competition," the annual demonstration of grass-roots initiative; Department Chief Koryakov; Victor himself. Four people. As planned.

"Are there any other suggestions?" Hint of democratic process. Silence. "No other suggestions, then. Shall we vote on the list as a whole, or on each individual?"

The appointed voices shouted, "By the list!" Of course. It's faster.

"Who is in favor of voting by the list?" A forest of hands. "Against?" No hands. "All those abstaining?" No hands.

"Who is in favor of the suggested presidium?" All the hands. "Against?" No hands. "Abstained?" No hands.

"The presidium is accepted unanimously. I ask the comrades named to take their seats at the table here." Those appointed to the presidium stood and moved to join Victor at the table, which had been provided with exactly four chairs. It didn't take long because they'd conveniently taken seats near the aisles.

Victor, the Chairman, sat in the center; the Secretary and the Department Chief on either side of him. The lesser comrade took the side chair.

Victor stood and went over to a separate podium where there was a microphone. He placed his outline in front of him. Contrary to the prevailing custom, Victor did not write out the full text of his speeches. Except in the case of very formal and important meetings, he preferred to speak extemporaneously. He cleared his throat, surveyed his audience, and began. "As you well know, the current international situation is extremely complex. Let me focus today on some key areas—those which are of particularly vital interest to the Soviet Union. . . ."

He ran through the usual roster: the United States, Europe, South America, the Middle East, South Asia, and Africa. Despite the grumbling from the Secretary that invariably followed his turns at the speaker's podium, Victor consistently defied the norm and brought his speeches in at just under thirty minutes. Forty was customary, and most other speakers were considerably more long-winded than that. His speech today was no exception. In his wrap-up, half an hour after he'd started, he concluded, "As you can clearly see from this overview of current events, international Imperialism is far from surrendering. America especially is not about to give in, and instead tries with all its power to advance. Examples of ever-increasing capitalist imperialistic aggression can be seen everywhere. Angola and Nicaragua are fresh victims. In the light of this evidence, it is the task of every communist—especially the communists in the KGB—to contribute as much as possible to the success of the Soviet Leninist foreign policy, as well as to the success of the defensive measures of our propaganda apparatus against Western propaganda, which, as we know, tries incessantly to corrupt our people and undermine our noble goal. Thank you." Modest applause. "Now, are there any questions, comrades?"

Although there was always a question-and-answer period following the main address at Party meetings, it was hardly a spontaneous exchange. The trick was to pre-arrange the proper questions and to avoid, or at least sidestep, the risky ones.

Victor knew from experience that in any organized group of people there are always a few characters who love to ask questions, regardless of the subject or their familiarity with it. He knew they'd be sitting somewhere in the front three rows. These people mostly liked to hear themselves speak in front of an audience, so their questions tended to be a rehash of the speech, windy and unthreatening. They were even useful because their questions lent a semblance of "democracy" to the proceedings and rarely caused ideological embarrassment.

"Our interest in Afghanistan is presumably based on the fact that it is on our southern border. Does our increased sensitivity and attention to Afghanistan indicate that we have information that the Americans are trying to infiltrate the country and use it as a military base?"

Victor was ready for the question. "Well, I don't have specific information to that effect. That does not mean, however, that the Americans are not planning such a move. But there is another reason, perhaps more important than that. Consider Afghanistan's location. If you remember your history, Russia has always tried to gain access to the Indian Ocean. Tried but never succeeded. Still, from geopolitical and strategic standpoints, access to the Indian Ocean is more important to us now than ever before. We had a chance with Pakistan, when Bhutto was on the rise, but our plans did not work out. We have hopes, unfortunately diminishing at present, with Khomeini, although it's not yet clear how that situation will be resolved. In any event, we need Afghanistan to gain access to the Indian Ocean. Therefore, we have a great deal at stake there. Strategically, it would be perhaps the biggest advance for our Navy. And there is the other crucial point: getting closer to the Middle East with its oil—a resource that is vital to the Western capitalist imperialists."

The questions dealt with, the concluding resolution was accepted—unanimously, of course: "To accept and approve the report of Comrade Sheymov. To devote all the resources of the communists of the Organization to the advancement of the foreign policy and propaganda efforts of the Leninist Politburo."

The second point on the agenda, "miscellaneous," produced only a few, unimportant matters. In another fifteen minutes the meeting was over.

As Victor left the conference room, Valentin was beside him. His friend teased him mercilessly, as always.

"What a performance, Victor!" he whispered melodramatically. "You were marvelous! Such perfect use of Party rhetoric—you almost sounded like you meant it! I congratulate you—you get smoother and smoother. Pretty soon I won't be able to distinguish you from any other Party functionary!"

"Come on, Valentin. The form must be observed. You know that." Victor was not in the mood to be needled. He was quite pleased at the way he'd handled the meeting, and he was eager to get away.

But Valentin was going to have his say. He took Victor by the elbow and half turned him to get his attention. He was no longer teasing. "Look, Victor, so we're all hypocrites, no question about it. The question is how far your conscience lets you go. It comes down to your personal moral standards. The hypocrisy of Party functionaries makes me sick. When I see you right in there with them, doing exactly the same shit—even more smoothly—it really bothers me. You're a decent man. Why are you doing this?"

The unsolicited lecture delivered with Valentin's characteristic passion angered Victor. Perhaps even more so because deep inside himself he was wrestling with the same questions. He asked caustically, "Do you have any specific suggestions? All I've heard so far are generalizations."

Valentin paused and stared hard at Victor. He said quietly, "No . . . ," then suddenly he tightened his grip on Victor's arm and added ominously, "Maybe . . . in a while . . . perhaps I will have some specific suggestions." He pulled Victor a little closer and added, "That is, if you have the guts to hear them."

Suddenly, Victor felt as if there were not enough air in the corridor. The conversation had taken an alarming turn. He had to stop Valentin. He pulled his arm free and said, "Look. You've been walking a dangerous line lately, and you know it. I've heard more than a few rumors about you, and as your friend I'm telling you your tongue is going to get your neck in a noose. You can say what you like to me, I don't give a damn. But it's not the same with the others who hear you. Your views could prove detrimental to your health—do you understand what I'm saying?"

"But, Victor, I just can't stand it. Look, I know I've gotten away with some remarks because of my last name. Because of my Central-Committee-goddamned-father . . ." He took a long pause and then said, "Victor, I've got to talk to you. We need a good, long talk. . . . Perhaps when you get back, OK?"

"Yes, all right, fine. But for God's sake be more careful in the meantime."

"Yeah. OK. I promise." Abruptly he changed his tune to a more cheerful selection: "So, when do you start your vacation?"

"We leave tomorrow morning."

"Well, have a wonderful time then," and he leavened his benediction with more than a hint of sarcasm, "you certainly deserve it."

Both laughed, and Victor grumbled, "Oh, go to hell. You're impossible."

Victor went home to pack.

The next morning Victor and Olga got themselves to the crowded Vnukovo Airport, where they boarded an Aeroflot plane. Aeroflot was the country's only airline and ran accordingly. As always, the plane was jam-packed, and the air-conditioning didn't work. The rudeness of the flight attendants was typical of domestic flights. The fact that it was also the start of vacation season only exacerbated matters.

Frequent flyer that he was, Victor was impervious to the discomfort. He still preferred flying to the train, on which the conditions were even worse and the suffering much more prolonged. Olga, on the other hand, was not a practiced traveler and quickly developed a headache. To complete the misery, the plane had to cross the Caucasus Mountains—the ridge shielding the Georgian shore of the Black Sea from the cold of the central Russian plains. This passage was always turbulent. All the passengers were greatly relieved to land at the Batumi airport.

Several taxis and a few private cars were available for hire at the exit. The unconcealed availability of the private cars was a striking challenge to the power of the Soviet government. Soviet law explicitly forbade the use of private cars for profit. The strict rule was vigorously enforced from time to time in Russia, especially in Moscow. In fact, it had gotten to the point where offering a ride as a favor could seriously backfire on a car owner. If, for whatever reason, the rider wanted to get the driver in trouble, all he had to do was claim that he'd had to pay for the lift—actual proof of payment was not necessary. The driver would then be heavily fined, given a stiff official Party reprimand, and warned that the next time his car would be confiscated. Goodwill rides had practically dried up in Moscow.

In Georgia, though, things were different. The ban on rides for hire, along with many other Soviet laws, was flagrantly ignored. Especially in the Georgian province of Adzharia, of which Batumi was the capital. If Georgia was one of the notably corrupt republics in the Union, it was still only half as corrupt as the province of Adzharia. Nothing could be accomplished there without a bribe. To make matters even worse, the Adzharians had perhaps one of the shortest tempers of any minority in the Soviet Union. There was only one notable exception to their hostility—if one were a personal guest. The responsibilities of the host were still held sacred there. And the tradition of "a friend of my friend is my friend" still applied.

Victor had long suspected that one of the factors behind the corruption in the republics was their resentment of the central Soviet government. His own experience with friends of various ethnic minorities helped him to understand that, like the Georgians, every Soviet nationality is intensely proud—on every possible level: personal pride, family pride, village pride, and ethnic pride. Almost invariably, the smaller the ethnic minority, the fiercer the pride. Victor was thoroughly convinced that this deep ethnic pride was in fact the primary reason that corruption in the republics was so much greater than in Russia. It was the clearest way for them to express their profound resentment of the arrogant assertion of Russian supremacy from metropolitan Moscow.

This was not Victor and Olga's first trip to this particular sanatorium. They knew exactly what to expect. They hired a cab. Victor said, "Mahindjauri, please."

The driver—a typical Adzharian—yawned insolently and responded in heavily accented Russian. "Where in Mahindjauri?"

Victor understood the question behind the question. Mahindjauri was a small village, about a mile long, with several resort facilities. Only one of them belonged to the KGB. That's what the driver was checking for. The locals always gave vacationing foreigners a hard time: overcharging them, trying to provoke the men into fights, harassing and embarrassing the women, and so on. But never the KGB people. Messing with them was taboo.

Victor answered nonchalantly, "Sanatorium 'Mahindjauri'" and watched for the impact of his response.

Instantaneously, the driver's yawn vanished, along with all the other macho mannerisms. He started the car immediately, and as they got under way he transformed himself into Mr. Nice Guy, happy to welcome the vacationing couple. At the end of the trip he even refused a tip, accepting only the exact amount shown on the meter.

Victor grumbled to Olga, "I wish I got that kind of respect in Moscow."

The Sanatorium Mahindjauri, formerly one of Stalin's dachas, was situated on a hill just above a lovely beach. The view of the Black Sea and down the narrow strip of land between the mountains and the sea was breathtaking. Olga and Victor were lucky. They'd been assigned a room with a seafront view instead of one facing the nearly vertical wall of mountain a hundred feet from the back windows of the building. This "luck" was the direct result of some foreign souvenirs that Victor had thoughtfully brought to the all-powerful Admissions Chief.

The splendid grounds of the sanatorium on this subtropical eastern shore of the Black Sea had been meticulously maintained for decades. Although not officially a botanical garden, it offered stiff competition to the main public botanical gardens of Batumi. The privacy of this generous estate was especially striking in contrast to the surrounding district, where the sea and the mountains squeezed the narrow strip of habitable land. The many pines, sequoias, and magnolias, along with the enormous variety of flora beneath, created an interlocking, mysterious shade. A complex harmony of floral fragrances completed an atmosphere that was both deliciously relaxing and exciting at the same time.

The sanatorium was famous for its eucalyptus baths, which were developed by its own excellent medical staff. Neither Olga nor Victor had any health problems, although Victor felt slightly fatigued after almost two years of nonstop scrambling and scheming at Boss's pace. Nevertheless, both of them were brought to medical justice by the very kind Doctor Xenia. She ignored Victor's "I'm as healthy as a bull" and prescribed the whole gamut of the spa's procedures. Eucalyptus baths, of course, some complicated inhalants, massage therapy, and the like. She was also adept at verbal fencing. To Victor's resistance she riposted tartly, "I am in command here, and I am responsible for the health of our invaluable Chekists. So please be good enough to maintain your subordination, and do as you are told, Victor." Doctor Xenia had treated Victor on previous visits, and he liked her very much. She reminded him of his mother, and she was one of the few doctors he'd met that he felt took the Hippocratic oath seriously.

By late afternoon of their first day, Olga and Victor had finished all the registration and check-in formalities and were ready to relax into their vacation. Good food; reserved seats in the dining room, where a courteous, helpful waitress would take their orders for the next day's meals; and a number of delightful activities: bus tours to spectacular local sites, swimming in the sea, or just sunning on the beach. The only minor inconvenience was the one-track railroad that separated the beach from the main grounds, but only a few trains passed through the village each day. There was always entertainment at night—concerts or movies. And lots of dancing. However, what Victor and Olga most looked forward to was hiking together. They loved to escape the sanatorium and walk in the natural beauty of the mountains.

It took several days for them to shed the pace and anxiety of city living, to reach the point where Moscow's conditioned responses grew less and less frequent and finally stopped altogether. They missed a few breakfasts and enjoyed the luxury of sleeping late. There was no second sitting in the regimented dining room, and when Olga suggested, "We could get a bite in the village . . . ?" Victor simply laughed and said, "I've told you, I'm not the suicidal type." The food in town was notoriously inedible. So instead they passed lazy mornings grazing on fruits and were hungry as wolves by lunchtime.

By the middle of their four-week stay, Olga and Victor felt genuinely refreshed. They began to feel that their minds and bodies were filling with new energy, which, in turn, led to more exercise—swimming and volley-ball. And more thinking. That relaxed but steady thinking when one sees things objectively. Not too far removed to miss the details, but with the perspective necessary to see the whole picture.

One day, when they were hiking alone in the mountains behind the sanatorium, they stopped to rest in one of their favorite spots, some two thousand feet above sea level, up in a nearby pass that cut through the mountain wall. The view of the Black Sea to the horizon and the rest of the deep valley stretching out below was spectacular. They had discovered this spot when they'd been on vacation there four years before. Victor chuckled to himself as he replayed the adventure they had stumbled onto back then—literally.

One warm summer morning a group of four vacationing KGB officers and their respective wives—or girlfriends—had embarked on an ambitious ascent up that same mountain path behind the sanatorium. Their goal was a pass. The view was said to be more than enough reward for the effort expended in getting there. It was a good long hike, and the day turned out to be a lot hotter than they'd anticipated.

The view from the pass had been truly magnificent. As they stood, breathless, both from the view and the climb, the door of the tiny, stone-and-wood cabin just below them opened, and the owner and his wife approached them. The couple had heard their voices and were eager to offer refreshment to the adventurers. This hospitality was typical of the native Adzharian mountain folk who, unlike their surly counterparts in the town, were open, friendly, and unbelievably generous. The couple would not be satisfied until the group agreed to stop, sit awhile, enjoy the view, and accept some "humble provisions." They seemed absolutely undaunted by the prospect of feeding eight hungry hikers. Victor and company were more than amenable to the idea. When they asked what would be acceptable payment for refreshment, they were repeatedly told, "No matter, no matter. Come." Clearly, money was not even to be discussed. Resolving to settle up later, they followed their host around the hut to a small patio overlooking the valley, while his wife disappeared inside. If anything, the view from this concrete slab was even more dramatic than the one they'd set out for. To start with, the edge of the slab extended beyond the tiny terraced square on which the house had been built. Although it was a sheer drop of hundreds of feet to the rocks below, there was no protective railing to guard against a careless misstep.

Having indicated that his guests should make themselves comfortable, their host also disappeared into the hut. As the group settled themselves, it happened that Victor took a seat near the edge of the slab, with his back to the view. When the host reemerged, he was carrying what looked to be a five-gallon flagon filled with a clear, light-yellow liquid. However, before he would pour what he called "young wine" for them, he insisted that Victor move away from the edge and face the valley. Not wanting to make an issue of it, Victor had obliged, and then wine was poured for all. All except for Olga, that is. She was three months pregnant with their daughter and asked for water instead. They talked and laughed and drank as they waited for their food, emptying the glasses several times. The "young wine" was fruity and refreshing, with no obvious taste of alcohol. They washed it down like soda pop. At last their hostess emerged from the hut laden with plates of the native bread known as "lavash" and a huge bowl of fresh local fruits. Having been content to sit, drink, and talk up to that point, no one had even tried to move. Now, they found to their amazement that they couldn't. All except Olga, who wondered why no one else stood to help themselves to the food. It turned out that one of the effects of the "young wine"—whatever it really was—was that it impaired one's motor coordination while leaving one's head absolutely clear. Olga watched in amazement as her companions—and her husband—lurched and staggered over to the table, only to reach for an object and miss it by a foot. It was quite clear why their host had been concerned about Victor's initial seat.

They had all thought it was hysterically funny, even as they paid for the feast with numb, fumbling fingers. Then it was time for the precipitous descent. Not surprisingly, it took them far longer to get down than it had to climb up. For the most part, it had been a "five-point descent" for everyone except Olga, who had had her hands full shepherding her loose-limbed charges down the mountain.

When they finally made it back to the sanatorium, exhausted and laughing hysterically, it was time to dress for dinner. The idea of any of them being able to fumble their way into the formal dining room with any degree of dignity was preposterous.

This time they had sat in silence near that very spot for quite some time. Victor assumed Olga was similarly lost in the same memories. He turned to her and was surprised to find her watching him instead of the view. Evidently, she had been for some time. The expression on her face indicated that something was up.

Once she saw that he was back in the present, she took a deep breath and, choosing her words with great care, began to speak. It was clear from her intensity that she'd given a lot of thought to what she was about to say.

"You know, my darling, I have absolute trust in you, in what you do. I know you always act according to your conscience. I don't know, and frankly don't want to know, exactly what your job is, or what kind of work you do. But I do know that you are aware of what's going on in the country—in the world, as well—far more than I am. There are many things I just don't understand. What I see around me is not what I've been told all my life." She paused, then added, "I'm confused." She faltered, looking at Victor, wanting to continue, but unsure how to proceed in this risky conversation. She was waiting for his response, some encouragement.

Victor was not sure where the conversation was headed, but instinctively he knew that it would be dangerous. He tried to tease Olga, to make light of her concern: "Well, I wish I had your confidence in what I do." He was instantly sorry. He could see his levity had disappointed her and dropped it immediately. He looked at the woman he loved reaching out to him for help. Whatever was bothering her had to be taken seriously. He touched her cheek tenderly and said, "I'm sorry. Joking aside, I'm grateful for your trust. I know how hard it must be for you not to ask questions sometimes." He paused, then as if reaching for the first glass of "young wine" all over again, decided to pursue her question, wherever it would lead. "What exactly are you asking me?"

Olga, relieved by his encouragement, fixed her dark eyes on him and plunged ahead. "Victor, what I mean is that the life I see all around us is not at all like what I've been taught life should be. Corruption is everywhere. I'm not talking about Georgia and the Adzharians; I mean Moscow. You can't buy anything without bribes or connections, unless, of course, you're privileged. Millions of hard-working, honest people are being screwed, either by the crooks in the distribution system or by government officials. Many women can only be promoted by sleeping their way up. I'm lucky. My superiors know that you're a senior KGB officer, so no one dares to harass me. It seems to me our whole society is rotting. It's awful. I've tried not to see it. But I can only keep my eyes closed up to a point. Victor, I think I've reached that point. You must be aware of what goes on; you have to be. How could you not know, doing whatever it is you do? Now I need to know what you think." Olga's eyes were feverishly bright.

Victor was deeply moved by her passion and by the courage it must have taken to broach the subject, breaking their tacit taboo. He was silent for a long time, trying to decide the best way to answer her—trying to sort out his own thoughts, now that she had unknowingly confronted him with the very conflict already simmering within him.

At last he said, "Olga, for some time now I've felt that we'd have to have this conversation sooner or later. I guess now's as good a time as any." He spoke slowly, in a quiet, steady voice. The step they were on the verge of taking would be irrevocable. It would either bind or split them. Either way, it would be dangerous. "Of course I'm aware of all you're describing. Perhaps I'm even more acutely aware than you just how pervasive the evil seems to be. I, too, have reached the point you speak of. From my earliest days in the KGB, isolated incidents have troubled me, but I was in too much of a hurry to stop and analyze them, or put them all together. Then just after I was appointed Deputy Party Secretary, I started reading up on my Communism so that I would know what I was talking about in my position. What I am finding is disturbing, to say the least. How can I describe it to you so that you'll understand? Olga, all my life I've been trained to evaluate things as objectively as I possibly can and not to jump to conclusions. I also know that things are often not what they appear to be at first glance. When I reached the point where, like you, I could no longer close my eyes to what I saw, I decided then that I had better study Communism properly. I mean, for myself this time, not for my job. You'd be surprised, but I can bet you that perhaps only one in a thousand Party functionaries really knows what Communism started out to accomplish, and how it was done. Most of them just mouth ready-made, predigested slogans." Victor paused to let his words sink in, then continued, "At least I can say now that I know basic communist theory reasonably well. What I've learned so far has shocked me deeply. It's clear that ever since the Revolution the leaders of the Communist Party have deviated more and more from the original Party goals. Now all we have is a bunch of bureaucrats who have usurped all the power and are doing nothing for the good of the country. And your humble servant is one of them. You asked for the truth? This is the truth. And it's not very pretty."

As Victor spoke, Olga's face was still as a mask, with an expression Victor had never seen before. She was profoundly shaken. Evidently, she had hoped to hear something soothing, something that would tell her that there was no cause for concern, no reason to worry. Instead, she'd received only cold confirmation of her disillusionment.

The silence between them was like a wall. At last, Olga broke it. In a thin, strained voice she asked, "If this is the case, how can you, a man whose conscience is so sensitive, be a party to it—be in the very thick of it? I cannot understand this, Victor. Forgive me, but all of a sudden it's as if I don't even really know who you are."

Victor tried to calm her, "Please don't jump to conclusions. First of all, I have nothing to do with the internal affairs of the country. My interests are abroad."

That sounded lame, even to him. A big tear rolled down her cheek as she gazed steadily at him, silently reproachful.

He tried another tack: "Olga, just think for a minute! If you take an action, naturally you expect to see some result, yes? You tell me: what options do I have?"

Her answer came instantly: "Quit! Just tell them what you've told me and say you quit."

Her innocence exasperated him, but her naivete was largely his fault. Where could he begin to give her the picture that he had concealed up to now? "I'm afraid there are some minor details to consider. If my views became known, I'd end up in a labor camp at a uranium mine—that's if I'm lucky. I can guarantee you that. I'd be dead in three years, at most. What is more likely, considering that I am a so-called 'carrier of extremely sensitive information,' is that I'd just face a firing squad with a blindfold and no cigarette. Olga, the views I've just described to you would qualify as 'state treason.' Furthermore, the fact that I've communicated these views to you, means that—in accordance with Soviet law—I have spread 'anti-Soviet propaganda.' Another treasonable offense. So, while express-ing my views openly and quitting outright is certainly an option, it's not a very attractive one. But even if I didn't care about the consequences to myself, what would I achieve? Who would benefit from my action? Only the person who would step into my privileged, well-paid job. Nothing else would change."

The alarm in Olga's eyes signaled that his words had gotten through to her. She said, "So, just quit, but make up an excuse, or leave without any explanation. Couldn't you do that?"

"Once again, what good would be accomplished by that? Would the system become any better? No. Of course, I would look like the noble hero to you, and to myself, but that's just narcissism."

"But tell me then," she pressed, "tell me, what good are you achieving by staying on? Is the system any better for your participation?"

"Who knows, Olga, maybe it is. I don't play their careerist games or participate in the corruption. I try my hardest to play it straight, and so far I think I've managed to remain myself. And believe me, that's not easy.

For now I'll have to keep up appearances. But at least the higher I go in the system, the more power I'll have, and the more good I'll be in a position to do. Besides, I'm sure I'm not the only one to have figured these things out. There are others, there must be. Of course, I can't discuss this with them, just as they wouldn't dare discuss it with me. But you can see who's doing what. You and I know a lot of honest people. I'm sure, deep inside, a lot of them are sick and tired of what's going on."

By now Olga had been so shocked by what she was hearing that there was little room for hope in her heart. She shrugged helplessly and asked, "Well, then, why can't people like you organize yourselves? I'm sure you'd have a lot of support. I mean, don't say what you've just told me, but instead word it differently, more discreetly?"

Victor smiled ruefully. "It's not so easy, my darling. The people on top aren't stupid. They would immediately smell what was up. Besides, they've already anticipated that possibility and taken steps against it. The Party Charter specifically states that one of the most serious sins is the formation of any faction within the Party. So such an attempt would be crushed. Ruthlessly."

Victor tried to put Olga's mind at ease—and to regain a semblance of control. "That's all I can tell you for now. Please don't do or say anything foolish, and don't breathe a word of this conversation to anyone. Be patient, and try not to torture yourself. You've nothing to feel guilty about, and there's nothing you can do at present. I'm doing everything I can. More importantly, I'm thinking. The only thing I can promise you is that I've never done anything corrupt or dishonest, Olga, and I never will."

There was no reaction from Olga. He was desperate to find a way to make her understand. They looked at each other, numbed by the enormity of what was at stake. At last, she reached out and put her arms around his neck. They sat there, holding each other in silence for a long time, watching the Black Sea stretch to the horizon, enervated by the conversation and apprehensive about its consequences. Then it was time to return to the KGB sanatorium.

This time the descent was precipitous for very different reasons. The danger lay ahead—as soon as they came off the mountain.

It took them a couple of days to digest the conversation. They both realized their relationship had entered a new phase as a result of it. Their trust in each other would become absolute. The cold, objective perception of the truth they had shared about the world around them brought them much closer. They had chosen to reject the easy way out—no blinders, no ignoring reality, not for them the self-imposed tunnel vision so successfully rationalized by millions of their compatriots. Their life as they had known it had come to an end. There was no way back.

On the surface, everything was just as it had been, and there was no way anyone could possibly notice the tremendous change that had taken place in the hearts and minds of the Sheymovs. As before, they swam, played volleyball, and danced. They continued to attend the spur-of-the-moment, late-night room parties, although now the inside jokes and stories seemed on a distinctly different wavelength.

One such spontaneous soirée took place in the Sheymovs' room. As usual, those who dropped in came in pairs. Even those vacationing alone had what were known as "temporaries," regardless of their marital status. It was perfectly acceptable socially. There was even a joke about whether it was better to have a higher rank, so that one could take one's spouse along on vacation, or to be just high enough to rate a single reservation and a "temp." It was referred to as an automatic equalizer that compensated for insignificant disparities in the country where "everyone is equal."

Most of the group this particular evening were from the Moscow Center, with only two of the men from peripheral KGB stations: a department chief from Siberia and a commander of a Border Guards frigate from the island of Sakhalin in the Far East. As always, after a few drinks had warmed up the neutral small talk, conversation turned to shop. Only generalities, of course. Someone brought up the subject of volunteer informants. Everybody agreed that despite their obvious value, they were generally real pains in the butt. There were so many of them, and their reports were usually packed with such petty garbage. More often than not they were trying to get at someone they didn't like. Many of them were genuinely mentally disturbed.

The chief from Siberia silenced the room by saying he'd found the definitive method for handling them. It seems an old man with a long psychiatric history had been bugging him with reports of a major counterrevolutionary conspiracy in his small town. He maintained that it was directed and funded from America. The old man was indefatigable. He wrote. He phoned. He came in. He was retired, so he had all the time in the world to track this conspiracy. The chief finally reached his limit and decided to get rid of him. Easy to say, hard to do. Finally, he invited the old man to a "briefing" in his office. It was clear the man was psychotic. The chief expressed his great respect for the old man. He said that he had in fact known about the conspiracy before the old man had started submitting his reports, but he'd only had a general picture. The old man's work had added critical details to the case. The chief said that he'd not responded to the reports because he'd wanted to keep the old man out of danger. The old man had no idea, he said, how dangerous these plotters were. The truth was, he told his informant, that these traitors were up to something of great danger and consequence. Perhaps even a new kind of weapon, capable of destroying the whole country. It would, therefore, be unwise to round these villains up before the KGB had learned everything about them and their project. He continued, saying that the case was so complicated that the KGB could not handle it without the old man's help. He must, however, warn his informant of the extreme danger. Would the old man be kind enough and brave enough to help his country and the KGB? Sure enough, the old man was delighted to risk his life for KGB and country. Well, then, the storyteller continued, his instructions must be followed to the letter. The old man waited. His instructions were these: "You will obey orders from me only. You will give your reports to me only. The most important thing of all: you do not, repeat, do not contact me. No matter what. We cannot take chances with an agent as important as you. I'll contact you when it's appropriate, but this case is so complex it may take months, even years. You watch and listen. Write down everything, do not rely on your memory. But please, don't take too much risk. Your safety is most important to us." The chief gave the old man a code name, wished him good luck, and never heard from him again.

Everyone laughed at the solution, and someone asked, "When did this happen?"

"About two years ago. Since then, I've put two more psychos on ice. It really works. The only problem is, I always forget the code name." More laughter.

After a few more drinks, the conversation naturally turned to politics. It centered on the issue of dissidents.

A man from the Second Chief Directorate grumbled, "I'd like to know why we keep all those Jews here. It's too much trouble for no good reason. If it were up to me, I'd let them all go, and I wouldn't let any back in." His opinion, which was a popular one in the KGB, found fans in the gathering.

The fellow from the Fifth Directorate—the directorate concerned with ideology—was in the minority. He obviously didn't share that view and remained silent as the talk swirled around the subject.

In the early sixties, when the Fifth Directorate was formed, it had been the laughingstock of the KGB. It was immediately nicknamed "The Anecdotic," a pointed reference to its solemn investigations into the ori-

gins of anticommunist anecdotes around the country. Inevitably, the officers of the Directorate soon became the best source for these anecdotes.
They shared them—very selectively. Even now, in 1979, very few people
had any idea of the considerable scope of the Fifth Directorate's activities.

When the man from the Fifth Directorate couldn't bear to listen to
such political misinformation any longer, he jumped into the conversation. "You all simply have no idea what you're talking about. If you let the
Jews go, you'd spoil the fruits of many years of careful planning and hard
work." That got everyone's attention.

"What are you saying?"

"What do you mean, it would spoil years of work?"

"Come on, what the hell do we need Jews for?"

"Of course we need them. Just listen. You all know they cause no
harm. What you don't know is how useful they are to us. There's no
counterrevolutionary danger from them; they just want to be left alone,
right? So. Where does the danger come from?" he asked his audience,
and without waiting for anyone else to speak, he answered his own question, "The real threat to Communism, friends, is from the Russian people
themselves. Why? I'll tell you why. Because they are the majority. They
have the power to be dangerous."

A few people nodded, agreeing. He continued, warming to his subject,
"All of us know that most Russians are not overly fond of Jews. I refer to
the general population, of course. I won't go into the reasons. Ethics
aren't the issue here. What matters is that it's easier to create a negative
attitude toward the Jews than toward the Russian and other dissidents.
And we've cultivated that prejudice ever since Stalin came to power. The
next step in the process was to deliberately confuse the terms 'Jew' and
'dissident' in the minds of Russians, Ukrainians, and Byelorussians. We've
been working on that for years. And we've succeeded. Look around. People are convinced that they are one and the same: Jews, dissidents—the
terms are interchangeable. Believe me, I know what I'm talking about.
This is how we've turned a lot of people against the dissidents before they
even started listening to them. So, you see?"

By now, the silence in the room was almost sober. Smiling victoriously,
the man from the Fifth asked the group, "Now tell me, do you still think
it's a good idea to let the Jews go? Then face dealing with the Russian dissidents?" The question was rhetorical. Even he didn't answer himself this
time. There was a low buzz as people murmured, "No," "I never thought
of it like that . . . ," "Imagine . . . !"

Victor knew the man was describing the manipulation accurately. He was reminded of how the Jews had consistently been the wild card in the Soviet political game.

The party gradually came back to life. It was quite late when the last guest departed.

The rest of the vacation passed quickly and uneventfully. Another Aeroflot jet returned Olga and Victor to the Moscow Vnukovo Airport, to resume life as before. For a while.

CHAPTER

VICTOR'S MOTHER HAD a long list of messages waiting for him. This was customary. Whenever friends couldn't get an answer on Victor's home phone, they called his parents and left word with them. One of the messages was an invitation from his old friend Misha Vainstein. Olga reminded Victor that they'd been unable to attend his last two gatherings. It would be rude to miss a third. Victor called him immediately.

"Misha, hello! It's Victor."

"Well hello, stranger. I suppose you're calling to tell me you're busy again?"

"No, quite the contrary. I'm calling to say I don't know how to kill all my free time, so since we haven't anything else to do, I think we should come."

"Splendid. As I told your mother, it's tomorrow evening. We're having a few friends in. Oh, and speaking of killing, I presume you've washed the blood of all those innocent people off your hands . . . ?" Misha was a dissident. He hated the KGB. Victor's joining their ranks had been extremely difficult for him to accept, and even though their long-standing friendship had survived that test, Misha never missed a chance to get his digs in.

"Well, I confess they're still dripping a bit, but I'll take care of that by tomorrow night. You won't notice a thing."

"Six o'clock all right?"

"Sure."

Olga speculated, "I bet they'll have a houseful of dissidents."

"I'm sure they will. They always have an interesting crowd—highly intellectual. Almost never boring."

"Victor, are you sure it's OK to socialize with them? I mean, so openly? What about your job—your regulations?"

She'd never worried about the political inclinations of their friends before. He hastened to reassure her. "Don't worry, it's absolutely fine. They're aware of my friends, but I'm beyond suspicion."

"But what I don't understand is why you can't come within shelling distance of a foreigner, and yet you can still have close social contact with friends who are known dissidents."

Victor shrugged. "It may seem paradoxical, but it's not hard to explain, really. I had many dissident friends before I joined the KGB, and even then I already had a high security clearance. Once in the KGB, my clearance became even higher. Anyway, most of the dissidents aren't perceived as all that dangerous. What they're after is more freedom to talk, to write, to create their art, to emigrate, and so on. They're not really questioning the foundations of the State, or the fundamentals of Party ideology. Besides, the KGB knows exactly what's going on in the dissident groups. So, my contacts with them are regarded as effectively controlled."

Olga was incredulous. "Controlled? How's that?"

"I'd say that at least a quarter of every dissident group reports to the KGB, independently one from another. So you see, the KGB knows perfectly well that I don't belong to any of these groups, and that I only meet old friends from time to time on a social basis. That they happen to be dissidents is purely coincidental."

Olga was still unconvinced. "Well, that may be, but as far as I know, none of your KGB friends have such contacts."

"Maybe some do. But then, I've always been perceived as a sort of maverick. At any rate, I know for a fact that it's viewed as harmless socializing. It's quite another story with foreigners. No one in my kind of work is allowed any contact with foreigners whatsoever, no matter how trusted he may be. And no one who knows as much as I do is trusted in that respect. *Doveryay no proveryay*: trust, but verify, remember? Actually, when you really think about that saying, it's idiotic. A contradiction in terms. Lots of people quote it—mainly those that are not too smart. I guess it just sounds good."

The next evening Victor and Olga headed for the Old Arbat neighborhood, where Misha and his wife, Nina, lived. Among diehard Moscow residents it was considered *the* place to live—the best place to be born and raised. Regardless of other qualifications, anyone with that credential was automatically accorded some social status. Old Arbat's claim to fame was that it was rightfully considered to be the mecca of Moscow's intellectuals. During the thirties and forties the neighborhood had been invaded by a horde of government and Party officials, but their presence had done little to change its intrinsic character.

It was 6:30 by the time Victor and Olga entered the old building and rang the bell of the Vainstein apartment. The hum of excited voices beyond the door told them the party was already in high gear. Nina opened the door. Tall and slender, with light-brown eyes, she welcomed them warmly, kissing them both as she accepted the proffered wine and flowers. She then stepped back and, with an air of exaggerated regret, raised her hands and sighed, "Ah well, to tell you the truth I was hoping that today we'd witness a miracle . . . but, no chance."

Olga fell for the setup, "Oh no, Nina, what was that?"

"That tonight you'd be on time for a change!" Nina pretended to scold them but couldn't keep a fierce face. They all laughed and hugged again, and she said, "Come in, come in and catch up. There are a couple of people I'd like you to meet. I think you know most of the crowd already." She was an engineer, the quiet, practical one of the pair.

She ushered them into the apartment. By contemporary standards it was huge—three rooms, perhaps six hundred square feet—jam-packed with people, all talking animatedly. Misha was not immediately visible through the smoke. He was sure to be right in the middle of an intense intellectual debate. They'd bump into him eventually when he came up for air.

When Nina introduced Victor to the people she wanted him to meet, he gave his most commonly used cover story—that he was a scientist specializing in military research. Well, it was once true.

A bit later, after a drink and a skillful slalom through the tightly wedged groups, they found Misha. As they'd expected, he'd only just extricated himself from a discussion. Six feet tall, strong and immediately likable, he radiated kindness. His eyes, already glowing with the excitement of intense mental exercise, widened with pleasure when he recognized the Sheymovs. He pocketed the handkerchief with which he'd been mopping his profusely sweating brow and embraced them affectionately.

"Ah, Victor! Olga! I'm so glad you've come! Victor, so tell me how you're doing?"

"Fine, Misha, fine, I guess. Nothing spectacular to speak of."

"Oh, I'm so sorry you couldn't make it last week. You know I had Sasha Zinoviev staying with me here for a couple of days. I wanted you to meet him. He's a great man. Really special."

"I'd have loved to meet him, believe me, but we were away."

"Abroad?"

"No, no, on vacation in Georgia—Mahindjauri. Before that I was in Poland."

Misha wasn't fazed by Victor's travels. He came from a privileged family himself. His father had been a prominent scientist in missile development during Stalin's time.

"So tell me, how are things over there?"

"Not good. The Poles are poor and angry at us."

"Do you blame them? Why don't we just leave them alone?"

"I certainly would, if it were up to me. . . ."

"I know, Victor, I know. You don't make the policy, you just implement it." Misha caught himself, "OK, OK, let's not argue about that again. Tell me, what's happening in Georgia?"

"Nothing much. Everything there is as usual: corruption worse than here; portraits of Stalin in every window and on every car. You know all that."

"Bastards. How I hate chauvinism!" Victor knew that Misha hated Stalin even more than chauvinism.

"Wait, Misha, I don't think it's as simple as that. For instance, there are no portraits of Beria, and he was a Georgian, too. I think the portraits and statues of Stalin are just one of the ways the Georgians show their resentment of Russian rule. They suffered under Stalin, like everyone else. And if you think about it, Misha, that resentment isn't unique to Georgia. Other nationalities are also expressing their discontent with similar gestures. It's a pervasive undercurrent in all the republics."

Misha looked sharply at Victor. "Interesting, coming from you. I've never looked at the issue from that point of view. I'll have to think about it." Unlike most of his guests, Misha listened to the ideas of others, as well as holding forth with his own. For now, however, he was off and running in another direction, "Listen, Victor, I've got something interesting I want you to read. Oh, by the way, Zinoviev is emigrating. Personally, I don't approve. He should stay here."

"How's he doing?"

"Badly. They don't let him work; he doesn't even have a place to live. He goes to friends like me. We give him food and shelter—as well as moral support."

And he should stay? For what?

Hearing Misha describe Zinoviev's predicament, Victor was prompted to begin the serious talk he'd wanted to have with Misha for quite a while. Taking his friend's arm, he moved Misha out into the warm summer night, onto the balcony overlooking the building's large courtyard.

"Look, Misha, you understand I'm not supposed to talk about anything I'm about to tell you. Things are heating up here. Brezhnev's death is imminent. No one knows what's going to happen next, but it's going to be rough. I see two possible scenarios: Number One—we revert to the Stalinist era, with all that that implies. Number Two—we play at democracy for a while and then cut straight to Number One. I don't want to see you hurt. It's a sad thing to have to say, but I think you'd better get out of the country while you can. You're half-Jewish, so you still have a chance to do it legally. You're a magician with the computer. You know you can always make a decent living abroad as a programmer. But I'm telling you, if you stay, you won't have a prayer. When the first order comes down to look for 'enemies of the people,' you'll be dead meat. You're too well known a dissident to have any hope of surviving a purge."

Misha fixed Victor with his big, sad brown eyes. He spoke slowly, for once. "Victor, I thank you. I know what it means for you to say this to me. But I cannot leave. This is my country, too. I must stay to fight for it—and die for it, if it comes to that. The fact that you're Russian and I'm Jewish doesn't make this country more yours than mine."

"Please don't get me wrong, Misha. I'm not questioning your patriotism. It's not just a matter of survival. It's a question of effectiveness as well. I know you believe strongly in what you stand for. But if you stay here, you simply die in vain. At least abroad you'd have a chance to influence what is happening here."

"No. I won't leave, Victor. It's as simple as that."

Victor shrugged helplessly. "Well, I've said all I can. There's nothing else I can do."

"You've got to try to understand, Victor. I wish I could get out, but something deep inside won't let me leave. I can't."

There was nothing more to say. In silence Victor put his arm around his friend's shoulder. The two reentered the apartment, where, like polarized magnets, they were immediately drawn into separate clusters. Victor found himself in the middle of a group loudly decrying Soviet policy towards Israel and the Jews. He remembered the party conversation in Mahindjauri. This was the other side of the coin. The other side of the topic was not exactly in the public domain. Israel had been one of the most striking Soviet miscalculations. As the Soviets maneuvered for a foothold in the Middle East at the end of World War II, they figured that with a large number of ex-Soviet Jewish communists in Israel they should be able to gain control of the new Jewish state. They figured that the relatives left behind would serve effectively as hostages, thus guaranteeing the loyalty of the emigrants. Tonight's group was triumphantly rehashing how wrong this judgment had proved to be. The Soviet authorities had badly underestimated the willingness of the Jews to sacrifice for their new nation. They'd also consistently underestimated the cunning of those departing. Victor knew only too well how the KGB had recruited and trained many "agents" among those bound for Israel, never to hear from them again. They were certainly not about to pursue those "disloyal" agents, having no desire to add the Mossad to the main-enemy list.

Victor found his mind wandering. His conversation with Misha had left him feeling very sad. The rest of the evening seemed sour to him, with endless, pointless discussions of the wrongdoings of the authorities. Everyone was full of complaints, but nobody offered solutions. In fact, everyone was talking and no one was listening. As usual. At these parties Victor generally liked to listen, and the dissidents loved him for it. Here even those Victor assumed from their provocative rhetorical style to be KGB informants were jabbering away. He wondered just how effective they could be as informants. By eleven, he felt as if he were in a madhouse. He'd had enough. He collected the prohibited books Misha had offered him and rescued Olga, who was being cornered by an earnest-looking bespectacled fellow, and they left.

Olga was equally exhausted and exasperated by the evening. When they reached the quiet darkness of the sidewalk, she sighed, "You know, sometimes I think these dissidents are so busy being intellectual that they lose sight of common sense!"

It took less than fifteen minutes for them to catch a cab. As they got in, Victor noticed the surveillance team that had picked them up as they left Misha's building. The sight of them spooked Olga but didn't bother Victor in the least. He'd grown accustomed to being followed. The surveillance people also cut him some slack. They knew who they were following and that he was considered a good assignment. Preventive surveillance of the most reliable KGB officers was understood to be an unavoidable formality. They knew that nothing would come of it, and often let themselves be noticed as a courtesy to their "target." In return, the target would not make any quick or questionable moves so that the guys could write a nice, smooth report. Everyone was reasonably happy with the arrangement. This particular evening, Victor and Olga were back in their apartment in less than half an hour, and the surveillance crew could head for home as well.

Back in the office, Victor found all as it had been before vacation: every issue was Urgent, every action was Rush. When he called Boss, the greeting was terse.

"Welcome back. And about time. Look, there are a few things I need you to take care of. But first I want you to prepare the Authorization Order for Retaliatory Action for the American embassy communication line. You'll find my memo and the briefing report with your 'in' papers."

"You want me to do it even before the updating?" After every protracted absence—longer than two weeks—Victor had to go through mandatory "updating" regarding any changes that had taken place in the international situation and the operational environment abroad during his time away. Usually that was the first thing to be done.

"Yes. I want that Order immediately." Boss was overriding the regulation. It must be serious.

Victor went to the Secretariat and signed for all the papers waiting for him. He had to sign for every single one. As he wrote his name over and over, he recalled a scrap of paper he'd seen a while ago—quite by accident—on the desk of one of his friends in the Middle East Department of the First CD. The paper was a receipt—a sort of IOU. All it said was: "I, Sheik so-and-so, borrowed two bags of money from Sheik so-and-so." That was all there was. No indication of currency or denomination, terms of the loan, or even the size of the bags. No bureaucracy. No paper trail. It was enviable. Thinking longingly of that simplicity, Victor grumbled to the secretary as he signed that the rules of handling secret papers needed to be modernized. He proposed that after being classified, the papers should be packed and distributed by weight. For example, a pound of Secret; two pounds of Top Secret; a pound and a half of Utmost Importance. Three signatures and he'd be on his way. Probably only two, really. He rarely handled anything less than Top Secret.

The secretary retorted tartly, "If you're so smart, Victor, while you're streamlining the system, why don't you change the idiot rule that makes me count the pages of every book and document that crosses my desk." That was the rule—when you signed for a book, you actually signed for every page of it. Officially, you had to count the pages. Few officers actually did, but the Secretariat ladies certainly had to.

Back in his office, Victor shoveled the papers into his safe and began to study the briefing report on the interruptions of the Soviet embassy's line in Washington, D.C. The Soviets had prohibited the American embassy in Moscow from using radio for transmitting communications. The KGB had decided that it was easier to keep tabs on cable traffic over the telegraph lines than over radio channels. Reciprocally, the Soviet embassy in Washington was not permitted to use radio for transmissions either. Each side was, therefore, forced to use the international telegraph lines.

According to the report, the Soviet embassy's line had been interrupted several times during the past month for no apparent reason. Boss's memo instructed Victor to prepare the Authorization Order, to be signed by Andropov, authorizing deliberate interruptions of the Americans' Moscow embassy telegraph line. The interruptions were to be longer and more frequent than the Americans' had been, by way of dissuading them from any future interference. There was a secondary benefit. After every interruption, the opposition was forced to restart their cipher machines' key generators, and that meant an additional opportunity to intercept the critical initial cipher key. Normally, that opportunity came only once a day.

After he'd read both documents, Victor dropped in to see Boss. As usual, Boss was talking on two phones at once. He nodded to Victor and indicated for him to sit.

Ending both conversations with his customary brusqueness, he greeted Victor. "So, hello, stranger. You still look refreshed. You had a good time?"

"Yes, thank you," answered Victor. "It was a bit short, unfortunately."

That was enough to get Boss roaring. "What! Four weeks is too short for you? If that's your attitude, I'll make sure that in a month you'll be dreaming of one day's rest!"

"I'm sure you'll see to that regardless of my attitude." They both laughed.

Then Boss got down to business. "What do you make of the interference problem?"

"One thing bothers me. The report is not too convincing about the fact that the Americans deliberately disrupted our communications. Is Andropov convinced that there are solid grounds for retaliation?"

"Don't worry, he's already been briefed and is convinced. Besides, as far as we're concerned, the point is that we need them to restart their cipher machines as often as possible for the experiment we're conducting on the offensive side. We need as many starts as we can get."

"But what about the Americans? Aren't they likely to retaliate in response to our retaliation?"

"No. They always back down—they're easily intimidated. Besides, their press would eat them alive if we made a big stink over their retaliation. And they know it. No problem there."

"All right. Off I go, then."

Victor prepared the Order, sent it to Boss, and began the process of updating.

Victor got in touch with Valentin the next day. They met after work and strolled together to the Chistoprudnyy Boulevard—a part of the Boulevard Ring that circles the Moscow Central District. It was one of the best quiet places to be found in the heart of Moscow. Well-spaced benches were tucked discreetly in between the trees along the rich green plantings of the beautifully maintained boulevard. They found an empty bench and sat down—for anyone who was watching, simply two men relaxing in the golden late afternoon of the short Moscow summer. The old babushkas with children and the young mothers with infants in carriages had all gone home. It was still too early and too light for the young couples seeking a romantic haven. So Victor and Valentin had the street all to themselves.

They had traded inconsequential small talk en route to the Boulevard, but it had been half-hearted and had died away in anticipation of the real discussion at hand. They sat quietly together in the diminishing warmth of the setting sun, neither knowing where to begin.

At last, Victor broke the silence. "Valentin, you've been reckless lately. There's a restlessness about you, and unfortunately it's not gone unnoticed. Even our mutual friend the esteemed Party Secretary asked me whether you were having problems. Said he'd heard about a couple of stupid remarks you made. You don't need that kind of reputation. Now you say you want to share a few of your bright ideas with me. So. Go ahead. Fire and fall back." Victor hoped to diffuse the rapidly mounting tension between them.

"I think you already know most of it, Victor. The fact is that I just can't live like this anymore." His words eerily echoed Olga's in Mahindjauri.

"Nothing new has happened to you recently, as far as I know. What exactly are you referring to? What do you mean you can't 'live like this'?"

"Come on, you know perfectly well what I mean. Our whole system is totally corrupt. What's left of the original communist dream? Nothing, that's what. It's a farce, and it makes me sick. The whole idea behind Communism was the power of the proletariat—the common people. You tell me where the power is today—it's concentrated in the hands of a bunch of crooks who, at best, can be called bureaucrats. The people are powerless—the masses are simply fodder for exploitation. From age three you and I were taught that we live in the most democratic society in the world. But—and here's the trick—for someone like you and me, who are inside the system and operating it, it takes us till we're thirty to figure out that it's all crap. But by then we've sold out. We're well on our way to becoming a part of the ruling elite. So, we stifle our consciences with the privileges of our position and continue up the ladder along with the rest of the crooks. The real tragedy is that most of the people out there never realize the system's bullshit, and that they've been duped. They spend all their lives enthusiastically working themselves to death to support that very elite—us! Then they die, happily thinking that they've served a noble cause. Pah!"

Victor knew Valentin hadn't done his homework and was simply shooting from the hip. Victor tried to quiet him. "Look, I basically agree with you. I do. We both understand the situation. But it didn't happen yesterday either, so I don't quite understand what makes you so jumpy now."

Valentin would not be calmed. "Holy Christ, Victor, look what we're doing abroad. We've screwed up the whole world! We'd support any rat on earth if it furthered our own interests. These Third World scoundrels are already corrupt, and then we corrupt them even further, giving them more power to do far greater evil. We buy them villas while their own people are starving. Never mind that our own people don't have meat either. I'm sure we've sponsored more death in the world than anybody else. And most of us, like you and me, who are in a position to know about all of this, hide our heads in the sand, playing our roles in this vicious charade, all in the name of the noble goal of Communism."

Valentin's accusations put Victor squarely on the fence. On the one hand, although Valentin's knee-jerk analysis irritated him, he was fundamentally in agreement with his friend's basic argument. On the other, however, as a result of his Party rank, Victor was privy to the real story behind the symptoms Valentin was attacking. And that's exactly what they were—symptoms. Soviet maneuvering in Third World countries was actually much more cynical and politically calculating than his friend could imagine.

As Valentin ranted on, Victor's mind flashed back to a recent "Party Active" seminar he'd attended. Access to a meeting of this inner circle was one of the few real bonuses of his new Party job. The seminar had been given in the Hall of Columns, the grandiose space that occupied the first two floors of the Appendix. There must have been a shortage of space that particular morning, for the hall was rarely used, and then only for very formal State occasions. Even so, the place was absolutely spotless. Sterile. The gloomy cavern lined with huge marble columns seemed better suited for State funerals and dwarfed the little group of thirty or so Party Secretaries and their Deputies.

Victor found that at the very least these seminars were good for networking, and some were genuinely interesting. There was no protocol, no calling one another "comrade," and some of the discussions were very candid and informative. The reason was simple: everyone was a member of the Party Active, the inner circle of the Party. There was no need for impressing anybody or "playing at democracy." The main lecture was usually given by someone from the Central Committee or the Highest Party School, someone knowledgeable about what was going on at the top.

While the speech given at that particular seminar hadn't offered much in the way of revelation, one striking insight had come out at the end, during the question-and-answer period. Someone had asked, "It's quite clear we don't have too many ideological 'brothers' in the Third World. Our clients are of little real value to us economically or militarily, and yet we're spending billions of rubles and dollars to support them. Does it really pay off?"

If someone had asked such a direct, provocative question at a Party Organization meeting, he or she would most certainly have gotten into serious trouble. Within this elite group of the "ideologically firm," however, the question was acceptable.

The candor with which it was answered was equally acceptable. "Yes, it's true these so-called 'friends' aren't much use to us in and of themselves. However, you have to remember both our primary goal and our Main Enemy. Suppose we spend a million dollars a day to support Country X. We may indeed never get anything from Country X in return. But consider the alternative: if we don't support Country X and withdraw, the capitalist countries will move in immediately—the Americans leading the way. They could probably find a way to make ten million dollars a day in pure profit there, thus significantly improving their economic and strategic position. Our 'friends' in Country X would probably be better off, too—but who cares about those poor bastards? In the overall struggle we're much better off if we spend the one million than if we give the Americans a chance to make ten million, however difficult that may be for us economically." Pure defensive strategy. Nobody argued with it. How could they? The logic was unimpeachable.

Valentin's voice reached an alarming pitch, jerking Victor's focus back to the present. Valentin was ready to hit the climax of his diatribe. "Don't you see? This is about as far from the original idea of Communism as you can get. Forget what Marx said. In fact, it's modern Communism that is the opiate of the masses."

Victor couldn't disagree. But neither would he stoke Valentin's furnace further by sharing the knowledge he possessed. It made him acutely uncomfortable to hold out on his friend when his own conscience would not permit him to defend the system. At this point, however, his primary objective was to talk Valentin into a more rational frame of mind. "Valentin, please listen to me. You're right, and I agree with most of what you're saying. I too am trying to figure out what is to be done. I've already given the problem a lot of thought . . ."

"Bah, Victor, you and your thinking. How long are you going to think? Till you retire with your pension, or till you die? Not me. I can't stand it anymore. Do you realize that we—you and I, Victor—are contributing to the putrefaction? Considering who we are and what we do, I'd say our contribution is not insignificant, either. Has this ever occurred to you?"

Victor struggled not to rise to Valentin's personal attack. "Yes, it has—of course it has, Valentin. Now calm down, please . . ."

"I can't calm down, goddammit, when I'm ready to blow up." He paused, eyes burning, and added ominously, "Or to blow up somebody."

This remark startled Victor. "Look, we've got to be rational here. Try and be objective for a moment. Yes, I understand the reasons for your anger, and they're absolutely valid. I also understand that you feel deceived—betrayed, even—by the top people of the Party. Believe me, I feel the same way. I'm angry too. But anger is an emotion. It's irrational. If we let ourselves be guided by our emotions, we'll be doomed from the start. We must use our brains as coolly as possible. I guarantee you that the only way we have any chance at all is if we take a cold-blooded approach. We've been trained to be professional under pressure, haven't we?"

Valentin's rage seemed to have subsided for the moment, and he nodded. "OK, so let's be professional. At least our training won't be completely wasted. And, Victor, what I just said, you know, about blowing someone up? That was nonsense, of course. Sorry—I got carried away."

Victor nodded, relieved to see his friend on a more reasonable track. "All right. So, what do we want to achieve, and what are our options? But note that the first question has to be, *what do we want?* It makes no sense to discuss options until we can answer that."

"But, Victor, that's impossible."

"How do you know whether what you want is impossible until you've determined exactly what it is you want? Besides, nothing is impossible."

Valentin laughed, almost himself again, "Ah! Sorry, I forgot you specialize in doing the impossible."

"So?"

"So, ideally, I want the Communist Party to return to its original goals and values. Any problem with that?"

"Not really. But I must admit that there's something about those goals and values that still doesn't make sense to me. Something's missing, some part of the equation."

"What do you mean? I know you've been studying communist theory like crazy for quite a while. Surely you've got all there is to get by now? And besides, I don't see the point. The results are obvious enough."

"There really is a problem. I haven't yet gotten to the bottom of what's bothering me. Actually, there are two things. One is that communist theory is totally unstructured. It's not a theory in any meaningful sense. It's just a potpourri of essays; I don't understand why it hasn't been pulled together. It's, therefore, extraordinarily difficult to analyze, so much so that sometimes it seems as if all this incoherence is deliberate. The other problem has to do with the very beginning. It's about Lenin."

"What?"

"I don't quite understand what he meant by his famous 'unique blend of flexibility and firmness,' as he put it. And there are some very loose ends in his other fundamental statements as well. I need to study more of the historical context, which is not easy to grasp. Every time there's a shift in the powers that be, 'history' is changed at least ninety degrees. And each time that happens the new powers insist they've restored the truth as it was revealed by the principles of Lenin. Valentin, I have to find out what really happened, and how."

It was Valentin's turn to be concerned by Victor's passion. "You'd better be careful. You are questioning the fundamentals. That's serious business. Even with your Party job you could arouse suspicion."

Victor nodded ruefully, "I know. I went to the KGB general library last month—one of the best in town. When I asked for a history book published in the twenties, the librarian asked to see my ID. I was surprised, but immediately I knew exactly what was meant. 'Certainly,' I said, 'just find the book for me. Meanwhile, I'll browse around a bit.' As soon as she went to get the book, I left. I'll have to get those books from other sources."

"Christ, there are informers in every dissident group, you know that."

"I know. Don't worry, I have some reliable contacts. Besides, I've worked out a good approach. The dissidents are passionate missionaries. You don't have to ask a dissident for a prohibited book—you only have to express a mild interest in it, and they'll force it on you. When I accept a book, I make a great show of polite interest—and then return the book very quickly. That way, if anyone is curious about the transaction, it's obvious there hasn't really been enough time for me to actually read it. In fact, I read very fast. And then on top of that I have a fallback scenario. From time to time I raise concerns in the Party Active seminars about the serious danger from dissidents, emphasizing how much we underestimate them, and that we don't know enough about their propaganda. So, my interest can easily be explained anyway."

"OK, say that you answer your questions to your own satisfaction. Then could you agree with the goal I've stated?"

Victor thought for a moment, then replied, "Yes, with that absolutely critical provision, I could."

"So, provided your questions are answered, what can we do?"

"Not much for now. But don't think that we are alone. There must be others. Not everyone at the top is a scoundrel. We just have to find the right ones."

"Yeah, right!" was Valentin's sarcastic response. "Come on, Victor, you know perfectly well everyone's scared to death to even think about insurgence. And you want them to discuss it? Are you willing to speak up yourself?"

"Not necessarily. But there just has to be an alternative. To stand up like Sakharov and throw it in their faces is precisely what they want. They want those who disagree with their line to expose themselves. There's no danger for them in that. They know quite well how to deal with it. An ordinary person finds himself in a mental institution, at best. You and I would probably face a firing squad. And what would be achieved? Nothing. That's the main point I'm making."

"You're right, I guess. But still, I can't stand it. My conscience is making my life a living hell."

"More than anything else, you must resist your impulsiveness, Valentin. There is no margin for error here. None. If your nerve fails, you're lost, and you're much too good to be wasted. If we take our best shot and lose, OK, but it must not be for nothing."

"Frankly, Victor, I don't really see any chance. I'm awfully tempted to stand up, throw what I think of them in their faces, and just say the hell with it all."

"Great. Noble intentions, the *grande geste*. And tell me, who benefits?"

"I don't care!"

"That's where you're wrong! You've got to care. Aside from wasting your life, what would be changed? What would be accomplished? Nothing! If you don't like what's going on, you change it, right?"

"Sure."

"Then for Christ's sake let's try to accomplish a change. A few have taken the route you're talking about—or simply committed suicide. Quietly. With all due respect to them, what's been the result? What damage have they inflicted on the system they oppose? Admiration for their noble souls aside, I don't think it's the way to go. It's not effective."

"But, Victor, let me turn your words on you: you're not suggesting any course of action, either. You're just criticizing. What do you propose we do?"

"I've told you, I don't know—yet. We have to think. There must be a way."

"You sound logical, no doubt about it. But you can sit and think the days away, doing nothing, and be at the same point twenty years from now."

"Yes, of course, but on the other hand what you're suggesting isn't any better. Just quicker. Perhaps more satisfying in the short run, but that's all. Even the Japanese kamikazes died doing damage to their enemies. At least their deaths accomplished something."

Emotionally spent by this point, both Victor and Valentin felt the need to end the discussion. Valentin, more tired than Victor, acquiesced: "OK, you're right, I guess. At least in theory. Let's see if you can come up with something realistic."

"That's all I was trying to hammer into your head. Meanwhile, I want you to promise me that you'll sit tight and do nothing rash. OK? I want your word of honor on that."

"All right, Victor, you've got it." The debate temporarily shelved, Valentin changed the subject. "How's Olga? I hope she enjoyed your vacation."

"Oh, she did—yes, she's fine, thank you. Of course she missed her favorite pastime—haunting art museums. She was upset at missing two excellent exhibitions in Moscow. Now she's trying like mad to catch up. You know how she is."

Valentin laughed. "Yes, I can imagine. I admire people who serve such an obsession. I bet she knows every painting in every Moscow museum."

"I wouldn't be surprised if she did. She spends all her free time at museums and exhibitions."

"She's lucky." Valentin picked his words carefully. "Politically, she can sit on the sideline, while her talent and her soul are nourished by Fine Art."

Victor considered this provocation and concluded gently, "That's right." No one, absolutely no one, could be trusted with Olga's secret views.

They didn't discuss Valentin's family life, which was not particularly pleasant. Not only was there the friction between him and his father, now exacerbated by Valentin's present frame of mind, but his arranged marriage—customary among the ranks of the political and social elite—was a constant source of unhappiness. In addition, his recent agitation had led him to drink excessively. Victor was concerned about this latest symptom but could find no appropriate way to raise the issue. And he figured they'd covered enough ground for one discussion.

The two friends shared a few moments of silence together, then rose from their bench. The sun had set, and now it was time for the nocturnal denizens of the boulevard to emerge. Young lovers strolling together, oblivious to everything except their happiness. And of course their pursuit of amorous ambitions. A fleeting thought crossed Victor's mind: "Is the society we live in really of any consequence? Who the rulers are? The evils they perpetrate? Does it matter at all?" He immediately answered his own seditious question: Yes, of course it matters! I can bet that many of these kids' parents were tortured and killed by the Stalinist gang—the slogans glorifying the "Father of Peoples" ringing in their ears even as they died. History might well be on the verge of repeating itself now. No! This has to be avoided at all costs. Something must be done. But what? And how? By whom?

These questions needed answers. And soon.

CHAPTER

14

ON FRIDAY AFTERNOON OLGA was waiting for Victor by the car in the KGB parking lot. On the way home they stopped to pick up their four-year old daughter from her kindergarten.

While Olga went inside to fetch Elena, Victor waited near the car and watched from a distance. He loved to see the two of them together and broke into a smile as he saw them bursting out of the building and laughing as they ran through the playground. As Elena scrambled into the car, Olga caught Victor's eyes. For a split second her face was grim, with no trace of playground merriment. Then, as if a mask dropped back into place, she laughed again as she turned to settle Elena into her seat. Soon they were back on the road. Fighting rush-hour traffic pushed the strange moment with Olga to the back of Victor's mind.

That evening, after she'd put Elena to bed, Olga was distant, preoccupied. Victor knew something had upset her, and her silence indicated that it was something they couldn't discuss inside. Victor dropped his earlier bravado about disarming the bugs when he needed to. Their policy now was no sensitive conversations in the apartment. It was strictly observed— now was not the time to take chances.

He proposed a morning walk in the park. "A good way to clear our heads, don't you think?"

Olga nodded. "Yes, I think that would be a good idea."

By ten, Elena was happily competing with the other children on the swing set in the park across the courtyard, seeing who could go highest. Olga and Victor sat together on a nearby bench.

"Victor . . . ?" She paused.

"What's up?"

"Victor, you wouldn't believe what a small boy in Elena's class said when he saw me yesterday, inside the kindergarten. It touches on something I've wanted to talk to you about."

This was unusual. Olga wasn't often rattled by the things Elena and her friends came up with.

"What was it?"

"You remember that I was carrying one of those foreign plastic bags? The kind that are popular now, difficult to get. You know how mine has 'KENT' written on it? Well, the boy pointed right at it, then cried out, 'Capital bag! That's bad!' Can you imagine? He can't even pronounce the word 'capitalist,' and he's already psychologically primed for a witch hunt."

"I don't see why you're so surprised, Olga. So-called 'political education' starts very early. Especially at the KGB kindergarten—the teachers must be terrified of being accused of not teaching the Party line correctly. I'm sure those kids start hearing Party propaganda by the time they're three. I certainly did—and I wasn't even in a KGB kindergarten."

This clearly was not the response Olga had hoped for. Her voice rose in anger. "Victor, I can't believe this doesn't bother you. Our own Elena—she's just a child, and she's already being brainwashed into a system that we've both agreed is wrong."

Victor was uncomfortable under her attack. "I know, Olga. I know," he said gently. He didn't like being put in the position of defending mind control. On the other hand, there was a substantial and pragmatic quid pro quo. He tried that argument. "Olga, just consider the alternative—we're very lucky to have such a place for Elena. It's a privilege, you know."

The KGB's kindergarten was indeed superior to any other kindergarten in Moscow, except, of course, the one for the children of the families and staff of the Central Committee. Its attractive building and playground, the clean facilities, and the excellent medical supervision made the place the envy of those parents who didn't have access to it—among those who knew about it. Along with the exemplary care and attention the children received, there was its unique flexibility. During the week the children could either go home at night or stay over, whichever the parents wished. During the three summer months the school moved to a splendid dacha in one of the most beautiful locations in the Moscow countryside, an exceptional amenity. Naturally, there was top-notch security for these children—all sons and daughters of officers in the KGB. And all for a nominal fee.

Olga studied him soberly, then asked, "Victor, how do you justify a privilege that comes at such a price? It's a wonderful place, to be sure, and it's certainly convenient for us, but Elena's being programmed there. Can we close our eyes to that? No. We must not. It's wrong, terribly wrong!"

"Olga, I understand why you're upset. But you have to look at this calmly and objectively—for Elena's sake. There is no school where Party propaganda isn't taught. That's a fact of life. It is also a fact of our life that we get to send Elena to one of the best facilities in the country. Can you suggest any alternatives? I can assure you there are none at this moment that would do any better by her. Or us."

Olga was visibly frustrated by the impasse, and she made no effort to conceal her irritation.

This was too much for Victor. He was angered by her persistence. Also by the way she'd managed to get right under his skin, once again calling him on the same moral conundrums he'd been wrestling with. The privileges that came with his position were more important to him than he wished to admit. And anyway, would they in fact be better off without them? And for what in exchange?

"Yes, it sickens me to think of Elena's being fed Party rhetoric when she's defenseless." He allowed his voice to rise, "But I refuse to act impulsively or irrationally, Olga. To do so would not only jeopardize her, but us as well." Then he spoke quietly, determined not to lose control—of himself or her. "By no means have I forgotten what we agreed." Returning to a softer, measured tone, he hoped to reassure her. "Have you noticed what I'm reading, Olga? *History* by Solovyev. One of the many books I've been studying since our return from Mahindjauri. You have to trust me. Let me think, let me complete the study I set out to do. And in the meantime, we have to leave things as they are. Do you understand?"

To his intense relief he saw that she seemed to agree. She met his gaze for a moment, then dropped her eyes and shrugged.

"Victor, I'm sorry. But to hear that propaganda coming out of a child's mouth . . . it's hard."

Victor was silent. There was nothing else to say. She had a point. So did he. Olga sighed and stood. She called to Elena, and they walked home in silence.

They'd planned to take Elena to the circus on Saturday afternoon. Her first, promised months ago as a special treat. And they were going to the Old Moscow Circus, too. The small one with the genuine circus spirit. Its intimacy was magic—every seat seemed to be ringside—the performers really interacted with the audience, and the lions were so close you could count their teeth! Like many of his fellow Muscovites, Victor preferred it to the huge New Circus—a state-of-the-art extravaganza that was currently the boast of the Moscow impresarios. As far as he was concerned, that vast arena was devoid of circus spirit. One sat safely out of reach of the clowns' shenanigans, needing binoculars to see the acrobats and imagination to smell the animals.

Just as they were headed out the door, the phone rang. Victor's inclination was to leave and let it ring. Discipline prevailed, however, and he answered it.

"Victor, hello. How are you doing? You're not going anywhere, are you?" Boss.

The only reason for Boss to call on a weekend was that he needed Victor right away. Victor followed the standard etiquette. "No, nothing in particular."

"Good. I'd hate to upset your plans, and I need to talk to you. Sorry I didn't mention it yesterday. You can't really talk during the week, you know. An interruption every five minutes."

"Of course."

"So. How long will it take you to get to the office?"

"About forty minutes."

"I'll be in my office in an hour. See you then." That was it. He hung up. Victor, still holding the receiver, looked at Olga and shrugged. Although she was used to Victor's abruptly shifting plans, this time there was a shadow of fear in her eyes.

In silence, Victor drove Olga and Elena down to the Central District and dropped them off at the Old Circus on Tsvetnoy Boulevard, not far from his office. Olga said she'd call him there after the show, to see if they could drive home together. What she didn't say was that she'd really be calling to see if everything was all right.

Boss was already waiting in his office when Victor got there. Without preamble he asked, "What do you know about China?"

"Not much, just the standard stuff."

"I mean, do you understand what's going on there?" Boss looked very serious.

"Not really," replied Victor cautiously, wondering if Boss was testing him. And why.

He was. He broke into a laugh. "Don't worry, nobody else does either." Boss paused. Victor knew that he was organizing his thoughts. He wasn't sure what Boss was up to, so he simply waited for him to continue.

Finally, he said, "What I mean is this: where the Chinese are concerned, we're in the dark—in every sense. We don't understand them politically. We don't know what they're thinking. We haven't got a clue what they're up to—what their intentions toward us are. They've shut us out for years. Very effectively. First CD intelligence has been totally inadequate. It's fiendishly difficult to operate against them from the embassy. Travel there is severely restricted. I'm ashamed to admit it, but right now we don't have a single Illegal inside China. In short, we have no reliable sources of inside information. We don't seem to be able to get even our toe in the door. The situation is intolerable."

Victor was really surprised. He had never seen Bosik at a loss before, and it had never occurred to him that the KGB machine could be frustrated to such a degree by anyone. "I had no idea that the situation was that bad. What about the intercepts?"

"Pure trivia. Our 'Crab'—the intercept station in the embassy—doesn't produce much. Just some military communications. Bits and pieces from their embassy here."

"And our own security? I haven't heard of any problems up to now." Victor had not been involved in the China operation.

"We're going to install the new communications system in the Beijing embassy, but it may well be a complete waste of time. We don't know what we're up against. We don't even know if they're attacking our conversations and our communications. And if they are, we haven't the slightest clue how. The bottom line is that it's absolutely crucial for us to answer these questions."

"What's to be done?"

"That's why you're here."

"I see" was all Victor said. It still wasn't clear why Boss had called him in. He couldn't read him.

"The technical team has just left for Beijing—routine debugging exercise. They've gone there every other year and haven't found anything yet. Not likely to come up with much this time, either. I want you to go and see what you can find out. If the Chinese are attacking our communications, or eavesdropping on our conversations, they must be using unconventional methods. This could be an interesting experience for you, Victor." His dark eyes glinted as he dangled the bait of doing the impossible. He knew his man.

Victor's mind was already beginning to race. He murmured noncommittally, "Interesting."

"There's one more aspect to your mission. Probably the most important. Andreyev was discussing it in the Central Committee. Our hypothesis is this: the technical policy of a country's intelligence service follows the style of the politics at the top. So, given a total lack of information on the latter, it should still be possible to determine it by analyzing the former. Right?

"For example, to make a gross generalization, on the offense, the American policy to a large extent is to avoid confrontations and risks. So, technically they much prefer to operate from an embassy, avoiding the risk of being caught and being trashed by their own press and liberal politicians. On the other hand, the Israelis pull stunts all the time. For them, virtue lies in open political defiance of everyone. Hence, they are as blunt in their technical operations as they are in their policy. Not even being good technically, they still take all the risks they can find. They don't mind taking a chance or being caught."

"OK, I follow you."

"I thought this approach would interest you. That was our main reason for choosing you for this mission. You'll have to look at things with the broadest possible perspective. Keep your mind open to every possibility."

"OK, I get the idea. How much time do I have to prepare?"

"You won't find much information on China to study here, believe me. But you'll have to wait for a visa anyway. A couple of weeks should do."

"Right."

"Remember: examine everything. Take nothing for granted. Look for correlations whether things seem related or not. Find the invisible connections. And, Victor, this assignment comes from the very top. Good luck."

"Thank you."

"There's one more thing. Unlike most of your missions, there's no risk for you here. Absolutely none. If you win, you're a hero. If nothing turns up, it's OK. We'll be no worse off than we already are."

Victor left and went back to his office. He was deep in thought when the phone rang. Olga told him that the circus was over. He collected his car and picked them up, tacitly reassuring Olga that all was copacetic.

During the drive home he was silent as Elena bubbled with excitement about all that they had seen. She'd been enthralled. Out of the blue she suddenly asked, "Papa, are you a clown?"

Victor and Olga looked at each other and swallowed their laughter. It was the first light moment between them since their discussion the day before. He managed to keep a straight face as he answered, "No, darling, not exactly."

Elena persisted, unwilling to give up the idea of her father's somehow being connected to the afternoon's magic. "But, at least you work in a circus, don't you?"

Victor was about to say, "I certainly do" for Olga's benefit, but he thought better of it. Chances were the car was bugged. And besides, a child's boast reaching the wrong ears could lead to some serious misunderstandings. All he said was, "No, darling, I'm afraid not."

Her excitement gave way to profound disillusionment—her first disappointment with her father. In the car's mirror Victor saw her eyes brimming, her lower lip out, and he tried to save the situation. He quickly added, "But I do know a lot of clowns." For sure.

A good move. Elena perked up at that idea. "You do? Oooh! I want to know them, too. Can I meet them, Daddy? Can I?" Olga was suddenly serious, watching Victor closely.

The smile died on his lips as he nodded ruefully. "You will, my darling. I'm sure you will. Lots of them."

His preparation for the trip to China produced no surprises. His research in other related departments pretty much confirmed what he'd learned from Boss's scant briefing. Not only was there virtually no information on Chinese intercept methods, there was no hard analysis in the files of Chinese intelligence priorities, nor anything significant about their modus operandi.

He did come across a grim rumor, though—strictly inside stuff—concerning Khrushchev and China. Around 1960 the Soviet leader had been desperate to save the deteriorating relationship between the U.S.S.R. and China. Characteristically acting on an impulse—according to the rumor—he'd ordered that the list of all native KGB agents in China be released to the Chinese government. Some of these agents were third-generation spies, whose grandparents had worked for Russian Intelligence even before the 1917 Revolution. It was a network that had taken more than a century to create, and allegedly, everyone on the list had been hanged within a week. In other words, Khrushchev had given away the store, wiping out the entire Russian intelligence network in China with one stroke. It was inconceivable to Victor. If this story was true, it meant that Khrushchev had committed an act of the highest kind of treason. During his preparations, Victor tried to discover whether there was any way to substantiate the rumor. He asked people who were in a position to know. Every person he queried had been resolutely tight-lipped about the matter. Their non-answers all carried the same warning: "No comment—drop the subject. Now." The mystery remained unsolved. Victor knew perfectly well that Khrushchev had revealed top strategic secrets during more than one of his long-winded speeches. He was fairly sure the allegation about China was well-founded, but he knew that his interest in the rumor had more to do with his own political curiosity than with its relevance to his assignment. Whether or not it was true, the fact was that there was no existing Russian spy network in China. He stopped asking.

When his visa finally came through, Victor had exhausted the Center's sources of information on China. He rarely left on an assignment without feeling like a student before an exam—not quite ready, wishing desperately for one or two more days' preparation. Not this time. He knew that two more days, or two more weeks, would add little to what he'd already learned.

Very soon after the Aeroflot jet landed at the Beijing airport Victor sensed that he'd dropped into a completely different world, and not a very friendly one at that. The moment the plane came to a stop a few hundred yards from the terminal, it was surrounded by soldiers with AK-47s. As the passengers exited the plane, the soldiers herded them toward waiting buses and packed them in tighter than Moscow commuters at rush hour. There was no anger on the soldiers' faces, just an impersonal determination to execute orders. Once inside the airport the official formalities were smoothly carried out—though still under heavy guard.

As usual, Victor was met by the embassy's Security Officer. During the ride to the embassy in the black Soviet Volga, Victor studied the surroundings with great curiosity. It was a gross understatement to say that everything was drab. The first surprise was the absence of trees. There was no grass either. Everything was dry—parched, like a desert—and covered with a thick layer of dust. The shabby, ramshackle buildings advertised a profound poverty, reproachfully contradicting the garish roadside billboards with their grandiose images in familiar socialist-realist style. Although Victor did not read Chinese, he could easily imagine how the pictographs would translate—inspirational Party slogans, communist sound-bites. Propaganda was propaganda.

Closer to the center of Beijing, the conditions began to change. The asphalt surface of the roads became smoother. The layer of dust thinned out. Clearly some effort had gone into maintenance. As they passed through the center of the city, Victor observed that Stalin's and Mao's architectural tastes had been surprisingly similar. He wondered if one's political views necessarily had any bearing on one's aesthetics. Then he remembered Boss's urgent admonition. The point wasn't to look for the similarities, like a sentimental tourist, but to find the essential differences between the two cultures.

The embassy's compound was huge, about seventy acres, and surrounded by a high wall. The grounds were guarded on the outside by a full regiment of the Chinese army. The Security Officer explained that because of the current tension between the Chinese and the Soviets the embassy even had a special complement of thirty plainclothes Border Guards. Embassy guards swung open the heavy iron gates.

Victor felt that he had entered yet another world. In startling contrast to the dreary desolation he had just ridden through, these grounds were lush and verdant. Two large ponds and a canal sustained a number of trees that were more than a hundred years old. These provided precious shade and created a very pleasant microclimate during the dreadful Beijing summer days when temperatures frequently soared over a hundred dusty degrees. The Ambassador's villa, with its rose garden and tennis court, was on an island in one of the ponds.

For everyone except the Russians in their Eden, Beijing truly was a Forbidden City of wretched summers, harsh winters, and endless dust. A saying of the local diplomatic corps had it that in Beijing one eats one brick's worth of dust a year. Not surprisingly, the Soviet embassy was the object of profound envy throughout the entire diplomatic corps. Not even the top Chinese government officials could dream of such accommodations. The reason was that the compound had formerly been the site of the Russian Orthodox Church Mission in China and had been meticulously maintained for well over a century. In grotesque counterpoint was the embassy building itself. It was much more recent, built around 1950, similar to the Warsaw embassy in its Stalinist Imperial style, except that this grey building was even more massive and ponderous.

Victor already knew that the KGB Resident, General Mikhail Markovich Turchak, was reputed to be one of the most brilliant officers in the KGB. Beijing had to be one of the most difficult intelligence postings in the world, especially because there was no functioning network of Illegals. Victor'd been particularly intrigued when, during his preparations for this assignment, he'd come across the fact that Turchak's background was similar to his father's. Like Ivan, Turchak had lost his parents during the Revolution and had also been raised in an orphanage. He'd also deliberately avoided the easy choice of a criminal career and had been saved and guided by his natural thirst for knowledge.

Turchak impressed Victor right away as one of the dozen most intelligent people he'd ever met, although he made no obvious effort to do so. Turchak was not interested in playing the usual intimidation game of rank and connections with Victor. His ego didn't need the stroking.

After Victor had outlined his assignment, Turchak said, "Welcome aboard. That's quite a mission you've been given. I'd like to know the answer to the big question myself. I'm afraid there are many things we Russians don't understand about this country. I'll do my best to enlighten you as far as I'm able." A modest statement, considering that it came from a man whom Victor knew to be one of the most knowledgeable experts on China in the U.S.S.R.

"Are you at all familiar with Chinese history and culture?"

"Not really. I've read about the history of China, of course, but only in rather general terms. I went over it again before coming here. I couldn't find anything of much help in Moscow—only the superficial stuff, you know, for tourists and business visitors. And, of course, now that Sino-Soviet relations are deteriorating, endless propaganda."

Turchak shrugged. "I'm not surprised. Well, I'd recommend that you start with the basics. Any objections?"

"Not at all. I was thinking along the same lines."

"OK. I'll give you a couple of guys who are well versed in Chinese culture and history." He hesitated for a split second, then added, "Let's say, reasonably well-versed." He was decidedly a perfectionist. A superb linguist, Turchak also spoke and wrote Chinese fluently. He continued, "They'll show you around, whenever they're free from operations. Also, there are a few really good internal embassy reports on China. They'll be helpful. My secretary will find them for you."

"It's most kind of you."

"When you feel you're ready to talk, drop by."

Victor spent a couple of hours in getting acquainted with his two guides, and together they worked out his itinerary. The reports Turchak had promised were delivered. Before he allowed himself to settle down and study in earnest, Victor paid a visit to the chief of the debugging team from the Center.

Victor was lucky. The guys on the team really knew what they were doing. He asked the chief to notify him of any doubt or hunch, no matter how far-fetched it seemed, and to operate on maximum alert—as if they were in the United States instead of China. The team was eager to cooperate.

Victor then went to visit a KGB Line X, technical intelligence officer, whose cover was the job of Deputy Head of the Trade Mission. Victor asked him to find out everything he could concerning Chinese purchases of any equipment that could conceivably be used for interceptions and bugging. Fortunately, only a handful of companies in the world produced quality equipment of that type.

Satisfied with his first day's work, Victor returned to his quarters in a modest apartment house to read the embassy's reports. To his surprise, the general had also sent along two rare Russian books on Chinese culture and history—published before 1949—from his personal library. Victor read late into the night.

The next few days were fascinating. His guides took him on an exhaustive tour of the highlights of Chinese culture in Beijing. Chinese counter-intelligence was obviously puzzled: who was this Russian diplomat, and why was he doing nothing but touring the city? The surveillance teams followed a hundred feet behind by car, ten feet behind on foot. When Victor remarked that they seemed a little too obvious to be very effective, his guide replied, "Don't be fooled—you can't see the ones who are really watching you. These guys want you to believe that they're a very simple, unsophisticated service, doing everything straightforward and by the book. But that's not true. They're actually quite good."

Victor was surprised to learn that crime is practically nonexistent in China. During one sortie he learned why. He and his guide-guard came across a huge crowd gathered in a large square. The people were pressing around a truck with its sides down. Three young Chinese men were standing on the bed. Their heads had been crudely shaved, and their hands were tied behind their backs. Ropes around their necks held two-by-three-foot placards with large pictographs scrawled boldly. When Victor asked his guide what was going on, he was told that the men were criminals. Assuming their offense must have been serious, Victor then asked what their punishment was likely to be.

"They'll probably be executed. The Chinese don't fool with prisons much. They can't afford them. The best these guys can hope for is ten to fifteen years of hard labor. And believe me, hard labor in this country is really hard. Before they're punished, though, they're shamed. That's what this is all about. They're usually carted around from town to town for quite a while, humiliated in the squares. It's an effective deterrent, I must say."

At Victor's request they got out of the car and walked to the rear of the crowd. The guide spoke fluent Chinese and asked one of the spectators what the three men were guilty of. Victor was surprised at the answer. "They stole money and have been sentenced to die. If they're lucky, their sentence will be reduced to fifteen years in a labor camp. But they really deserve to die." Victor asked how much money was involved, figuring they must have stolen a considerable sum. The answer came as a shock: "Ten dollars between the three of them."

Seeing Victor's reaction, the guide explained, "It's all a matter of how you look at it. You see, these people feel that stealing is stealing. The act is morally wrong regardless of what or how much has actually been taken. This kind of harsh and very public punishment consistently applied over the centuries is the reason why there's practically no crime in China."

Victor said nothing. *I suppose on a moral continuum, stealing ten dollars is more serious than making a joke at the expense of a head of State. It's an open question as to which system of values is more civilized. And which is less.*

As Victor's Beijing education continued, he began to notice other remarkable things about the Chinese. They were incredibly hard workers. He respected them for that. Even more impressive was the fact that they could work the way they did even though it was clear that most of them were suffering from malnutrition. It was also obvious that the military and the police fared much better. It didn't take Victor long to be able to distinguish them from ordinary civilians. It wasn't a question of a uniform instead of the standard blue or green work robes. Sleek cheeks and an obviously healthy appearance were the giveaway. When Victor was told what the diet of the average Chinese worker consisted of, he was appalled. He doubted that a Russian worker could survive six months on such meager rations—or if any Russian could. He was told that the situation in the provinces was much worse.

With practically no mechanization, the Chinese workers resembled ants in the construction sites. They worked incessantly, trying their best, but they were not physically capable of lifting or carrying half of what an average Russian worker could easily do.

The effects of widespread malnutrition were also evident in the traffic laws. For example, a driver was permitted to continue through an intersection without stopping if he was within one hundred feet of it at the time the light turned red. This rule compensated for the average reaction time of Chinese drivers. At last, Victor fully appreciated the story a fighter-pilot friend of his had told him long ago: During the Korean War, Soviet instructors had trained the Chinese pilots. In the early days of the program there had been quite a number of crashes for which no cause could be determined. Each, however, had occurred shortly after a sharp maneuver and had been preceded by an abrupt loss of communications. The suggestion was made that perhaps the Chinese pilots were more susceptible to G-forces than the Russian pilots and were simply blacking out.

The question then was why. As an experiment, the Chinese pilots were put on Russian rations. The crashes stopped within a month. The Chinese government had taken the lesson to heart. Hence, well-fed police and military personnel.

Victor frequented the so-called "Friendship" store—the Chinese shop open only to foreigners. The merchandise he found there was far superior to the customary souvenir stock. The objects were truly representative of traditional Chinese arts and crafts. Victor was astonished at the quality, and his eyes were opened to the meticulousness, patience, and skill of Chinese craftsmen. He noted that the same skill and painstaking attention to detail evidenced in their crafts would be of significant value to the intercept business.

But there were many skills they did not possess. Peter, one of his guides, told him of an acutely embarrassing example. "When Chairman Mao died three years ago, the Chinese wanted to have him embalmed in the same manner the Soviets had preserved the body of Lenin. But no one in China knew the technique. For political reasons, they couldn't turn to the Soviets for technical assistance. They knew that the Soviets had helped the North Vietnamese preserve Ho Chi Minh. The Chinese assumed the Soviets had trained the Vietnamese in the art. So they asked Hanoi for help. The Vietnamese had not in fact been trained by the Soviets. As a matter of fact, the Soviets used that as a point of political leverage—the preservation process required continuous maintenance, so the Soviet morticians were indispensable. Apparently, not wishing to offend or disappoint Beijing on the one hand, and not wishing to disclose their dependence on the Soviets on the other, the North Vietnamese sent an ordinary embalmer to Beijing. He performed his work as usual, and Mao looked appropriately serene and lifelike. But alas, as the weeks went by, the Chairman began to change color, and his skin began to wrinkle. When he shriveled and turned a ghastly hue, the authorities had to remove him from public display."

Victor was professionally fascinated by a famous tourist attraction at the Forbidden City—two pagodas surrounded by a brick wall several feet thick. The wall enclosed a circular yard about one hundred and fifty feet in diameter. Since ancient times, this facility had been used for formal receptions, mostly diplomatic. The trick was that from one specific place near the wall one could clearly hear a whisper from anywhere inside the courtyard. *One high-class job! Christ, these people knew more about acoustics centuries ago than we do now! They got their results without the fancy equipment or complicated formulas that we're so proud of.*

After he'd done his homework thoroughly and had sniffed around Beijing for a couple of weeks, absorbing everything he could, searching for any direct or indirect clues about possible approaches to Chinese intelligence, Victor felt ready to approach General Turchak again. He found the general friendly and encouraging.

"Well, what have you been up to, Victor? Getting a feel for this country?"

"I must say, it's one hell of a place. It's unlike any place I've ever been. I'm lucky to have the chance to visit it under these conditions. A once-in-a-lifetime experience."

"I'm glad you appreciate that. I like this country very much. And you're right, it is unique. The culture's different, the psychology's different. You'd need ten lives to study it adequately, to understand it. This country is my hobby. Luckily it happens to coincide with my job."

"Well, to open this discussion, let me say that I've picked up on a few things that might be relevant to our problem. For instance, from the merchandise I observed in the Friendship store, I got the distinct impression that the level of Chinese craftsmanship, and their obsessive attention to detail, would suggest that they are more than capable of doing a fine mechanical job in interception. The workmanship bears witness to incredible patience. Would you say that's a safe assumption?"

"You know from your reading they're famous for it."

"Well and good. Now, I asked for records of Chinese transactions involving equipment that could conceivably be used for either interception or eavesdropping. These purchase reports indicated that the Chinese have been buying audio intercepting, recording, and analyzing equipment on a regular basis from the two top international manufacturers for years. Mostly indirectly, using Chinese nationals all over the world. One peculiar detail was that most of the purchases have been large pieces of equipment—items designed for use in a lab. Another peculiarity was the complete lack of evidence of any electromagnetic intercept equipment."

The general was silent, listening closely.

Victor continued, "I'm relieved by what turned up in the reports concerning their work in the electromagnetic field—or rather, what didn't turn up. There were no indications of any related purchases."

"Did that surprise you?"

"No, it didn't. As a matter of fact, their lack of interest in the field of electromagnetic interception is easy enough to understand. The level of Chinese technology in the field makes it practically impossible for them to compete with us, or with the other technologically advanced countries, for that matter. The embassy seems to be clean—at least in that respect."

General Turchak interrupted him, "What do you mean 'at least in that respect'? Have you found something somewhere else?"

Victor took a breath and dived into the heart of the problem. "The thing that has me stymied is in the area of acoustics. Let's go back to the purchase records. They indicate that the Chinese are buying the same acoustic equipment that we are—highest quality. But no sensors, no miniature microphones. And they certainly haven't got the technology to manufacture them themselves. So why are they buying the other acoustic equipment if they don't have sensors and microphones? It just doesn't make sense."

"This is very interesting. I've never looked at the problem from that angle."

"Well, I must admit, I'm really puzzled. I've visited that reception courtyard with the two pagodas in the Forbidden City five times now— you know, the ancient one in the reception yard with the unbelievable acoustics. It's most impressive. I wonder if there isn't something there. Something that could help us crack this problem."

The general smiled, "Oh, that old tourist conversation piece. Neat trick, isn't it?"

"Actually, Mikhail Markovich, there's more to it than that. I managed to use a calibrated microphone to measure the structure's conduction of an acoustic signal. That ancient system is technically flawless. The attenuation is almost zero, and . . ."

Turchak leapt to his feet, interrupting Victor, "Are you aware, young man, that you are not permitted to operate personally? At least not according to my instructions."

Victor immediately affected a guilty demeanor and hastily tried to downplay the incident. "Oh, well, it was just a minor thing, you know. Nothing risky, really."

"You can cut that crap right now. This is a serious violation, and you know it. You should have asked to have someone else run the test for you."

"I just wanted to make sure that it was properly executed. It's a pretty tricky procedure, especially in the field."

"So what! The last thing I need is for you to create trouble. The Chinese are totally paranoid about foreign services operating here—did you know that? They are perfectly capable of grabbing you, regardless of any diplomatic immunities—which, by the way, they don't give a damn about in the first place. They could keep you locked up for a day or two, and do you understand what that would mean for you and me?"

Victor nodded.

"Did your guard know what you were up to?"

"No." That was true.

"Damned blind idiot! I'll remember that. Who was with you?"

"Peter. Mikhail Markovich, it wasn't his fault. I've told you, I was very careful. Even you wouldn't have noticed, I can assure you, with all due respect. Look, nothing happened, so there's nothing to blame him for."

Victor was genuinely sorry he'd mentioned the incident. He certainly could understand the general's reaction. From his point of view, Victor had placed them all at risk—one false move and the Chinese would have made a circus out of it. Turchak's career would have been wrecked. Even though Victor had his own priorities to consider, out of deference he'd have to be more careful.

For now, he had to get back into Turchak's good graces. Victor broke the uneasy silence. "I'm really sorry. I shouldn't have done it. It wasn't a very smart thing to do. Chalk it up to the act of a Russian bull in the China shop."

Turchak was not amused. "Look, I'll let you off this one time, but I want your word that nothing of this nature will happen again."

"It won't. You have my word."

The general relented. "All right, how can I help you out?"

"I need to know about anything you can think of that might be even remotely relevant. For instance, have you ever had any reason to suspect that information might be leaking to the Chinese? Speaking off the record, of course."

Turchak thought for a while and then said slowly, "Perhaps. I took part in the negotiations concerning our Permanent Government Delegation here. Deputy Minister Kapitsa is the head of it." Victor nodded, and the general continued.

"It's just a gut feeling, nothing more. Instinct, if you will, but on many occasions I felt that the Chinese knew more than they should. Funny, that feeling intensified when we changed our position in the negotiations. There's no way to prove anything."

"I understand."

"And there's one more thing. The famous Marchenko case. Are you familiar with it?"

"Not very. That was the Far Neighbors' case, not ours." Far Neighbors was the code name for the GRU, the military, just as Close Neighbors was the code name for the KGB.

"Yes, and the Far Neighbors got a raw deal, too. The Chinese considered it a significant victory for their counterintelligence. Briefly, the Far Neighbors had an agent, a Chinese. Quite a promising development. To be precise, they were about to finalize his recruitment. They goofed—made the operation too complicated. It was late at night. Three of them—a man and two women—set off for town. The women were in the back seat, and Marchenko, their control, was lying on the floor of the car under their feet. They dropped him off. No surveillance was detected. Marchenko, dressed like a typical Chinese worker, walked to the meeting place. It was late at night. The meeting place was under a bridge. When Marchenko approached the Chinese agent, the show started—literally. The Chinese turned on high-intensity movie lights—installed underneath the bridge specifically for the occasion. Both men were arrested as commercial movie cameras recorded the whole scene. Crazy stuff. Only the Chinese would do such a thing. Major embarrassment, you know. Caught red-handed. Preserved on 35-mm film for posterity, no less."

Victor was reminded of the scene in the square where the authorities had exposed the three young, shaven-headed thieves to public ridicule.

"When the case was analyzed, blame for the failure was ascribed to the fact that the agent had been a double right from the start. It was rumored, however, that that was not the real story. My own hunch was that the Chinese turned the agent around in the middle of the affair. The tricky detail is that the operation was discussed in the room adjacent to the living quarters of the Head of the Permanent Government Delegation here in the embassy. And that room was not soundproof."

Like a hound, Victor smelled a fox. There was a silence.

The general cut into Victor's train of thought, "By the way, how's the debugging team doing?"

"As before, they've found nothing. They haven't even put a question mark on anything. By the way, this team is an exceptionally good one, and I asked them to proceed as if on triple alert. Still nothing. You'll have the report in a couple of days."

The general dismissed that idea. "Pah! Those reports. If you read through all the rhetoric, you'll see that all they're saying is, 'We didn't find anything.' Nobody says, 'There are no bugs.'"

Victor smiled. "You're right. On the other hand, everyone plays the same game. You won't tell the Center, 'There is no coup coming in China,' you'll say, 'We couldn't find any evidence indicating a potential coup.'"

Turchak laughed, "OK, we're even."

Victor then asked the general for his sense of how far the Chinese would go to get something they wanted.

The general's response surprised Victor. "They'll go as far as it takes. They don't seem to mind jumping through any number of hoops to accomplish a goal. You mentioned the patience evident in their crafts? Let me give you an example of how it's applied in our business. Recently the East Germans discovered how the Chinese got into their embassy. A spectacular penetration. The Chinese had dug a tunnel under the basement of the embassy, then cut through and made a manhole in the floor of the basement. The craftsmanship was so good that when the cover was in place, it was invisible. When they wanted to get in, the Chinese simply lifted the concrete cover with a hydraulic mechanism in the tunnel.

"Then, they cut the same thing in the floor above, working from the basement at night. Again, the cover was undetectable, even from the surface: the edges perfectly matched the parquet of the floor. Now, here's how they used the setup. At night they lifted the basement cover and sent a man in. Then, they closed that cover, and the man set poles between the first and the second cover. They jacked up the basement cover and so opened the first floor cover, and the man climbed up onto the first floor."

"Christ!"

"Wait, this is the part of the story that speaks to your question. The whole operation was done just to get into the Ambassador's office. But secret papers were never left there overnight, and they'd known that. The office was secured on the outside, so they couldn't go anywhere else in the embassy—which they'd also known. The whole setup was just to get access to scraps of paper in the wastebasket and to the Ambassador's official calendar!"

Victor was astonished. He didn't say a word.

Turchak said, "Now, perhaps, you have a better sense of the ends to which they are prepared to go?"

"Yes, much better," he paused, "Why didn't I see anything on that in the Center?"

"The East Germans didn't notify us. Perhaps they found it too embarrassing. This story was recently obtained from our agent in their embassy."

By the time Victor left Turchak, he had an uneasy feeling about this assignment. He had no frame of reference for dealing with this adversary. He realized that for once he just might fail. He knew that Bosik's rhetoric about no risk was just that—rhetoric. They were all on the line: Andreyev, Bosik, Victor. This failure could backfire as well as any other. Another crazy problem.

The next day Victor got the debugging team together in a soundproof room.

"Guys, we've got some more work to do here."

One of them responded, "Come on, Victor, we've gone over this place with a fine-tooth comb, and we've found zero. What else do you want? You're looking for a ghost. There are no ghosts. At least not here. Let's just pack our bags and go home."

"No. There are indications that the Chinese are getting stuff from us. I'm pretty confident they're not working with electromagnetics. There's not much left, the answer has to involve acoustics."

"Are you saying that they're so good that they've got mikes here we can't find?"

This was getting sensitive. Victor didn't want to impugn the experts' professionalism. He countered quickly, "No, of course I'm not saying that. You didn't find any mikes because there aren't any. They don't use them. At least, they haven't bought any. I've checked that out. But they have bought a lot of stuff for recording and analysis. Lab type. Top quality. Any bright ideas why they might be buying it?"

The guys were puzzled. One tried to make a joke: "Maybe they just love hi-fi."

"Sure. And I'll be damned if we don't find out just what that hi-fi is." Victor turned to the leader of the team. "Nikolai, have your guys go through all of the embassy's maintenance and building records. Pull all references to any digging on the embassy compound. Any construction. Analyze them to see if anything looks remotely fishy. Check for any indications of tunnels. And now let's you and I do some brainstorming."

Nikolai just said, "You got it."

The meeting was over.

Nikolai and Victor went for a walk around the embassy grounds. Nikolai, who had supported Victor's determination, confessed, "To tell you the truth, it's not clear to me what you're looking for."

"I wish I could say I knew. It's just a hunch I've got. There must be something here."

They were headed toward the corner of the compound that was farthest from the embassy. Victor said, "Now, let's look at the building from a distance, like the Chinese do. If you want to hear what's being said in there, you need a mike of some sort. With no conventional mike available, what would you use? Think."

When the two men reached the fence, they turned together and looked back at the embassy building. Then it hit them both simultaneously. They looked at each other, confirming with smiles that they'd each figured it out. With the Chinese guards less than ten feet away on the other side of the wall, Victor and Nikolai didn't say a word. Slowly, they walked back as if nothing had happened. They had their answer, though. The building! The building itself had to be the microphone.

When they reached a place where they wouldn't be overheard, they talked excitedly about their discovery. Nikolai swung his arms and whispered hoarsely, "We were such damned idiots! They've been using the whole building all along! Damned ingenious."

When they'd calmed down, they looked at the building again, Nikolai thinking out loud: "Now, just what, exactly, is different about this building—unusual?"

The building in front of them was a typical monumental monster in the Stalinist style. Victor turned and looked at the boiler house just behind them. The sight of the ugly, barnlike concrete structure halted the flow of his thoughts. He looked at the embassy building again. Something was anomalous. Again, he looked at the boiler house. Back at the embassy. The chimneys. The boiler house. The chimneys on the embassy. Lots of chimneys on the embassy. If there was a boiler house, why would there be any need for chimneys? With so many chimneys, why the boiler house?

As soon as Victor mentioned it, Nikolai said, "That's it."

They went to the building-maintenance engineer and asked for the construction blueprints. Their request surprised him. In his five years on the job no one had ever looked at those documents.

The dusty books and drawings documented that the Embassy had been built by the Chinese around 1950 in accordance with Soviet plans. The only deviation from the original blueprints had been the addition of—the chimneys. They had been proposed by the Chinese as an additional feature. They had solicitously suggested that it might be wise to safeguard against a failure of the central heating system. Just in case. The suggestion had been gratefully accepted by the Soviet side. A necessary concession to the local conditions. So that's how it had come about. The Chinese had then volunteered to cut through the usual red tape and make the design changes on the spot.

The team's report on their research of the embassy's records indicated only one incident worth noting. When a trench had been dug for a new power cable in the mid-sixties, the workers had hit a small tunnel, which went from the compound wall to the embassy building. The tunnel was too small for a man to get through, and it was assumed that it was a left-over from the building's construction. The trench had cut off the tunnel. The incident had been duly recorded, but nothing had been reported to Moscow, as the matter had seemed insignificant.

Closer scrutiny of the chimneys showed that they had been constructed in such a way that would have precluded their ever being used as such. Each one narrowed from base to crown, forming a stretched bell shape that would have kept smoke inside the rooms instead of conducting it out-side. More to the point, their bell shape would have contained sound almost as perfectly as smoke. The inside of each chimney turned out to be lined with an acoustic clay, never used in regular chimneys. The bricks of the wall that separated the chimneys from the rooms they were supposed to conduct smoke from, were also made of an exceptionally good acoustic material, hitherto unknown to the KGB experts.

Victor ordered the tunnel reopened, and with only his small tape recorder managed to produce hi-fi quality recordings from several rooms in the embassy, including those mentioned by Turchak. And this was from close to the edge of the compound. Having closed the tunnel, the team then sealed one of the chimneys from the top and tried to suck air with a pump from inside its fireplace. Air continued to flow freely—a clear indi-cation that another tunnel had been dug and was functioning.

The mysteries of the Marchenko case and the uncanny Chinese aware-ness of the Soviet position through the Permanent Government Delega-tion negotiations had been solved.

General Turchak was excited by the discovery. "You realize that the most significant aspect of your discovery is the fact that the Chinese per-petrated this invasion right at the peak of our relationship with them. This has extraordinary political significance. You've just shed consider-able light on the way they operate."

"Wasn't that supposed to be the single most important objective of this assignment? The possible political extrapolations from the technical stuff."

"Yes, and you certainly delivered. You can count on my sending the highest commendation."

"Thank you."

"It's been a good day all around. I have other reasons for cheerful telegrams to the Center."

Victor didn't need to ask what the reason was. He already knew. Not long ago, the first Soviet Illegal, a Chinese national raised in the Soviet Union, had secretly arrived at the embassy after penetrating the Soviet-Chinese border and crossing China. After a few days' rest in the embassy, he'd successfully made his way back. Victor nodded knowingly. "I heard.

Congratulations."

Soon after, Victor left for Moscow. The debugging team stayed behind to fill in the chimneys with dirt.

Olga was waiting for him at the airport. As always, it was easy to spot her slim, graceful figure standing slightly apart from the crowd of waiting people. Getting into the cab, she asked, "So, it went well for you?" Victor smiled and nodded. He'd tell her about China later—but even then, without any operational details. That taboo had to remain in place, for her sake. The more she knew, the more of a hostage she would be.

She started on another tack: "I saw Mother while you were away. We had quite a talk, Victor. . . ." Something in her tone set off an alarm in Victor, and he shook his head. She got the message and finished lamely, "She said everyone is well, and wondered when we could get together for a family visit." Her glance said, "We have to talk about this later."

So they chatted about Elena, Olga's job, and Moscow news. Real conversation would have to wait. Victor wondered about the clowns at the Center and smiled to himself.

CHAPTER

VICTOR RETURNED TO THE CENTER a winner. The few who knew about the assignment congratulated him on his discovery of the Chinese "listening chimneys." Of course, that was just the tip of the iceberg. Andreyev and Bosik were aware of the larger purpose of Victor's mission and the extrapolations to be made.

He immediately went to Bosik's office to report. Boss was more excited than Victor had ever seen him. He shook Victor's hand, slapped him on the shoulder, and exclaimed, "Well done! Great job."

Victor demurred, "Well, it was luck more than anything else, really."

Boss insisted. "No, Victor, it's you. Andreyev is happy." The highest praise of all.

Even though he both liked and respected Andreyev, Victor could not resist a little dig. "This may be the first time in his life. What it takes to make him happy would transport an ordinary mortal to nirvana." Andreyev's reputation for being a tough, exacting taskmaster was legendary. He never raised his voice or used strong language, yet all his subordinates feared him. Even Bosik. During the previous two years, three Chiefs of his Secretariat had retired early after suffering heart attacks.

Boss laughed. "Come on, he's fair, give him that much. And he's almost always right. You and I certainly have nothing to complain about." That was true.

Then Boss cut the pleasantries short, eager to begin the debriefing. "So tell me, what did you manage to learn about China—in terms of our overall problem?"

Victor grew serious. "It's quite clear that our criteria for evaluating the Chinese intelligence capability are irrelevant, even dangerously misleading.

"In most areas they are obviously far behind us—but they can be ingenious to the point of genius. They are superb craftsmen—unbelievably patient. They can work as hard as anyone I have ever seen—and they will go to any length to accomplish an objective.

"They don't have that consistent level of performance that we are used to dealing with in other services. They give the appearance of operating at a generally low level, with the occasional wild success—apparent flukes. Like the Marchenko case, for example."

Bosik just rolled his eyes.

"Right. They're very effective at taking advantage of our tendency to underestimate them. They do their best to get us to let our guard down. I saw that with the two sets of surveillance teams they put on me: the one I was intended to see operated rigidly by the book; I never even caught sight of the other.

"In my view, it's their inconsistency that makes the Chinese especially dangerous. As a result, they are capable of real surprises. In their own, idiosyncratic way, they are a force to be reckoned with. We must take them seriously, regardless of how they appear. They are not the proverbial peasants in straw hats. Did you read my cable on their acoustic-intercept capabilities?"

"Yes. Go on."

"I discussed this with Turchak, who as you know is one of the most sophisticated experts we have on China. He explained to me how this business with the chimneys is a perfect expression of their general modus operandi. Let's face it, during the construction of the embassy building they fooled us completely. And they succeeded because our guard was down at the time. I'm sure we would have caught on to what they were up to if we'd been on the alert, watching for it. But we weren't. This brings us to what must be the most important political extrapolation: that their bugging of our embassy took place right at the absolute apex of our relationship with them—our two countries were as close as brothers. The point is not how they outsmarted us, but that they chose to try at all, especially during that period. In doing so they were risking not just discovery but maximum international scandal. Considering that Stalin was in charge, it was much more dangerous for the Chinese to play such games then than at any time since."

"That's certainly a discovery. Go on."

"In my opinion, there are two possible interpretations for their duplicity. One: even then they had already planned the break in relations between our countries. Or two: taking advantage of us when we had let our guard down had a higher priority than safeguarding the relationship. My hunch is that there was no reason for them to plan a diplomatic break, since they were getting whatever they wanted with us as close allies, so the second interpretation seems to be the more likely. As I say, it's only a hunch. Even after studying their history and culture I'm not confident I can read them. I've never encountered a mind-set that seemed so different and alien from ours. Somebody better qualified than I should study this problem carefully."

Boss was uncharacteristically quiet. He reflected for a long time before breaking the silence. Finally he said, "Yes, I agree. We'll take it from here, but you've given us a promising new angle—something solid to work with. All this will be reported to the Politburo very soon. I am sure you'll be rewarded for this assignment."

Victor acknowledged Boss's praise with a slight nod, smiling, outwardly pleased. Somewhere in his head he heard Murphy: "The best things at the worst time . . ." They chatted briefly about China, and the things Victor had found particularly strange or exotic. Tourist talk. Then assuming the meeting was over, he stood to leave.

Boss stopped him at the door. "Oh yes, one more thing. That chimney business presents a bit of a political problem. It's extremely embarrassing that the Chinese have been listening in on us for all these years. Our defense failed. We have to handle it in such a way that it's not too big of an issue, you know. Otherwise it'll require a lot of explaining and a scapegoat. But don't worry, we'll take care of that. Just keep in mind that it must be played low key."

Victor nodded, "Of course." He understood.

As he'd expected, his "in" box was heaped with fires to be put out. There were problems with the Washington embassy and the construction of the new communications center in Ottawa. After he'd dealt with the various crises, sending urgent telegrams and making phone calls, he decided he'd done enough for the first day back. He'd start his report on the Beijing trip tomorrow. He and Olga were going to a concert that night—one of a series they attended regularly at the Tchaikovsky Hall. A quiet supper with her beforehand was too attractive a prospect to pass up. He phoned her to say he was on his way to pick her up and take her out.

On his way out, Victor bumped into Valentin in the corridor, eyes bright, face flushed, in a state of feverish excitement.

"Hi, welcome back!"

"Hi."

"The grapevine's been buzzing—I heard you did well."

Victor smiled, a little warily. "I heard something to that effect myself."

"Congratulations." Innocent enough.

"Thanks, Valentin. So how are you doing?"

"Not bad—not bad at all, I'd say. Listen, Victor. Yesterday I had quite a little chat with my ancestor. Laid out exactly what I think of the system, of him, and all the other members of the illustrious gang."

Victor knew that "ancestor" was Valentin's slang for his father. The "gang" was the Central Committee. He was stunned. Valentin had promised to sit tight.

"What?! Are you crazy?"

"Well, maybe I am, but I just thought it might be useful for a member of the Central Committee to hear what the common folks are thinking."

Victor couldn't believe his ears. "Come on, Valentin—since when are you 'common folk'?"

Valentin ignored the needle. "God, I wish you could have seen his face. He looked like a fish, just opening and shutting his mouth, unable to speak. I told him things I'm sure he's never heard anyone say out loud before." Victor could well imagine. Valentin raced on, "I don't know which gave me more pleasure—his reaction or the relief of finally calling a spade a spade. In the end, I told him that I was close to deciding on a course of action."

"Are you sure that was a smart thing to do?"

"Know something, Victor? I don't care! Besides, what's he going to do? Turn in his own son?"

"No, just put you in a mental institution. Oh, but don't worry, it will be a good one. Not where the 'common folk' go." Victor tried to defuse the tension with a joke, but Valentin was wired. Victor tried another approach. "Listen, Valentin. Why don't we get together next week. No politics, no ideology, just for fun. With wives."

"Sounds good to me, but I'd rather bring a girlfriend. Do you mind?"

"Not at all. That's your business." Victor was well aware of Valentin's marital difficulties. He also knew that both Valentin and his wife were quite liberal about extramarital relations. Open marriages were not uncommon, especially among the elite. Divorce was almost certain to derail one's career.

"OK. Call me tomorrow, and we'll settle on the day."

"All right. Talk to you tomorrow, then."

Their supper together was not the celebration Victor had anticipated. They seemed to be at odds—Victor flying high on the kudos from Boss, and Olga strangely preoccupied.

The concert that evening featured an all-Rachmaninoff program. The turbulent music seemed to intensify Olga's mood. Afterward, she suggested a stroll through the streets of old Moscow. Victor knew she'd been upset by the conversation with her mother that she'd mentioned in the car while coming home from the airport. They'd not yet had an opportunity to discuss it. Victor wondered if that was what was bothering her.

She was silent as they turned down Gorky Street, passing the monumental statue of Mayakovsky, the Bolshevik revolutionary poet, who despite the mediocre quality of his political poetry had achieved fame thanks to Lenin's personal support of his procommunist sentiments. The Mayakovsky monstrosity dominated the intersection of Gorky Street and the Garden Ring, an ugly inner-city conduit for cars. Victor and Olga didn't even need to glance at the statue to feel its oppressive presence looming over the square. Like a macabre nightmare image, it seemed to represent much in their life that they had been reluctant to look at, but which they'd felt shadowed by nonetheless.

Victor didn't press Olga, figuring that whatever was bothering her would surface during the course of their walk.

She began casually, "As I started to tell you, I saw my mother during lunch break the other day." That was nothing unusual. From time to time they met in the center of Moscow. Both women were busy, holding jobs and running households, so their visits were usually no more than short chats, touching base and catching up. Often Olga's mother would bring clothing she'd made for Elena. Sewing was her hobby, and she was quite good at that.

Victor didn't respond, knowing that this piece of news was only the preamble.

They walked on, and after a while Olga continued, "We met just near my museum, in that tiny park by the corner of the KGB building." Another pause. Victor noted to himself that she normally referred to the Center as "your building."

By way of encouragement, Victor asked, "So, how's she doing?"

She didn't even hear the question. "That building is so oppressive. Sinister, even. Looking at it today, I suddenly recalled all those stories about the purges and the Revolution. The stories that people only dared whisper to trusted friends. I told my mother what I was thinking, and observed how so many Russian families had suffered in those days, and how all their suffering was directly related to that building. Then I added that, thank God, our family had not been touched. Do you know what she told me?"

"What?"

"She gave me a strange, sad look, and said simply, 'I'm afraid that's not true.' Naturally, I asked her what she meant. She said she thought the time had come to tell me the truth. It seems the truth is that my great-grandfather—a father of eight—was killed by the communists during the Revolution."

"What for?"

"I asked her that, and she said, 'For nothing. As an example to terrify others.'"

"Was it to protect you that they never told you that before?"

"Yes."

Victor nodded. That was typical behavior for families throughout the country. Parents everywhere shielded their children from the truth about relatives who had been repressed, imprisoned, or murdered. These family members were simply not spoken of. They became nonpersons. If children were told anything about their absent relatives, it was that they had died of a sudden illness or some other natural cause.

Olga interrupted his thoughts, "Victor, that's not all. My grandmother's brother didn't die of pneumonia after all. He was in the White Army in the Civil War and was killed. He was nineteen."

A few months ago Victor might have been mildly worried by the potential damage Olga's family's record could do to his career. Now, however, he was disturbed for very different reasons. Her story went straight to his heart.

They'd been walking along Gorky Street and now found themselves in Pushkin Square. As they passed the statue of Pushkin at the intersection with the Moscow Boulevard Ring, Victor reflected that it was an appropriate setting for him to receive this latest piece of news. Even as they strolled by this celebrated dissident, his thoughts were heading down the forbidden path to questions about the very foundations of the Soviet system.

In silence they turned to Tverskoy Boulevard, each lost in troubled thoughts. By the time they'd reached the Arbat Square, it was past midnight. Reluctantly, they caught a cab and headed home.

The next morning Victor had a rough commute and was fifteen minutes late in getting to the office. At a quarter past nine the corridors were empty. Victor raced up the stairs instead of taking the elevator. He was about to pass the hallway where the Leadership of the Directorate had its offices when out of the corner of his eye he caught sight of a standard three-by-four-foot sheet of white poster board on the wall. In the middle of it was a three-by-five-inch photograph mounted in a thick black frame. Underneath was a stand, covered with red cloth, with flowers on it. It was an obituary display—the customary way of announcing the death of an officer in the Directorate. Victor approached, curious as to who it was. As soon as he was close enough to see, his blood ran cold and his body went numb. Valentin.

The fat, black text on the white paper blurred in and out of focus as he forced himself to read:

DIED OF A SUDDEN ILLNESS.
THE LEADERSHIP AND THE DIRECTORATE PARTY COMMITTEE
EXPRESS THEIR SORROW AND EXTEND THEIR CONDOLENCES
TO THE FAMILY OF THE DECEASED.

Victor read the announcement again, then one more time, and still he could not believe his eyes. He felt a tightness in his chest and realized he'd been holding his breath. When he exhaled, he began to pant as if he'd run a mile. He stood in front of the display, dumbly staring at the picture of his friend. Then he slowly turned and walked heavily up the rest of the stairs to his office. Those four flights felt as long and steep as Everest.

In the office, the first person Victor met was Michael. He was visibly agitated and practically pounced on Victor. "Have you heard about Valentin?"

"I've just seen the obit." Victor was still trying to pull himself together. "What happened?"

Michael usually got to the office before eight. By the time the workday officially began at nine, the Department's unofficial minister of information had already had his ear to the ground for an hour.

"They say it was a heart attack. I just can't understand that. He was the best cross-country skier in the Directorate—a great athlete, in terrific shape, healthy as a bull. Can you imagine?"

"When did it happen?"

"Last night. The guys did a super job getting the obituary together so quickly. It was already up when I came in at eight."

"Really?"

"Sure. They must have started working on it around five in the morning."

That was probably true. The large photograph was of Valentin in uniform. Someone had gotten Valentin's official KGB photograph from the file in Personnel and then had it enlarged. That was how things were usually done for an obituary display.

"Any other details?"

"No. Everyone's buzzing about it, but so far no one really knows anything." Michael knew that Valentin and Victor had been friends. "Why don't I go and sniff around. Maybe more grist has been fed into the rumor mill." Then he vanished. He was at his best in such situations— harvesting the grapevine.

Victor automatically went through the ritual of opening his safe, took out the papers inside, and sat down at his desk. He couldn't work. The loss of his friend was a stunning blow. But he knew there was something else about Valentin's sudden death that troubled him. He tried to calm himself. *Come on, heart attacks are always unexpected. Lots of guys get them before they turn forty. This is a classic case. The obituary appeared awfully quickly, but so what. The guys just did their best for him. Everybody liked Valentin. Don't get paranoid.*

But Victor couldn't get past Valentin's "chat" with his father two days before. He had no idea if anybody else had known about it. Probably not. Yesterday Valentin had said that he'd more than clearly expressed his disgust for his father and the whole communist system. God only knew what he'd said about his "intentions."

Michael stormed in. "Victor, it's incredible! Listen to what I've just found out. It seems Valentin was reading in his armchair around nine last night. His wife was in another room. She heard a noise, like something falling. She knew he'd had quite a lot to drink, and she figured he'd probably stumbled or knocked something over. Apparently, he'd gotten quite defensive about his drinking, and she didn't want to provoke a confrontation by checking on him. When she finally did go in an hour later, he was on the floor, unconscious. She called an ambulance. The team tried to revive him, but it was too late. He was dead." Trust Michael to reap every gory detail.

Victor simply nodded. It was difficult to absorb the story. He sat thinking for a while, trying to decide what to do next. When he'd made up his mind, he put his papers away, locked the safe, and went to see the Party Secretary.

The Secretary was hard at work. He seemed unusually glad to see Victor. "Ah! It's good you're here. I was just about to call you—you know, about Yegorov, I'm awfully sorry, but I'm tied up with the quarterly report. I'm going to have to leave it to you to handle it. You know, visit the family, observe the formalities on behalf of the Party, make the necessary arrangements. . . ."

It came as no surprise. The Secretary wasn't the only one to sidestep unpleasant matters. There were certainly no brownie points given for observing the amenities, and all it meant was witnessing someone else's pain. The job of handling the formalities for a KGB officer's funeral was usually fobbed off on the deputies. Deputy Directorate Chief, Deputy Department Chief, Deputy Section Chief, Deputy Secretary—Deputy Whoever's Available. That was fine with Victor. It was exactly what he'd been counting on. He wanted to check out a few things himself. Quietly.

He played along with the Secretary, feigning annoyance. "So, I guess the whole unpleasant business is going to be dumped in my lap—again?"

The Secretary laughed, "Afraid so. I'll handle the next one myself. I promise."

"All right."

"And don't worry, there won't be that much to do. The Central Committee is taking care of the funeral. His father, you know . . . Look, I've already ordered a car for you. Take it and do whatever is necessary."

As Victor got into the car the driver asked, "Where to?"

Victor had planned to go to Valentin's place. Abruptly he changed his mind. "The hospital."

"Ours?"

"Yes." The KGB Central Hospital.

As they approached the hospital, Victor said, "No, not the main building. Go to the morgue."

"Ha. Sounds like 'Go to hell.' "

Victor didn't join his laughter. He left the car and entered the building, which stood about a hundred yards apart from the main hospital plant. In the gallows humor of the patients it was commonly referred to as the IPD, the Institute of Precise Diagnostics.

Victor entered the administrator's office, showed his ID, and asked about the preparations for the funeral ceremony of the late Captain Yegorov.

"Everything is in order, Comrade Major. Nothing to worry about." Primly, she handed him a copy of the orders concerning the scheduled formalities. Victor pretended to study it carefully. He wanted to appear as intimidating as possible. He was really calculating his next move.

"Well, it all seems to be in order, as you say. Just make sure that the band is here on time." He knew perfectly well that there would be no band at the morgue. He was just trying to get her off balance.

"I'm sorry, Comrade Major, the custom of bands here was canceled by order of the Leadership quite a while ago. Perhaps you haven't been here since. The funeral music had a depressing effect on the other patients."

"Yes of course, I'd forgotten. Now, I need to see the body to make sure that the makeup is satisfactory."

"It's too early for the makeup to be applied."

"I want to see the body anyway."

The woman tightened her lips, offended by his high-handedness. She sniffed, "Just a minute," and disappeared into the room behind her office.

When she reappeared, there was a look of triumph on her face. "A viewing is impossible."

"This is highly unusual."

"I'm sorry." Clearly she was not. "Only by the order of a Deputy Chairman."

Victor allowed himself to explode. "What is this? Another new rule of yours?"

"No, Comrade Major," now her voice was infuriatingly patient, patronizing. She'd verified her orders in the back room and was now smugly wrapped in the security blanket of bureaucratic procedure. "It only applies to this particular body."

"And who gave the order?"

"I'm afraid I don't know."

He knew the answer anyway. It had to have been one of the Chairman's Deputies.

"All right, at least show me the autopsy report."

"That's impossible."

He had to carry the charade to its logical end. "What?! That's ridiculous! What do you expect me to put in the obituary?"

She checked her book. "Just what has been cited here, Comrade Major. Heart attack." She snapped the book shut. The confrontation was over. She'd held the fort. However, thanks to Comrade Cerberus, Victor now knew a great deal more than he was supposed to. Her roadblocks had been more helpful than she could have imagined. Victor left, grumbling that he would certainly lodge a complaint to the Party authorities about the kind of treatment he—a Party official—had received from her. Outrageous!

Back in the car, Victor ordered the driver to go to Valentin's apartment on Kutuzovsky Prospect. He did not want Comrade Cerberus to see where he went next. When they'd gone two blocks he instructed the driver, "Wait. I've changed my mind. Go back to the hospital. I just remembered. A friend of mine recently had an operation here. I'd like to drop in on him. Use the entrance over there."

They approached the hospital from another side, one not visible from the morgue. Victor headed for the reception desk. Now he needed to call in a favor. On the hospital phone he dialed an old friend of his—a coroner in the morgue he'd just visited. Fortunately, he was in his office.

"Pavel, hi. It's Victor Sheymov."

"Hi, Victor. What can I do for you? I hope you're not about to need my services personally . . . ?"

"Are you kidding? I'm going to live long enough to have to rely on self-service!" Victor joked back. "Listen, Pavel, I'm at the reception desk here. Can I see you? It'd better be somewhere other than the morgue. I've just had an unpleasant tango with your dragon lady."

"No problem. She's a piece of work, huh?"

Five minutes later they met in the hospital garden and started to walk.

"Pavel, one of our guys is a guest in your place—Yegorov. Does that name ring a bell?"

Pavel looked at Victor sharply. He didn't answer for a moment. Then he lowered his voice. "A captain from the Eighth CD, right?"

"Yes."

"What do you want to know?" His voice had dropped. Victor pressed on quickly. Momentum was crucial.

"Did you do the autopsy?"

"No, it was done last night. They'd finished before I came in at eight this morning. I don't really know much about the case."

"Are many autopsies performed in the middle of the night?"

"No. It's quite unusual, actually."

"What was the hurry?"

"I'm not sure."

"Did you see the report?"

"Well, yes and no. I signed it, but I only saw the last page, where the signatures go. See, the boss only brought it to my office because it needed another signature."

"Does that happen often?"

"It's pretty much standard operating procedure. We're shorthanded, you know. More signatures are required per case than there are people actually involved."

"Who performed the autopsy?"

"The boss, I guess."

"Does he often operate at night?"

"No, never. I was surprised."

"Did you see the body yourself?"

"No."

"Anything else unusual about this case?"

"Well, Victor, I must say there's something fishy. I asked my boss about it—indirectly, you know—and he just ducked. He said the guy was the son of some big chief. Embarrassing death, discreet cover-up. So he put 'heart attack.'"

"What was embarrassing about it?"

"Well, according to my boss, Yegorov got dead drunk, threw up, then choked on his own vomit and suffocated."

"Jesus Christ! Are you the only one he told?"

"No, as a matter of fact, he told a few others around here as well."

"Was there any need to tell the others?"

"No. I was surprised myself. It was almost as if he wanted them to gossip."

Victor realized what was going on. Pavel's boss had carefully provided substantiation for the rumor he had planted.

"So, I guess the rumor will hit the open air soon?"

"Yeah."

Victor looked him straight in the eye and asked, "Well, which version is true? Death from heart attack or death from drunken suffocation?"

Pavel hesitated, too uncomfortable to meet Victor's gaze. Then he replied, "Neither. For God's sake, don't quote me, but the cause of death was something entirely different. Now, please, don't ask me to go any further."

His words confirmed Victor's worst fears. It was his turn to lower his voice. "Pavel, I understand that you know more than you can tell me. That's OK. But please, just answer one more question. Would you say Yegorov died of unnatural causes?"

Pavel looked at Victor, then slowly lowered his head, as if nodding in very slow motion. Then he said, "Victor, you understand, of course, that it's not my case. OK? I cannot comment on such a question. . . ."

There was a long pause as they looked at each other. Pavel, alarmed by what he saw in Victor's eyes, broke the silence. "Listen, I don't know what you're up to, but let me give you a little advice: Stop digging. Quit right now. You're dancing close to dangerous territory. Please, for your own sake."

Despite the *Valentin was murdered!!!* bells and sirens going off in Victor's head, Pavel's message got through. Victor said simply, "Thanks, Pavel. Don't worry. By the way, you understand, I'm only here to make sure the body looks good at the funeral tomorrow."

"Of course. Why else?"

They parted. Victor got back in his car and told the driver to take him to Valentin's place. He stared out the car window, seeing nothing, unable to bring his thoughts to order. The only thing he knew was that he had to know more.

Valentin's apartment was filled with people—relatives and friends. Victor approached Valentin's wife—widow now. He barely recognized her. She wore no makeup and had obviously been crying for hours. She nodded to Victor, and he simply shook her hand. There was no point in polite commiseration. Anything he'd say along those lines would sound false to both of them. Instead he tried to distract her with small talk.

After a couple of minutes, however, when he saw her relax a bit, he asked gently, "Why did you say that you were at home?" He was bluffing, but he had a hunch.

In her present state of shock, her reflexes were slow, and she didn't realize that there'd have been no reason for Victor to doubt the official story. She said simply, "They told me to."

There was no point in asking her who "they" were. It would only trigger her suspicion. Besides, she wouldn't know their true identities anyway. Victor continued softly, "But why? I don't quite understand."

She lowered her eyes guiltily. "I . . . well, I came home late, you see. They said that . . . ," she gulped back a sob, then poured the rest of the story out in a whispered rush, "that if I hadn't been out with another man—if I'd been home with my husband he wouldn't have died." She paused for a shuddering breath, then continued weakly, "They said their story would help me avoid embarrassment. Oh God, I feel so guilty." She leaned against Victor and started to weep again.

Victor tried to calm her. "Believe me, Tatyana, there was nothing you could have done. No one can escape his fate. You have nothing to feel bad about. Your guilt won't bring him back."

"Do you really think that's true, Victor?" As she wiped her tears, her eyes reflected a glimmer of hope—some way to be able to live with herself.

"Yes. Yes, I do." He paused, then asked Tatyana, "When did you really get home?"

"About half past eleven."

"What did you see?"

"Valentin was lying on the floor in this room, near the chair, face down. The chair was overturned. He wasn't breathing. He'd . . . ."

Victor interrupted, "This chair?" He indicated Valentin's favorite armchair: massive, low center of gravity, impossible to overturn by accident. It would have taken a deliberate effort—or a violent fight.

"Yes."

"Was anything else knocked over?"

"No." She was answering automatically. So far, thanks to Victor's gentle, sympathetic tone, she'd not even realized she was being interrogated.

Now he had to press a little harder. He was in a hurry. They could be interrupted at any time. Later, when she was less vulnerable, she would not be so compliant.

"Did you call an ambulance?"

"Yes. No, I mean, I called two of them."

"Which ones?"

"The Central Committee one and the KGB's."

"Which one came first, and how long did it take to get here?"

"The KGB ambulance. It arrived in less than five minutes." Impossibly prompt. Victor knew what that meant.

"Then, did the other one come later?"

"You know, it just occurred to me—no, it never did come. That's strange. . . ."

"Oh, they probably radioed each other, you know." He didn't want to alarm her. "What happened next?"

"They told me he was dead. But I knew that already. He was cold." She shook her head and said, "Poor Valentin—and that nasty bruise."

"A bruise? Where?"

"On his face, just under his eye. He probably got it when he fell."

"Ah, I see." *He must have put up a fight. Bastards!* He asked, "Did someone from the KGB come right away?"

"Oh yes. Two men—just after the ambulance arrived. One was a duty officer. I don't remember their names. They talked to me for a while. They're the ones who told me what to say."

At that moment, someone across the room called to Tatyana, and she excused herself. Victor was boiling inside. *Those shits! Not only did they murder him, but they didn't even take the trouble to make a clean job of it. Why?*

Before leaving, he confirmed the fact that the Central Committee staff was handling the funeral arrangements and did not need any help from the KGB.

The driver dropped him off at Dzerzhinsky Street, and Victor went back to his office. He ordered the official memorial wreaths from the Directorate. He felt restless, uneasy, desperately in need of a walk, to be alone for a while, to sift through everything he'd learned so far.

He went out. At Kirov Street he reached the Boulevard Ring and turned right. He walked to the place where he and Valentin had had their talk, just after Victor had returned from Mahindjauri. Their bench was vacant. Victor sat. *There's something odd about this place.* This was where Victor had lectured Valentin on being too impulsive. Now he had to bring his own emotions under control if he was to make sense of Valentin's death.

It had all the earmarks of a deliberate KGB liquidation. If the KGB wasn't responsible, then why bother with the cover-up? But if the KGB was responsible, why such a clumsy execution? Valentin didn't drive, so they couldn't have staged an accident, but they easily could have used any one of their numerous "quiet" methods. They had an arsenal of extremely sophisticated poisons—Victor knew that—surely they could have slipped Valentin something to simulate death by heart attack. One possible explanation is that they still would have had to deal with the doctors. Whenever an officer at Valentin's level dies, the KGB autopsy is very thorough. In any case, why not a clean kill? Why all the footprints?

As Victor's mind raced through these calculations, the one thing he was sure of was that Valentin had been murdered. There were too many coincidences pointing in the same direction. And it had to have been a KGB liquidation.

Suddenly, Victor was stopped by a chilling thought. *Could it be a trap? The only conceivable reason they'd leave footprints for someone like me to find is to flush out any possible co-conspirators.* His own phrase stopped him. Someone like him.

Victor wondered if he'd left any footprints of his own. Immediately, he began a methodical review of his behavior since learning of Valentin's death. He concluded that his actions had been risky but, so far, not incriminating. He'd been careful to cover himself. Now he'd have to take extra precautions. And he'd do no more sniffing around. No talks with duty officers.

He left the bench and caught a cab back to Dom 2. He stormed into his office and shot a scowl in Michael's direction to make sure he was paying attention. He was. Good. Victor grabbed the phone and called the Party Secretary. He began to complain loudly, "I don't know what's going on with our hospital! The place is going to hell. It used to be a good operation, but I'm telling you, you wouldn't believe what it's like now. Just this morning I tried to make sure that the makeup on Yegorov would be done decently, and you know what? That idiot of an administrator at the morgue wouldn't let me see his body! Not only was she insufferably rude, but she mumbled incoherent garbage about the Deputies of the Chairman, and God knows what else. Maybe the formaldehyde fumes got to her—I don't know, and frankly, I don't care. I want to register an official complaint about her. That bitch should be fired!" By the end he was almost shouting—the image of righteous indignation.

"Hey, Victor. Calm down. I know what they're like over there, and I agree with you, it just gets worse and worse. But don't waste your time and energy worrying about it. It's not worth it, you know. Oh, and you don't have to worry about the funeral arrangements, either. Didn't I tell you that already? The Central Committee staff is taking care of it. You've done all you need to do. You did go and see his wife, didn't you?"

"Of course."

"How is she holding up?"

"All right, I guess. Under the circumstances. I talked to her—tried to comfort her. You know. What else could I do?"

"Nothing else, of course. The main thing is that you went over to offer our condolences. Nobody can accuse us of insensitivity now."

Right. "Are you going to the funeral?"

The Secretary sighed. "I have to. I'll give the speech, of course. You don't have to worry about that."

"Thanks." Victor knew exactly why the Secretary suddenly had the time to attend the ceremony and give the eulogy. The Leadership of the Directorate would be there. Valentin's father's presence was the reason.

Out of the corner of his eye Victor saw Michael heading for the door. The minister of information was on his way.

Then Victor made a similar phone call to the Chief of the Personnel Department. Preventive measures. Now no one could accuse him of snooping around. On his way home Victor thought about Valentin's father. Just how much did he know? The thought that he might have ordered the murder of his own son—even indirectly—was inconceivable. Perhaps their conversation had been intercepted. That was his tentative conclusion.

At the funeral, Victor watched Valentin's father carefully. Throughout the entire ceremony Victor was unable to discern a single sign of emotion from the old man. His face might as well have been carved in stone. What he did notice was that Valentin's father did not once look at his dead son's face—not once. Nor did he give him the traditional kiss on the forehead just before the coffin was closed. All the other relatives did.

By chance, right in the middle of the funeral, Victor found one more piece of evidence to support his conclusions. When he approached the open coffin to take his turn as one of the four honor guards, he clearly saw the mark under Valentin's left eye. It had been pretty well covered by makeup—almost invisible from a distance—but he could tell it had been a nasty blow. Then, as he took his place just behind Valentin's head, he glanced down again at his friend. As usually happens after death, Valentin's neck had become thinner, shrinking away from his collar. His head was resting on a low pillow in the coffin, his chin slightly lifted. From where Victor stood—behind and to the side of Valentin's head—he could clearly see another bruise through the gap between the neck and collar, just underneath the Adam's apple. Then Victor focused on the Adam's apple itself. There was something odd about it. It was barely noticeable, almost flat. But Valentin's Adam's apple had been quite prominent. . . . And then Victor knew. His own face paled and became still, expressionless. Inside, he felt a rush of adrenaline—pulse pounding, blood racing to his head. He looked straight ahead, and said his silent good-bye to his friend. *Sorry, Valentin. There is nothing I can do now, but I won't forget. I'll get to them.*

Five minutes later Victor was relieved of honor-guard duty, and he rejoined the crowd. Within an hour, Valentin was buried, the funeral was over, and the mourners drifted away.

Victor's first instinct was to nail Valentin's killers. But the more he thought about it, the clearer it became to him that any attempt to discover who had actually committed the murder was irrelevant. Eliminating the hit men wouldn't be much of a revenge—they were most likely regular KGB officers simply carrying out orders. Men much like Valery. Besides, he thought, who knows what they'd been told about their target? Probably some blood-curdling lie about Valentin, implying that even murder was too good for him. The KGB was skilled at psychologically immunizing officers before such assignments. In Valentin's case the killers undoubtedly would have been convinced that they were eliminating a dangerous subversive—perhaps even a traitor. Even if it were possible to get to whoever had actually ordered the hit, it still wouldn't really change anything. There was no lack of able and eager candidates waiting in the wings for a golden opportunity to further their careers. Simple revenge would only be an ego trip. Victor decided to postpone any action until he could think through a truly effective way to strike.

CHAPTER

16

VICTOR RESOLUTELY PUSHED Valentin's murder to the back of his mind. Now he appreciated the lesson he had learned in Beijing: he was certain that the deeper meaning of Valentin's death lay somewhere within the culture and history of the system itself. Once he understood that, he'd be able to act. But he was now under the gun. Although he was reasonably confident that he'd left no footprints during his investigation of the crime, he knew very well that there was no certainty of that. It was no secret that he'd been friendly with Valentin, who hadn't been too discreet about his opinions and may have been under particular surveillance. And given his execution, it was probable that all his contacts had been noted and carefully assessed.

These possibilities made Victor realize that he was unlikely to get away with his ongoing study of Communism and communist power for much longer without arousing attention. Anyone who set out to acquire a mass of political literature ran the risk of provoking official suspicion. At any time a routine look at the information that was accumulating on Victor as a matter of course could trigger the Second CD to begin an in-depth analysis of his activities. End of game for Victor. His unconventional social life could easily be turned purposefully against him. No matter how careful he was, Victor realized that if the authorities compiled a list of his readings he'd quickly find himself transferred to Lefortovo, the KGB central prison. For starters.

Even though Victor still went to his office every day, he was working strictly on automatic pilot. He performed his job, his projects went forward, crises got solved. There was no outward sign that his mind was elsewhere, engaged in another, formidable task.

The literature was massive, the propaganda shrill, and the rhetoric ponderous, and it all took considerable deciphering. As he tried to pick his way through the tangled web of disinformation, he was baffled by the gross manipulations of the "truth." In one simple exercise Victor compared entries in the successive editions of the Soviet Encyclopedia published under Stalin, Khrushchev, and Brezhnev, which he found in his father's library. He was fascinated by the way articles covering the same subjects juggled quotes from identical passages of *pervoistochniki*—the works of the founders of Communism—and derived totally different conclusions from them. What one source presented as solid fact was dismissed by the next as lies and fabrication, and a new scenario was hammered into place.

Like solid, familiar objects seen in a nightmare, the "facts" of the world as he had assumed it to be dissolved right before his eyes. One after another, many of the ideals and truths instilled in him since childhood were shattered. His whole frame of reference began to disintegrate. He became increasingly disoriented.

Victor persisted. Gradually, a coherent picture emerged from the shards of his reality. It was horrifying. Even with the evidence staring him in the face, he could not trust himself to accept the next logical step. Now he really understood Dostoyevsky's *Idiot:* it was beginning to seem to Victor that he was the only sane person around—a sure sign that he must be the one who was going mad. To maintain his mental balance Victor withdrew into himself.

Olga gave him space, letting him alone as he struggled. He saw that she'd noticed the change in him. She didn't question him, and he was grateful for her sensitivity. Even so, it was hard for him to see her deliberately avoiding his eyes so that he wouldn't be pressured by the silent questions in hers. He couldn't help feeling those questions whenever they were together.

Victor was trained to try and establish the truth beyond any shadow of a doubt. As a professional troubleshooter, however, he'd grown used to making rapid assessments under pressure—decisions based on deductions from often-insufficient data enhanced by well-honed intuition. The assignment he faced now seemed to be truly impossible: how to make sense of the patchwork of communist "history" and draw solid conclusions.

Those conclusions finally fell into place. At long last Victor felt that he finally understood his reservations about Valentin's position. Here was one more proof, he mused, of a fundamental lesson he'd learned in his scientific training: We rarely make mistakes in analysis. We usually make them in our assumptions. He was convinced that Valentin, like most of the dissidents, was not searching deeply enough and so couldn't see the root of the problem. It wasn't simply the corruption of the leadership. The evil in the system was fundamental, inherent in its nature.

He was satisfied that he'd achieved the first part of his quest. Now he had to talk to Olga. He took her for a walk in the park nearby.

Victor turned to her with a rhetorical question: "So. What have I learned? Let me list my answers." He'd been at this exercise for so long that at first he sounded as if he was talking out loud to himself.

Olga couldn't help smiling. "Ah, yes, the list."

"To begin with, the basic idea of Communism was just one of many utopian responses to the fact that there are many unhappy people on earth, and it wasn't particularly original. According to most sources, Marx was a genius as a social analyst. So he must have been smart enough to understand the human fundamentals. Yet his proposed system was a deliberate perversion of reality. For instance, he branded all forms of inheritance as evil. He surely must have also understood that protecting one's children—including giving them a secure inheritance—is a universal human instinct. If you deny everyone that opportunity, you'll make everyone fundamentally unhappy. And that can only produce an unhappy society. Marx had to have understood that." Victor went on: "Or, take competition. Marx damns it as an evil of Capitalism—but he certainly knew enough to comprehend that the driving force behind human progress is competition. It's another basic human instinct. If you eliminate it, you frustrate everyone and stifle progress."

Olga was uncomfortable with these large statements. "But we also have competition; you have to compete in order to be successful."

"Our competition is about who shouts communist slogans the loudest. That's the way to success here, but it's not the point. The point is that there's the idea of Communism, and there's the theory of Communism. But the first thing you have to do is to separate the idea of Communism from the theory of Communism. That step is crucial for understanding all the rest, and the amazing paradox is that the theory has almost no connection with the idea.

"Marx presented the idea of Communism as an historical inevitability, but his disciples didn't want to wait for History. They said, in effect: 'This is the way we'll make Communism happen.' That was the birth of the theory. But if you really examine the theory, you'll find it's not a coherent theory at all. That's the most astonishing flaw in Communism, and nobody seems to have focused on that. It's what kept derailing my attempts to analyze the theory. It was only when I tried to get a fix on the basic assumptions of Communism that I was lucky to hit on the right approach. So, there's just no way of getting around the fact that there's a world of difference between the idea of Communism, and the theory of Communism."

"I don't understand. How could the one be different from the other?"

"That's just it! That's the massive deception! Right from the beginning, any time anyone questioned the theory, the communists would immediately switch the discussion of the theory to a discussion of the idea. So people got confused. How could you possibly criticize the idea of everyone's being happy? It's the classic magic trick. The magician puts a chicken in a hat. You think it's a chicken? No, out comes a bouquet of plastic flowers."

"How come nobody noticed?" Olga was skeptical.

"It's sleight of hand. A trick, built in, right from the beginning."

"Do you mean that this 'trick' started with Marx?"

"Not exactly. Marx started it by providing a convenient foundation, and the Bolsheviks, notably Lenin, invented the trick and made it into a party policy."

"You don't think that maybe someone else twisted it all much later?"

"No. Absolutely not. Marx was much too smart not to see that problem. I'm sure he knew precisely what he was doing. I think he was a profoundly bitter and angry man, angry at the whole world. Now, clinically speaking, there are plenty of angry people out there. But Marx saw himself as a prophet and undertook to prove that revolution was inevitable. I think he was embittered by the fact that he couldn't achieve this revolution himself. Perhaps when he wrote the *Communist Manifesto* his goal was to put a time bomb under society, just to make everyone suffer. In the hope that someone like Lenin would come along, use his theory as a weapon, and set off his bomb.

"Lenin was another angry man. He didn't wait for History to follow Marx's prophecies. Lenin was a tremendously skillful manipulator of Marxist theory—he was a compulsive manipulator, period. Incidentally, Lenin committed the greatest of crimes himself. He betrayed his country in time of war. He came to power with the help of the Germans, who were desperate to do anything that would weaken their Russian enemy. His political and terrorist activities at the time were financed by German intelligence.

"That was a time when people in many countries were exhausted and demoralized by economic failure and the horrors of World War I. They desperately needed hope—and a dream. Lenin was ruthless. In his drive to seize power, he used a tactic that often works for charismatic political leaders. At least in the short run. He simply promised everyone whatever they wanted to hear. He didn't worry too much about the need to deliver on those promises. Anything to win. This approach has become a hall-mark of the communists, and it serves them well. As soon as they succeed in taking power, some of the communists—the idealists, who haven't done their homework on the theory—realize that it will be impossible to honor the promises they have made. But the leaders of the gang are never ideal-ists; they never have any intention of honoring those promises in the first place. Once they seize power, they know that the only way to keep it is to eradicate all opposition—especially those among their ranks who insist on the fulfillment of the communist promises of justice and democracy."

"People like my great-grandfather?"

"Well, he probably wasn't a part of any kind of formal opposition. Most likely he was simply a 'class enemy'—liquidated because he was born in the wrong political category."

"That's grotesque."

"It's also amazing to see how Lenin got away with complete ideological U-turns. The same man who preached pacifism when he urged Russian soldiers to stop fighting Germans in World War I, on the grounds that the proletariat must not fight among themselves, then did a quick about-face and issued a call to arms in the even bloodier Civil War. Never mind that the Red Army soldiers were fighting their 'proletarian' counterparts in the White Army. These gross inconsistencies were papered over with slogans. If the latest one was shouted loudly enough the people would forget the previous ones. And anyone who even mildly questioned Lenin's judgment or logic was labeled a demagogue and was disgraced—or worse—while, in fact, he was the greatest demagogue of all.

"To achieve their goals the Leninists allied themselves with anyone who was useful at that moment. This facile pragmatism was such a suc-cess that pacts of expediency became a standard trademark of communist policy."

"But I've always been under the impression that our country has lived by its ideological principles."

"Well, that's just the point. Lenin was the first to really appreciate that most people in the world get their information from the mass media. He was the first to realize that in the mass media truth competes with lies on equal terms. He calculated that by controlling the media, the communists would control the minds of the people because everyone's decisions would be based on 'communist information.' If you controlled the 'truth,' you controlled the country. That's why propaganda became a major strategic weapon in the communist arsenal."

"But what about those people who knew the real truth?"

"Only a tiny percentage of people ever had access to the real truth—the very few who witnessed it firsthand. People who proved impervious to propaganda and questioned communist 'truth' were simply liquidated."

"The Red Terror?"

"Yes. Communist 'truth' didn't provide a strong enough evidence of loyalty to satisfy Stalin. Stalin was a really paranoid bastard. He took Lenin's ideas about controlling information a huge step further: he converted the entire country into an information prison. It was sealed off. At vast expense, the communists used extraordinarily tough measures to keep Soviet citizens from hearing any information from the outside world. People were sentenced to years in prison simply for listening to a foreign radio broadcast. Those gangsters knew all too well that objective information would be their downfall."

"Come on, Victor, 'gangsters'?"

"Sure. They were gangsters. Still are. Their mentality and deeds still are purely criminal. Adolph Hitler once declared: 'Soldiers, I free you from your conscience.' The communists went one better. They invented a new entity: the Party conscience. It was more subtle, more sophisticated—and much more dangerous. It was to be superior to any other reasoning—including conventional human conscience. Since the Party's advertised goals are by definition most noble, it follows that the Party conscience is also noble. Party conscience has two meanings. One is, any action that benefits the Communist Party is noble. Regardless. And don't worry if something is moral or immoral—the Party will be the judge of that. But there's also the second meaning: certain rules do apply, but only for communists. Where others are concerned, there are no rules. Isn't that just the same as the criminal 'code of honor'? As a criminal you have to follow the rules strictly when dealing with your fellow criminals. But when it comes to others, there are no rules—you can do whatever you want to them. Outsiders are fair game. No rules."

Victor took a breath and continued: "Think about the sheer number of heinous crimes committed in the name of Communism. That there would be a sufficient number of genuine sociopaths living in any one country to accomplish the murders of so many tens of millions of people is statistically improbable. But Party conscience gave millions of 'normal' people an incentive to commit otherwise-unthinkable atrocities for 'the good of the Party.' Did you have any idea that Communism has killed *many times* more people in the name of equality, and the proletariat, than the Nazis ever killed for their evil cause?"

"Victor! How can you even compare the two!"

"Listen, Fascism and Communism are closer to each other than most people realize. Both are energized by anger against the injustices of the present. Communism seduces with the promise of the future; Fascism dwells on the glories of the past. In the early stages especially, both ideologies attract those who regard themselves as victims of the existing order, whether they are actually wronged, exploited, or generally 'underprivileged.'

"Communists always manipulate this question of the 'underprivileged' by transforming it into an intellectually seductive cry for justice and democracy. Because it proclaims universal equality as its main goal, Communism has always appealed to a much broader audience than Fascism. But in both ideologies the underlying appeal for the 'underprivileged' is that they promise to provide permanent personal security. Both promise their followers that in return for 'satisfactory performance,' the Leader or the State will take care of them. That arrangement is especially attractive when it turns out that the major criterion for 'satisfactory performance' is no more than unconditional loyalty, that wealth and power will be redistributed in proportion to ideologically loyal performance. For the many who would feel threatened in a more competitive society, a loyalty oath looks like a relatively painless trade-off for security.

"In this country alone the communists have turned tens of millions of otherwise normal individuals into psychological cripples. As a result of all the brainwashing, it's now ingrained in our people that they don't have to work in order to succeed. They simply receive everything they need from those who are empowered to decide what those needs are. How hard they work makes no difference at all to what they are allowed to receive. And now the main thrust of our society is not directed toward achievement; it's toward preventing others from succeeding. Just think of it. If all of a sudden, by some magic, communist power vanished tomorrow, you'd have a country full of people whose main concern would be no more than preventing others from living better than they do. It's going to take a lot of time to change that attitude."

Olga was silent, shaking her head.

He pressed his point. "Don't you see? The communists actually created a new form of slavery state, based on the most insidious kind of evil.
In the ancient slavery states at least the slaves knew they were slaves.
Their anger and resentment of the ruling class made their labor inefficient and led to frequent revolts. But in the communist state the slaves'
natural desire for freedom is repressed. They remained unaware of their
slavery. Since generation after generation had never experienced freedom, they were ignorant of what they were missing. Like anyone born
and raised in captivity, these inmates assumed the rest of the world was no
different from their prison. Their idea of getting to the top of their 'free'
world was to become the equivalent of a prison guard."

"You mean like in the GULAG."

"Those in the GULAG at least got a kind of a break. Once they managed to get to the GULAG, they still had a chance of surviving further.
Others never even made it there. Millions of them." Victor stopped. A
nightmarish vision had filled his mind, one he had long repressed. He fell
silent, thinking about those stories of the stone-crushing machines in the
basements of the KGB prisons around the country, machines that were
used to pulperize the bodies of prisoners, and of how the remaining pulp
was flushed into the sewers. Stories difficult to verify and impossible to
forget. He couldn't bring himself to speak of them to Olga.

Olga stared at him intently, trying to read his thoughts.

"Olga, I'm sorry. I'm not through—it gets even worse. Beyond the tens
of millions slaughtered, and the hundreds of millions more enslaved—literally and figuratively—the greatest evil of all perpetrated by the Communist leaders was the deliberate corruption of the very souls of those
who survived the Communist Terror."

"What do you mean?"

"The ultimate symbol of this spiritual poison was the way the communists destroyed the Russian Orthodox Church. Like everyone else, on the
basis of the so-called 'information' and 'history' available to us, I believed
that the Church had eventually come to accept communist rule after the
Revolution. Nothing could have been further from the truth."

Victor took a deep breath and continued, "The unholy Synod we have
in Russia has nothing to do with the Church. It was created illegally by
the communists. The real Synod emigrated to escape liquidation. None
of the Patriarchs after Sergiy was legitimate. Lenin realized that he could
not compete with the Church in either ideology or credibility. It's a basic
tenet of communist ideology that you cannot believe in God and be a
communist, and vice versa. So Lenin followed his usual line: 'If the

enemy doesn't surrender, it must be destroyed.' It's hard to find out exactly how many, but at least six thousand priests were murdered immediately after the Revolution. But even that didn't do the job. Many people still kept the faith. So all Church property was confiscated, believers were purged, and there was an unprecedented campaign of atheist propaganda. Anyone openly displaying faith could only hope for the most meager kind of job.

"Soon after the Civil War the Church as such had been destroyed, or was presumed to have been. Then the communists discovered that many believers had gone underground. That posed too great a danger to the regime. So the communists intensified their infiltration of the Church—what was left of it. At first, they had recruited informers, using the usual carrot-and-stick incentives. Not fully satisfied with the results, they started sending KGB officers in as priests. They infiltrated every level of the Church hierarchy, especially the top echelon. So by now the hierarchy of the Soviet Orthodox Church is nothing more than an extension of the KGB. Just listen to the preaching of the hierarchs—both here and abroad. Their sermons are nothing more than Party cant—with an occasional mention of God.

"And take the ROCOR, the Russian Orthodox Church outside of Russia, which was organized by the émigré Holy Synod—the legitimate Russian Orthodox Church. It's one of the KGB's prime targets. The ROCOR really frightens the communists, small as it is. They know that the parishioners of ROCOR are truly dangerous to the regime: they are passionately patriotic, but they have their own ideology—and they are among the very few who understand the true nature of Communism. They aren't fooled by communist propaganda stunts.

"Pretty soon the communists will start promoting this rotten Soviet Church. It'll look like they've decided to tolerate religion again. But it will be just another trick to smoke out naive believers and fool credulous Westerners.

"So it's truly demonic: Communism has not only tempted people to sin, it's coerced them into it. Blindered and brainwashed by propaganda, the slaves have killed, tortured, and repressed their fellow slaves in the name of democracy and equality. Those who have passively gone along have been forced to be silent accessories to these crimes. As a result, the entire country has been transformed into the largest concentration camp in history. It's even surrounded physically by a barbed-wire fence and other less tangible barriers that make the border practically impregnable—to anyone who wants to get out."

"But, Victor, we've been under siege ever since the Revolution. We're at war, aren't we? And you yourself are in the thick of it. So is your father. Even you have never suggested that the West doesn't want to destroy the Soviet Union."

"Yes, we are in a kind of total war—it's supposed to be an ideological struggle. But now I know the ideology I've been fighting for is fundamentally wrong. It's based on lies. You see, the communists always need an outside enemy to justify what is virtually a wartime regime. The reason is that from the very first Lenin viewed the export of revolution as an essential defensive strategy against hostile Western governments. As a result of our help, Communism in one form or another has flourished round the globe. And I assure you it will continue to consume many lives."

"If it's flourishing, then doesn't that mean there must be something to it? If it's as obviously wrong as you say, why would people still be attracted by it?"

"Communists have never had to look too far to find comrades-in-arms. Wherever they strike, they target two distinct groups of people. First, the local dissidents, necessary to lend political legitimacy to any communist-incited potential revolution. For the most part, these are angry intellectuals who become enchanted by the facile logic of communist slogans and are too lazy to do their homework. They are also usually the first to become disillusioned by the practical application of Communism once the system is in place. No matter. After the revolution they can easily be eliminated. They've served their purpose.

"The other group—the core essential to any coup—consists of those who realize that the communists offer them the chance of a lifetime to grab power and wealth without ever having to work for it. Just kill people, shout slogans, flatly deny any wrongdoing, and you'll have it all. The ultimate opportunity. For those with a criminal bent, it's more profitable than a gold mine. And this basic modus operandi is how Communism has managed to gain a hold in countries around the world. In fact, I couldn't find a single criminal-scoundrel-turned-head-of-state in the whole world with whom we wouldn't deal and support.

"And look at how communists have played a huge practical joke on the whole world. With their prestige as a superpower, and with their propaganda, disinformation, and 'active measures' abroad, they've provided legitimacy to many real criminals. It used to be that a person who committed a crime was called a criminal. Not anymore. Taking advantage of the open-mindedness of democratic societies, and their willingness to listen to opposing views, the communists have managed to create situations

in which terrorists and other criminals can claim to be the 'political opposition.' And most of them get away with it. Of course, in the West it's
much better to be a 'political prisoner' than a plain criminal. You get
much better treatment. Even respect."

"But at least we are a superpower, so you've got to admit Communism
must have done something right?"

"Our success has come at a horrendous cost. We'd surely have become
a superpower long ago without Communism. This is a huge country, and
we had all the resources imaginable—once. Just look at our economy
now. One of the reasons it's so inefficient is the absence of private property. But the communists simply can't afford to allow it. They know all too
well that as soon as anyone becomes economically independent, political
independence will follow. That's why most absolute monarchies have
fallen. Economically, this system is not terribly productive—it certainly
can't compete around the world. Probably as many as 60 percent of the
so-called workers produce nothing at all. The gangsters at the top have
behaved like any other criminal parasites: their appetites have kept
increasing. They've bled the country dry. Only the extraordinary natural
wealth of Russia has made it possible for them to go on doing this for so
many decades.

"Then, just like any criminal gang, after investing heavily in arms, they
started robbing other territories in the name of defense against the West,
but in reality it was just to keep the budget balanced. When they run out
of prey they'll get into serious trouble. Remember the joke—Will there be
stealing under Communism? The answer is, Yes, if they haven't stolen
everything during Socialism."

"Victor, I just don't understand how the communists have been able to
sustain this kind of total control. Why don't people rebel?"

"First of all, it's fear. And of course, there's dissent. We ourselves know
many dissidents. But many of them are effectively impotent. If you look
carefully you'll see that what most of the dissidents want is only to modify
the system, not do away with it. They don't see the real problem. What
they're preaching amounts to applying Band-Aids to a cancer lesion.
They don't understand that the system itself is evil and must be destroyed.
You have to consider the massive, endless propaganda, together with the
transformation of Communism into a compulsory pseudo-religion, the
sealing of the country's borders, the threat of the GULAG, the psychiatric
'hospitals,' the endless state of total war. Most of the public dissidents are
understandably intimidated. As a result, their objections are feeble. They
amount to no more than the mild proposition that there's been some

deviation from the original communist ideal. It's been practically impossible to go any further and still stay out of jail—or alive. This harsh suppression has resulted in the virtual absence of any attempt to question the root of the problem, the basic theory and practice of Communism itself."

As he heard himself explaining his conclusions to Olga, Victor was struck by the full force of what he was saying. And the danger he was in by simply coming to this brutally simple series of conclusions. For the first time he understood just how strong the system was, with its endless layers of defense against any possible expression of rebellion. He understood the real reason for the massive KGB penetration of society: any threat to absolute communist authority—any form of questioning—had to be exterminated in embryo. The paranoia was not illogical. Victor now knew from his own experience how one small chink in the armor could eventually corrode the whole system. He knew how one tiny compromise could eventually collapse a network. Finally, he understood why so many millions of people had been murdered and executed, or buried alive in jails, labor camps, and mental institutions.

They were lost in their separate thoughts. Olga broke the silence. "I'm sorry, Victor, you've been thinking about all of this for some time now. You've had time to accept it. I think that's as much as I can absorb for now."

Obviously, the starkness with which he had outlined the whole horrible picture had shaken Olga, but he was confident she wouldn't back away from the truth. Their friends who generally thought of her as a friendly, charming, sociable young woman would have been surprised by her quiet courage. He knew that she had the strength to digest what he was telling her. She'd just need a little time.

It was Friday, so Victor arranged for Elena to stay with his parents over the weekend. Both he and Olga were so disturbed by their conversation that they could not sleep that night. But the rule of no sensitive discussions in the house was strictly observed—now more than ever.

In the morning, after a mug of strong coffee, they went to the park again, Olga shivering with nervous apprehension.

Without any preamble she said, "Victor, as I see it, the worst part is this: if everything you've told me is true—and I'm sure it is—why didn't we figure it all out sooner?"

"Well, remember, Olga, I've been at war, the Cold War, since I was a kid. And my father has been a military man at war for forty years. One hundred–percent loyalty is at the heart of the military code."

"Yes, but you're hardly rank and file."

"True. But that's the genius of the system. You have to know enough about everything that's going on to be able to draw such clear conclusions. For that kind of big-picture perspective, you need to be pretty high up. To have gotten far enough to be trusted with a peek behind the wall of propaganda means you're already steeped in sin."

"Are you saying that everyone at the top sees as clearly as we do now?"

"Maybe not everyone. Most of those at the top are probably afraid to think too much. But if you're reasonably smart, at some point in your career you're faced with a choice: either you follow your conscience and do something about what you know, or you put blinders on and continue climbing higher up the ladder."

There was a pause, then Olga asked quietly, "Victor, where is that point?"

Hearing the question for what it was, he met her gaze steadily and answered, "It depends on who you are and where you are. The system is organized so that most people remain isolated, compartmentalized. There's no opportunity for an objective, comprehensive point of view. I'm sure for me the point of decision is arriving sooner than for most. First, because I'm in the KGB, where one learns more—sooner—than in other jobs. Secondly, because I'm relatively close to the top and in an unusual position. It's my job to know the big picture."

"But for the others older than you who are in a position to see and know—how can they live with themselves and do nothing?"

"Don't forget the baggage factor: by the time they reach that position, they have a great deal to lose—children, family, relatives, friends, position, power, money. Everything. They're effectively paralyzed by the privileges of their position. The system sees to that. If their conscience persists, the devil steps right in and presents them with the first stage of a Faustian bargain: 'Look, you're a good guy. There are lots of bad guys above you. If you play along and keep climbing, you'll get to where you are in a position to do more good.' And that's the trap. It sounds plausible, but it's really just a convenient rationalization for staying on and supporting the system."

Olga chided him, "Victor, in Mahindjauri, when we first talked about this, that was your argument, wasn't it? To stay and try to do things right. Wasn't that your devil rationalizing?"

Victor nodded ruefully. "I'm afraid it was."

"But that's terrible."

"There's worse, the second part of the Faustian bargain. You get in so deep that the easiest solution is simply not to think about the dilemma at all, to wipe it out of your mind. At least your dependents are protected. Even if they can't inherit, your children will survive. And that's just what most people do, I'm sure. Or drink, like Valentin."

It had always puzzled him that there were so many suicides among the upper echelon. Now he understood. These were the people who could see no way out. Their consciences would not allow them to simply carry on; neither could they come up with a viable alternative. For them, the Faustian bargain proved fatal. This was the conclusion that Victor did not share with Olga.

There was a long silence. They walked slowly, not looking at each other.

He thought out loud. "There just has to be a solution for us. It has to be there. I may not be able to see it yet, but my experience, my training, my very being tell me there has to be one. I simply don't believe in hopeless situations."

"Victor, I have faith in you, as I've said, I believe in you. But it does sound hopeless, as if there's nothing we can do, and if that's true, then what you're discussing is an impossible situation."

"Olga, nothing is impossible! I'll have to keep looking, but I will find a way. Believe me. One of the lessons I've learned from rock climbing is never to make any sudden moves when I'm in shaky balance. I think that's an especially good rule for us at this point. We just have to hang on tight—for now."

Olga was silent for a while, thinking. Then she turned to him and said, "I'm afraid it will take me more time to fully comprehend what you're telling me."

"Don't worry, most people never do. I'm not even sure that it was a good idea for me to share all this. It's already cost you your peace of mind."

"Oh, come on, Victor. What 'peace of mind?' You and I have always been honest with each other. I hope we always will be. Believe me, I'd rather know what you're thinking than be left in the dark. I prefer being troubled to being lonely."

They returned home, and Victor tried to give Olga some space. She needed time to sort things out for herself as Victor had. He was always nearby, available if she needed him. In turn, he was relieved and reassured by her strength.

CHAPTER

17

ON MONDAY VICTOR WENT BACK on automatic pilot. Just another routine day at the office. Around 5:30 Boss summoned him.

The moment Victor entered, warning flags went up. He saw the signs of serious trouble: Boss was calm and was not on the phone. Then the black monkey eyes suddenly drilled him. Victor met the look firmly. Mentally, he prepared himself for the worst. What could have given him away? *OK, if you want to play poker, let's play. At the very least I won't give you the pleasure of a psychological victory.* The twenty seconds of silence that followed felt like eternity.

Finally Boss said in a crisp, dry voice, "Sit down."

Victor took a few stiff steps forward and sat upright in the chair in front of Boss, still looking him right in the eye. Victor concentrated on making sure that his own eyes did not betray the slightest hint of insecurity—no flicker of "What's wrong?"—which Boss would have immediately interpreted as a sign of weakness. He deliberately controlled his breathing. It was calm and even.

"Well, what explanation can you give me this time, Comrade Sheymov?" Boss demanded in his meanest, most insinuating voice.

Victor's voice was firm and official, "I am not aware of anything that would require my explanation."

Suddenly black was white. Boss exploded into laughter, his black eyes shiny with merriment. In between bursts Boss said, "Totally mobilized for battle, as always. Relax, Victor. Everything's just fine." Once again, Victor had underestimated Boss the actor.

Boss explained, "For your exceptional and consistent performance, especially during some of your most recent assignments, the Leadership has decided to promote you to the position of Section Chief. Congratulations."

Victor's guard was up so tight that it took him a moment to grasp Boss's about-face. His automatic pilot came to the rescue. Numbly he said, "Thank you very much. It's a great honor." That was the KGB speaking. The civilized people. According to the military code he should have stood at attention and answered, "Serve-the-Soviet-Union!"

Still laughing, Boss continued, "Now you are officially going to be a member of the Leadership, especially considering the Section you'll be in charge of."

"Which one is that?"

"The Third Section. It's mission is going to be redirected. Your responsibilities will include the overall security of the KGB's cipher communications with all the residenturas abroad. Including the technical, physical, and personnel aspects of that security. The construction of the new communication centers in our embassies will also be your responsibility. Victor, this is the most important line job in the Department, and you're the youngest ever to be given such a position. On most aspects you will report to the Department Chief; on a few others, directly to me."

"Who's to be my deputy?" Key question.

"Davydov. He's a good guy. I'm sure you'll get along fine." Just over forty years old, Major Anatoly Davydov came from the Sixteenth Directorate, an expert at placing bugs in the foreign embassies in Moscow. But his strongest trait was his total loyalty to Boss. He was Boss's favorite. He'd be there to keep Victor in check.

"The responsibilities you've just indicated are considerable. Such a section will require a good many people."

"Don't worry, we will see to it that you have plenty of support. Besides, you will have the pick of the Directorate."

"That'll be a help."

"Again, don't worry about the details. Everything that is necessary will be done. What's more important is that politically, this job is highly sensitive. On the one hand, you'll have a lot of exposure to the Leadership. On the other, there's a great deal of risk out there. You'll need to maneuver skillfully. And you'll have to be firm and flexible—as the saying goes."

"I'll do my best."

"That's all for now. Go home and celebrate."

Victor thanked Boss again and got up to leave.

Boss stopped him at the door, "Oh, Victor? Just one more thing. Everyone is sure of your total loyalty, but some of your numerous connections make the Personnel Department nervous. As a member of the Leadership now you'll need to be more selective. I hope it won't be a problem for you. I'm sure you get my meaning."

"Yes, of course." Victor knew precisely what was meant. Faust, Part II. "Wonderful. That's all."

He left and went straight home, brooding on the irony of his situation. Not very long ago this promotion would have thrilled him. Victor realized that this final stroke of "luck" was going to push him past the point of no return.

That same evening Olga and Victor went for another walk in the park. The air was still and unusually humid, almost tropically thick and oppressive. Strange weather for Moscow. They made small talk, avoiding the subject that preoccupied them both.

Finally, Victor stopped and faced Olga, smiling wryly. "By the way, I've just been promoted to Section Chief." He shrugged. "So I'm supposed to be congratulated."

Automatically Olga asked, "What's the job?"

"Oh, it's pretty good. The highest position for a lieutenant colonel. The next one up means colonel. This gets me into the Directorate's Leadership. I'll be the youngest there. The Chief of that particular section is *nomenklatura*, appointed by the Central Committee. Most guys never make it that far."

Olga smiled sadly and took his hand as they started to walk again. "Should I cheer for you? You know, Victor, with all you've been telling me, I simply don't know how I am supposed to react."

"Neither do I. Believe me. For Christ's sake, Olga, this is exactly what you and I have been talking about! The second Faustian bargain. The choice couldn't be purer. And I have no one to blame for my situation—I certainly haven't got the excuse of being an ignorant victim of the system."

"So, what do we do?"

"I don't know. What I do know is that I just can't continue to be a part of this system, feeling guilty all my life. Even if I were to try, my conscience wouldn't allow it. I'd lose my self-respect and be finished as a person." After a long pause he continued, "Sometimes I almost wish I'd never tried to understand the communist system. But the plain fact is that I do understand it now, and Olga, I can't forget what I've learned."

"I know that, and I feel for you. But, Victor, ideology aside, we have to face the practical question: what are we going to do? There's not much I can contribute, except my moral support. It's really up to you."

"Yes, I know. But I agree with you that we have to make our decision soon. And then we'll know how to act." Victor knew all too well that he'd be playing for time at work. Once he had made up his mind and chosen a course of action, he could continue there for only a while, keeping up appearances and carrying out his job. But without a clear plan—and a clear head—he wouldn't be able to fool sharks like Bosik and Andreyev. They were much too smart and too experienced not to sense that Victor was up to something. Feeling as strongly as he did, sooner or later he'd be bound to reveal himself.

"But what can you do, Victor?"

"It's not just deciding what to do. The very first thing I need to answer is whether I just want out quietly, or whether I actually want to take on the whole system. There's an enormous responsibility involved. This has to sound presumptuous, I know, but my responsibility here is not only to you, to our daughter, to our parents, relatives, and friends, for God's sake. Some individuals are given great opportunities—tests, if you will. How they respond to these tests can make a real difference. The question is, how do I turn a potential personal disaster into a meaningful act. Simply escaping this jam doesn't seem enough, somehow. I feel an obligation to those who are already slaves to the system—as well as to those in other countries who run the risk of becoming slaves if their eyes aren't opened. They must understand the threat of Communism and take it seriously."

He paused for a moment, his train of thought interrupted by a new idea. "You know, I often think of those Germans who tried to assassinate Hitler. They were very courageous men. But killing one man, even if he was the dictator, would not abolish the whole Fascist system in Germany. Such an act only emphasizes the futility of isolated individual gestures, no matter how heroic. The system is what has to be destroyed."

"Victor, are you saying you can destroy the system? That's hardly realistic, surely?"

"I'm not sure how much I can do, but I know what needs to be done."

"Well, knowing you, I can't imagine you taking half-measures."

He acknowledged her observation with a rueful smile. She continued. "How about helping the dissidents, or getting together with other people like yourself?"

"I wouldn't have a prayer. The dissidents are completely penetrated by the KGB. The KGB is even more thoroughly penetrated by the KGB. . . ."

Olga winced at the joke.

She hesitated. "I would be terribly afraid for you, but what if you were to take a public stand, the way Sakharov did? Maybe a lot of publicity would protect you."

"I couldn't pull that off either. I'd be put away instantly. And besides, Sakharov's like the other dissidents. He's only trying to improve the system, not abolish it. I have tremendous respect for his courage. I don't know if I have that much myself. But the bottom line for me is that he's a liberal, a 'democratic' communist—which as far as I'm concerned is actually a contradiction in terms. That's why he's still alive." Victor stopped, then said slowly, "You see, Valentin was going to do exactly that. Take a public stand. That's why he was murdered."

"What?" Olga was stunned.

"Yes. By the KGB. I didn't want to tell you. You had enough pressure."

Olga's knees buckled, and Victor thought she was going to faint. Maybe it had been a mistake to tell her about Valentin. He held her tightly, and slowly they started back.

On the way home he said, "Olga, I don't know exactly what I'm going to do. But I do know that the only way to deal with Communism is to bring the real truth about the system to people—open their eyes. I have to find a way to rip the veil of secrecy from the operating methods of the Party's Central Committee and the KGB. That's the cortex of the whole system. By chance, I happen to be one of a relative handful with unusually powerful leverage in this respect. I must find a way to use it so that I maximize the damage I can do to the system. That's my overall goal. Now all I have to figure out is how to achieve it." *Right—a minor detail.*

The next few days were difficult. Olga was trying to catch up and absorb the implications of their latest conversation, and Victor was trying to gauge its impact on her. And he was desperately looking for a solution. A practical one. They almost stopped talking altogether. It was as if there'd been a death in the family.

Finally, Victor felt that they were both ready to take a new step.

He realized that their frequent walks and quiet but obviously intense discussions in the park were becoming a pattern that might attract the attention of his watchers. And not just the formal surveillance. There were plenty of volunteers in their KGB apartment building. To break the pattern they went to Gorky Park several days later after work. Not the main entrance, though, where all the tourists grazed in one large herd. There was another part of Gorky Park that few tourists knew about, private and beautiful, stretching out behind the Academy of Science on

Leninsky Prospect. They took the Metro to Gagarin Square and doubled back a few blocks toward Krymsky Val on the Garden Ring by the left side of the Prospect. The narrow and little-known Titovskiy Proyezd street led to the entrance of Niskuchny Sad, the more-secluded section of Gorky Park. Niskuchny Sad was on higher ground than the rest of that portion of Gorky Park, so there was a gentle and pleasant downhill walk toward Krymsky Most.

They both knew why they were there, and it wasn't for the romantic environment. Victor came straight to the point. "I've done all the thinking I can. Theoretically, we have five alternatives."

"Theoretically! You mean that you've already made your decision."

Victor laughed: "You know me too well." Then he paused and added more gravely, "You're the only person on earth who could know me so well and still not make me uncomfortable." Then he continued: "Seriously, these are my options: one, to resign for 'reasons of health'; two, to stand up and throw the truth in their faces; three, to establish an underground anticommunist party; four, to commit suicide; and the fifth is to escape from the country." He interrupted Olga's reaction with a gesture of his hand and continued, "Don't worry, I said I was speaking theoretically. The first four options amount to suicide anyway. If I resigned, they'd smell something fishy and come after me, but that's not the point. The point is that it wouldn't achieve anything anyway. As for number two, you know what happened to Valentin. As far as organizing a party, the country is riddled with informers. At a rough estimate, I'd have about two weeks. So, since I'm not the suicidal type, the only viable alternative is to escape. It's the only choice."

Olga was astounded. "Do you understand what you're saying? That's . . . ," she stammered, unable to say the word "desertion."

Victor had anticipated her reaction. "Desertion? No, absolutely not. Deserters run away from a fight. We're going to run *in order* to fight."

"It's still hard to comprehend, Victor."

"Think about it. This way we don't surrender. On the contrary, we'd surrender if we stayed, because then we'd have zero chance of destroying the evil. So, realistically, I don't think I have a choice—it's my destiny, if you will. I have to do everything I can to destroy this communist system. Or at least to inflict the greatest possible damage on it before I die."

Olga was speechless.

Victor rushed on, "Thanks to the system, we don't really know much about those people in the West. Maybe they're good, maybe they're bad. I've never given the question much thought, actually. They've simply been The Enemy. Now, frankly, I don't care what the answer is. I can work with anyone short of the devil himself to achieve my goal."

"Darling, I'm scared."

"Don't be. This goal is worth shooting for, and whether we win or lose, fear is irrelevant." It hurt him to see her wince at the harshness of his professional response, but it couldn't be helped. She had to know the reality.

They were approaching a crowded part of the park, so they switched to neutral chatter—quite a strain, given the turmoil in their minds. They made their way to the main gate. Catching a taxi home was surprisingly easy.

Over the next few days Victor's brain worked nonstop. He was sure the same was true with Olga. Finally, on Saturday afternoon, she whispered, "I can't take it anymore. Let's go outside."

They walked silently down the stairs, back to the park. No director could have created a better backdrop for the scene. Dark, leaden clouds made the middle of the day seem like late twilight. With no wind at all the scene looked surreal.

Olga started the conversation. "Victor, I understand the logic of what you're saying, but I just cannot comprehend a step like defection. Maybe, it's my own lifelong brainwashing, but I cannot imagine us leaving all our relatives, our friends, our country, for heaven's sake. Never seeing any of them again? What are we going to do abroad? No language, no anything. Even the thought of it is unbearable."

"I know. I never said it would be easy."

"And what about our daughter? What can we give her there? What will happen to her if we fail?"

"OK, Olga, suppose we stay? Say we somehow manage to pull off the charade. She'll continue to receive her communist brainwashing with our support and encouragement." He followed that thought to its inevitable conclusion. "Any break in our facade, any slip, and our own little communist could inadvertently blow the whistle on us. Even worse, she might even deliberately turn us in. Just remember that boy in her kindergarten, the one who upset you so much."

"Even to think about Elena as one of them is more than I can bear."

"The way I see it, every step in this logic takes us deeper and deeper into a living hell. If we stay we face a life of cynicism and the total loss of our self-respect. The most profound isolation. It would destroy us." He did not add his next thought out loud: suicide would seem to be his only way out—the ultimate defection, but no solution. Suicide would stigmatize Olga and Elena and inevitably lead to questions—and conclusions.

"Victor, I'm confused. What will our friends and relatives think of us? Won't they see us as traitors?"

"As long as I'm absolutely convinced that what we're doing is right, I don't care who thinks what. But I'm sure many of them will understand that the real traitor of the country and the people is the communist government." Victor paused for a long moment, and reluctantly added, "Eventually."

There was a long, long silence. At last, Olga broke it. "I just cannot bear the uncertainty any longer."

"Well, let's go over it again then. We're not running away from a fight. We're trying to escape a situation we have no hope of surviving. Even if by some miracle we did, we would not be able to live with ourselves. We're leaving so that we'll be able to fight. There's no cowardice in that. As a matter of fact, we're risking everything." It was a classic understatement.

Quietly, Olga said, "I understand."

Victor just nodded. He knew that there was no way in the world for Olga to understand how slim the odds for their success really were. He'd have to bear the responsibility for the decision.

Suddenly they noticed that they were talking louder. There was a strong wind now. Olga looked up. "Look, Victor! There's almost no sky there."

He pressed on: "Olga, believe me, this is the only way we have a chance of doing some real damage to the system. It's certainly a very slim chance. But it's much better than having no chance at all, like those millions this monster has already killed."

She leaned against him. "This is terrifying for me. I'm sorry, but I need time."

He put his arm around her and said gently, "Let's go home."

Slowly, they headed back to their building. Victor sensed that Olga had already made her decision, and he was grateful for her courage and her love. He knew now that they were walking to a place that was no longer home. The storm was about to break.

Part II

THE MAZE

CHAPTER

1

TIMEOUT. That was precisely what Victor needed. Not that the pace of the game was too fast—he knew all too well it would get much faster, and very soon. He just needed a short break, to reflect on where he was, where he was going, and how he was to get there.

It was mid-morning, and Victor found himself sitting at his desk on the seventh floor of the Tower. No major earthquakes. He was mechanically turning the pages of a report, comprehending neither what was in that report nor even what it was about. Automatically, Victor recalled that Boss and Koryakov, among other members of the top management of the directorate, were in Fili, at the Eighth CD Headquarters, getting injections of energy and wisdom from Andreyev. Some meetings of the Leadership were all-inclusive, others were arranged according to the Leadership's inner categories. A top-level meeting for a Chief Directorate included only chiefs of the Directorates, their deputies, and the Chiefs of the Departments. Since Victor wasn't in any of those categories, he hadn't been invited.

Victor thought for a moment. Luckily, he'd come to work by car, and it was parked just downstairs, in Vorovsky Square. He put the report in the safe and locked it with both locks. A sure sign he wouldn't be coming back today. Five minutes later he was on his way to the countryside.

* * *

Abramtsevo. One of his and Olga's favorite places around Moscow. They'd been here together many times. It was almost strange for Victor to be in Abramtsevo without her. Victor didn't even bother with the museum. He needed to be alone. Using familiar paths, he went to a remote part of the magnificent estate. Not that it was formally grand; it was simply a perfect country retreat. The most attractive time here was the fall, but even now the color of the foliage had become just a shade warmer. In a short while the leaves would turn to gold. The natural and unregimented beauty of the park slowed Victor's pace and brought his wandering thoughts into focus.

Yes. The decision had been made. They'd have to defect. There was no other way that would give him a shot at the profoundly evil system.

Victor found himself in an unfamiliar moral territory. So far, when he'd taken chances, he'd put only himself at risk. Now it was very different. Victor was talking to himself: "Now, calm down. You've got to be absolutely cold-blooded. Cool as a cucumber. No emotions. Any emotion can cause an error. Any error can kill you. And your family. Yes, your wife and daughter. You certainly have a right to risk your own head, but do you have a moral right to risk your family? Especially when they aren't capable of comprehending the level of risk. Even Olga, no matter how much you tell her about the KGB, doesn't have a chance of understanding it. You have to be in the system, and high up, for that. So there's no way even Olga can make her own relatively informed decision."

A long time ago his father had given Victor a good maxim: "If you have something worthwhile to risk for, go ahead, take the chance. Even if it's one in a million. If the goal isn't worth the risk, don't take nine to one." Good guideline. For yourself. How about others? How about those you love? Easy, when you're a commander and you have to send your troops to an almost certain death. Soldiers know what they're in for. Children do not. Soldiers can fight. Children cannot. *Here we go again. Moral choices.*

Victor came upon a large tree stump and sat on it. The possibility of failure weighed on him. The possibility of being cut down by the system, of going down the well-traveled path followed by so many. Leo Tolstoy had philosophized, using an oak as a model. "Our generation has to settle for an oak stump," Victor mused. He put his hand on the wood. "This used to be an old oak. Cut down. But the more you grow before being cut, the better foundation you make for someone else. And you never know in what way. If I'm lucky, even having failed, I can be of use to somebody down the road, in some unpredictable way, like this stump, so comfortable for my butt. At least that's something."

OK, let's stop wobbling. Sort things out. Make decisions and act.

"So, the Number One question is: Do I have a moral right to put my family at risk, and to a degree they cannot comprehend?" Victor considered this for a while. Then the answer came to him: "For lack of any better idea, let's consider the alternative. If I want to avoid the risk to my family, I'll have to continue working for the communist system, contributing to its strength. I simply cannot do that. And if I didn't, my family would suffer almost as much as if we fail to defect. Moreover, even if I could keep on doing business as usual, my daughter will continue getting those massive doses of brainwashing and, God forbid, will become a devoted communist. So the answer has to be yes, at least by default. But in the end I'll probably never know the answer to the big one. And God help me not to have to face it when it's not academic."

"Now, to question Number Two: Where to defect to? Given that the goal of the defection is to fight the communist system, it only makes sense to defect to a country strong enough to do so. Besides, there are practical operational restrictions. There are only a handful of countries in the world with intelligence services really capable of pulling off an exfiltration operation from the Soviet Union: the United States, Great Britain, West Germany, and perhaps Israel. Realistically, that's about all," he concluded.

Israel would not fit the bill overall. Victor also knew that West Germany was thoroughly penetrated through the East German service, and the danger of walking into a waiting trap was too great even for Victor's taste. On top of that, even knowing it was wrong, Victor couldn't overcome his prejudice, the aftertaste of World War II. To say nothing of the fact that it was the Germans who had played a major role in helping the communists to usurp power in Russia during World War I. So, the last two on the list were out.

Choosing between the United States and Great Britain was difficult. To some extent it might well be academic since the whole approach was chancy at best, and it was impossible to predict what kind of opportunity would come Victor's way. But still, priorities should be set.

There was no clear-cut choice between the CIA and MI6. On the one hand, being much bigger, the CIA should statistically have the larger set of operational alternatives. Also, the famous British "fifth man" had still not been located, nor had other possible "deferred payments" Great Britain might yet make for some of its elite's flirtation with Communism. On the other hand, in a large organization like the CIA there was a much greater chance of a bureaucratic slipup, which could prove deadly in an intelligence operation. Besides, the fact that no "four men" had been discovered in America didn't mean that "all five" weren't happily operating there. So Victor felt it was hard to choose between the two organizations. *Let it be a draw for now.*

When it came to weighing the pros and cons of the two countries themselves, Victor felt distinctly at a loss. Even though he was better informed than most on the Main Enemy's positions on geopolitical issues, he was appalled at how relatively uninformed he was about real life in the West. He'd never even spoken to an Englishman or an American. Now more than ever he was irritated by the fact that what he did know was based on communist propaganda. Finally, to his dismay, Victor had to admit that the only sense he had of the difference between the two countries was that America had a tradition of offering a relatively safe harbor to foreigners, most of whom were fleeing trouble in their native lands, for one reason or another. English society, he reckoned, based on his limited knowledge, was notorious for being static, structured, and elitist—a tough place to start from scratch. On the basis of these superficial impressions, Victor concluded that he and his family would probably adapt more easily to a new life in America.

One more consideration crossed Victor's mind. He recalled that Oleg Penkovsky, the army colonel executed in Moscow for espionage, had initially worked with the British. Later, that became a joint operation with the Americans. Considering the extreme sensitivity of the matters Victor was involved in, it was absolutely essential to limit the number of people in any intelligence service who even knew of his existence. He concluded that the British were very likely to get the Americans involved, while the Americans most likely would not even give a hint of his existence to the British. If you double the number of people "in the loop," you at least double the risk.

OK, the Americans are the first choice. The British will be our backup.

Victor stood up and started walking slowly, in no particular direction. *Two down, a hundred to go.*

Now, question Number Three: How to contact the Americans? His wife and daughter were hostages, forever forbidden to leave the country. They couldn't even travel into the Soviet Union's own backyard, such as Bulgaria. So, there was no point in even considering the three of them simply walking into an American embassy anywhere in the world—which would have been nice and easy. The American embassy in Moscow was too heavily guarded around the clock: it was out of the question to try to penetrate its KGB guards—even alone. A lot of people tried that without knowing what they were up against, and paid dearly. If all else failed, which was inconceivable, the guards simply shot to kill. Even if somebody were to have the incredible luck of getting inside, then what? Sit out the rest of your life in the embassy? No, that was no way to go.

Bearing all of this in mind, he still had no choice but to contact the Americans and make the arrangements for all three of them to get out at a later date through by far the most tightly guarded border in the world.

Generally, outside of the Soviet Union, Americans are much less intensely surveilled, and their embassies are much less closely guarded by the host country. That seemed to present a possible opportunity. However, because of his job, Victor had to stay on the premises of the Soviet embassy during his trips abroad, and could go outside it only if he was accompanied by a KGB guard, usually the Chief Security Officer of the embassy. The prospect of attempting to contact the Americans under such conditions, and on top of that to return back for his family, made Victor shiver. "No, no, too crazy even for my taste," he mumbled.

Well, the only thing left is Moscow. I've got to contact an American here. So be it.

There were hundreds of Americans in Moscow. But Victor knew that there were Americans, and there were Americans, with a world of difference between them. Some of them were intelligence officers, some were diplomats, some were businessmen or tourists. Some of them were honest, some were not. Some of them came on their own, and some were lured or just brought in by the KGB. And the KGB was working on all of them. Relentlessly.

With the problem of Soviets' traveling abroad well under control, the KGB's biggest problem in Moscow was the physical proximity of foreigners to the Inner Ward Members, the "carriers of the secrets." That proximity suggested possible opportunities to those who would want, for whatever reason, to volunteer to cooperate with the West. The KGB took this problem extremely seriously and devoted a great deal of energy to it. As with most things the KGB focuses on, its efforts were remarkably effective.

Characteristically, the KGB attacked the issue from both ends, intimidating Soviets and foreigners alike. Unless they happened to be a KGB officer or an informer, Soviet citizens were aggressively dissuaded from any contact with foreigners. And any foreigner who in the KGB's view was too active in his contacts with Soviets was given a really hard time. As a result, people on both sides developed a Pavlovian reflex, and became extremely cautious about their contacts with one another.

Suppose Victor did manage to contact an American. The first danger awaiting him was that the American might be "friendly" with the KGB. The second danger was that the American might be justifiably frightened of a KGB provocation and make a big stink out of Victor's approach. Then the KGB would unquestionably find Victor, and quickly. The third, and more likely, possibility was that the American might just be someone who wanted no part of any spy games. And then all the risks he had taken to establish the contact would have been for naught. Victor had no illusions that if any attempt by him to contact an American were noticed it would be misinterpreted. Any professional would know there could be only one reason for Victor to try to contact a foreigner, especially a NATO-country native: Espionage. He'd have zero chance of getting away with it. So the only type of contact Victor was interested in was an intelligence officer.

So, Victor concluded, here's my immediate task. Contact an American KIO—known intelligence officer—and offer my expertise in exchange for exfiltration and political asylum for me and my family. He realized that this mission, far beyond any other he had ever attempted, should be classified "impossible." *What the hell, why not pull off one of these for a good cause for a change?*

It was time to go home.

Olga was waiting for him. After supper, Victor suggested, "Let's go downtown and stroll around for a bit, see what's going on."

"Sure." Her eyes narrowed with tension; she knew exactly what the "stroll" would be about. Olga was getting into the game.

They got out of the Metro at Marx Prospect and started walking down Gorky Street.

Half-jokingly, Victor asked: "So, no regrets so far?"

"Of course not. Did you have doubts about me?"

Victor laughed. "No, just checking. I just want to make sure you understand a few things."

"Victor, please. I know what you're about to say. I know it's dangerous, so don't try to scare me even more. Let's get down to business. How can I help?"

As so many times before, Victor realized he had underestimated Olga once again.

All right. Perhaps you're right. Perhaps I'm just subconsciously trying to shift some of my responsibility to you. I suppose I'm just kidding myself. The responsibility rests with me. Period.

He continued, "At least we should set the ground rules. There is one thing I want to make sure that you understand. I can assure you that in our circumstances the risk—the probability of failure—is much greater than you think. No matter what you think it is. And once we've started, the time bomb is set. It's a race against the clock." He grinned and added, "With one minor detail—we'll have no idea how much time there'll be between the start and the bang."

Olga tried to be cheerful: "Well, uncertainty does add excitement."

"Believe me, you'll have all the uncertainty you can handle. Remember when I asked you to marry me, I told you I couldn't promise you anything like prosperity or happiness. The only thing I did promise you was you wouldn't be bored."

Olga laughed. "Sure, I remember. It was an unusual proposal."

"Now that's truer than ever." Victor paused for a second. "Now, the ground rules. You have no earthly idea what I am up to, OK?"

"Now wait, Victor. We're both in this together, and I don't need any shielding. I know what I'm doing. As I already told you, I'm convinced it's the right thing to do. So, I'm prepared to take my full share of the responsibility for it."

Victor looked at Olga. *Oh, God, if she could only imagine what that "responsibility" means if we get caught.* He said, "It's not a matter of you alone. It's our daughter too. If we're both caught, the State will take her. And they will make sure she grows up a perfect communist. The only chance we may have to save her is if you're out of it. So I want you to swear one thing to me. If I am caught, you will publicly denounce me, express your outrage, demand a divorce, and say whatever they tell you to."

Olga's face froze. Her steps became stiff, mechanical. Unshed tears shone in her eyes. His heart was breaking at what he had to put her through. But he had no choice. She could barely speak. "Do you understand what you are asking me to do?"

"Fully. When you think about it, you'll realize there's no other choice. Olga, you can call it a sacrifice for our child. I don't want to discuss it any further, not now or any time later. I want us to settle this once and for all. Swear you'll do it."

There was a long, long pause. Finally Olga whispered, "I swear."

That hurdle cleared, Victor tried to lighten the mood. "Oh, by the way, did I mention before that I'm not the suicidal type? What I mean is that I promise you I'll do absolutely everything in my power to succeed. Besides, do you really believe I'd start this if I didn't believe we'd win?"

"I'm sure you'll find a way, Victor. It's just the thought of a failure that's so painful." She paused and took a deep breath. All business now, she asked, "What about the ground rules?"

"As we already agreed, Rule One is that as far as anyone on earth is concerned, you haven't the faintest idea about either my ideological convictions or what I'm doing." Victor continued without pausing: "Rule Two. No more ideological discussions or doubts. No emotions. They're distractions. We'll need to concentrate all our energies on the task at hand."

"Agreed."

"Rule Three. Total discipline. I run the show. You'll help me, but only when I ask. No volunteering."

"OK."

"Rule Four. No changes in our lifestyle. I mean, visible changes. That's not as easy as it sounds. You'll have to analyze all your habits and very deliberately stick to them. Everything must stay absolutely the same, with only one exception."

"What's that?"

"Morally, we have to protect our closest friends. So for their own sake we'll have to provoke a chill and separation. We'll have to do it extremely carefully and as gradually as we can."

"But that's a contradiction of what you just said. By doing that we'll change our habits."

"True. As well as whatever I do to contact the other side. But the one is an operational necessity, and the other is a moral responsibility. So we've got to do it, and try to do it very smoothly, minimizing the risk. As far as our friends are concerned, this is actually a good time. With my promotion I am 'entitled' to become a bit snobbish, to get rid of some chaff among old friends. It happens all the time, particularly with that psychological type who can't take success in stride, who believes that all of a sudden he's a superior person because he's climbed higher up the social ladder. I reckon no one will be suspicious. Perhaps just some of our old friends will be disappointed."

"But that's disgusting! It'll be so hard to be so low. I'd be ashamed."

"Sure. Any better ideas?"

Olga thought for a while. She was taken aback by Victor's being so matter-of-fact about such emotional issues. "I guess not. But how can you be so cool about it?"

"Just remember Rule Two."

Olga said nothing, only nodded and sighed.

They were approaching the Belarussky station and it was rather late, so they went inside and caught the Metro back to their apartment.

CHAPTER

VICTOR'S IMMEDIATE TASK was clearly defined: to establish contact with an American KIO, a Known Intelligence Officer.

Victor wondered which was the better way: to know all the strengths of the enemy and use that knowledge to try to defeat him, or not to know anything and just take the plunge and hope for the best. He recalled how several years back the Soviet border, assessed as "impregnable" by most of the world's experts, was penetrated in a most embarrassing way.

In the middle of the night a flash cable from the Helsinki residentura had arrived at First CD Headquarters. The cable stated that the Finnish police had contacted the embassy about a group of political-asylum seekers, asking what the Soviets wanted done about them.

The defection per se was no surprise to the KGB; defections had occurred many times before. Neither was the fact that the Finns asked the embassy what to do with the defectors a surprise—little-publicized "cozy" arrangements like that between the two governments were well known to all concerned within the KGB. The startling fact was that the group hadn't jumped ship but had managed to sneak across the border—by definition impossible. An even more startling detail was that the group consisted of four teenagers, aged between fourteen and nineteen, who all came from the same village deep in the middle of nowhere in Russia. The teenagers had surrendered all the equipment they'd used to penetrate the border: a two-by-three-foot general map of the Soviet Union and a hiking compass. The KGB resident in Helsinki, at the end of the cable, hinted at the possibility of a practical joke by the Finnish police, but taking no chances, he made his report to the Center and took off to see the perpetrators.

The story proved to be absolutely true. It was the ultimate embarrassment for the famed Border Guards and cost a few careers. During the investigation the KGB extensively interrogated and intimidated the teenagers, then offered them anything they wanted if they would repeat the trick—just to find out how they had penetrated the border, and in a way that had left absolutely no trace. To no avail.

Much as he envied those teenagers, Victor still preferred a different approach, with exact knowledge of the full strength of the enemy and no illusions. He also felt that if one can be intimidated by the enemy's power, the battle itself is pointless—in effect, one has already been defeated. Victor made sure he wasn't intimidated.

But the enemy was powerful indeed. Victor fully realized that he was going to be operating in a distinctly hostile environment. Still, it wasn't the hostility per se that worried Victor most of all. It was the uncertainty. He understood the deviousness of the KGB better than even most of its insiders. The most dangerous aspect of the KGB style was its layered structure. You could begin to see it when you were deep enough in the know. Victor was, all right. By then you usually knew how many and what layers were below you. But you never knew about the layers above you—neither what they were, nor how many. Everything tempted you to conclude that you knew the "real truth." Even at Victor's level of access this wasn't always true. *Christ! It's like trying to find and defuse a land mine which is booby-trapped which is booby-trapped which is booby-trapped.* . . .

Victor's troubleshooting experience had taught him that no matter how carefully you make a plan in advance, things go differently, and usually by the end of an affair there's virtually nothing left of the original plan. While the jury was still out on the issue, many felt planning in such situations was a formality and really wasn't worth pursuing seriously—just enough to satisfy the bureaucrats. Victor felt strongly, however, that meticulous planning in any uncertain situation was absolutely essential, even if one knew in advance that everything would go differently. When you don't have the time to think, you can only act and react. Your reflexes and instincts are better if you've done your homework. The issues you're dealing with become an extension of your mind and your body.

With that conviction in mind, Victor began to lay out his plan and organize his homework. First of all, the term "establishing a contact" had to be defined. It needed to be defined precisely, every phase of it, every motion. It was not a question of just finding a number in a phone book and making a call.

Right. Victor sat in an armchair in the living room after supper. *Let's sort things out. Question one: Do you know the playground?*

He had always assumed he did. After all, Moscow was his turf. Probably more so than for even many KGB counterintelligence officers—the guys he'd be directly up against. He also knew a lot about the KGB and its operations. The trouble, he realized, was that while his understanding was solid, and he could see the big picture, his knowledge of the finer details of counterintelligence operations was more sporadic. The reasons were simple: first of all, counterintelligence wasn't his cup of tea; secondly, he'd always tried to stay away from "internal affairs." *But who cares about the reasons why you don't know something? Facts are what count. Details, especially minor ones, are what kill you in intelligence. As a matter of fact, I can't recall a single major failure in intelligence caused by a major mistake. Each one of them was caused by a minor error in a minor detail.*

Well, what exactly do you know about the operational environment in Moscow? Victor started to think.

To say that Moscow was an operational nightmare was a gross understatement. Every foreigner visiting the city was surrounded by troops of the countless army of KGB informers. A safe assumption was that more than half the foreigners' Soviet contacts were reporting to the KGB. Those informers were in addition to the KGB officers, who paid specific attention to those foreigners who were more interesting than others either because they were suspect or because they presented a good potential for recruitment. Naturally, NATO countries' nationals were given vastly more attention than the others'.

For instance, most restaurants frequented by foreigners had sufficient "*literniye*" or "marked" tables to accommodate them all. Those tables were permanently equipped with listening devices, which were connected to tape recorders in the "object control" room—the room at the "object" or facility where all "internal intelligence" such as these taped conversations was gathered.

The same type of hospitality prevailed in the hotel rooms for foreigners, often with the addition of optical devices permitting full observation. Many foreigners assumed that to be the case, so the natural solution for doing something without being observed seemed to be the bathroom. As a result, hotel bathrooms were the KGB's most productive sources of information. The KGB's observation of a guest's activities during the first couple of days of his or her stay, coordinated with intelligence received from abroad, played a major role in deciding on a further course of action.

So if a Soviet citizen were to approach a foreigner out of the blue, the probability was very high that that foreigner was either in the company of a KGB informant or was under surveillance. The procedure followed by a surveillance team in a case of even the most casual approach, such as someone's asking for a light, was very simple. The team split up, and one part followed the contact until he or she was "homed" and fully identified. Then there'd be an investigation. If the contact belonged to the Inner Ward or was a relative of someone who did, even if the foreigner was the most innocent student or tourist, a major case was under way.

A KIO was an entirely different game. The surveillance team for a KIO could comprise as many as sixteen or even up to twenty teams in cars as well as others on foot. That was in addition to the stationary surveillance, sometimes disguised as the traffic police who frequently manned major intersections. On top of that there were *visirs,* surveillance stations armed with powerful optics.

And more: homing devices were planted on many foreigners' cars, so their movements were very closely followed by the central control station, with the aid of several monitoring towers with direction-finding antennas.

Is that all? Victor asked himself. *It's all I can remember for now. And I just don't know if there's anything else. That's the trouble.* He laughed to himself. *For any reasonable person there should be enough trouble in what I do know about, without worrying about what I don't. But then I haven't been considered a reasonable person too often.*

He knew that no matter how powerful the defense was, to a professional the most dangerous thing was something unexpected, however simple. It's entirely possible to circumvent the most sophisticated security system, only to knock over an empty beer can in a dark room.

Anything else, anything trickier? Victor searched his memory.

Oh, yes. The decoy cars. The decoy cars were yet one more KGB technique for catching would-be defectors. Cars, usually American, with the diplomatic plates of the American embassy, "D-04," roamed aimlessly around the city, parking from time to time. The foreign-looking drivers would get out of the cars, take a walk or buy something, and then get back into the cars. All that just to lure would-be defectors. The drivers, of course, were KGB officers, and their job was considered among the best in the Seventh, the surveillance Directorate.

"Now, let's see how one can approach a KIO," Victor asked himself.

"The telephone is out. Foreigners' phones are eavesdropped on around the clock. A letter is also out. Every letter addressed to a foreigner is 'per-lustrated'—opened, read, and analyzed. The only option left seems to be a personal contact. Perhaps, with a variation of dropping a note. Handing it directly to a KIO or dropping it inside a car. That would shorten the contact. OK, at least that's a place to start."

Victor shook his head at the unfolding picture and started to figure out which of the two options was the better. "Obviously, a note is incriminat-ing. If it somehow gets into the hands of the KGB, it's more than likely the game will end shortly thereafter. First of all, a small note dropped into a car might not even be noticed by the addressee and could be found by the KGB during the next search. Foreigner's cars, especially KIOs', are searched pretty often. Secondly, there are all those horror stories about Americans who get tired of KGB provocations and, afraid each contact is just another one, might well turn such a note over to the KGB, and make a big stink out of it for good measure. One of those stories that are impossible to verify. Sounds stupid, but who knows? Besides, there's that nagging pos-sibility, sitting in the back of every intelligence officer's mind: What if you somehow become unconscious? Just a traffic accident, robbery, or some other dumb reason. The hospital personnel will then find the note or what-ever other 'sexy' stuff you might have on you. End of game.

"On the other hand," Victor continued thinking, "suppose there's no note. What must I accomplish with the first personal contact? One, estab-lish my bona fide; two, establish a clandestine means of communication; three, get away without being noticed by the guy's surveillance. How much time do I need for that?"

After he thought a minute, the answer came: "Well, at least ten min-utes. On the assumptions that the guy is sharp and speaks Russian very well." Victor didn't like the idea of betting his life on such assumptions. Besides, ten minutes was too much to expect. Handing over a note, on the other hand, would take just a few seconds.

"All right," he concluded, "a note. So be it. I'll have enough trouble stealing even those few seconds." He sighed, "It would be nice to cut those seconds down to one or two."

Victor was so deep in his thought that he didn't sense Olga's coming up behind him. "Let's catch some fresh air before we go to bed."

"With pleasure."

They went along Tepliy Stan Street. As always, the sidewalk along the park wasn't crowded. They met a neighbor who was walking her meticu-lously clipped poodle. Victor mumbled, almost talking to himself, "These days they're even using pet dogs like this one for surveillance all over town."

Olga was startled by his remark and broke into laughter: "Victor, I've lived with you for a long time, and I still can't get used to your sense of humor."

Victor had just realized the situation was really funny. "That's because I'm not joking."

Olga laughed again, than suddenly stopped. "What?"

"They are. Some kind of new, very secret program. I've no idea what they're up to. Something sophisticated, a cross between new tech and an old dog."

Olga was incredulous. "You know, this kind of environment could drive anyone crazy. I don't know how you still manage to stay normal."

Victor shrugged. "I'm not sure I am."

They walked silently for a while, Olga still smiling, trying to envision a KGB heavy with a joyful poodle, both on the KGB payroll.

Then Olga asked, "Any news?"

"Not really. Just trying to sort things out. I figure I have to approach a known American intelligence officer. Here, in Moscow. As a practical matter, there's no other choice."

"So, you're saying we're going to America?"

"I think so. I hope you don't have any objections."

"No, but it's a little scary. There's so much crime there, so many poor people. You see it in the papers all the time."

"In our papers. Propaganda." Victor smiled. "The only thing I know for sure is that that can't be true. The real situation must be either better or worse. In any case, don't believe propaganda."

She picked up his teasing tone. "You know, you've a habit of making fun of me when I'm in dire need of your loving support. You are not a reasonable husband." She stopped, looked at him, and reiterated: "You most certainly are not!" Then she laughed happily and kissed him.

After a short pause Olga said: "Now, Victor, please get serious. What do we do next?"

"I've told you, I've got to hand a note to an American KIO. Then we'll see."

"How many of those do you know?"

"To be precise, none."

"Can you find out about them?"

"No."

Olga was getting irritated. "Victor, please, stop it. I am very serious."

"So am I. The KGB is highly compartmentalized. I may know a lot of secrets, but any specific information of that kind is beyond my need to know. Any attempt to find out will immediately trigger very strong suspicion. They know all too well there are only two reasons for someone in my position to fish out a KIO: espionage or defection."

"So, in other words, you haven't a clue?"

"Well, luckily enough, I hope I do have one clue. Not long ago I bumped into a surveillance guy whom I met abroad at a KGB station. He showed me an American KIO passing by. I still remember the car, the place, and the time. Sounds like he might be my man."

"How can you track him down?"

"I don't know yet. I don't even know if he's still here. That kind of guy generally doesn't last in a country for too long. Besides, he'd be under constant heavy surveillance. That's true, though, for any KIO. But there are other possibilities as well. Bumping into an opportunity, for one. Sometimes you recognize an intelligence officer by some nuances in his behavior. Intuition. Hard to explain."

"Well, you have to be the judge. How long will it take to find such an opportunity?"

"Might be forever. It's just a matter of luck. But it's the least risky way."

"What can I do?"

"Not much. I can't take you with me on a hunt. But I'll need to do a lot of driving around. Just give me as many reasons as you can for me to use the car so it doesn't seem unusual. Make sure our in-house ears hear you send me out on errands. If I resist—and I will from time to time—just insist. I'll choose the routes and take care of the rest."

"How about the 'change of lifestyle'?"

"Good question. We'll have to just do the best we can. We don't have much of an alternative at the moment, do we?"

"No, not really."

"Meanwhile, I'll be working on other possibilities."

They turned back toward home in silence.

"What're you thinking about?"

"Not much, just trying to assess the timing." Victor wasn't sure he wanted to scare Olga any further.

"What about it?"

"You remember, they decided to promote me?"

"Of course. It's ironic, isn't it?"

"Yes, but that's not the point. As you know, I'm under periodic surveillance, as are all the guys in my category."

"Yes, but you've always laughed at it. It's rather obvious."

"It is. But only when they want it to be obvious. Sometimes it may be, just may be, not so obvious. In any case, they wouldn't expect to see any 'criminal' activity as such. They're looking for patterns, and changes in those patterns. Patterns indicating something odd or unusual in my behavior. And that's exactly what I'll be doing. They don't need to see me literally talking to an American KIO. Seeing me all of a sudden going often to places I haven't been to before, especially those frequented by foreigners, is enough for them to become suspicious and to put a blanket coverage on me."

"So what can you do?"

"Whatever I can to avoid creating patterns. Which by definition decreases my chances for a lucky accidental contact."

"But what does all this have to do with timing?"

"Well, there's a little catch here. Usually my surveillance is random, and not very frequent. However, just before any promotion becomes formal, surveillance is mandatory, and the candidate requires a new security vetting. Promotion to a higher category, as in my case, means the entire process is even lengthier and more thorough."

"Then, isn't it wiser to wait a little bit?"

"That's precisely the dilemma. At first glance, yes. But there are other factors as well. First of all, our task is not just to get in contact with the Americans. We have to get out of here. Any exfiltration operation is very difficult, at best. Remember, the Olympics are here next summer. That means the border control will get tighter. Even if it doesn't, many border security procedures will be changed. That will only multiply our difficulties."

"I almost forgot about the Olympics. But isn't it easier to get through in the confusion?"

"Not likely. It might be, if we tried a frontal 'hurrah' assault. But with a professional operation it will add too much uncertainty. Unless, of course, the whole border-control system is an open book for the Americans, and they'll know every change immediately. I seriously doubt that. But even then, it's very difficult to change things on the fly. Every detail is usually planned well in advance."

Victor paused, and then added, "There's one more factor. The psychological pressure on us. After a while it will begin to wear us down, and we'll start making mistakes. I don't like to think about it, but it's a reality."

"Are you saying we have to hurry?"

"Well, we have to hurry, and we have to wait. There's no clear answer— at least I don't know one. My instinct tells me to move as fast as we can."

"You know, my instinct tells me the same. Let's get it over with as soon as we can."

CHAPTER

GOING TO THE OFFICE seemed the same as always. But any other time Victor spent in the streets had become very different. Watching yourself from aside, as objectively as possible, gets to be second nature in intelligence. His self-control was tighter than ever. Then Victor realized that he was now looking at Moscow, his city, with totally new eyes. Moscow had somehow changed. Victor didn't notice exactly when, but it was a different city. It wasn't just his inability to suppress the unwanted sense that he'd soon be leaving the city, never to see it again. There was something else as well. Disturbed, Victor searched himself but couldn't quite catch it. Finally it struck him that he was now looking at his environment with the eyes of a spy. A street was no longer just a street. It was a place to conduct countersurveillance. A long and branching alley was a place for a brush contact. A corner phone booth became a place to set a signal.

This discovery worried Victor. It might mean that he was developing the bright stamp "SPY" on his forehead. That is, for the professionals to notice. The members of the worldwide club of intelligence operatives had long developed a sixth sense for recognizing their brethren. It isn't for sure, but it's there. Something in the eyes, or the posture—who knows. Whatever it is, it's dangerous. For the offense. The defense enjoys it.

Then there's the seventh sense, the complex and most disputed sense of surveillance. Even if you don't have any objective indication of being under surveillance, sometimes you can somehow feel it. That is, if you can manage to distinguish it from simple paranoia. Of course, the defense hates this sense—it can spell the failure of their operations.

No one wants to admit these senses exist, yet not many professionals would want to fully deny their existence. So both these "extra" senses represent a classic dilemma. In a business where so much emphasis in training is devoted to objectivity, where every intelligence officer checks and double-checks constantly that he hasn't been carried away by his feelings and instincts—which can be rather easily manipulated—it's extremely difficult to draw the line between intuition and subjectivity.

However, Victor's concern at the moment was very far from philosophical. It was quite pragmatic. He was swimming with the sharks. He was afraid of giving himself away. His command to himself was simple, and the only course available to him. *Tighten your controls. Make sure you look and move just as you've always done. Too bad—such a performance, and not even a remote chance of an Oscar.*

Leaving his office for the day, Victor stopped at the main stairway of the building. He looked down through a window. The inner court looked like a well. The asphalt at the bottom was clean and empty. Suddenly, he recalled what in his early days at Dom 2 an old hand had told him at that exact spot: "You know, having windows into that courtyard is pointless. No one here ever looks out of them. Most of us even pretend not to notice we even have windows in our offices. Once, though, I saw faces crowding every single window here. That was when they got Penkovsky out of his cell in the jail below and took him for a date with a firing squad. Funny, nobody was supposed to know, but that grapevine never fails. The guy's head was totally white. When they caught him, he didn't have a single grey hair. Bastard. I wish they'd mutilated him. Alive." Victor shivered. *The KGB spirit, alive and well.*

Victor's thoughts turned to Penkovsky. Who was he? What was his motivation? The closest Victor had come to the case was an acquaintance of his who worked with Penkovsky's daughter. She had been given another identity and was heavily "supervised" by the KGB, which was "doing its best to be her 'adopted father.' Children, you see, cannot suffer for the deeds of their parents. We must be very humane."

Don't get sentimental. Victor didn't like where his thoughts were heading. *Stay cool. Concentrate. You'll have the time to think about that—if you get caught.* He rushed out of the building.

Victor headed for the Children's World store, which also faced Dzerzhinsky Square. He bought a toy for Elena and stopped at the stationery section. He bought the softest pencil available and two note-books—different, but both of poor quality. Good-quality paper doesn't dissolve easily in the mouth and takes a long time to swallow. *Time. That's precisely what I won't have.* He'd test both types of paper later, keeping one and disposing of the other.

At home Victor got busy. He faced simple-looking tasks and was working on the details. *A detail, that's what kills.*

The paper from one of the two notebooks dissolved better, but it tasted even worse than the other. After a moment's hesitation Victor chose function over delicacy. Besides, the color of the bad-tasting paper was absolutely perfect. Dirty beige with an olive tint, it wouldn't catch any-one's eye even if it was thrown, unless someone was watching really closely. Elena would get the other notebook for a weekend's drawing practice, and then it would be promptly disposed of.

Well, how much paper supply was needed? Several pages, no more. On the one hand, extra inventory could be harmful to one's health. As soon as the note was thrown, the rest of the paper must be dumped in the toilet immediately. Heavily incriminating evidence. Too much supply could take too much time to handle. On the other hand, the note would probably be written several times. It wouldn't be good to keep it over the weekend, for example. So, some supply of paper would have to be main-tained. Well, the rest of that notebook would go to Elena as well. The first part, of course. Loose sheets of the same paper lying around in the apart-ment for a long time would be odd. As well as a notebook with the first pages in place and the last ones gone. So, Olga would be given a difficult diplomatic task, to have Elena use most of the notebook and to rescue the last several pages, avoiding a demarche from the youngest Sheymov. Olga would manage.

Now, carrying the note. Several considerations would apply. One, it would have to be well hidden. No sticking out or accidentally dropping it. Two, it would have to be easy to take out and then either to deliver or to swallow. In some traditional place for hiding poison used by determined movie spies, like a shirt collar. Three, it would be nice if it could not easily be found by emergency hospital personnel or volunteers if he were to become unconscious in some accident.

Victor started experimenting. He put on a dress shirt and a jacket and began fussing with a piece of paper, putting it in one odd place after another. Olga didn't say a word. She just watched him with understand-ing but laughing eyes. He must have looked hilarious. After a while, frustrated, he threw the paper on the floor and fell into the armchair. Automatically, he touched his neck. Something was missing. The tie. He jumped up and grabbed a tie and for the first time in his life began studying its construction.

Surprisingly, it offered plenty of opportunities. The solution was quickly found. A thread would have to be attached to the lining inside the tie, without piercing the fabric, of course. Then the thread would be looped through the note, which would be folded three or four times so that the lower edge would hang about an inch above the inside opening of the tie. Difficult to find, even if hand-searched, and easy to take out. Just insert two fingers of either hand inside the tie, pull the knot, break the thread, and you're ready to go.

Another problem would be the note. Even without thinking about it, Victor knew it would present a tough dilemma. The Americans had been getting a lot of these notes. Most of them were KGB provocations. On the one hand, the note would have to convince them that it was genuine. It should include a "teaser" of verifiable information too valuable to be given away by the KGB. On the other hand, it would be nice if the information wasn't traceable back to him. Considering how tight was the circle of people with access to the same information as Victor, this would be a tough one to solve. *OK, I'll think of something.*

The final point was the delivery. There wasn't too much hope of an opportunity to hand a note to someone. Besides, many guys would make a scene, assuming he was working for the KGB. The last thing he needed. Dropping it in an unattended car would be almost suicidal. The KGB would be much more likely to retrieve it than the Americans. So, what was left was to look for a chance to pitch it into a KIO's car—perhaps near a traffic light. Luckily, this time of the year most cars would have the driver's-side window open.

Over the weekend Victor used his father's car garage for "repairs." The garage was one of two hundred in a compound within a five-minute walk from his parents' apartment. A luxury by Moscow standards. The entrance had a gate and an attendant. The one-story structure contained several rows of individual garages, each with its own doors. With the garage door partially opened, the only way to see the car and Victor in it from the outside was to stand right in front of the garage. In that case Victor would undoubtedly see the visitor in a rearview mirror. Victor put a "target" on the side wall inside the garage and practiced pitching a note at it without any visible motion on his part. By mid-Sunday he was pretty good at it: Twenty out of twenty with just a flick of his wrist. Good enough for a garage environment, but maybe not quite for the street and under pressure. He'd practice more later.

On Sunday night he set out to write the note. He took a marble slab from the kitchen, a present of unknown purpose from one of their relatives. One of those things too good to throw away yet too silly to actually use. He cleaned it thoroughly with alcohol, so there was nothing on it to imprint his writing. Then he laid a thin sheet of rubber from his father's extensive garage supplies over it. That became his desk. He pulled on rubber electrical gloves, also from his father's garage. Because Moscow's power operated at 220 volts, many people kept such gloves handy in case they needed to make electrical repairs. He'd keep them for the time being, but they'd have to be disposed of quickly after the delivery because the invisible chemical compound they would impart to the paper could be traceable. He started writing on a sheet of paper from the chosen notebook.

> Hello.
>
> I am a KGB officer with access to highly sensitive information. My ideological and political convictions demand action. Since we seem to have a common enemy, I suggest we join forces. To establish my bona fide, I would like to inform you that a substantial flow of information is being intercepted by the KGB from the Mediterranean region, coming from the U.S. 6th Fleet.
>
> If you are interested in cooperation, meet me at a tobacco kiosk near the Old Novokuznetskaya Metro station every Thursday between 6:07 and 6:08 p.m. for the next three weeks. Your officer should hold a rolled-up magazine in his right hand. My password will be "finally" in Russian. I do not speak English.

Victor read it over. *Not quite Cicero, but for the purpose it should do.*

CHAPTER

VICTOR'S MORNING HUNTS for a KIO involved relatively little risk. The probability of Victor's having his own tail was very low—where would he be going, except to his job? A KIO, Victor's prey, wasn't likely to have a heavy surveillance either, for the same reason. Most likely he'd have only a routine and obvious tail, probably only one car, just to "keep him honest." That was perfectly fine as far as Victor was concerned, as was the fact that a KIO's morning commute should be pretty much on a regular schedule and route. He wouldn't want to make his watchers nervous for nothing.

People who commute by train see the same faces every morning. Sometimes they get to know one another without even speaking. Though less obvious, the same is true of people driving in the morning rush-hour traffic: the same cars travel the same routes every day, with only a few minutes' deviation. Over time one can even pick out the driving habits and get-ready-for-work routines of quite a few fellow commuters.

Since Victor knew neither who his target was nor his target's departure time, to find a KIO he'd have to cover as much of the morning rush-hour traffic as possible. The earliest departure he could manage without changing his own patterns was 7:45. The latest would be about 8:35. Victor needed to cover as large a part of the morning traffic as possible. He knew he couldn't go straight "up and down" in his departures and show a pattern—he'd mix them up nicely so that they'd appear random. If one day he started at 8:13, the next day it would be, perhaps, 7:52 and not 8:20. He also figured he needed a "dragnet" with a cell of about seven minutes. Riding with the traffic exposes very few cars to you. So one has to either go slower than the traffic or faster. Going slower would clearly be a change from Victor's previous driving habit. With some skill, he figured, he could catch up about seven minutes of an average commuter on his way to Dzerzhinsky Square. So he divided the target period of fifty minutes from 7:45 to 8:35 into eight departure times, with one minute to spare. It would take eight trips to comb the traffic on one route—sixteen if he included the alternate route to his office. Three weeks for one dragnet operation. A lot of time, not even considering the rainy mornings when car windows would be rolled up. Precision and a carefully kept mental log would be essential.

Victor pulled away from his parking space, thinking of the fundamental dilemma he was facing. On the one hand, he had to be very methodical in his search if he wanted any chance of success. On the other hand, he couldn't show any pattern. His departures must look random.

This morning Victor chose the Leninsky Prospect route. Luckily, he lived close to both it and Vernadsky Prospect, another major traffic artery leading to the center of Moscow, so he could cover both of them, alternating without any problem. There were areas favored by foreigners along both of them, and many diplomats lived there. Most of the route to the American embassy coincided with his own drive to Dom 2.

As he made his way in the traffic, Victor was moving quite fast, but not fast enough to attract attention. After all, everyone was in a hurry in the morning. Luckily, diplomatic license plates were easy to spot, and their registration codes made it clear which country the diplomat was from. Decoy cars were unlikely to be in the streets that early in the morning. Victor was interested primarily in D-04, the United States, and D-01, Great Britain.

While passing one Frenchman at the beginning of Dimitrov Street, not far from the French embassy, Victor had looked out of the corner of his eye through his open passenger-side window. The Frenchman's driver's-side window was open, as in most of the cars. Good. However, even at a slow speed it was obvious there was absolutely no way to throw the note into another car on the move. A light piece of paper would simply be blown away by the onrushing wind. *What a way to learn a practical lesson in aerodynamics. So, it's got to be a full-stop situation.* Attaching the note to something heavy, like a metal ball, would certainly scare any driver. Victor wanted to practice an "accidental" simultaneous pull-up at the next red traffic light, but decided against it. *Stay away from him. Do it later, and not with a diplomatic car.*

By the time he had driven by the Borovitsky Tower of the Kremlin, he figured he had passed four diplomatic cars: two French, one Bulgarian, and one he wasn't sure of—probably some new African country.

Victor was approaching Dzerzhinsky Square. *Well, typical of intelligence.* You go through a hell of a lot of thinking and preparation—just to discover that nothing, absolutely nothing comes of it. What a disappointment for lovers of the spy genre. For a professional the excitement in intelligence doesn't come from wild car chases and broken surveillance. *It's a chess game. Well, sort of. So just be patient. And don't blow your chance when it comes. If it comes.*

Since he'd arrived rather early, finding a parking space at Vorovsky Square was easy. *At least something's going my way.*

In the office his thoughts kept coming back to the note inside his tie. Psychologically, it bothered him less than he'd thought it would, but still, it did make him a little tense. *Relax. You've got to get used to this thing. It's going to be your dog tag for a while. Maybe a long while.* He resisted a strong temptation to touch his tie.

Boss's call came at mid-morning. "Victor, drop by for a few minutes." As always, no clue.

There were two men sitting in Boss's office. Both rose from their chairs when Victor entered. Boss said, "These comrades are from the Second Chief Directorate." Counterintelligence.

Victor's heart jumped. He felt a strong urge to touch his tie, or at least to glance at it. It was hard to resist. He only raised his eyebrows, quickly trying to figure out his line. The men introduced themselves, and Victor reciprocated. As soon as Victor realized what unit of the Second CD they were from, he knew he probably didn't have to worry about them. One of them, Alexander, was Victor's neighbor from the same apartment complex. Compartmentalization—neither of them had known where the other worked.

Boss said, "Victor, we've got to help our colleagues."

"What kind of help? I've never worked with the Second CD. I'm not sure if I can be of any help." He tried to sound as lame as possible.

One of the men said, "We're installing a couple of computers. We need to protect them."

Victor's heart returned to its proper place. He looked at Boss questioningly. Boss was all business. "They're installing the computers here, in Dom 2. And they understand it's potentially dangerous. The control zone is very small, only about twenty meters to passing cars and a hundred meters to parked ones."

"All right, I'll see what we can do for them."

"Very well, guys. You all go and work out the game plan. Sorry, but I've got a meeting in five minutes. Victor will make sure everything is top notch." The protocol was being followed closely. These men were not on Boss's level. Somebody on his level probably called and asked him to see them. So Boss referred them to Victor. Keeping levels equal was important.

They thanked him and left. As he reached the door Victor heard, "Oh, by the way, Victor, drop by in an hour or so. I need your progress report on 'Diamond.'"

Victor turned and said, "Of course." There was no project "Diamond." Boss was giving him a message not to commit to anything, to find out as much as he could, and to get his real marching orders later. Victor'd understood his orders without the reminder.

After a long chat with the two, Victor was back in Boss's office. "Alexey Leontyevich, what's this whole thing all about? It's not our cup of tea."

"Of course not. Since the protection of computers seems to be falling into our lap anyway, Grigorenko called Andreyev and asked if it would be safe to install the computers here. Andreyev couldn't say that it would be. He couldn't lie to a Deputy Chairman, which the Chief of the Second CD also was by statute. Naturally, Grigorenko asked for help. You can guess the rest. By the way, did you find out what they need those computers for? Grigorenko just said it was sensitive."

"They certainly think it is. We had a good chat. At least we parted on a friendly-enough note." Victor neglected to mention that he needed to develop these guys, for his own new personal interest in counterintelligence. So he'd been more accommodating than he might otherwise have been. It was admittedly a long shot, but still bits and pieces of information accidentally picked up from the Second CD could be more than a little helpful. For his own project. "They finally decided to get out of the Dark Ages and are installing a computer to manage a new centralized system with files on all their informers in the country. A second computer will be used to clean up the Border Guards mess. You'll love this one."

"The Border Guards?"

"Yes. Someone decided to check on how many people are going in and out of the country. I reckon it was some sort of Central Committee request. Probably mostly out of simple curiosity. Obviously, you can never get the literal balance. You can only get snapshots. And then a hilarious thing happened. For many years now each year has produced the same pattern. Several hundred more people have been entering the country than are leaving it."

Boss laughed: "I can guess what happened next. Wish I could've seen the faces of those who had to report it to the Central Committee."

"Sure enough, the border is sealed like a submarine, but on paper it looks like several hundred spies a year are coming here and never leave. I guess some idiot goofed in the methodology and got a systematic error. To make a long story short, they've decided to computerize the records of border crossings, and are installing the central computer here. The funny thing is, they don't realize that unless they change their methodology, at the end of the day they'll get the same results."

"Yeah. So, did they take a hit from the Central Committee?"

"No, they know better than that. They've sat on the results so far, claiming the system is in transition, as they prepare to accommodate the flow of people coming to the Olympics. And they're paddling like hell, trying to get it fixed before they have to report." The Olympics. That's what bothered Victor. That had a direct impact on his personal project.

"Now I see where we are."

"So, what do we do? We don't have any enclosures to spare."

"Do we have a choice?" Victor did not respond. "Get hold of the enclosures somewhere. Dance a little with the scheduling for overseas. Get them installed quickly."

"What about defense?" That was the skunk on the table. Boss didn't want to hear it, but he understood that Victor had been around long enough not to let this consideration go by him.

"None. Just have it welded. That's all."

"What if they find out later from somewhere?"

"From where?" Boss's voice turned terse.

As usual, of course, Victor would get the short end. *If the Second CD makes a big stink about not getting full protection, it'll be me who took a shortcut without ever informing my superiors. And jeopardized sensitive information.*

"OK. You're the boss."

On his way home Victor started practicing his stoplight pull-up approach. A simple task that proved to be quite tricky. He had to spot a car pretty far ahead, which in the case of a real target would automatically put him in very close proximity to the surveillance car. Then he'd have to keep an eye on the traffic lights. Best of all would be if he could manage to move steadily but a little faster than the target, to position himself slightly ahead of it on his right, and then "suddenly" get a yellow at the traffic light. If at that time he was too close to the intersection, he'd have no choice but to keep going and try again some other time.

After three days of practicing on unsuspecting targets, Victor became pretty good at the maneuver. He figured that on average he was able to put himself in a throwing position eight times out of ten within two traffic lights. He was confident that the procedure wouldn't trigger the attention of the most scrupulous surveillance team.

A major danger Victor had to look out for—and one unknown to Western intelligence—was not even part of a KIO's surveillance team. It was the stationary surveillance, which was particularly dense on the two routes that Victor was working. One well-known and virtually open part of it was the "traffic police." On the routes frequently used by foreigners, some of the traffic police at major intersections were in fact surveillance officers of the Seventh Directorate. Their observation posts were danger- ous places for Victor. Sitting at one of the corners of the intersection in *stakans*, or "glasses"—round metal booths with glass caps raised about six feet above the ground level—these officers were able to scan good stretches of the streets and, more dangerously, they were able to see what was going on inside the cars. Victor had to make sure he didn't try any- thing at those intersections.

There was another, invisible, and much more dangerous part of the stationary surveillance. These were the optical *visirs*, or monitors—basi- cally powerful zoom telescopes with fast lenses—set up in some of the buildings along the main avenues, usually near major intersections, in a room on the second floor. The image was projected on a mat screen, sim- ilar to a mat glass in a reflex camera. The telescopes themselves could be zoomed and controlled vertically and laterally, giving a well-controlled, close-up view of passing cars. And the slightly elevated position of the telescopes provided a good angle for looking into the interiors of automo- biles, to see what the occupants were doing. Communications between all these optical stations and the control center were conducted by telephone, so no radio emanations could give away the presence of the surveillance. The *visirs* were a typical KGB surprise backup system. Victor recalled one good example of their effectiveness. A certain Western intelligence officer, not having anything mounted in his car, surely looked "clean" to his sur- veillance team, and he was obviously confident of having a free run. He put his attaché case on the passenger seat, which was nothing unusual, and as he passed his target he partially opened the case and manipulated the controls with his right hand, without making any motions visible to the surveillance team. But a *visir* operator caught him in the act, and a seemingly flawless operation was halted. Such a failure is not only bad in itself, it prompts doubts about the operation's security—and the apparent possibility of the KGB's penetration of the service—a situation every service would be obliged to seriously look into. The resulting investigation would be extremely disruptive of other ongoing operations, and the KGB would have achieved its goal.

Those *visirs* were a major factor affecting Victor's scheme. So he studied the buildings that lined his two routes like a hawk every time he went by. He spotted a few posts, projected their view fields, and added those "red zones" to the ones covered by the "traffic police." This stationary surveillance severely reduced his operating space within the already limited routes. So he not only had to make a perfect approach while driving, he had to do it strictly within the "green zones." *Hell, those are more "yellow" than "green"—there's no way I can guarantee I've spotted all the observation posts.*

Victor decided not to try any methodical approach on his commutes back home after work. People aren't nearly so consistent in the evening commute as they are in the morning. They often leave earlier or later, depending on the day's particulars, and they often go to different places on their way home. *Too many variables to design anything even remotely systematic.* Instead, Victor relied solely on dumb luck—driving sometimes straight home, sometimes stopping somewhere to carry out errands conveniently required by Olga.

CHAPTER

AFTER TWO WEEKS of meticulously following the procedure he'd designed, Victor began to feel he was on a wild-goose chase. He took Olga for their ritual walk.

He turned to her and said, "Remember I told you that this stunt wouldn't be easy or simple?"

"Yes."

"Well, that was probably the only thing I've been right about so far. This whole KIO car-hunting business has turned out to be a silly exercise, at best."

"What's happening? You haven't been too eloquent lately."

"I reckoned that the most difficult problem would be to choose the right guy. Not even close. I thought I'd have the opportunity for a contact every other day or so. I grossly miscalculated the probability of a meeting, and now I feel like an idiot."

"So, how many American diplomatic cars have you seen so far?"

"Not one. To be precise, the closest I came was when I spotted a very attractive Frenchman—attractive for my purposes, that is—I saw him twice—and an American school bus."

Olga laughed and said, "That strange-looking thing with the wide black stripe along its sides?" The American school bus looked ridiculous in the streets of Moscow, especially when carrying children. The reason was that as there were no funeral limousines in Russia, except for State funerals, caskets were transported in buses that looked very similar to the American school bus. These buses came in various colors, so to distinguish the funeral buses from the rest a wide black stripe was drawn along each side, just below the windows. Inside, a single row of seats lined the aisle, while the casket was placed on a long table in the middle. For whatever reason, the Americans had drawn the exact same wide black stripe on their bus. Muscovites were mystified at first, but now just chuckled when they realized that it was the school bus.

"Yes, and in all my wisdom I made a difficult decision: not to proceed with delivering the letter to the bus driver."

Smiling, Olga suggested, "Well, maybe the KIOs are on vacation."

"Sure. They just closed the CIA station and posted a 'Gone fishing' sign on the door."

"Well, what about that Frenchman?"

"No way. First of all, as far as I remember from my days on another job, the French service is pretty well penetrated. Secondly, and this I know for sure, their ciphers are an open book for the KGB. Andreyev would have a copy of their very first communication about me on his desk before it reached their headquarters in Paris."

"So, what's our next game plan?"

"First of all, I'll continue my hunt for a little longer. Stupid projects like this sometimes just get lucky. I think I can keep at it for another week without making anyone suspicious. At the same time, we'll try something else as well. I think I've got an idea."

"Let me guess. You'll dress as Santa Claus and walk straight into the embassy. Who could suspect Santa, especially in September?" She wasn't being sarcastic—she was just trying to ease Victor's tension. She knew how difficult failure was for him.

"Oh, no. Much better than that, although you may be onto something there. The Americans have a dacha right near Pirogovskoye Reservoir. I bet they go to the reservoir fairly often to picnic and row boats. Why don't we go there and check it out. It'll be easier to throw a letter into a boat than into a car."

"I'd like that. I always like to mix business with pleasure."

"So would Elena. You two'll get the pleasure, I'll do the business."

The following week Victor "accidentally" bumped into one of his old friends—Nikolai—a former teammate from the University, who just happened to live in his parents' house on Pirogovskoye Reservoir from May through mid-October. Sure enough, the conversation turned to the reservoir, and Nikolai invited the Sheymovs to visit him and his family on the following weekend. "Let's have some fun. Have a party, rent rowboats, spend the day on the water." Victor was a little hesitant, Nikolai insisted, and Victor had no choice but to agree.

On Saturday the weather was beautiful. Had it rained, the whole exercise would have been for naught. The Sheymovs started off early in the morning. The Ring Road traffic was very light, but Yaroslavskoye Shosse was a pain in the neck, as always. While passing the turn to Bolshevo, Victor thought about the work he had done there. The memories were vivid, but detached. As if from another life.

Victor resisted the temptation to turn left at Tarasovka. That route would have led them past the American dacha between Cherkizovo and the reservoir. There would have been nothing unusual in going that way, but Victor didn't want to leave any footprints. His license plate would be registered, and who knew when and how it might be the last straw that would tip the counterintelligence scales and draw their undivided attention. He just glanced at the "traffic policemen" at the intersection and passed through without slowing down.

He turned to Olga and said, "You know, I haven't been in this area for ages, but this route is full of places I used to go often."

"I know you used to work in Bolshevo, but what else do you mean?"

"Oh, Mytishci—we passed it—is where my cousin used to live. I stayed over with them sometimes. But the real fun was in the late fifties, when they lived in Ivanteyevka, out in the country. I spent a lot of time there during the summers. That's a little farther down, just after we're going to turn. Also, a good friend of mine had a dacha in Tarasovka, which we just passed. His folks were very tolerant, so we spent a lot of time partying there when I was at the University."

They were turning toward Klyazma, and Victor continued, "And here's a very well known military 'Dom Otdykha.' It's mostly for the families of the military elite and some lucky young officers. Very popular in winter. I've been there many times."

"I see. That was before my time, and frankly, I'm not too eager to know all your previous recreational activities." Olga was teasing him, but something in her voice was unusual.

"Are you jealous?"

"No, just not interested."

They passed Ulyankovo and would soon turn to Sorokino, their destination. That way was longer, but more secure. Soon they pulled into the drive of his friend's house. Except that Nikolai's parents looked older, and his son and daughter had grown up beyond recognition, nothing seemed to have changed there since Victor's last visit, more than five years before.

Nikolai immediately suggested, "Let's have some healthy activity before we begin partying. It would be a shame to miss this beautiful weather." That was precisely what Victor wanted. Without delay the two families went off to rent the rowboats. Victor's first dilemma was deciding on his boat crew. On the one hand, even if an opportunity presented itself, he couldn't risk having Olga or Elena in the boat when he threw the letter. On the other hand, he hesitated to make a big deal about seating—only to find there was no opportunity for contact anyway. He decided on a compromise.

While they were walking to the pier, Victor made his pitch: "Nikolai, I bet you're getting too fat to race."

"Who, me? I'll tell you something. I can outrow you any day by two boat lengths in five hundred meters. Wanna bet?"

"Sure."

The two families eagerly took up the challenge. The kids got excited about seeing their fathers compete. Then Nikolai's wife jumped in: "You guys settle your accounts any way you want. Just don't forget that we want to have fun too. Don't spoil our outing with your rivalry. Besides, you're both old men, so stop bragging and carry your kids into the boats."

Victor didn't want to give up: "OK, we'll settle this later. After everyone's had some fun."

Nikolai put on his fiercest face: "Deal."

The boarding began. Now Victor would have the second run without anybody else in the boat. That is, if he could find his target on the first reconnaissance run.

The lake was fairly crowded with lots of boats of all shapes and sizes. Of its total area—roughly a mile wide and five miles long—a small section not far from the rental station was designated for rowboats. Laughing and chatting with Elena, Victor was carefully studying the surroundings. Most of the boats were filled with Russians. Most of them, like the Sheymovs, in rented rowboats. But he could pick out three motorboats, evenly distributed over the rowboat portion of the lake. They were meandering through the crowd of smaller boats, not going out onto the lake's greater open space. Each contained two nasty-looking men with dull faces.

A few rowboats carried couples who didn't seem to be having any fun either. No smiles, very watchful eyes looking around all the time. They never looked at each other, even while talking. Their conversation consisted of brief remarks. It was impossible to hear what was said. Whenever another boat came close, they fell silent.

Victor spotted a Zodiac in the distance, obviously carrying foreigners. It was being followed by two motorboats. There were a few other row-boats with foreign-looking people, but each one had those no-fun people in the immediate vicinity. In addition to these, from a couple of cabins on the wooded shore, when the angles were right, he could spot the telltale sparkles of powerful optical devices. *Must be about one-meter telescopes.*

"Daddy, do you think you're going to lose?" That came from Elena.

Victor almost flinched. "What?"

"Your face just turned sad. I guessed that you're afraid Nikolai will beat you. He's much bigger than you."

Victor was mad that he couldn't even control his face. He smiled. "No, darling. I wouldn't say that. We're old friends, and we were just joking when we heckled each other. We used to compete a lot on track. Some-times he won, sometimes I did. We're old rivals. No, I just have a little headache. Nothing to worry about."

"Poor daddy," Elena sighed, "you have to take medicine and go to bed. Isn't that right, Mama?"

"Of course, darling. As soon as we get home."

Victor was upset. There was no way he could approach any of the boats with foreigners without being photographed and "homed." Then, in a few days, bingo, "Why don't we take a good look at this hotshot? After all he had no business there." A good career opportunity for a vigi-lant counterintelligence officer. So he stayed clear of those boats. It took considerable effort for him to get through the outing in reasonable humor. At least Nikolai's wife helped him duck out of the race that he had bargained for and now no longer wanted.

On their way home Elena slept, exhausted. There was dead silence in the car.

Victor was thinking that he was running out of relatively sane options. The situation was growing desperate, and desperation was one of the shortest routes to failure.

At home his emotions gradually turned to thoughts, then his thoughts quickened. He had one more plan, which he didn't want to share with Olga. He didn't want to make her too nervous. Just one more plan.

Suddenly a new idea struck him. "Maybe two," he mumbled.

"What?" Olga was surprised. It wasn't really Victor's habit to talk to himself out loud.

"Nothing, just thinking of some things I don't want to forget in the office on Monday."

On Monday Victor was all business. He went to one of the younger guys in his group. "Eugene, something's come up. We need to get hold of a couple of enclosures for the Second CD. Go to the 'Forest' and talk to the North Yemen Section of the Eighteenth Department. See if they can wait on the installation in San'a."

"Come on, Victor. First of all, they'd never agree. Secondly, that's more on your level than mine." The guy was smart, and he was absolutely right on both counts.

"Well, I have to report on something to Boss tonight. And now I've got to go to Personnel. I can't duck this one. So, we don't seem to have any choice." Victor hated to give anybody stupid assignments, but he really had no alternative now.

Eugene resorted to his last line of defense. "But I've got to go to Sheremetyevo to give the instructions to the courier and the driver and to see them off for the Helsinki delivery."

That was precisely what Victor was after. The Helsinki delivery. "Damn. What time did you schedule them for?"

"One thirty."

"All right. Look, I'll cover for you. Just give me all the papers and go to the 'Forest.' Call me around four." A hint that he didn't have to come back and could leave early.

Eugene's face brightened a bit. "You got it."

It wasn't a bad deal for Eugene after all. Ten minutes of humiliation at the line department in exchange for a trip to a place much better than the dreadful Sheremetyevo. And perhaps an early end to the day.

For Project "Case," the Eighth CD had to deliver huge quantities of equipment and materials to other countries—up to twenty tons at a time. By diplomatic mail only. When Helsinki's turn came, the MFA notified the Eighth CD that restrictions on diplomatic mail to Finland would allow only a few bags per delivery. Delivery by regular diplomatic mail via Aeroflot would take more than a year. The solution came unexpectedly. Some joker suggested the shipment be delivered in a sealed truck, as to the Warsaw Pact countries, but with a diplomatic courier and a declaration of "One diplomatic package." So what if the package was a bit big— was actually a truck body? Andreyev's decision was to go ahead and try. "If there's any complication, backpedal immediately." Surprisingly, there were no complications. Apparently, the Finns were rendered speechless by the "package."

There were two deliveries left. One was ready to go, and the second would leave in a week. That was the one Victor was interested in.

Victor showed up at the Eighth CD warehouse twenty minutes before the truck was due to depart. The diplomatic courier had known Victor for some time.

"Victor, what a surprise. This doesn't look like a promotion."

Victor laughed: "It sure isn't. But don't write me off yet. Eugene just heaped too much onto his plate. He's a young guy, you know. Besides, I've wanted to see what you guys do here for a long time. I just never found the time. So, show me the truck."

"Come on, Victor. We packed everything nicely, locked it up, and sealed it. And you want us to unravel it again? You've never been big on formalities. You've known me for a long time. Do I look like a sloppy guy?"

"No, of course not. Nothing personal. But I've got my masters too, you know. And I have to report to them once in a while. If one of them asks a question, I don't want to look too stupid. So, open up the damn thing. And don't worry, it won't take too long."

The courier sighed, "All right, all right, I always get the short end." They went to the truck.

The truck body had only one back entrance, through a pair of hinged doors. Tightly closed and latched, they were also protected by a standard MFA seal, "*valiza*." A cord about a tenth of an inch in diameter was tightly looped through the latch, then laid across an eighth-inch-deep groove in an inch-and-a-half-diameter standard MFA sealing plate. The cord was sealed into the groove with hardened burgundy sealing wax. The hanging plate, along with the lock, was wrapped with plastic and tied to and covered the "ears" of the latch.

The courier started to cut the cord, the only way to free the latch. Victor said sharply, "Wait a minute, the sealing plate is supposed to be hanging free, clearly visible at all times."

"Victor, don't be a pain in the ass. You know as well as I do that on a truck it'll be torn away after fifty kilometers. What do we do then? I lose my job, and you wouldn't know what to do with the stuff. Is that what you want?"

"OK, but there are regulations. I don't remember you guys clearing the rule waiver with me."

"Somebody cleared it with your beloved 'Boss.' Ask him if you don't trust me."

"Well, then, are you sure it's really safe enough?"

"Of course I am. The truck is guarded all the time anyway. Just don't worry about it. I've been in this business for twenty years and, knock on wood, haven't had a single mishap yet."

"All right, all right. You guys always want some kind of a waiver. Give you a free hand and you'd start sending the pouches through the god-damn mail and taking trips with your girlfriends instead."

Now Victor knew that the sealing plate wouldn't be unwrapped, nor the contents inspected before the delivery to the embassy in Helsinki. *That's encouraging.*

The next thing was the lock. That was a delight. Just a regular hanging lock from a hardware store. *Easy to pry open. Then I can pour some good glue in and, while the lock's being pushed to, the glue will adhere, so the lock will look locked and normal. That is, of course, until someone tries to open it. But by then it'll be too late. OK, so far, so good.*

The latch was a simple one. *If I hold it steady above its proper position with a piece of steel ribbon, I can carefully lower it in place from inside the truck, through the rubber gasket of the closed door.*

Then the real problem popped up. There was no way to put the lock and the sealing plate back because the cord had to go through both matching holes in the latch. Finally, Victor found the solution. *After I replace the lock, the cord need only go through one hole of the latch, and the lock can simply hang there on the cord, maybe reinforced so as not to be accidentally torn off. It'll swing a bit more compared to normal, but it won't be noticeable until the truck is moving. I can also pad the lock slightly underneath the plastic wrapping, so it won't knock too much on the door. Good.*

As Victor was making these calculations, he'd been going through the stuff inside the truck. Most of the material was packed simply enough, but boxed equipment was first put in tamperproof KGB packaging, sealed, and then put in the outer MFA packaging and sealed again. Victor was checking those MFA seals. He'd already spent about fifteen minutes in the truck. The courier was losing his patience.

"Anything else I can give you to double-check my diligence? Victor, I never knew you were such a bureaucrat."

Victor had gotten everything he was after. "Sorry. They're giving me a hell of a hard time too, lately." It wasn't too clear who "they" were, but the argument usually worked. "Don't get mad; I'll make it up to you. Let's go inside and finish off the instructions business. It won't take long."

They went inside, and in just fifteen minutes Victor had given them all the necessary instructions. To be precise, he simply repeated all the instructions they already knew by heart. The courier was still disgruntled when Victor waved them off.

That same evening Olga and Victor took another of their walks.

"By the way, I made a reservation for a trip to Finland for all of us. I hope you don't mind."

"Be serious, Victor. We need to do something, and time's running short."

"I am serious."

"What?"

"See, we're sending a truck with our toys to Finland in a week. One of those huge things with a full metal body. It will go under guard from Sheremetyevo to the KGB headquarters in Leningrad and spend a night there. Then it goes on to Helsinki, also under guard."

"How are we going to get in and out?"

"Getting out is easy. The truck shouldn't be unloaded or opened until the next morning. It'll be parked at the embassy in Helsinki. They can't back it flush to the wall—I've already checked. So, we get out at night and climb over the back fence. By the time they react—and they only will if they notice us on their security TV monitor—we'll be gone. Then we hide till morning and go to the American embassy.

"Now getting into the truck is a bit more complicated. There's no way to do it in Sheremetyevo. But they notified us that they have no space in Leningrad in the inner yard of the KGB building. Someone agreed that the truck may be parked just outside, in front of the entrance. That's where we can get into it."

"It's probably guarded. We could get caught right there."

"Sure, we could get caught. Anytime, anywhere. But it's too bold, you see? Nobody in his right mind would seriously believe that the truck would be tampered with at the KGB HQ. Besides, they don't have outside guards. I know the building. They'll park the truck just in front of the main entrance, and we'll be shielded by it as we're getting in at the rear door."

"Go on."

"I took a look at one of those trucks today. I've figured out how to open it and close it and replace the lock and the seal back from inside. We should be all right."

"If you can pull this one off, you can compete with Kio. I thought he was the only one left after Houdini who could do something like that." Olga was obviously excited.

"Well, Kio or not, I'm running out of options." Victor paused. "There could be one problem though. Air. The truck will be only about 10 percent full. It's not completely sealed either, so we should have enough air in there. But I think we should take some with us, just in case."

"How?"

"Well, I know a place in the country where you can buy scuba-diving tanks without any registration. I'll go there on the weekend. And I have a friend who's a welder. He'll fill them with oxygen, no questions asked."

"My God, is there a profession in the country where you don't have a friend?" Olga laughed.

"I'd have to think. There probably is one."

"So you're going to carry oxygen tanks to Leningrad and run all over the city with them at night?"

"We can do it by train. Day trains aren't at all crowded. We don't even have to buy tickets in advance. As far as 'all over the city' goes, it's not a problem. I have a friend who just happens to live a couple of blocks from the KGB building there. We can have a little party till eleven or so, and then go."

Olga just shook her head and laughed. "Well, what can I say? You can't die twice. . . ."

Two days later Victor came up to Eugene. "How are things going on Helsinki?"

"Fine, no problems at all. We'll make the last delivery early next week. The team's ready to go."

"Look, we can't afford a screw up now. If we forget to put something in the damn truck, I'll have to do a lot of tap dancing to explain how it happened."

"I understand."

"Keep me fully informed, would you?"

Eugene bridled, professionally offended. "You mean you think I can't handle this?"

"Not at all. If it were up to me, I wouldn't bother asking you a single question. But Koryakov keeps asking me about it all the time. I have to stay current. Come on, I know you well enough."

That seemed to mollify Eugene. "All right. Here's the last cable from Leningrad. Came this morning. Everything is tip-top."

Victor glanced lazily at the cable. In cables sent inside the country, code names were not used.

BOSIK.

WE ARE PREPARED TO PROCEED WITH THE ASSISTANCE OF THE
DELIVERY TO HELSINKI AS PREVIOUSLY AGREED.

ACCOMMODATING YOUR PREVIOUS REQUEST, WE WERE ABLE
TO ARRANGE THE OVERNIGHT SAFEKEEPING OF THE TRUCK
INSIDE OUR INNER YARD.

WE EXPECT THE TRUCK TO ARRIVE AT THE HQ BUILDING AT
ABOUT 20:00 ON TUESDAY.

KALUGIN

Victor carefully put the cable back on Eugene's desk.
"All right, let me know if anything changes."
"Sure thing."
That was the end of that idea. However, Victor also felt lucky to have
seen the cable. It had saved him a lot of aggravation. And visiting his
friend in Leningrad, carrying oxygen tanks.
Back to square one.

CHAPTER

ALL DURING HIS ATTEMPTS to contact the Americans Victor had been working on a last-resort permutation of his note-passing scheme.

The idea was based on something he'd accidentally learned in the spring, when Victor had emerged from a late-afternoon meeting in the MFA building on the Garden Ring. He crossed the street and ran into an acquaintance whom he'd first met in Czechoslovakia while on TDY, or temporary duty. This man was a Seventh Directorate—surveillance— officer, working there as an operational driver.

Interrupting their standard chat, the man suddenly pointed to a black Chrysler with D-04, the U.S. license plates, passing by. "See that bastard? One of the most active in the CIA station here. Looks so innocent, goes home like a choirboy, right on time. It would be easy to take him for a stupid 'clean' diplomat, but under the surface he's paddling like hell. We had to go through God knows what to follow him the other day, the son of a bitch."

Mildly curious, Victor asked, "And he probably lives in the midst of our people, instead of in a compound for foreigners?"

"No, that's the thing about him. Lives just like the 'clean' diplomats do, in a building full of foreigners on Vernadsky Prospect. I told you, he's a very innocent-looking guy."

With such an introduction, Victor had automatically memorized the license-plate number. Now he was trying to utilize what was for him a rare piece of information. For some time now, whenever he'd had the chance, he'd been studying the various routes and traffic patterns from Smolenskaya Square to Vernadsky Prospect, making test runs on each of them.

With nothing else sensible left to try, it was time for Victor to draw on his contingency plan. The meeting today at the MFA started at three. It hadn't been difficult to bring the witness he'd need without arousing any suspicions. The MFA was always trying to get more control over their newly installed cipher systems, an eternal and eternally fruitless goal of the MFA's. The KGB didn't want to surrender that control to them, the eternal and eternally successful KGB response. The day before this particular meeting Victor had called Personnel and asked someone to accompany him: "Your prerogatives may be involved." Predictably, Personnel was eager to be represented. Seldom invited, they always wanted to be involved; they wanted to know what was going on in the line jobs.

Boris, the man in Personnel to whom Victor had spoken about the matter, of course managed to come himself. It was prestigious to go to a meeting at the MFA, and not simply to one with their Personnel. Besides, it broke up the routine of Personnel work. What Boris didn't know was that he possessed one qualification that was especially important to Victor: he lived right between Victor's apartment complex and the end of Vernadsky Prospect. He also possessed another useful qualification—he wore thick glasses and still couldn't see well at all. So on that particular day he was the perfect companion for Victor.

The meeting itself was a bore, as always. That was fine with Victor. He could simply provide his physical presence, half-listen to the blab of the MFA's communications department deputy chief, and concentrate on mentally checking and rechecking the details of the upcoming operation. So most of the time Victor was silent. Boris was silent because Victor was silent—which added to the tedium of the meeting.

16:40. Victor finally stepped in: "Comrades, I understand the reasons for your concerns and requests. However, you are putting me in a rather difficult position. I have no authority to change the status quo. I'll have to report your requests to our Leadership, which, I'm afraid, is not predisposed to change anything. All I can say is, I'll do my best in presenting your position."

Everyone in the room must have thought, "The hell you will." The senior MFA man promptly and politely adjourned the meeting. *16:46.*

Don't rush it. Don't take the initiative yourself. It was natural for Victor and Boris to go down in the elevator together. The two of them emerged from the building. *16:51. Don't start it. Wait.*

Victor's patience was rewarded. Boris looked at his watch. "Too late to go back to the office. Victor, where are you going?"

"Tepliy Stan. And you?"

"Vernadsky Prospect, almost the same place."

"I didn't know we were neighbors." *16:53.*

"OK, let's go to the Metro."

"Well, actually, I drove in today."

"Well, why don't you give a ride to a poor colleague?"

"Sure, let's go."

On the way to the car Boris made conversation. "Must be nice to work in Directorate A. Lucky bastards. Almost all you guys have cars."

"Well, I don't complain." *16:57.*

They crossed Smolenskaya Square. *It'll be much better if he has a close surveillance today. They'll be distracted for a moment, but they'll feel confident they've seen everything.* Victor's Zhiguli, a Soviet version of the Fiat-124, was well parked. Victor could easily see the southbound traffic of the Garden Ring through both mirrors. He'd spent ten minutes driving around to get the spot. They got into the car.

"Just a second." Victor got out of the car, opened the trunk, and leaned into it, as if looking for something. He put the second and third fingers of his right hand inside his tie while holding the tie with his left hand. The folded note was easy to find. Victor squeezed it between the middle knuckles of the two fingers. That way there'd be no fingerprints on the note. He pulled gently, and the thread broke. Victor held the note in the same manner with his left hand and inserted it into a folded handkerchief inside the left pocket of his jacket. *17:02.*

Key into the ignition, start the engine. 17:04. Good, now I'm ready. Let's play the waiting game.

Victor made sure Boris fastened his seat belt and started fiddling with his own. In fact, he couldn't have it on. He'd need to get out very quickly right after the collision. He unbuckled his seat belt and reached over and opened the glove compartment to get some chewing gum for Boris—a low-denomination bill in Moscow's unofficial currency. Of course, he'd forget to put the seat belt back on.

Two D-04 cars passed. The traffic was getting heavier. Suddenly, Victor spotted the black Chrysler. *Hard to tell from this distance, but that looks like a surveillance Volga faithfully following it. 17:07. Mark 0.* Victor started moving, picked up speed, and then quickly made a sharp right.

"Where are you going?" Boris asked. It wasn't the usual way to their destination.

"Oh, quicker this way, through the embankments. Rush hour, you know." That was true.

Victor had run both this route and the conventional ones many times at this hour. He knew the time the conventional route took was fixed, plus or minus two minutes. By going through the embankments he could be at the intercept point up to five minutes earlier. More important, he could control his speed—the traffic wasn't nearly so bad as it was on the Garden Ring and Vernadsky Prospect.

He certainly couldn't afford to follow the car. The chances of his being noticed by the surveillance before he could properly position himself for the collision were too high.

Thanks to the landmarks he'd selected during his test runs, monitoring his progress relative to the American's was easy. They passed Moscow State University and turned toward Vernadsky Prospect. Approaching it, Victor knew he was thirty to ninety seconds ahead of the American. He entered the Prospect. Taking the middle lane, he positioned himself for slower going.

Come on, I need a little luck. The important thing is not to be going too fast just before the collision. He glanced at Boris. Relaxed and chattering away. Victor responded with occasional remarks, so it seemed to Boris like a lively two-way conversation. *Now, run through it all again. The key is not to get hit too hard. Spare the American; he can ram me into the front car. I'm OK for the rear hit, but without the seat belt I'm not protected from the whiplash. I could black out. So if I get hit too hard, I must swallow the note before I pass out. Only then can I afford to collapse. So, the bottom line: immediately after the collision, get out of the car. If you feel bad, swallow the note, and only then can you collapse. If you're OK, make an angry face and jump out of the car and rush toward the "offender." Before he manages to get out of his car, put your hands on the door, hand him a note with your left hand, then open his door with the right one and start shouting that he's an idiot.*

At last. There it was in his rearview mirror, the black Chrysler, about two hundred yards behind and cruising in the left lane, standing out like a sore thumb in the Moscow traffic. Victor swerved into the left lane right in front of the Chrysler less than politely. In his rearview mirror Victor saw the American expressing some thoughts in regard to Victor's driving manners. *His seat belt's on. Good.* Victor was in a "green" sector, with no *visirs*—at least, none that he was aware of.

Ready? All right, let's go. He made a show of turning his head to the right, pointed in that direction with his left hand, and exclaimed to Boris, "Look, what a crowd!" Then he slowly took his left hand away and put it his pocket. He retrieved the note from the handkerchief with his fourth and fifth fingers and casually rested his left hand on the side of the seat, next to his pocket. No way to change gears now, but he didn't need to shift again. Boris was looking to the right where Victor had pointed, and so was Victor. Out of the corner of his eye he saw he was coming up very close to the car slowing down in front of him.

At the critical distance, going about thirty-five miles per hour, as he had practiced so many times, he hit the brakes hard, on the verge of locking the wheels.

The next thing Victor was aware of was the shadow of the black Chrysler on his right, passing him in the middle lane, horn blaring angrily. Victor's Zhiguli narrowly missed hitting a Volga in front by a couple of inches. The car that had been behind the Chrysler barely managed to avoid hitting Victor's Zhiguli.

He slowly put his left hand into the side pocket of his jacket.

CHAPTER

7

AS USUAL, VICTOR WAS SUMMONED by Boss with no hint as to the subject. As usual, it was only after waiting for fifteen minutes for Boss to finish his phone maneuvering with another Chief that Victor got Boss's undivided attention. As usual, the subject came out of the blue.

"How is the most recent modification of 'Case' going?"

"Almost on schedule. The preliminary research was completed about six weeks ago, with some questions remaining. Those are to be fine-tuned during the lab testing. We'll have the hardware from the factory in about a month."

"How long should the tests take?"

"The people in the Sixth promised to finish within another month. But we have a problem with the supply of the enclosures because of that business with the Second CD, so it'll take a couple of months longer, I guess."

"Too long."

"I tried to get extra enclosures. No way."

Boss thought for a few seconds. Then he made his decision. "The first installation in a month from now—where's that scheduled for?"

"San'a, Yemen. They've been moved back for about a month because of the Second CD."

"OK, we'll do the testing right there." That wouldn't be the first time a new system was tested in the field instead of in a lab because of the frantic pace of Project "Case," but it still violated the very basic security procedures. Victor knew Boss too well to have much hope of changing his mind. *Let's see if he buys this one.*

"Well, this time it may be difficult to get a special waiver of our own security rules. I reckon Andreyev didn't like it much last time."

"Don't worry, he'll agree. Especially if you're going."

"Me?" Victor almost jumped out of his chair. "My plate's full for the whole year ahead. Besides, what would I do there? I'm not a technical expert."

"Come on, nobody's asking you to do the testing. You'll just make sure everything's all right. It's still a violation of the rules, and we don't want any slipups there, do we? And it's only for two-three weeks."

"But the Sixth Department has said the testing will take a month—that's the best they can do. And that's in a lab in Moscow. Who knows how much time they'd need in the field?"

Boss shrugged: "Not to worry. Andreyev will ask them to be a bit quicker. I can arrange that much."

"So, I've got to go?" With his personal project in a shambles, and time running seriously short, Victor was trying every trick in the book to duck the trip.

"Yes." Suddenly, Boss looked Victor straight in the eye. "By the way, why is it you don't want to go?"

Careful, you've already shown too much. Play it smoothly. "Well, I really have a lot to do here. Besides, what's the fun in babysitting a few scientists?"

Boss appeared to have bought it. "Oh, come on. It's not such a big deal. You haven't been to the Middle East yet, have you?"

"No."

"Go, it's fun. Very interesting. You'll like it."

This time Victor wasn't driving. He met Olga, and they took the Metro to his parents'. After supper, on the way back home, Victor suggested a walk. They went along Profsoyuznaya Street, which led almost to their apartment complex. It took Victor a long time to put his thoughts together before he started.

"You know, I think it's about time to summarize the results so far."

"Yes, but frankly, I don't see much to summarize. God, I wish I could help you. I'd do anything."

"'Not much to summarize'—that's precisely the point. There are no results, but we already have some information. So we should analyze it." Victor took a deep breath and continued, "You don't know it, but I can tell you I haven't had a failure yet in my line of work. It's not that I'm bragging to compensate for a failure, it's just a fact. Maybe because I couldn't afford one. In our snake pit you either win or you're down and out. So I literally had no choice but to win every time. It has actually served me in a positive way. They forgive me a lot for my performance. They forgive some defiance, my being something of a maverick—they even forgave me my divorce. You know, I know of only one other case where a divorce didn't derail a career. They haven't flat out forgiven all that—the payment's just being delayed until I fall for one reason or another. But that's an entirely different matter altogether. The real point here is that having gotten used to winning, I feel very embarrassed professionally to lose so miserably, especially when it's the most important project of my life."

"I don't see any reason for you to feel embarrassed. You said yourself the task is enormously difficult."

"Yes, but who cares. I've failed, and that's the fact."

"Don't be too hard on yourself. Better we should find another way."

"It's not that. It's neither the emotions nor my professional pride that bother me the most. It's the objective evaluation. Look, I undertook four operations."

Olga automatically interrupted him. "Three."

"Four. There was something else too." He saw Olga just glance at him, but she said nothing. He continued, "And every time I tried to be careful. But still, I'm sure I've left some footprints, and it's only a matter of their discovering them. The only question is when. I've started the clock."

"Are you saying they're looking for us?"

"No, I didn't say that. But if I attract their attention, in conjunction with other things, it could prove bad." Victor paused for a second. "The fact of the matter is that if I'd done nothing, we'd be better off now."

"But you tried."

"Well, that's a minor detail of my biography, no more. I should have known better. Just that one trip to the lake tells it all. It doesn't take a Ph.D. to figure out that any Americans there would be covered like a hand in a glove. And that it was stupid of us to pop up there with a lousy excuse, just to present our faces for a surveillance photo-op."

"You think it can hurt us now?"

"It's anybody's guess, but it could, and you'd never know if, how, or when."

They'd been walking along the street for quite a while now, but neither of them felt tired.

After a prolonged silence Victor sighed and said, "OK, I guess the real point is that we have to do something, and fast."

"How about trying to go through somebody? You have a lot of friends."

"Absolutely out of the question. I can't trust anyone, I mean anyone, with Elena's and your lives."

"Then I don't see what else we can do."

"I think I've got an idea. Let's start with the concept. We seem to have enough information to say that it was probably not simply four failures in a row. It's more likely one conceptual failure. Up to now, whatever we were going to do we were going to do as carefully as we possibly could. That was the priority. Now, let's look at the problem. In short, given the restrictions on our lifestyle, it's crazy to try to defect, particularly the way we're trying to do it. In other words, what I am trying to say is that this problem is crazy enough to demand a crazy solution."

"I don't know what you have specifically in mind, but what you're saying makes me shiver," said Olga with a tense smile.

"Just wait, this is only the beginning," laughed Victor. "So, let's just imagine: what's the craziest thing I could do in the circumstances, bar something like going to the American Moscow embassy, which means going straight to the KGB?"

"Trying to do it abroad?"

"Yes. I can't think of anything crazier for me. Can you?"

"No, not really," said Olga slowly. Victor saw a silent question in her eyes, the question she would never ask out loud, even to herself—*What happens to Elena and me if you go into an American embassy somewhere, get noticed, and can't get out?*

Victor knew this was a possibility. He knew also that in that case he'd do whatever it took and either get them out or die trying. It might take years, but he'd do it. As much as he was sure of his determination, he was also sure the subject couldn't be discussed. There was no sense in assurances; they'd sound false.

"Are you ready for that?"

"You mean you're going to escape your guards, go into the embassy, and come back without knowing whether or not you've been burned?"

"Yes." And he quickly added, "But I promise, I'll be careful."

Olga laughed wholeheartedly, despite the high tension of the situation. "Coming from you, particularly under the circumstances, that must be the joke of the week."

"So?"

"You've just said we'd better do something and quickly. For lack of any crazier idea, I think this one should suffice." That took real courage, which Victor could only admire.

After several minutes Olga broke the silence. "Well, where are you going to do it?"

"I guess the best place would be somewhere in one of the Soviet Bloc countries. Of course, the surveillance on the Americans is stiff there, but it's not nearly as stiff as in Moscow. But the main point is that KGB security is a little lax in those countries in comparison to the rest of the world. Probably because they feel their position there is too strong. They're overconfident. As always, the weakest link of every security system is its human element."

"But even in a Bloc country you still have to be accompanied by guards all the time, don't you?"

"Sure. But there must be a chink in the armor. You just have to find it. You have to feel it."

Olga was dubious. "How're you going to get there—wait for a convenient assignment?"

"No, we don't have time for that. I have to actively manipulate the system to draw one."

"Do you have a country in mind?"

"Sort of. I'd prefer Prague or Warsaw. I know both places reasonably well. The American embassy in Warsaw is better located, it's on a busier street, so that's probably my first choice." What he didn't say was that there was another, personal reason for that choice. He still vividly remembered that cable ordering the KGB Resident to prepare the assassination of the Pope, as well as Valery's story about the scientist—who was doing his time somewhere in Siberia, if still alive. He wanted to beat that dreadful crowd professionally, and beat them badly. They should realize that whacking a naive and too trustful scientist isn't reason to feel professional pride, even in the KGB. *Try me; we'll see who's worth what.* Victor didn't like the fact that such an emotion was in the back of his mind, but it was there. And there was nothing he could do except pray that it wouldn't cost him a mistake at a crucial moment.

They noticed they were very nearly home, but all of a sudden they realized they were exhausted. They jumped on a bus for the two-stop ride home.

The next morning Victor was ready to move fast. The San'a trip had scrambled his cards. The Olympics were getting closer every day. He went to see Boss.

"Alexey Leontyevich, I'd like to brief you on Warsaw."

"Good, I was about to ask you about it. How's it going?"

"Fine, I don't see any problems. That is, except one little one."

"What's that?"

"Eugene is going to be in charge there. He's a good guy, but this is his first trip in that capacity. We have to brief him very thoroughly. You know the ambassador, Karlov. The SOB is awfully vindictive. I'm afraid he still hasn't forgotten my visit. In other words, I don't want to set Eugene up for a quick trip back without his even knowing why."

Boss grasped the situation instantly. "Who's the smart ass who gave that assignment to a rookie?"

Actually, it had been Boss. "Smirnov, I reckon. But he didn't know the particulars of my visit there. You didn't want me to brief him."

"I see." Boss paused for a few seconds. "Victor, you've got to go there, to pave the way for Eugene and make sure the whole process is irreversible. Then you can come back."

Victor feigned mild outrage. The danger was in overdoing it. "But I'm supposed to go to San'a."

Boss didn't blink. Nobody could shake him with such a petty detail. "So what? Warsaw won't take you more than two weeks. The team is leaving pretty soon, isn't it?"

"Yes, in four days."

"So, you come back and then go to San'a."

"All right then, I guess it's about time for me to pack my bags." Victor stood up to leave.

Boss looked up at him. "Victor, I realize you're doing a lot. You'll get rewarded."

I hope so. Victor left.

CHAPTER

WARSAW AIRPORT. Nothing changed here. Victor instantly spotted Valery, who this time was not just his sentry but his immediate opposition, and a man not to be underestimated. They went straight through, without wasting any time on formalities, almost exactly as the first time they'd met.

When they had settled themselves in his car, Valery laughed: "You know, you've got a reputation as a major troublemaker here. Folks are wondering what's coming this time around."

"Any troubleshooter is a potential troublemaker," quipped Victor, "but there's not much coming this time. Just showing the flag, that's all."

"Intimidation?"

"I'd rather call it deterrence."

"I'm glad you phoned Kuritsyn before you left. He seems to be taking it in stride. By the way, I reckon the team is arriving tomorrow?"

"Yes. Did you get decent quarters for them?"

"Sure. I'm still in charge here, so don't worry. We'll put them in our compound, three blocks from the embassy. They're OK."

"Thanks. How're things in the capital city of Warsaw?"

"Nothing new, just more of the same. How about Moscow?"

"Same. Brezhnev gets sicker and sicker."

"So I've heard. Who's running the show?"

"Yu. V. seems to be. But Chernenko is driving hard too."

"I hope Andropov takes over. Our man."

"He probably will."

They came to the familiar embassy grounds. Now, in the fall, the monstrous Soviet embassy building looked even more grim than it had in the spring. Victor noticed that the new Soviet Trade Mission next door, a tasteful modern building with a lot of glass, was almost complete. Its mere presence compounded the dreadful appearance of the embassy. Victor settled into his apartment—the same pirate's cave, still spotless and depressing in its uncoordinated and senseless luxury. Then he went to see Kuritsyn.

In what he considered a friendly tone, the stocky general barked, "Welcome back. I think you're right in coming here for a while. The Ambassador surely hasn't forgotten the number you did on him last time. Besides, quite a few people are mad at you for being thrown out of that wing. Are you going to be very busy?"

"Not too much." Victor's plan was to show his presence, but to have plenty of time outside of the embassy compound. He was deliberately tempting the general. And he knew what was coming next.

"I'd like to take advantage of your being here, to assess more specifically the technical threat from the Americans."

"Officially, I'd need authorization for that. Unofficially, I'd be glad to help. I owe you one anyway."

"Good. What do you need for that?"

"Americans work mostly from the embassy, so I should take a closer look at their compound, somehow. I want to see their antennas and all that kind of stuff."

The general thought for a moment. "That's easy. Valery will take you around. Anything else?"

"Whatever you've got in your files that's pertinent. I guess that's all."

"Sure. If you need anything else, let me know."

"Thank you."

"Oh, by the way, how long are you going to be here?"

"Only a couple of weeks, I hope. I've got to be off on another trip by mid-November."

"Hah, busy-busy?"

"Yes. My chief has an acute sense of time." Victor left, fully satisfied with the arrangement.

* * *

For the next few days he was busy with the team, helping Eugene to assume his position as team leader. On the one hand, Victor's priority was to free up time for himself for a few days so that he wouldn't be tracked down with a question every half hour. On the other hand, he really did want to help Eugene settle nicely into his new and difficult position, especially considering the inheritance Victor had left him after his spring visit. And after all, he was the one who'd trained Eugene initially. After a week the team and Eugene seemed to be working comfortably together. Now it was time for Victor's personal project. He ordered himself to fend off any emotions, and even thoughts about such things like the KGB's plan to assassinate the Pope.

One morning Victor came to the *residentura* to see Valery.

"Hi, Victor. Haven't seen much of you lately."

"Yeah, been working with the team. Now you're going to see too much of me, maybe. I need to snoop around the American embassy."

"Oh, yes. The general mentioned it. What's it all about?"

"Nothing much. He just wants me to slave for you guys again. He needs an assessment of the Americans' technical threat here."

"I'm swamped with paperwork. Besides, the November 7 is getting close. Look at this." He pointed at a cable on his desk. It was several pages long.

Victor laughed: "You don't need to read that stuff. You should know it by heart by now." They were referring to the standard "Increase-Security-Measures-before-the-Holiday" cable that was sent year after year to all the KGB residenturas around the world before State holidays—May Day, Victory Day, and Revolution Day. Each of these fat cables was virtually a copy of the previous one, elaborately calling for increased vigilance in the face of possible provocations by the imperialistic enemy forces.

Valery sighed, "I still need to send back a long reply, detailing what additional security measures have been taken in light of the glorious holiday. You know that."

Victor kept teasing him. "I also know you'll send a copy of your last holiday cable, adding one more security measure. And that's what's bothering you now—you haven't come up with a new one yet." Victor took a breath and continued, "I also happen to know you're violating the ciphertraffic security requirements by keeping a copy of your last-year's cable."

Valery laughed mischievously. "How did you know?"

"Because everyone does the same thing. I can bet you're slightly changing the first and the last paragraphs, and you'll add that new security measure just before the last paragraph."

Valery put back his head and laughed. "You know, you're dangerous, Victor."

Victor smiled, "Not when I'm friendly."

"All right, all right. When do you want to go?"

"It's not that I want to go. As a matter of fact, I'd rather not. I'm not too thrilled at the prospect of rummaging through the dusty attics and crummy apartments around the damn thing. It's your chief who wants that, not me. Seriously, why don't we come up with an excuse, such as the great holiday that's coming up, and scrap the whole idea?" Victor was taking a chance.

Valery didn't disappoint him. "No way, not with the old man. He's too heavy-handed. Easy for you, you don't work for him. I can't afford that kind of stunt. Let's do it by the book."

"All right, as you wish. Then, the sooner, the better. I'm leaving in a week, so we'd better hurry."

"OK, let's go now. Are you ready?"

"Sure."

They took Valery's car.

When they approached the American embassy, a glass and concrete, but mostly glass, building on a corner of Ujazdowskie Street, Valery asked, "Well, what's the game plan?"

"First, just make a couple of large circles around it."

On the second circle Victor said, "Pull over close by."

Valery stopped. They looked at the building. One glance was enough for Victor to dislike it. The entire ground-floor facade was covered with glass, making a clear statement: "Look, we are very open; you can see anything inside." A semicircular cobblestoned driveway, starting at the sidewalk, led to the front entrance and then continued on to the exit. A Polish police booth, a wooden shack so small that one person had barely enough space to stand in it, was at the left side of the drive, just back from the street. It was manned by one policeman armed with a handgun. Through the glass of the lobby, in the middle of the opposite wall, one could see an American flag and a uniformed marine standing guard. A receptionist's counter was visible at the left side of the lobby.

"What's so interesting for you here? A facade like any other. Surely they wouldn't run anything from here."

"I'm just looking to see how many windows are curtained on the upper floors. Seems to be a lot."

"Yeah. Want to take a closer look?"

"Sure. What observation points are available from this side?"

"See that thing high on the lamppost? That's a Polish surveillance camera, not a traffic camera. Switches from normal to infrared, so it covers around the clock. It's hard to get the pictures off that camera from the Poles, though. You have to go through all the formalities. Takes forever. There's an observation post on the second floor of the building across the street. See those three windows with light curtains? Supposedly, it's manned around the clock. We can get in there to take a look, if you like."

The two second-floor windows belonged to a building across from the embassy on Ujazdowskie Street. They were off the center of the embassy's facade, almost at the intersection with the small street beyond. Victor calculated that it gave the watchers about a twenty to twenty-five degree angle of observation on the center of the lobby. "It doesn't give a frontal angle. Do the Poles have another one on the other side?"

"No. Do you want to go inside and take a look? They have pretty good optics there."

"No, thanks. It's too low, only the second floor. You can't see anything on the embassy's upper floors by looking up the building."

"Well, I'm afraid they don't have anything else on this side."

"What's that door into the left wing from the side street?"

"That's the entrance to the Americans' kind of cultural section. All sorts of people go there. The Poles cover it point-blank. Anybody exiting faces their observation point across the street. But it's low as well, so it wouldn't do for your purposes. They just cover people, you see."

Victor didn't need to ask if there was a surveillance unit attached to the observation posts. That was standard operating procedure. He also knew that he shouldn't push his luck any further. "It's imperative to take a look from above."

"Then let's go behind the complex. The Poles have a couple of facilities there."

"OK. But I'd rather not show my face to the Poles. Let's first see if there's anywhere we can take a look at the American roof without using the Poles."

"I doubt there is." Valery paused, and suddenly said, "Wait. I think there is such a spot. I ran into it last year."

For about five minutes they drove around the American embassy, seemingly at random. Valery kept mumbling, "No, not this one." Finally, he said, "That's it." They drove into the yard of an apartment complex and parked. Valery hadn't been here many times before, perhaps once or twice, and then only by chance. Yet he seemed entirely at home. That was just his style. He entered the front door as if he went through it twice a day. Victor followed. They took the elevator to the top floor. Valery looked up in the stairway. There was a small fire-escape ladder that led to the attic. He shook his head: "No, there are no windows in the attic. We could go to the roof, though. But let's try this window first." He led Victor one flight down the stairs to a stairway window. The whole place was filthy, and the window was no exception. Suddenly, through the dirty glass of the window, they saw the roof of the American embassy just below and in front of them.

"Splendid. This is precisely what I need." Victor took out a notebook and started making notes.

No one bothered them; nobody even passed through the stairway. At this time of day the building looked deserted. Though clearly bored, Valery waited patiently.

Victor put the notebook and the pen in his pocket. "That's it. We can go have a beer now."

On the way out Valery asked, "Do you need a photo?"

"Not really. If the general had wanted me to write a report, he should have sent a cable with a request to my boss. He's never had permission for this work officially granted, and he knows it. So it'll all be oral. For that, I'm OK. Besides, if you think I like this extra job, you're dead wrong. Let's just get out of here."

As they were having a beer in a small dark restaurant just off Marshalkovska, Victor asked, "By the way, remember I ordered reading glasses for my father on my second day here? The shop isn't too far from here, is it?"

"No."

"I wonder if they're ready yet. The guy said next Wednesday. Should we check on them now? I'm afraid he won't finish them before I leave."

"Don't worry. I've known the guy for a long time. He's a regular chronometer. If he said Wednesday, it'll be Wednesday. No sooner, no later."

"All right then, we'll pick them up on Wednesday, the 31st. And I do need to do some shopping, you know. Preferably during the daytime— fewer people in the stores. Why don't we do it at the same time?"

"Sure. How about right after lunch?"

"OK."

"Oh, Victor, why don't you come over tomorrow for dinner?"

Victor hated himself for allowing his emotions to influence his choices. But he still couldn't forget his last dinner at Valery's. And Victor had another good reason as well: dogs often feel other people's attitudes toward their masters, and Valery's King was a smart dog. "Thanks, but I'll have to duck it this time. I need to spend time with the team."

Valery felt slightly offended. "OK, as you wish. My role is to suggest."

CHAPTER

VICTOR AWOKE EARLY and slowly. His eyes wandered over the absurdly ornate bedroom ceiling. *Wednesday, October 31, 1979. The movie starts at 17:30.* Victor knew all too well that this day would be the watershed of his life. He was determined to make it a positive one. He was going to focus on details and didn't want to let himself even begin to consider the larger implications of success—or failure. It was going to be a busy day.

He'd completed the basic preparations for his plan, and now he had till 17:30 to attend to the final details. The glasses, for one. The heavy-framed glasses were going to be an essential part of his disguise this evening. Because Victor had 20/20 vision, it would have been suspicious for him to possess a pair of glasses. But there was nothing unusual about Russian travelers' buying glasses abroad for relatives back home, where good lenses were difficult to come by. So Victor had taken his father's prescription for reading glasses and ordered them upon his arrival in Warsaw. To be picked up on the 31st. Today.

He'd also quietly bought thin leather driving gloves a few days before. Again, there was nothing unusual about that—everyone knew that it was impossible to buy driving gloves in Russia. They were stowed with some other purchases in his suitcase.

He'd spent the previous Saturday morning at the library. Both the library and a movie theater were in a kind of Soviet cultural center, located a short distance from the embassy. While he was there he'd inspected the bathroom carefully. It had a double-casement window with white-painted glass that looked out onto the street. It was locked from the inside with latches, and for extra measure two nails had been driven through the outer sash, to make sure that it was permanently shut. A redundancy for a place that required little security, and an annoying one for Victor. To his dismay, it had taken him half a day to find the two rusty nails he wanted to use for substitutes. Both nails had been carefully broken to size and were now waiting in Victor's pocket.

The movie starts at 17:30. He ran through his mental checklist again. All that was left to do was to buy a beret, pick up the glasses, and prepare the window.

Over breakfast, Victor mentally double-checked his whole approach. On the one hand, his preparations might seem a bit extravagant, perhaps a little nineteenth-century, but on the other hand, he was certain there was no way he could escape unnoticed from the embassy compound itself, with its massive security and closed-circuit TV. He would certainly not be able to get back in. *Whatever works—let it be even from the Stone Age.*

And there was no way to enter the American consulate. It was too logical for a walk-in to go to the consulate, and the consulate was too heavily covered by the Poles. So that was out.

Victor realized that by far the most difficult and the most dangerous part of his plan was getting by the Polish police guard at the embassy driveway. His only chance was to bluff his way through. Apart from official visitors arriving in chauffeur-driven cars, not too many nonemployees walked up to and through the main entrance on any given day, perhaps a dozen. Of course, no cab would be allowed near the main entrance. In theory, every visitor was supposed to be stopped by the guard and checked out. If Victor was challenged, he couldn't make a run for the door—the sixty-foot stretch was way too long. He'd be shot in the back as a "terrorist," the usual excuse given by the unfriendly guards at American embassies. Nor could he just run away. If he was stopped, the only slim chance he'd have of escaping would be to take over the taxi, drive to some crowded spot nearby, and disappear from there.

I'll just have to bluff my way through.

The time for thinking was over. It was time to act.

He spent more than an hour with Eugene, checking plans, until he was sure that Valery had gone off to his regular meeting with the Polish Service. *10:30. The movie starts at 17:30.* On his way to the general's office, Victor dropped by the technicians' storage closet. Nobody was around. He picked out a pair of pliers and two good chisels and put one in each inside pocket of his jacket. Now he was ready.

"What's up, Victor?" The general's secretary was friendly as usual.

"Nothing much. Is Valery around? I'm really in the doghouse."

"No, he left half an hour ago for the meeting with the 'friends.' What's wrong?"

"Oh, I took this book out of the library on Monday. The librarian was very nice and let me have it overnight, even though she's not supposed to let reserved books out at all. I swore up and down I'd bring it back yesterday, but I forgot. Completely. I'm so embarrassed. I was hoping Valery could give me a quick ride over there so that I could return it and apologize in person."

"Don't worry, that lady's a friend of mine. I can call her right now for you." That wasn't part of Victor's plan.

"Please, don't. This is a matter of principle. I'm the one who's personally responsible. You know what? Are any of the operational drivers available for about fifteen minutes?"

"Of course. But are you sure it's worth it?"

"Absolutely. At least I'll feel better about it."

The ride was very short. Out of the embassy compound, one block up Belwederska, one block to the left, and one block up 1 Armii WP. The driver stopped at the cultural center's entrance.

Victor noticed that from his seat the driver had a clear view inside the building and could easily see the door of the men's room. "Why don't you park over there; it'll be about ten minutes." Victor pointed to a parking space some thirty feet beyond. He entered the building, turned right in the lobby into the library, returned the book, and chatted awhile with the librarian. His body language indicated that he had nothing but time. More important, he wanted to create the impression of having spent more time with her than he actually did. Then, with the leisurely gait of a man who does not know how to kill all his spare time, he ambled out of the library and back into the lobby. He noticed that the car couldn't be seen from the librarian's desk, so the driver hadn't been able to see him. Nor could he now.

Victor quickly turned and strode into the men's room, putting on the driving gloves as he went. There was nobody in the center at this time of day. Taking out his tools, he walked briskly down the aisle, checking the

empty stalls as he went to the window at the end. First, he unlatched and
pulled open the center pair of inside windows. Then, using the blades of
both chisels, he carefully eased out the head of the first nail from the
frame of one outer window. If he had used only one chisel, the nail would
have bent and made a small but irreparable mark on the wood next to it.
The nail squeaked and started to move. One eighth of an inch was
enough. He took the pliers and steadily pulled the nail straight out without bending it and put it in his pocket. He was very careful—old rusty
nails have a nasty habit of breaking. That would be a major setback.

Having pulled out the second nail and put it away, he peeked through
a scratch in the paint. There was nobody outside near the window. He
carefully unlocked the latches, and holding the sharp ends of the substitute nails in his right hand, he used his left hand to softly push the left half
slightly open. Then he inserted a half-nail into the hole of the old one in
the sill and pushed it down with the flat side of a chisel. He quickly
repeated the operation on the right part of the sill and closed the window.
Victor stood still, his hearing tuned to the door of the bathroom. The driver could be a problem. Silence. He pushed the top halves of the nails
into the frames with a chisel, using a small piece of soft cloth to prevent
leaving any shiny marks on the heads. He looked for any telltale signs of
the work he'd done and, seeing none, closed and latched the inner windows. The tools went back into his pockets. Victor looked at his watch.
Just under five minutes. Not bad for working carefully. He took off the
gloves and returned to the car. The driver was reading a book, obviously
not counting minutes.

"All right, let's go." Valery appeared after lunch, as planned, all set for the
shopping expedition. First, they stopped at the optician's. To Victor's
quiet relief, the glasses were ready. The hard case was handsome. More to
the point, the frames were heavy and dark. Not only would they alter his
face, they were likely to make him look older.

Then they headed into a department store. As Victor had hoped, it
wasn't crowded. Both men had started out in good moods, but by the
time Victor had tortured the middle-aged salesman for better than ten
minutes with his requests to see yet another scarf, Valery's patience began
to wear thin. "Look, Victor, I'm going over to the sports department for a
minute, OK?"

"Sure," Victor replied automatically, not even turning to answer. He
was deeply absorbed in choosing a scarf. Glancing at the mirrored wall
behind the salesperson, he watched Valery disappear. Victor then imme-

diately settled on the longest and thickest scarf. It would require a bigger bag. He swiftly turned to the object he was really after, a black beret. One of those nondescript accessories that no one ever notices—or remembers. Besides, it could be adjusted to jut out a couple of inches to cast a sizable shadow over his face. As luck would have it, these hats were in fashion that season, so a large number of Warsaw men were wearing them. Black berets and trench coats exactly like Victor's.

Victor added the beret to the scarf, and the salesperson—relieved and thrilled with Victor's "That's all"—quickly completed the transaction, before his customer changed his mind yet again. Of course, Victor made sure the scarf was on top in the bag.

Valery was back. "Well, anything else?"

Victor went on buying souvenirs almost without looking at them. Valery was happy when they finished in another half hour. So was Victor.

"By the way, Valery, my team's going to the movies tonight. I thought I'd go too."

"Where?"

"Our club, or center, whatever you call it, on 1 Armii WP."

"Now that's funny, I was thinking of going there as well. It's rather early, too, at five thirty, so we'd better be getting back."

A complication. Victor hadn't counted on Valery's being there. *Had he really planned to go, or had he made that up on the spot?*

15:50. The movie starts at 17:30.

On the way back Victor started complaining: "Have you ever tried to figure out what they put into the food in the embassy dining room? My stomach's been hurting ever since lunch today." *Set it up. You need a free run at the bathroom.* "This is the second time it's happened to me on this trip."

Valery was sympathetic. "The food there is lousy, everyone knows that. Trouble is, no one knows what to do about it. This whole place is corrupt, you know that as well as I do. Everyone on the kitchen staff is a thief. But none of us seems to be able to do a damn thing about it."

With that, the conversation faded and never quite picked up again. The two men were silent for the rest of the ride. Valery dropped Victor off and promised to pick him up at ten after five.

The movie starts at 17:30. Victor was praying that Valery wouldn't be late. He wasn't. They bought their tickets and started circulating separately among the people standing in a courtyard, smoking and socializing. Victor went from one group to another, his black trench coat on his arm, hand in his pocket. This way the coat attracted practically no attention.

He was keeping an eye on Valery's movements—no easy task, given Valery's gregarious nature and wide range of interests. *17:25.* Although a few scouts had gone into the auditorium as soon as the first bell rang—holding seats for their pals—the main crowd didn't even start moving in until the third bell sounded, as usual. As Victor had planned, Valery was about four feet behind him in the line; luckily, some of Eugene's team were the same distance behind Valery. Victor half-turned, spotted Eugene, and started to make his way back toward him, crying, "Eugene, where did you disappear to? I've been looking for you!"

Valery had to turn slightly to let Victor pass behind him. The crowd was getting squeezed into a single line to fit through the narrow door to the theater. The distance between Valery and Victor increased, and Victor was now much closer to the end of the line. As he talked, quietly now, to Eugene, Victor suddenly dropped his lighter. He quickly stooped down to look for it, saying, "Go on, I'll catch up with you inside." Eugene was pushed along by the crowd surging toward the door. Victor groped about on the floor and finally found his lighter. Standing up, he held out his hands. Everyone could see him stare at the grime in dismay. He shook his head and looked around. He was relieved to find himself standing right by the men's room, and he immediately went inside.

Moving to a basin in the front section, he turned on the water and started to scrub his hands. The last men in the bathroom went out past him into the lobby. In less than a minute everyone had disappeared into the auditorium.

Victor wiped his hands roughly on the roller towel, quickly moved down to the last stall on the left near the window, and locked the door. *The lights in the theater should be out by now. Some people would be finding their seats in the dark. 17:32. The movie ends at 19:15.* The left-hand frame of the window he'd fixed was partly inside the stall. From his less-than-glamorous vantage point, through the clear inner pane of the double window and a small scratch in the paint of the outer glass, and at a very sharp angle, he could just glimpse the motion of cars passing by outside.

17:34. All quiet. Fortunately, the window couldn't be seen from the door to the lobby. Victor unlocked the stall door, came out, and put on his trench coat and gloves. All was still quiet. He opened the inside windows and secured the latches so that they wouldn't lock when the window was closed. *If somebody sees that and locks them again, I'll have a major problem.* He attached a thin thread to both latches. Then he unlocked the outer window. He opened it slightly, just enough for him to be able to see round to the street corner. He couldn't just jump out. There might be Polish surveillance, or a Soviet passerby. Jumping out of a window isn't exactly inconspicuous. *17:35. The movie ends at 19:15.*

Suddenly, a large truck, not unusual there, started to make a lumbering turn into the street. The truck's cabin slowly passed level with the window. *Now.* Victor swung the window open. *Don't step on the window sill. Step on the radiator just below it.* In a second he was on the ground outside. He quickly pulled the windows as closed as he could, then pulled the threads to shut them tightly. He pulled harder, breaking the threads. He wouldn't need them anymore. By this time the truck had almost passed him, slowly picking up speed. Victor sprinted to the left. An elderly woman had just turned into the street. *Nothing wrong; lots of people hurry.* He came to the intersection with Marshalkovska. *Danger zone.* He quickly crossed the most popular street in Warsaw and walked briskly through some smaller streets. He didn't see any surveillance. Victor put on his beret. *Now slow down; your breath must be very even.*

He spotted a taxi near the corner. He walked around the small block, slowly approaching the corner behind the taxi. He glanced behind. *Very unprofessional. Doesn't matter now. Nobody.* He turned the corner slowly, then quickly approached the taxi, simultaneously putting on his father's glasses. Now his disguise was complete.

How do Americans behave in such a situation? Most taxi drivers have had experience with American customers. OK. Take charge. He opened the back door and in a gruff, no-nonsense voice ordered in English, "American embassy."

"What?"

"American embassy." *Start the engine, dummy.*

"Americanske?"

"Yes." Now he'd have to start drawing on what he had learned in his weekend gleanings from his English dictionary. The taxi started rolling. Victor saw the driver studying him in the rearview mirror. *He's hoping for dollars, but I don't have any. I suppose I'd better give him an outrageously large amount in zlotys, to keep up the American image.*

17:47. The movie ends at 19:15. I must have just set a world's record for recklessness in intelligence. Ten minutes' checking on surveillance instead of the minimum two hours. The taxi pulled up to the embassy driveway. That was as near to the entrance as the driver was permitted. That put Victor ten feet from the policeman. *If he asks for your papers, end of game. The key is how you carry yourself. You have to look like you own the place. Your only chance here is to be so intimidating that he doesn't dare ask to see them.* But suddenly Victor realized that he had another problem. The taxi was a model he wasn't familiar with, and wearing his father's strong prescription glasses, he couldn't see the handle to open the door. He pawed at it desperately but still couldn't find it. *It's not the big mistakes that do you in, remember. Major failures come from small errors.* The last thing he needed now was to be clumsy. The helpful driver saw Victor struggling in the backseat and came to his rescue. He reached over, and flipped the door handle. But then the ungrateful passenger gave him a stack of zlotys.

"Dollars?" the disappointed driver demanded.

"No dollars. Zlotys." That certainly didn't sound too American. The driver looked at the fistful of money, made a quick computation, then quickly got out of the car and ran around to further assist this loony. Victor mumbled, "Dyakuii" as he opened the door.

Victor turned toward the entrance and looked at his watch. *17:56. It's OK to look at your watch. After all, it was the edge between the workday and the evening.* Then he started moving very confidently almost straight at the guard, aiming just slightly to the right of him. Finally, at the last possible moment, he looked up and acknowledged the presence of the guard. Victor glanced at him as he would glance at some fixture. Then, very slightly and a bit more slowly than he would normally do, he nodded to the policeman, while still moving toward him. The policeman had to take a half step back to let Victor pass, and he saluted. *The most important salute I've ever received.*

Victor had been lucky so far. His first crucial five or six steps toward the policeman had been on a smooth asphalt surface. Just as he passed the policeman, however, the driveway became cobblestone. Because he was seeing the ground through his father's glasses, it was a miracle that he didn't fall down. His walk became uncertain at best, but he was already in the clear. More or less.

17:57. The movie ends at 19:15. Victor opened the front door. There was a receptionist at the counter near the left wall of the lobby. *Probably Polish. Speak softly.* He went straight forward to the prototypical young marine standing guard. Victor quietly said the phrase that he'd practiced so many times to himself: "I need speak to the representative of American Intelligence." He wasn't sure how openly the Americans would admit to such a thing.

"I am the representative of American Intelligence."

Victor smiled. He'd expected something like that, though perhaps not so bold. He used his backup line: "Then I need speak to duty diplomat."

The marine nodded, apparently not the duty diplomat as well. He picked up a phone and said something quickly into the mouthpiece. Then he told Victor, "Wait, please," and indicated the row of chairs along the glass front wall.

That was not in Victor's plans. As he walked over to the chairs, he'd have to face the window. And the watchers. All of a sudden, the problem escalated. The bright lights in the lobby went on. There were no curtains. Now the whole scene was an illuminated fishbowl, every detail visible from the outside.

Since he had no alternative, Victor adopted an easy, almost swaggering posture, and slowly unbuttoned his coat. Then, still keeping the glasses and beret on, he started moving crabwise, slightly sideways, while constantly looking at something very interesting on the wall. The oddity was that there was nothing on the wall, nothing at all. He knew that he had to keep his head turned about twenty degrees to the right of the axis of the building all the time. This way the surveillance would get only the back of his head. Dancing his way across, he finally reached his destination and sat down on a chair, still faithfully facing twenty degrees to the right.

18:03. Five minutes. Nothing was happening. This was something Victor was totally unprepared for. *18:10. Twelve minutes. The movie will end at 19:15.*

18:12. A man came out of the elevator near the receptionist's desk and walked up to Victor.

"How can I help you?"

"I do not speak English."

"Do you speak Polish?"

"A little." Actually, Victor spoke some Ukrainian, which has much in common with Polish.

"So, how can I help you?" This time in Polish.

"Can we talk somewhere else?"

"Sure."

He led Victor past the receptionist and through a door to a room beyond.

"I would like to ask for political asylum."

"Where do you work?"

This had been Victor's major concern all along. He was sure that at this juncture they couldn't take him into a room protected for a secure conversation. He wondered how the Americans would solve the problem. Victor took out a piece of paper from his pocket and scribbled: KGB.

Instantly, the man's manner changed. He led Victor down a short stairway to the basement. Then through a corridor to another stairway. All of a sudden, Victor heard voices. Another unexpected problem: several workers, obviously Polish, were coming toward them. Reflexively,

Victor turned his face straight to the wall and stopped. *My God, they really do let local workers into the building. Surely, more than half of them are local counterintelligence officers. There's not much that's more stupid and more dangerous than that.* The workers passed on by, and Victor and his host went up the stairs. To his surprise and admiration Victor found himself in some kind of storage room. *That's really smart. Who would bug a storage room?* A second man soon appeared.

"None of us speak Russian, so let's make do with Polish," the second man said.

"OK."

"Do you have any time limitation now?" *Professional approach. Good.*

"Yes, I have to be back no later than 19:10."

"Can we meet at a later date?"

"No, I'm leaving for Moscow on Friday."

"OK. Sorry, but we have to observe the formalities. Who is the Resident at the KGB station here?"

"Solovyev."

"Who's running line X?"

Victor answered a few questions of that nature, which he knew were necessary to establish his bona fide, or at least to verify that he wasn't a crazy. Then Victor offered the men his passport. "Make sure you get good pictures of it. There are some special signals in it; we'll discuss them later." The first man disappeared with the passport and soon returned.

"OK, we're satisfied. What's your line of work?"

"Cipher communications." The Americans looked at each other. They could hardly contain their excitement. They knew then that they had a big one.

"Are you a cipher clerk?"

"No, I'm responsible for the security of the KGB cipher communications abroad." *Are they going to verify my bona fide in this field? Probably not. They surely don't know enough about it to ask intelligent questions, and they don't want to look dumb.*

"Well, I don't think we need to comment on that. What can we do for you?"

"My wife and five-year-old daughter cannot travel abroad. Security restriction." The man nodded. "I need you to help us get out; to guarantee us political asylum in the U.S., citizenship, and a comfortable living."

"Given who you are, I think it can be arranged." Victor nodded. The man continued. "Are you sure you're clean, coming here?"

"I think so. Who can be sure?"

"In other words, are you sure you want to go back now? You know the level of risk. Why don't we just get you to the U.S. right now?"

"Out of the question."

"OK, it's your neck. Anything else?"

"No, just meet me there." Victor took a piece of paper and wrote out the conditions of the meeting in Moscow. He passed it to the man asking the questions.

"Personal meeting?"

"Yes." Victor looked the man straight in the eye. "I know you think I'm crazy. Maybe I am, but as you just said, it's my neck."

The man looked down at the note again. "Why such a long time from now?"

"I'm leaving for Yemen soon and might get stuck there for a while."

"Any chance of a contact in Yemen?"

"Absolutely not."

"OK." He looked at his watch. "I guess you have to get out. Here's your passport. Thanks."

"Yes. How?"

"We'll give you a ride. In a 'clean' car. Where do you want us to drop you off?"

Victor gave him the address.

As they went back downstairs, the man asked, "By the way, have you ever heard of Halloween?"

"No, what's that?"

"It's an American holiday. Today is Halloween. You've pulled one hell of a trick-or-treat."

"I'm sorry?"

"Oh, never mind, you'll find out." And he probably thought, "If you're very lucky."

Before Victor crouched down onto the backseat floor of the car, the man said, "Good luck." He started to leave, then turned back to Victor. "Hey, be careful, OK?"

Another man drove Victor away from the embassy and dropped him off at Oleandrow Street.

19:05. The movie ends at 19:15. Victor walked briskly to the side street. *19:10.* At the window he had to wait another minute for the street to clear. He was going to test his luck one more time. He pushed the window open noisily and peeked inside. Nobody. If anyone had been inside, they'd have responded. Victor hoisted himself onto the sill and jumped down inside. He closed both sets of windows, pulled off the remnants of the threads, and locked himself in a stall. A different one. He finally had time to take a deep breath.

The movie was late letting out, so he had to wait five more minutes for men to start coming in. He felt tired. When the bathroom started to fill, he emerged from the stall, trench coat on his arm, hand in his pocket. He approached a sink and washed his hands and face.

At the bathroom door he bumped into Valery.

"Hey, man, you look like shit."

"I told you, you better check out what they put into the food in the dining room. It's just about done me in."

Victor was exhausted. All he wanted to do was get back to his pirate's lair for a luxurious hot shower and sleep.

CHAPTER

AT SHEREMETYEVO, Olga's eyes were just one big question. Victor pretended not to see it until they were in the taxi. Only then did his own eyes indicate "Yes." She was tremendously excited. Victor could imagine how difficult it would be for her to wait until it was safe to talk.

That evening they went out for a walk and finally she could ask: "How was it?"

"Just fine. I popped in, we had a nice chat, and we agreed to meet here later to work out the details."

"Did they agree?"

"Of course. In principle."

"How did you manage to escape?"

"Oh, it's a long story. But, in short, it seems the best way to escape from this system is through a toilet."

Olga laughed, not realizing that the description wasn't all that far-fetched. "I know this has to sound silly to you, but are you sure nobody noticed?"

"If anybody had, I wouldn't be talking to you now." *I wish I could be as certain of that as I sound.* He knew the KGB could go on playing a cat-and-mouse game for a while. It was their turf. No risk for them. But Olga was already under too much strain. He didn't want to add any more.

"When are you going to meet with them?"

"In February."

"So late? Why?"

"It's not that simple, you see. I have to go to Yemen very soon. They wouldn't have had enough time to prepare for the meeting before I leave. I'm not sure when I'll get back, so to be on the safe side I asked for mid-February."

"But the Olympics will be so close."

"Yes, but I really don't have a choice. Of course, I could have requested one for early January, with backups, say, every two weeks after that, but what if I didn't make it back before that first meeting? They might think I was in some kind of trouble and put the case on ice for six months. Or they might decide the whole thing was a KGB hoax and drop the case altogether. Unfortunately, both are likely professional responses. I cannot take those kinds of chances."

"So, we'll just have to wait it out." Olga was obviously disappointed. She was afraid too. Victor knew she was thinking of the clock running. *Much faster than you could possibly imagine.*

Even if he hadn't been identified during his visit to the American embassy right away, he still could be. Analysis of information normally takes a long time. There was still a chance that the Poles would identify him when they analyzed their surveillance tapes and other information, putting together the pieces of the puzzle. There was no way of knowing if or when it might happen. Even if it didn't happen, there was no guarantee that the Americans weren't already sufficiently penetrated, or wouldn't be tomorrow. The KGB didn't need his full identity. A few vague leads could be enough to snare him. He knew that during his unfortunate trip to Yemen he'd be thinking a lot about that accelerating clock.

"I'm afraid we don't have any choice."

"What do we do for now?"

"Nothing, absolutely nothing. We've got to keep as low a profile as possible. I really regret those stupid stunts I tried here in Moscow, but there's nothing we can do about them now. So, Olga, just keep to your routine as consistently as you can."

"What if for some reason you or they can't make that first meeting; will they be able to find you?"

"I would hope they wouldn't try. They should know better than that. Realistically, the only way they could find me would be through Moscow 'Information.'"

"Those kiosks all around the city?"

"Right. It's the only public way available to find someone's address.

First, you have to request the address in person, and then you have to wait an hour. Do you understand why?"

"I suppose it's because they're so inefficient?"

"Not at all. In fact, 'Information' is all too efficient. Say you ask for the address of someone who happens to be on a special list—which I certainly am. When you come back to pick up the address, they give it to you, all right. But by then surveillance is in place, waiting to follow you to find out who you are and why you need that address. The procedure doesn't generally produce much, just old friends and distant relatives. But it's one more system in place and operating."

"I hope the Americans are aware of that."

"So do I. But don't worry, I gave them 'perpetual' meeting conditions, which means that if, for whatever reason, we don't meet at the designated place and time, then I will be at a certain place at a certain time every once in a while with no limit. That's standard operating procedure."

"When do you leave for Yemen?"

"In a week or two, I guess. I don't know what's been going on at the office. Of course, I'll do my best to get ready as soon as possible, but there are a lot of variables beyond my control." He paused and continued gently, "Olga, I want you to forget the whole thing for a while. It's extremely hard to wait, especially when you know that there's absolutely nothing you can do, no matter what. But you have to try. Otherwise, without any release, the tension will wear you out. And then you'll become a nervous wreck. And you'll start making mistakes."

As it turned out, Victor couldn't leave Moscow for another three weeks. And then the business in Yemen took longer than he'd counted on. The one question, "Do they know?" haunted him the entire time.

For a week after Victor's return from Yemen everything was peaceful and quiet. Then one night the telephone shattered the calm. Victor picked up the phone and glanced at the clock. Just after three in the morning.

"Victor?" A female voice. Sobbing.

"Yes."

"This is Tanya Yermin."

"Oh, hi. How are you?" *What the hell's happened now?*

"Yuri's dead."

"What?" Victor's friend, Yuri Yermin, was an engineer from an enterprise that did a lot of contract work for the KGB. He'd just been with Victor in Yemen.

"Sorry, I couldn't wait till morning. I just got a call from the Militia.

They said Yuri collapsed in the street, and that he was dead by the time the ambulance came. They told me I could come after noon and pick up the papers from the morgue."

"Which one?"

"Sokolinaya Gora." She sobbed. "Oh, God, what am I going to do?"

"Tanya, I'm very sorry. He was a friend of mine. How can I help?" Victor hated how lame he sounded.

"I don't know," she sobbed. "I've called the relatives, and they're coming soon." Suddenly her sobs increased in intensity, and she blurted, "Victor, do you think he could've been killed?"

Victor hesitated. "Tanya, I'll try and find out first thing in the morning. We'll investigate this to the fullest extent. Please, try to calm down now. You're going to need a lot of strength. Try to rest." As an afterthought, "Tanya?"

"Yes?"

"Did you call anybody else about this, besides the relatives?"

"I tried to call Sergei, but nobody answers. Maybe his phone's out of order." Sergei was Yuri's best friend, also a member of the team that had just returned from Yemen.

"I'll try to reach him and have him come to you right away. Meanwhile, you try to rest."

They hung up. Olga was awake and watching him, having heard his end of the conversation. She understood what had happened and simply asked, "Who?"

"Yuri Yermin."

"My God, he's barely thirty! What happened?"

"She doesn't know for sure. Collapsed in the street."

Victor dialed Boss's home. "Sorry to disturb you, Alexey Leontyevich. It's Sheymov."

"Not at all, I was just thinking of calling you." Boss's sense of humor.

"I've just had a call from the wife of Yuri Yermin—an engineer who was with our team in Yemen. He's dead. Collapsed in the street."

"I remember the name. He's been quite involved in the program all along, right?"

"Yes. Do we want to give this to Investigations? At this point we have a head start—it's only a Militia case."

Boss was thinking. The pause lasted several seconds.

"I'd rather not. Keep it quiet if you can. I don't want to attract any attention to the program. If it's bad, then so be it, there's nothing we can do about it. If not, let's just close the case. Go to the Militia and the morgue, see what you can do. Call the duty officer, take a car from the CD pool."

Good. The last thing I need is for Investigations to start poking around everyone who's just been to Yemen, building wild theories and shaking everyone out.

"OK, will do. Again, sorry for the late call." Victor hung up.

It was close to 4:00 A.M. by the time Victor arranged for a mutual friend to roust Sergei out and tell him to go help Yuri's widow, and to see what kind of help their enterprise could provide. Then he called Sokolinaya Gora hospital.

"Morgue, please."

"Connecting."

"This is KGB Major Sheymov. Do you have the body of Yuri Yermin?"

"Just a minute. Yes, we do."

"Which Militia precinct sent the body in?" The rule was that if anybody died in a public place before the ambulance arrived, the Militia had to come before the body was moved.

"Sokolniki Precinct."

"Thank you."

Victor made tea for himself. *What the hell's going on? Every time somebody comes to me and voices doubts about the system, he turns up dead in a hurry.*

Victor was thinking about how just two days before the team left Yemen, Yuri had come to his apartment. Late. Drunk.

"How do you always manage to get the coziest accommodations?" The grim building was a former palace of a former brother of a former ruler of Yemen, and was now part of the Soviet embassy's compound. The walls were of thick stone, which made it warm in winter and luxuriously cool in summer. But what Yuri was obviously referring to was the ominous hook in the ceiling by the entrance to Victor's apartment. During a coup, the ruler's brother was said to have been hanged from it. It was anybody's guess what else the hook had been used for.

"Yuri, you're drunk again. Sooner or later this is going to get you into trouble."

Yuri sat down in a chair and was silent for quite a long time. Finally, he spoke. "Victor, can you tell me what's going on?"

"What do you mean?"

"You know."

"No."

"Look, old man, we've worked together in more than a few places. You know you can trust me, and I know I can trust you."

"Sure." Victor sensed trouble.

"Then tell me honestly, what's going on in our damn country? Are there any decent people left?"

"I don't understand what you're getting at."

"Oh, sure you do. You know this regime is rotten; you know that everyone's corrupt. You just don't want to talk about it. You don't trust me after all, do you?"

Victor had to think fast. Coming out of nowhere, this was dangerous. *Is this a provocation? Shouldn't be—Yuri's not the type for a setup. Is this just drunken candor? Probably, but either way it spells trouble.* "Yuri, you know something? You're so drunk I can't understand a damn thing you're mumbling. Why don't you get some sleep, and we'll talk over whatever's bothering you in the morning? Deal?"

With considerable difficulty Victor managed to escort Yuri back to his room. Nothing transpired in the morning.

Victor was at the Sokolniki Militia precinct at seven. His task was relatively simple. If Yuri had been murdered, there was nothing he could do. The murder of an Eighth CD contractor involved in a sensitive project would not be taken lightly, especially after his having just returned from a project abroad. There'd be a full-blown KGB investigation. In a potentially high priority counterintelligence case, no one would be above suspicion, particularly with the bait of a once-in-a-lifetime career opportunity for the investigators. For Victor it would mean that the KGB would start scrupulously investigating him—along with the others—at a most inopportune time. If he could establish conclusively now that it wasn't murder, he'd have a chance of closing off the affair quickly, and so preventing anyone from looking into it "just in case."

As usual with the Militia, it took Victor two hours to locate the case and the sergeant who had inspected the body the day before. Victor studied the few pages of the report.

"Where are the photos?"

"What photos? You must be used to your fancy place. We just use sketches."

There was a sketch showing the body in a small room. The body was half-sitting against the wall near the door.

"I heard he collapsed in the street. You have a transcript of the phone call to the emergency service saying the same thing. But this sketch shows a room."

"It's not a room, it's the small entrance hall of the apartment building. Look, it was twenty-five below zero outside. Someone with a heart must have brought him in. Nothing unusual."

"Who called the ambulance?"

"Let me find out." The sergeant picked up the phone as Victor continued to go through a list of the few personal effects found on Yuri.

By the time Victor was halfway through the list, the sergeant hung up. "No name given, just a female voice."

Victor had finished with the list. There'd been money in the wallet and an expensive fur hat. While it wouldn't have been unusual, under the circumstances, for some things to have disappeared, nothing indicated a robbery. However, there was something missing. Victor thought for a moment. The watch. He recalled that Yuri had bought himself a Seiko in Yemen.

"Did you turn all possessions over to the morgue?"

"Yes."

"Any chance that something might have slipped out?"

The sergeant took offense at the question. "Absolutely not."

"OK." Victor returned to the drawing. There was something odd about it, but he couldn't quite figure out what it was. "All right, I've got to go now. I'd like to have a copy of this sketch."

"We don't have copying machines here."

"Then I'd like to take the original."

"Against regulations."

"Look, let's not make a big deal out of this. Let me take the picture. I'll send it back to you today, promise." Victor took a pack of Marlboros out of his attaché case and put it on the table. "Let's have a pipe of peace."

The sergeant considered his options. The peaceful one was apparently more attractive. He put the Marlboros in his pocket. "Done."

Victor left for the morgue.

In the car he kept studying the sketch. Finally, it hit him. The body was leaning against the outside wall. Apparently, it had been dragged into the hall from within the building, not from the street. And it had been dragged by one person, otherwise it would have been set down less awkwardly. Yuri weighed around two hundred pounds, and whoever had pulled him in was none too strong. So Yuri had collapsed somewhere inside the building, not in the street.

In a hospital the shortest route is always from the top down. When he reached Sokolinaya Gora, Victor went straight to the Chief Doctor. Luckily, he was in and alone. Ten minutes and one phone call later Victor was talking to the Chief Pathologist.

"I'm sorry, Comrade Major, but we've just finished the autopsy. Nothing unusual. Heart attack."

Knowing he was in command, Victor demanded, "Then I must request a secondary autopsy." Victor felt decidedly uneasy. Watching a standard autopsy was unpleasant enough. A "secondary" was far more extensive, and Victor would have to watch the entire procedure. It's much harder to take when it's being performed on a friend. But he had no choice. He had to wrap things up quickly and cut off every possible reason for reopening the case, which the lack of the extensive autopsy could become.

"Right now?"

"Please. This way I'll be off your back much faster. But first, I have to examine the clothing." A standard procedure.

Victor went off to check through Yuri's possessions, and the doctor left to prepare for the autopsy.

The clothing looked normal, but Victor noticed that an upper button on the coat had been freshly torn off, and that the back of the coat and trousers were covered with thick dust—the kind of dust found in stairways and halls, not in snowy streets at twenty-five below zero.

The secondary autopsy was gruesome.

"So, everything is exactly as I told you. By the way, this guy would've been dead in six months anyway. His liver was falling apart. Do you still want a toxicology analysis?"

Victor did not. "What do you think?"

"I think you'd be wasting your time."

"All right. Can you clearly state your certainty in the report? I'd like to have that report right away."

From the morgue, Victor went to pay his respects to Yuri's widow. After spending half an hour there, he took the dead man's friend Sergei outside.

"Does this address mean anything to you?" Victor showed him a piece of paper.

"No." Sergei avoided meeting Victor's eyes.

"Look, I don't have time to play games. You were Yuri's best friend, and he wasn't the type to keep secrets from his best friend." Victor's voice was terse.

"Well, it looks familiar, but it's hard to recall exactly, you know."

"You've been to this address this morning?"

Sergei looked scared. "How do you know?"

"Educated guess. She's his girlfriend, isn't she?"

"Yeah." And then he quickly added, "But they were more like friends, you know. Kind of like drinking buddies. It's probably hard for you to understand."

"What happened?"

"Well, her husband was away. They were sitting and drinking. Then he collapsed. She was afraid their relationship would be exposed, so she led him outside her first-floor flat and called the ambulance."

"Not exactly. He had a heart attack, and the bitch, instead of calling the ambulance, got him dressed and dragged him out into the hall to die. Then she called the ambulance."

"How could you know that?"

"Go over to her place right away and get Yuri's new Seiko watch. She forgot to put it back on his wrist. And tell her to get rid of the button that came off his coat. Must be somewhere near the door. Then take Tanya to the morgue to collect Yuri's possessions. Slip the watch in quietly. I'll see you at the funeral."

"What'll happen? It wouldn't be good for Tanya to know."

"She won't. If you keep your mouth shut."

At Dom 2 Boss was available.

"Well?"

"Nothing funny. It's clear he died of a heart attack. The pathologist is quite certain."

"Anything we should be concerned about?"

"Only one minor thing. Apparently, there was a girlfriend involved. That raised a couple of teasers, but I managed to sweep them under the rug. We don't want Investigations jumping in and playing with the case for a couple of months, and then coming to the same conclusion, do we?"

"Of course not."

"I cut off all the angles. You'll have my report by the end of the day. No funny stuff, of course. Clean case. It'll be closed before Investigations even hears about it."

"Well done." Boss paused, leaning back in his chair. "Life's strange, isn't it? We learn much more about people when they die than we do when they're alive."

Later, Victor revisited the sergeant, who was happy to close the case.

Olga and Victor went to the Rossiya movie theater. It was perfectly natural to take a walk after the movie, so by nine o'clock they were moving slowly along Strastnoy Boulevard toward the Kirovskaya Metro station.

"Victor, are we just out for a stroll, or is there somewhere you want to go in particular?"

"In particular, but we'll talk about it in a minute. Right now, we need to assess our situation."

"But aren't we just waiting at this point?"

"Yes, we're waiting, but we still have to do our homework. I did quite a bit of thinking in Yemen, and I'm tempted to add an extra touch to our plan."

"That's just the kind of remark that gets me worried."

Victor laughed. "Nothing to worry about, this time. But it occurred to me that it would be nice if our departure wasn't noticed. To be precise, if the KGB could be persuaded that we were dead."

"Not a pleasant thought. But why?"

"You see, for someone like me to defect is a very serious blow to the KGB—but it's nothing in comparison to the damage I could inflict if they don't know about it."

"Well, obviously. They wouldn't think of taking steps to protect their secrets because they wouldn't know they were in jeopardy."

"Precisely. There'd be no damage control. See, it's every intelligence service's dream come true to talk to somebody like me for even half an hour. And it's the KGB's worst nightmare. If the other side could have access to me for a year without the KGB suspecting it, the impact would be many times greater."

"But they could still shift things around to make the information worthless, couldn't they?"

"Some. But there are other things that take years to change, and then others that virtually cannot be changed at all."

"I see. So that's why they're so paranoid about your security?"

"Right. The point is that if my ultimate goal is to inflict the greatest possible damage on the KGB and the communist system, then the best way for me to maximize the damage is to work with the Americans with the KGB assuming I'm dead."

"Could that make life easier for our friends and family here?"

"Absolutely. The KGB would have no reason to do anything to them. That's very different from what would happen to them for being closely related to a defector."

"Well then, Victor, how on earth are we going to convince the KGB we're dead? You wouldn't just leave three bodies behind and hope to fool them."

"That's the catch. It's just professionally inconceivable to pull something like this off—too far-fetched. But leaving bodies is out of the question. Aside from the lack of spare bodies, modern investigative techniques are so sophisticated that that's just not worth thinking about. So we'll have to find a way to convince the KGB that we're dead without leaving any bodies. And the only way to do that is to deny them any hard evidence, and to mislead them with circumstantial evidence."

"Is that realistic?"

"I think so. You see, if I just disappear, a whole lot of people will be in hot water. You can't imagine how many people's careers will be threatened, not to mention the imminent prospect of jail for some of them. Most of those people are very senior in the hierarchy. They'll be desperate; they'll do whatever they have to to save their own hides. So there's plenty of incentive for them to believe I'm dead. All we have to do is help them along."

"Well, it's an intriguing idea. But it does sound a little academic to me—if not downright crazy."

"Maybe, but the fundamental concept is sound. We just have to find a way to pull it off, and you'll have to help me."

"I'll do whatever I can, but I haven't a clue what that might be."

"That's my job. I have to set the frame for the investigation and very carefully steer them to the proper conclusion. We have to anticipate all the opposition's moves beforehand. For starters, you should understand right away that we mustn't leave the smallest clue about our intended departure."

"I'm not sure I get it."

"For example, how often do you go up into that little attic in our apartment?"

"Oh, gosh, twice a year. Why?"

"There's a layer of dust over everything up there, right? One of the first things they'll do will be to check whether that dust has been disturbed during the last month or so. People store things in an attic that they rarely need, but they are likely to fetch something down if they are planning to leave. That's KGB experience. So if you're going to want to take anything with you that's in that attic, get it out now, and don't go near the damn place again."

"I'd never have thought of that. Anything else like that that I should be aware of?"

"We'll go through it some more later. Right now I need to study the area we're coming to."

They were crossing Kirovskaya Street. The rotunda of the Old Kirovskaya Metro station was in front of them. They went around it and came to the Griboyedov statue, at the beginning of Chistoprudnyy Boulevard. Even though he had still been a relatively young man when he was murdered during a raid on the Russian embassy in Teheran, Griboyedov had made quite an impact and had joined the ranks of the country's classic writers. Characters from his works were cast on the statue's base.

"This is the area where I'm going to meet the Americans in exactly three weeks. I need to study it carefully." Victor looked at his watch. Just past ten.

"I thought you already knew this district pretty well."

"I do, but for the purposes of an operation you have to know every back alley, every yard you can pass through, which buildings you can get through via the back door, and which you can't. You have to know which attics are left unlocked, and a lot of other details as well. Even so, every place is different at different times of the day, and even on different days of the week."

"Why did you choose this area and this time?"

"Because it's Old Moscow. Lots of small old buildings crammed together, a maze of passageways. Not too much street crime here, and no highly sensitive buildings with tight security. In addition, there are lots of ways to get in and out of the area. As for this time of day—it's too late for people to be coming back from work or shopping, and too early for them to be returning from theaters and parties. It's a time when very few people are in the streets. So surveillance would have a hard time blending in. This isn't going to be a brush contact, you see. It's a long meeting."

"How long will it be?"

"I'd say at least half an hour. Maybe an hour."

"That doesn't seem too long."

Victor smiled. "It's very long. Any clandestine meeting in Moscow over five minutes is too long, believe me. Look, I need to go to work now, and you're going to help me."

"How?"

"First of all, simply with your presence. As a couple, we won't attract anyone's attention. Secondly, look for anything that strikes you as unusual. I might miss something. Just keep your eyes open."

They walked around the neighborhood for more than an hour, passing through narrow alleys, sometimes running into dead ends instead, going into buildings, but taking care every time to exit through the same door they went in to make sure they looked normal. Shortly after eleven the streets began to fill with people on their way home.

Victor was satisfied for the time being. "That's enough for now. Let's go home."

"Good. I'm cold, tired, and hungry. Let's take a taxi."

Warsaw and Yemen had really jammed his schedule, so between carrying out his job during the day and preparing at night for the upcoming meeting, Victor felt that the three weeks flew by. Almost before he knew it, the appointed day had arrived.

For all the time he had spent on his preparations, Victor wasn't sure what to do about countersurveillance just before the meeting. A huge question. Properly, he should first take a long, long route through different parts of the city, all justified. The last thing anyone wants is to get caught checking on surveillance, so one should check without ever showing it. Secondly, he should have somebody waiting at designated points to see if the surveillance is following him far behind, and if that's the case, to warn him with a prearranged signal so that he can abort the mission. Ironically, sometimes intelligence officers can check for surveillance thoroughly for several hours, making sure they'd "got black," only to pick up "floating" surveillance just before or at a meeting, with all the consequences to follow. These "floating" teams are extremely dangerous. Usually they consist of the most experienced surveillance officers, who know the KIOs and a lot of other frequently surveilled people by sight. These "floaters" are dispatched on random searches, looking for targets of opportunity and relying heavily on their experience and intuition. They're like floating naval mines in a narrow strait.

Victor's situation was particularly dangerous because his face was familiar to many surveillance officers. He knew it, but he also knew that there was nothing he nor anybody else could do about it. It came with the job.

The countersurveillance route was another problem. First of all, he didn't have support people to man the checkpoints. Olga didn't have any experience at that and so couldn't be much of a help. Besides, he wanted to expose her to as little risk as possible. Secondly, a long route took a lot of time, increasing the probability of picking up a "floater." On top of that, his long and unexplained absence from home could be noticed by his routine "security observation," and correlated with something the other surveillance teams picked up elsewhere.

Trying to tackle the problem from every imaginable angle, Victor still didn't see a clear solution. Either way, it was a judgment call. Victor prepared both scenarios and decided to choose at the last moment. Olga was fully briefed and ready.

On his way home after work he made his choice. *Let it be quick. In and out. No more doubts.*

After supper he lay down, closed his eyes, and tried to relax, all his senses in suspended animation.

20:35. Victor rose and slowly started to dress. The advantage of the short scenario was that he knew exactly how much time he'd need. There'd be very little chance of a slipup with transportation. *At least the system's good for something.* Five minutes to catch the bus, eight minutes to Belyayevo, two minutes to get a taxi, fifteen minutes to double back, thirty minutes on the Metro, three minutes to double back, two minutes to the statue. Sixty-five minutes plus five to spare.

20:50. All ready. He cued Olga.

"Victor, would you please take out the garbage?" Reasonably loud and distinct, for the benefit of the "house ears." The garbage-disposal chute was in the stairway, one flight down.

Victor needed to register his presence at home and still account for the absence of his voice. He also had to provide justification for the front door's being opened twice.

"Sure." All the appropriate sound effects followed, including the grumblings of an irritable spouse performing an unpleasant chore.

"Hell. I've got a splitting headache." The front door opened. Victor put the garbage in the chute and returned. The door was still open. "Olga, I think I'd better go straight to bed."

"Of course, darling. Try to get to sleep as soon as you can." A grunt of gruff agreement. The sound of the door's closing. Olga inside, Victor outside. He rushed soundlessly down the stairs. *It's amusing. At last I've found one positive use for the KGB's security system. I'm using their eavesdropping at home for a free ride to establish my alibi.*

Having successfully avoided meeting anybody in the stairway, Victor was outside. A brisk walk to the bus stop toward Belyayevo. This way, when he doubled back in a taxi, he'd be able to see the window from a normal passenger's view. The bus came quickly.

21:07. The bus pulled in at the Belyayevo Metro. The approach to the entrance of the Metro was an asset; it was through a passageway under the street. Once inside the station, Victor quickly crossed over from the crowd flowing into the Metro to the stream heading out to the street. Concealed in the throng, he emerged from the underground pass back on the other side of the street. The taxi stand was just sixty feet away. As he'd expected at this time of night, several cabs were waiting in line. Victor jumped into one of them. Back seat, right side. "Yugo-Zapadnaya, please." The taxi headed back down the route Victor had just been riding by bus.

21:13. He could see their apartment complex on the right. The kitchen window was dark. *No light is the green light.* Olga had watched Victor leave. If any person or vehicle had followed him, she'd have turned on the kitchen light to warn him.

21:25. The taxi pulled in at Yugo-Zapadnaya Metro station. Victor rushed in. *Careful. Quite a few acquaintances live around here.* He took a seat in the corner of the car, moved his fur hat lower, and put his chin down into the fur collar of his coat. His scarf was slightly sticking out. He was consumed with reading a booklet.

21:42. Kropotkinskaya station. The train stopped, the doors opened. A few people left the car. The characteristic sound of the car's pneumatic doors indicated that they were about to close. Suddenly, Victor raised his head from the booklet, looked intently out at the station, jumped up, mumbling, "Damn, Kropotkinskaya!" and squeezed through the closing doors. Nobody came off the train after him.

Two and a half minutes between trains. After climbing a flight of stairs, there was a long marble corridor with another short stairway ahead before the escalator. The incoming and outgoing crowds were separated by a series of square columns down the center. Right where the incoming crowd was thickest, Victor stepped quickly in front of a column. His move couldn't have been observed from behind because he'd just walked briskly up the short, twelve-step stairway. He turned and maneuvered himself to the right edge of the stream heading for the trains.

Along with a few people in front of him he ran to catch the train, making sure there was nobody running behind him. The train he caught was going in the same direction he'd just been riding.

21:51. Dzerzhinskaya Station. Victor felt a little tense. *Not only am I using KGB eavesdropping for a free alibi, I'm practically going through Dom 2 to get to this meeting. I wonder if irony has its critical mass. If it does, I hope I don't reach it.* All quiet—no familiar faces. Victor was still consumed with reading the booklet.

21:54. Kirovskaya station. Victor jumped off the train at the last possible moment—the same trick as before. *A good joke repeated becomes stupidity. You should have done something different this time, dummy.*

21:57. A long escalator carried Victor out of the deep station. He stopped near the map next to the ticket cashiers—a traditional meeting place. He studied the map, turning his face away from passersby.

He knew that he could easily have been burned already. The place could be crawling with KGB. Worse yet, perhaps the guy he was about to meet would turn out to be KGB. He'd have to test him somehow. *Not that easy without a long relationship.*

21:59. No one around. No passerby glanced at Victor for that telltale extra fraction of a second in that intense, abbreviated stare that was still considerably shorter than the gaze of a curious innocent. Victor unfolded his booklet, rolled it up in such a way that its pages would be clearly visible in the dimly lit area outside. He put it in his right hand and took a deep breath. *Well, as they say, you can't have two deaths, and you can't escape one.* He walked purposefully through the doors and up the stairs, wondering whom he was about to meet, the CIA or the KGB.

22:00. Victor came to the statue of Griboyedov, ninety feet from the station rotunda. He paused for ten or fifteen seconds and glanced around. Nothing unusual. The phone booth on the corner was empty. *Good. Any surveillance wouldn't have been able to resist the temptation to use it.* He slowly moved toward the alley off Chistoprudnyy Boulevard and put the booklet in his pocket.

Out of the corner of his eye he saw a male figure in a dark overcoat and fur hat approaching from behind.

"Victor Ivanovich?" A voice with an accent.

"Yes."

"Good evening. I'm Misha." He extended his hand.

Right, and I'm Napoleon Bonaparte. "Good evening, Misha. Nice to meet you."

They started walking slowly along the boulevard. After a pause, "Misha" broke the silence.

"I'm very happy to meet you. We're pleased that you could make this meeting and that you didn't change your mind."

"Changing my mind is not on the list of my sins. I'm glad you could make it too."

Another pause. "How much time do you have tonight?"

Professional. And a good sign. The KGB wouldn't think to ask the question. "No restrictions. How about you?"

"Same here. But we still have to contend with the dangers of meeting in the Moscow environment. I'm sure I don't have to remind you."

Victor nodded curtly. "Before we start, let me ask you a question."

"Please."

"Where did I approach your service?"

Misha smiled. "Warsaw. Do I look OK now?"

"Certainly much better."

"Do you mind if I turn on a small tape recorder?"

Trying to be nice. I wasn't born yesterday though. What difference would it make if I said no? "By all means. I'd like us to avoid any misunderstanding."

Misha put his hand into a coat pocket. "Do you mind if I am very direct with you?"

"I'd appreciate that. We don't have time for diplomacy."

"As you understand, we're very impressed with your offer, and satisfying your request in all its aspects is not out of the realm of possibility. However, as a professional, you must also understand that what you are requesting is a very serious and difficult undertaking."

"If it weren't, I wouldn't be asking you." Victor smiled.

"Of course. So we have to have a better understanding, what your field and level of expertise are, before we make a final decision."

"In other words, you want to make sure that I'm for real, and to find out how valuable my expertise is?"

"If you will."

"It's a reasonable request. Shoot."

The question-and-answer session continued for a while. Finally satisfied, Misha said, "I guess that's enough. Obviously, I'm not qualified to evaluate your answers. They'll be analyzed by our experts. But I'm sure everything'll be fine."

"I also would like to ask you a few questions."

"Please."

"How many of your people know of my existence?"

A pause. "Eight in our agency, perhaps five or six outside. Six know your identity, two of them from the little visit you paid in Warsaw. That's about as few as we can get away with. This case has been assigned the highest priority."

"You have to understand my position. Intelligence information has a nasty habit of finding its way back. So I'd be reluctant to provide you with any information you'd be tempted to act on immediately."

"Let me assure you that we wouldn't use any information coming from you while you're still here, even if you were to provide it."

"Given bureaucracy and high-priority political considerations, you can never be sure. But I'm glad we understand each other."

"Now, what can we do for you meanwhile? Do you need any help?"

That sounds right. The KGB would either ignore the subject or simply try to hand you money.

"No, thanks, I'm all right."

"Well then, how shall we communicate in the future?"

"Simple. Personal meetings."

"What? As a professional, you surely know that any personal meeting in Moscow is extremely dangerous and should be avoided at all cost. We have numerous very secure means of communications. As a matter of fact, I've brought some with me today."

"Yes, I am a professional, and I'm fully aware of the dangers involved. I also happen to know a few facts on the subject. For instance, not long ago I attended a CD Leadership counterintelligence briefing. They read out a very long list of KGB counterintelligence successes. That's to say, a long list of people who had failed in working against the KGB. The litany of causes was quite telling: 'caught on a dead drop, caught on a letter drop, caught on a brush contact, caught operating radio,' and so on. And you know what? Out of all of them—dozens—there was no mention of anyone being caught in a personal meeting."

"Well, I don't know. It's still very dangerous, for you more than anyone else."

"I can tell you the reason behind those statistics. It's because a personal meeting is a high-stakes event—for both the case officer and the station. Two in a year per contact is at least one too many, right?"

"Right."

"OK, so when a case officer approaches a personal meeting, he gives it all he's got. He's operating in high gear. With 'secure means,' like a letter drop, he might relax just a bit, get a little casual, and that's where the trouble starts."

"I can assure you . . ."

Victor interrupted him: "Look, let's not waste time. We'll communicate through personal meetings only." Victor paused. "Oh, another thing. All communications about me between the Moscow Station and Washington must be done by pouch. No telegrams."

Misha looked at Victor very carefully. He spoke slowly. "You realize, don't you, that if that's the case, this whole operation will take much longer?"

"I'd rather be safe than sorry."

Misha laughed. "You know, you're a very interesting cross of extreme caution and outright recklessness." He paused, and then added, "All right, it's your neck after all. We'll do everything in our power to help you and to assure your security. You're the one who's in the cold, and we'll play along."

"Thank you. I don't want you to feel offended, but because of my peculiar situation I'd really prefer to do it the way I feel comfortable."

"OK, now tell me, how many people on your side know about your contact with us?"

"Only my wife."

"All right. How are you going to manage these meetings with no operational support? We'll need at least two more."

"My wife will help me."

"Does she have any operational experience? And forgive me if I ask if you're sure you can rely on her."

"She is completely reliable, and smart too. As far as experience goes, she'll have some opportunities to gain it."

"Well, needless to say, I'm concerned. If there's any way we can help, tell me."

"I appreciate that, but I'd rather play it alone. Don't worry, we'll manage. What bothers me is the timing. In my position I won't last too long, as you know. And the Olympic Games coming up aren't going to make things any easier."

"That's for sure. With what we're looking at, I guess a month is a good bet for the next meeting."

"I agree. Let's say the same place and the same time four weeks from today?"

"All right. I agree—reluctantly. If we don't connect, then every two weeks. Same conditions. If I can't make it, Pasha will." The man took an envelope out of his pocket and handed it to Victor. "This is a letter for you from Washington. The paper is water soluble, so be careful. There are some additional questions there, as well as a few other ways you can find us if you need to—emergency signals, meeting conditions, you'll see. Disregard the part about communications."

"Thanks."

Misha turned to Victor and suddenly smiled broadly. "I'm really happy to have met you. Good luck and be careful, OK?"

"Same back. Good night."

Misha turned down a side street as Victor continued along the boulevard, crossing over to the sidewalk. They had parted at the end of Pokrovsky Boulevard, which was very close to Victor's clearing point after the meeting. The point in the route where surveillance would be forced either to show itself or to fall away. He heard the noisy rattle of a trolley car approaching down the rails behind him. The stop was about two hundred feet ahead, and a few people were waiting. Victor slowed down, to let the trolley pass him. It stopped. Then he sprinted and leaped onto the departing trolley. He stood in the rear and looked back. Nobody behind him. No cars. He felt a great relief.

Victor's return route was tricky. Anyone following the trolley by car was in for a rude surprise. One stop ahead, just before a small bridge, the street suddenly narrowed and became passable only by trolleys. The cars detoured along the bank of a canal for at least fifteen minutes. However, the next trolley stop, after the bridge, just two minutes away, was right by the entrance to the Novokuznetskaya Metro station.

There were no cars following. Victor jumped out of the trolley, dashed into the Metro, rushed through a tunnel full of people changing trains, and just caught a departing train. The Belyayevo line. He exited at Academicheskaya, threaded a complicated path through his parents' neighborhood, caught a cab, and headed home.

He had the taxi let him off at the building next to his and walked toward the entrance. Without raising his head, he saw a shadow in their window. Olga, waiting for him.

Exactly twenty seconds later Olga said loudly, "Victor, Victor, wake up."

A muffled growl in return.

"I'm sorry, but I heard a strange sound just outside the door. Please get up and take a look."

Another growl.

"I'm sorry, darling, but I'm scared."

The sound of the door opening. Victor stepped in. "Not to worry, there's nothing there now. Must've been some teenagers." A long pause. Victor closed the door firmly.

"How's your head?"

"Better. Look, now that you've woken me up, would you be kind enough to make some tea?"

"Sure. Sorry, but I really was scared."

"It's OK." He looked at her, silently indicating that everything was, in fact, OK.

Olga prepared the tea, shaking her head and looking at Victor as if to say, "Not only do you get away with this little stunt, but you want tea catered as well!"

Two hours later the letter had been read and the conditions had been memorized. One sentence in particular pleased him: "If you need any help, such as Western medicine, please let us know. We would be happy to provide it." This was far more considerate than the KGB would ever dream of being. One more proof that he was not dealing with the KGB. These were Americans. He put the letter in the sink and turned on the faucet. In a few seconds the letter had disintegrated into a light jelly, and then quickly disappeared down the drain. As if it had all been a dream.

CHAPTER

11

THIS TIME THEY WERE ABLE to connect. Misha caught up with Victor as he was slowly walking away from the statue of Griboyedov.

"Good evening, Victor."

"Good evening, Misha. I reckon you were under the weather last time?"

"Yes. We weren't sure whether I got black or not. Obviously, we couldn't take any chances."

Victor nodded.

"Well, I've got good news for you. Our experts were quite impressed with your answers. We've been given the green light for the exfiltration. My superiors asked me to tell you they have great admiration for your courage and are looking forward to meeting you in the States."

"Thank you."

"Meanwhile, this operation has been assigned top priority; our foremost concern is for your security."

"I appreciate that. Here are the answers to the questions in your letter." Victor handed Misha a pack of cigarettes and continued, "You'll find some important details missing. We can fill them in when I'm in the United States."

Misha shrugged: "I've noticed you don't like to tempt us. Don't worry, we've put a total blackout on any information you provide until you're safely out. How're you doing? Any problems?"

"No, not really. But time is running out for me, especially since I pulled a few stunts while trying to contact you. You never know if you've left any footprints."

"We understand that, and we're doing everything we can to accelerate the operation."

"In the package I just gave you you'll find our photos for passports and clothing sizes."

"Splendid."

They were walking through a maze of narrow lanes just off Kirov Street, both men automatically checking their surroundings. Everything looked peaceful and quiet. There was no sign of surveillance, those constantly changing but ever-present people deep in the background. They were on their own. Victor felt at ease.

"Victor, do you have any preferences about how you cross the border?"

"Not really, but I do insist that all three of us cross together."

Misha just smiled and shook his head. "Right. It seems to us that the simplest way to cross is to do it openly. Suppose we supply the documents and you three just fly out?"

Victor didn't need to think it over. He'd already considered that scenario. "Too risky. I've been to Sheremetyevo on business too many times. A lot of KGB people there know my face. Besides, there are built-in security measures designed to deal with that precise eventuality, as I'm sure you know. And they might easily be changed before the Olympics."

"I see. How soon after you've gone will they start looking for you? How much time will we have?"

"Taking a day or two off from work is not a good idea, right?"

"No."

"Then, the best I can do is from 7:00 P.M. Friday to Monday noon. Any time beyond that would be taking chances. Would you like us to get to the border under our own power?"

"Any problem with that?"

"No, but I can only do it by train. We can't fly."

"How come?"

"By regulation I have to report any trip out of town. If you fly, you have to show your passport to Aeroflot."

"OK, train it is. You'll arrange the tickets?"

"Yes."

"Good. That's settled."

Victor nodded, then introduced his embellishment. "Good. Now, Misha, I will need your help on something else. We'll have a tremendously greater advantage if the KGB is not aware that I'm in the United States." Victor paused. "How about leading them to believe we're dead?"

Caught completely off guard, Misha stared at Victor, trying to see if he was joking. He wasn't. Misha chuckled: "Look, let's just keep this professional, OK? We don't have time to fantasize."

"Misha, just listen to me. I think we've got a real opportunity here. For example, the three of us could go to the countryside, rent a rowboat, and capsize it. If it's abandoned near a large water system with a fairly strong current, it would be perfectly natural not to find our bodies. I know for certain that in a number of such drownings every year the bodies simply never turn up."

"No, Victor. Now you listen to me. Without mentioning the fact that a stunt like that would rob us of at least eighteen hours' lead time, I can guarantee that nobody in Washington is going to approve it. Our highest priority is to deliver you safely, without taking any avoidable risks. So just forget it, and let's concentrate on the task at hand."

"OK. Next question. What happens if the border crossing is aborted for the date you've set, and we then have to return to Moscow and try again later. We've got to get back to Moscow before Monday."

Misha thought for a moment. "You've got a point there. That narrows our options to only three possible borders: Poland and Czechoslovakia on the west, and Finland on the north. I think we could live with that. How do you feel about driving across one of those borders?"

"Fine with me. I was actually thinking along the same lines."

They turned into Khmeleva, a long, narrow street lined with old three-story houses that had been converted into apartment buildings after the Revolution. They saw them simultaneously. Their worst nightmare. Two hundred feet ahead, under the mushroom canopy in a playground sandbox. Two men. They could be anybody, but Victor and Misha knew instantly. Surveillance.

They looked quickly at each other. Victor's mind was racing through his options, and he was sure Misha's was doing exactly the same. The instinctive, human choice was to bolt and run back to the main street. *Surveillance is often obvious just before they make an arrest. Maybe the game is over.* The environment was not favorable. If they chose to run back, there'd be no place to hide. The street behind them, Sretenka, was a busy one, heavily patrolled by the Militia. They'd not get very far. The nearest yard with a through passage to another street was right by where the two men were standing. To get to it they'd have to pass only ten feet from the men. Without exchanging a word, Victor knew Misha would give him the lead.

After all, this was Victor's turf, and his stakes were much higher.

A hundred feet to the men. Victor's thinking accelerated. *Stay calm. Don't trigger their guard-dog instinct. There still may be a chance.* Then Victor noticed something about the men. Something that didn't quite fit. And then he got it. They looked cruder than the KGB surveillance. There was a decisiveness, a little too much self-confidence announcing, "This is my territory; don't mess with me." KGB surveillance is less obtrusive. It's trained to blend into an environment. *There may be a chance that these guys are just Militia. Still dangerous. They are rude, often jumpy. They can demand documents from anyone. Think fast. Just don't trip their alarm.* Then Victor looked across the narrow street and noticed another man emerging from the dark entrance of a building. Cocky and flashily dressed, he had the air of one who'd recently hit a jackpot. As Victor watched, the man spotted the guys in the playground. He was none too pleased to see them. In fact, he was clearly pissed off. *A criminal.* Like Victor and Misha, he seemed to be trying to decide what to do. *OK. Verify.*

Victor took out a cigarette. Without any warning, he turned sharply to the left and crossed the street. Misha simply stopped and watched. Victor approached the guy and asked him for a light. The fellow fished for his lighter. Victor nodded slightly toward the pair and whispered, "Your hounds?" Using professional criminal's slang for the Militia, he immediately established common ground.

"Mine. Bastards."

"Thanks." *They shouldn't go after us, then. I'm way too well dressed for them to suspect this is a criminal contact.*

Victor returned to Misha and whispered, "Don't worry, just shut up, and let me do the talking." Misha's American accent would certainly trigger a document check—every militiaman's secret dream is to catch a spy.

OK—he's my brother-in-law, and this is an emergency family meeting.

With the men now only fifty feet away, Victor became agitated. "Look, I understand that you're her brother, but tell me how a woman can do something like this to her husband? Don't you understand? I can't look my friends in the eye anymore!" Victor paused for a quick breath, "And don't you interrupt me!"

Misha, looking slightly stunned, hadn't made the slightest attempt to interrupt.

Victor continued his tirade. "I have no idea what to do now! Your fool sister doesn't seem to understand that I'll get an official Party reprimand if she takes this ridiculous business any further, and I guarantee you it wouldn't do her any good, either." *A simple domestic dispute. A husband* who'd been caught fooling around, whose wife had complained to the Party Committee. Common enough.

Victor's outburst carried them well past the men. As they'd gone by, he'd noticed they were dressed identically in warm coats, heavy boots, and reindeer-fur hats. They'd been prepared for an extended outing in the cold streets. Out of the corner of his eye, he saw the two men start to move in on Victor's savior. *Too obvious. The KGB's better than that.* Victor let his agitation subside. He and Misha turned the corner of the shortcut to the next street.

Victor and Misha looked at each other.

"Criminal surveillance. The Militia."

"How did you know?"

"Just a hunch."

"Boy, that was a close call. Do you still like personal meetings?"

"Sure. Now, where were we?"

"I was about to say that we need another month to get ready. Next meeting I'll bring your instructions. Let's shoot for mid-May." Misha was in no mood to prolong the meeting. Neither was Victor.

"All right. One more thing. If you'll bring me a miniature camera, I can take a lot of pictures before I leave."

"Jesus, Victor! We've never had a heart attack at the station yet. Please don't make one happen. I've told you, it's your expertise and experience we need over there, that's the most important thing to us. Anything that jeopardizes that has to be avoided. We appreciate the offer, but in this particular case it's a bad idea to take any unnecessary chances."

"OK, it's your choice."

Misha handed Victor an envelope. "Here's another letter for you. Next meeting in four weeks?"

"Sure. Thanks."

"Do you need any money?"

"Thanks. No need."

They parted, and Victor started his checkout routine, taking a route that would assure him of breaking whatever surveillance might by chance have picked him up at the meeting, but not yet identified him.

In the park, Elena was running and playing on the path in front of them as Olga and Victor talked quietly. They had much to discuss.

"So, we're leaving in six weeks?"

"Yes—but that's approximate."

"What did your contact think of our 'dying'?"

"According to the Americans, 'playing dead' is not a good idea. From a conventional point of view, I suppose I have to agree. And that idea with the rowboat has to be abandoned. We can't pull it off without the Americans' help. Besides, they've got a point, it would rob us of eighteen hours. Nevertheless, I'm still determined to try to lead the KGB to believe that we're dead. I'm going to do my damndest to pull it off. The fact is, there's zero risk in it. If we succeed, we'll have a tremendous advantage—not to mention that it would make things much easier for those we leave behind."

"Victor, I hope you know what you're doing. Speaking of those we're leaving behind, there are a few mementos I'd like to take with me. Is that OK?"

"Unfortunately, no. That's precisely what they'll be looking for. Missing memorabilia, photos."

"Victor, I'm sorry, but I think that you're too involved in the game to realize what a huge emotional toll this emigration is going to take on us— on you, too, not just Elena and me. Not to have even a family album is going to make it harder still."

Victor thought for a moment. Olga had a valid point. He was already putting a huge burden on them, so why make it worse?

"You know, maybe you're right. I think there just might be a way. Suppose I photograph all the pictures you want to keep, and we take the film with us. How about that?"

"I think it's a good solution. I also want to take some pictures from our families' albums, in the same way, of course."

"All right, but be very careful, and do it right away—don't wait until just before we leave."

"Is there anything else we need to do now?"

"Not really. The main principle is the same: keep as low a profile as possible. Don't make any preparations. We can't take anything of value with us: no money, no jewelry. Nothing. And no matter what, don't disturb the places in the apartment that you rarely poke into. As I told you, they'll study all the dust in the apartment very carefully."

Olga smiled mischievously. "You mean I don't have to clean the apartment anymore?"

Victor laughed. "That's taking unfair advantage of the situation. No, seriously, just clean things as you usually do."

Olga brightened for a moment, then sighed, "I'll miss my work at the museum."

"Of course. But who knows, maybe you'll get serious about your talent and become an artist."

"Well, I'm afraid to dream. At least till we're there."

Olga looked at Victor. Her smile disappeared. "By the way, all our friends are buzzing about your quarrel with Alexey. It breaks my heart to see you hurt him as a part of your plan. How could you be so cold-blooded? He's always been so loyal to you."

"And that's exactly why I have no choice. I must protect him. With some friends it's enough just to stop seeing them, but not with him. I only hope someday he'll understand. At any rate, I'm doing what I have to do, and I'd rather not discuss it any more."

They walked silently for a while. Victor was thinking of the relatives and friends they were going to leave behind, most likely forever. *Forever. I'd never thought much about it before, but that's a very sad word, "forever."*

He shook off his melancholy. *No emotions—too dangerous. The rule still applies, now more than ever.*

"By the way, there is one thing that you need to take care of right away." Back to business. "Elena could be a major problem during the operation. I'm afraid we have no other alternative but to sedate her with some kind of sleeping pill during the actual border crossing."

Olga just stared at Victor. No words were necessary to describe her feelings.

"Olga, don't look at me like that. I understand how you feel. I'm her father, for Christ's sake. But we have to face reality. If we cross by car, and we probably will, the slightest motion or sound at the wrong time could easily turn out to be a disaster. By definition, a five-year-old child is completely unpredictable, and we can't just hope for the best. There's too much at stake. There are plenty of perfectly safe medications for children that would do the trick. It will be no different than if she's slightly ill and has to take medicine."

Olga did her best to suppress her instinctive maternal reaction to the idea. "Well, I suppose there's nothing wrong with that. After all, it's for her sake as well as ours. . . ."

"That's right, and you need to get the medicine in advance—the sooner, the better. And please, don't ask my mother for the prescription."

"Right." Olga was eager to change the subject: "Do we need to buy anything special?"

"Only the luggage for the trip, but we'll do it later and very carefully. I don't want it in the apartment for long." After a pause he added, "You know, I've just had an idea. We're going to need every possible trick to throw them off our trail. Why don't you buy some boy's clothes for Elena—not specifically for boys, that might trigger questions if anyone saw you—but the kind of boys' pants and shirts and things that wouldn't be questioned if they were bought for a girl."

Olga smiled. "What kind of father are you? First you want Elena to sleep through the most interesting time, and now you want to deny her the chance to be a sleeping beauty!"

"Just make sure you do it, OK? We'll play a game with her, one that has her try and fool us by pretending she's a boy."

Olga just shook her head. "I'd like this whole thing to be over and done with before you come up with any other ideas."

"Not a chance."

The planning session had ended.

His final meeting with Misha was short.

"Misha, I'd like to extend my sympathy for that misfortune in Iran." Victor was referring to the mission that had failed to rescue the American hostages from the Teheran embassy.

"Thank you. It was a case of rotten luck. Hopefully, we'll be more fortunate with this one." He paused, then handed Victor an envelope. "Here's a letter with all your instructions. If everything's OK, and you're ready, you give us a mark signal one week from today. One day before the date, we'll also give you a green light with a mark signal."

Victor put the envelope in his pocket. "All right. Anything else?"

"We want you to know that we have done—and will continue to do—everything humanly possible to ensure the security of this operation. We're even going to run several decoy missions as a special precaution. But there is still plenty of risk, and we all know it, right?"

Victor was caught by surprise. "Illusion is not one of my sins. But why the decoys?"

"In the unlikely event that there's been a slipup in security, we'd be more likely to detect surveillance if we have several simultaneous exercises."

"I appreciate what you're trying to do, but couldn't one of the decoys tip off the KGB? Isn't the probability of that happening directly proportional to the number of decoys operating?"

"True, but only the decoy detected would attract their attention in this case. In regard to the actual operation, as all the decoys will start running at the same time as you, even if one was detected, the KGB wouldn't have time to link it to you and respond. All things considered, we're convinced it'll be safer for you this way."

"Well, your play."

"So, you don't mind giving us a sign, and then receiving ours? I remember how much you love our 'secure means of communications.'"

"How can I refuse you at least a couple?"

Misha laughed, then grew serious. Almost shyly he said, "Victor, we're worried for you and wish you all the luck in the world. Hey, it's better to be lucky than good, remember?"

"I'll take both. My theory is that God will help out, if you're doing the right thing, and then only after you've done your part to the limit, and then some. Even so, I will take all the luck I can get, though."

"You'd better go now. See you in Washington."

"Thanks, Misha. Thanks for everything."

The next day during a late-evening stroll along Tepliy Stan Street, Victor related the gist of the meeting to Olga.

"I was so relieved last night that they hadn't decided to abort the operation. I mean, after that crash in the Iranian desert, it's a real risk. I have to take my hat off to President Carter and whoever is running this operation in Washington."

"Do you mean political risk?"

"Yes. Not many people have the courage to undertake such a potentially politically damaging operation, having just failed one. Especially in an election year. I'm sure the Americans realize that if we fail, the KGB will make a huge stink, accusing them of kidnapping me, along with my wife and child. Can you imagine the fallout? I can guarantee you that ninety-nine out of a hundred people wouldn't have the guts to do it."

"I understand what you're saying. I've got to be grateful too. But, Victor, the whole business, the ordeal for the hostages, is terrible."

"Yes, it is, and not just this particular ordeal. There's a lot of terrorism going on all over the world. And by the way, most of those terrorist groups have been encouraged—in some cases organized—with direct or indirect help from the Communist Party and the KGB."

"But these people are animals! First, they hit defenseless civilians, then they exploit the limelight to blab their political rhetoric."

"I couldn't agree more. I don't think anyone who hurts innocent civilians in the name of a cause deserves the rights and privileges of a human being, no matter how righteous his political claim. And I'm convinced that civilized countries are far too considerate in accepting their 'political goals.' At this point, of course, it's a matter of legality, but I think it's time to change the legal definition of war. Given modern means of destruction, a small group can inflict every bit as much damage as a small nation could a while back. Consequently, any attack on a country's population should be regarded as an act of war against that country. Any attack against innocent civilians should be declared a war crime, and that's exactly what it is. As soon as one accepts that fact, the rest is unpleasant, but relatively easy. If the rules of war were applied to terrorist groups, these groups could be dealt with effectively. When pirates became a real threat, the world did just that and exterminated them. And believe me, sooner or later it will happen, there's no other way. You'd be surprised how quickly after that terrorism would go out of fashion."

"But wouldn't dealing with them on their own violent terms bring civilized society down to their level?"

"Absolutely not. Terrorists don't understand the concept of goodwill. To them, restraint is a sign of weakness. Those who are better educated cold-bloodedly exploit the patience of democratic societies."

"I don't know, Victor. Maybe that's too radical."

"Not at all. I can give you an example. None of these groups mess with the KGB, even when they're at odds with them and would love to. Why? The answer is pure and simple: because they know that the KGB would hit them back so hard that they would be annihilated—and fast. Like it or not, the only language terrorists understand is the language of brute force. And as long as their own language is not applied to them, they'll go on prospering, hurting innocent people everywhere."

There was a lengthy silence as Olga digested his words.

Victor broke into her thoughts. "Look, we'd better tend to our own sheep. We've got quite a task ahead of us. Olga, you probably have no idea how much you've already helped me. Now I'll need your help more than ever."

"I'm ready. You know that."

"This is the first time that you'll have to operate on your own. That's a big difference. We need to buy train tickets. Without my official privileges to swing around, and given the general level of confusion and incompetence of our transportation system, it may be much more complicated than you think. And we've only got about two weeks left."

"I'm sure I can manage it. I don't mind standing in line—I'm not a spoiled Moscow girl, remember?"

"Lines will be the least of your problems. Here's what you'll do tomorrow: in the early afternoon, slip away quietly from the museum, but leave your purse, scarf, or whatever will convince people you haven't left for the day. Can you do that tomorrow?"

"Sure."

"Go to the largest ticket office on Leninsky Prospect. I don't want you to look around behind you or anything like that, but still try to make a couple of sharp detours on your way there."

"No problem."

"Once you're in the building, go into the bathroom and change the way you look. Then buy four tickets—an entire sleeping compartment—on the evening train to Uzhgorod, for Friday, May 16. Not first class, though, just a regular sleeper."

"What if those seats aren't available?"

"Then buy them in two different compartments—or even two different cars, if necessary. But no first class, OK? We'd be remembered there for sure."

"OK."

"Then return to the bathroom, change your appearance back to the way it was before, and go to Ploschad Nogina Metro. If you have any extra time, kill it, but you must be there at exactly a quarter to six. Please, try to use the conventional definition of the time, not yours."

Olga laughed at Victor's gibe at her chronic tardiness. "All right, all right. Of course, you couldn't resist that one."

"I'll be there to watch for anyone following you. If it turns out you've been tailed, we'll have to do some fancy tap dancing to explain the trip, but I think I know someone who lives in Uzhgorod."

"So, where should I go then?"

"Walk slowly to the corner of your museum, go back into the museum, collect your stuff, and leave. I'll meet you at the entrance, and we'll go home."

"Easy."

"We'll see. Three days later you'll do the same thing, buying two return tickets for the Saturday evening train. They'd be looking for the purchase of three tickets—two adults and one child—so we can buy anything but that. Besides, we have to break the connection between the two sets of tickets. That should do it even if they're smart enough to look for two-way tickets bought simultaneously, with the return part unused."

Olga nodded, and Victor continued, "I want you to practice changing your appearance. You'll be doing a lot of it."

"But I'm not sure I know how. I always look the same."

"That's only because you choose to. As a matter of fact, women are much better at altering their appearance than men—they have more options. That's one of the reasons that where surveillance is concerned, women are more dangerous than men. Did you know that?"

"No. Why?"

"First of all, women can do different things with their hair—they have more to play with, and a different hairstyle alone can radically change an appearance. For example, Olga, with your hair down, loose, you can hide your neck, forehead, ears, and partially obscure your eyes. If you draw it straight back and pile it on top of your head, you automatically appear a couple of inches taller, and your features appear to be much sharper, more austere. These are just the two extremes—there are many variations in between. Not to mention that for women to wear a wig is not unusual; a wig can dramatically change the color of the hair, as well as the style.

"Secondly, women's clothing offers an infinite variety of colors and shapes. Normally, women take advantage of this flexibility to conceal deficiencies in their figure, but it could certainly be used for the opposite, to exaggerate physical eccentricities, or even to create an appearance of those, only to be used to conceal those same features later on.

"Third, there's the macho mentality. How can a macho intelligence officer concede that a pretty little woman can harm him? This attitude leads him to underestimate her—one of the most dangerous mistakes he can make. All in all, women can really change, take my word for it. Just do your homework, OK?"

"Of course. Now you've intrigued me. I'll start practicing right away. Maybe one day I'll be able to fool you!"

Suddenly, a black Mercedes passed them at tremendous speed. Victor chuckled, "Just like in the movies! That's something you don't see very often these days." Then he heard the distinctive roar of a charged eight-cylinder surveillance engine at full throttle. A black Volga flew by, obviously trying to catch up with the Mercedes.

From the sound of the Mercedes' engine, and the squealing of its tires, Victor figured that it was circling back.

"I wonder who the guy is—he's not exactly inconspicuous," he mused. They were about sixty feet from their building when the sound of the approaching Mercedes abruptly changed to an ear-splitting screech of brakes. Victor looked back and saw the car stop about two hundred feet behind them. As he watched, two dark figures jumped out and started a dash for the park a hundred feet away.

"Run!"

"What?"

"Run!" He almost yanked Olga off her feet, and they started their own dash to their building. Having made his drop, the driver of the Mercedes gunned his engine and made a fast getaway. Just as Victor and Olga had rounded the corner of their building, they saw the black Volga. *I don't think they saw us.* But he wasn't sure whether or not the surveillance had seen the drop.

"Victor, what was that all about?"

"The guy dropped off two people that surveillance had noticed in his car. They could have been agents or dissidents, who knows? The point is that the surveillance could have easily mistaken us for them."

"But that's ridiculous! We were just taking a walk."

"You explain that to the surveillance. Even now they can turn the whole building upside down and put everyone here under suspicion." *Damn, this is exactly what we don't need right now. On the other hand, it could be worse. Classic case of being in the wrong place at the wrong time.*

Olga and Victor quickly and quietly went upstairs. Luckily, the lights in their apartment had been left on, so they did not need to sit in the dark for a long time.

Another day, another problem. Victor was sitting in his office, getting ready to post the mark signal on his way home. *Charcoal. Damn. These guys are really something.* He'd only just realized that he'd overlooked a small but critical detail. The mark was to be made with charcoal. *Where the hell do I get charcoal in Moscow? There's none anywhere. A piece of coal might do, but even so, I'd need to go a hundred miles just to find that. Besides, it would seem a little eccentric for me to carry a piece of coal in my pocket. A piece of chalk would certainly be able to make a mark, but the Americans might go bananas figuring out what I was trying to say by using a color that was different from the one we'd agreed upon. So, black it is.*

He searched through his desk drawers. He found one black marker—too thin. He found another one that seemed OK. He tried it. Fine. He walked to the window, pushed the curtain aside, and looked out. It was pouring. The ink from his standard-issue marker would be washed away in no time. Victor knew the place, and it did not make him happy.

He walked two doors down from his office to the outfit that was traveling with Brezhnev. He wandered in, ostensibly for a little break. As he bantered with an officer there, he spotted it on top of one of the desks: a black waterproof marker, the widest point available. It would do.

He grabbed it. "Gee, this is exactly what our guys at Sheremetyevo need to mark boxes."

"Hey, Victor, this is larceny. We've got a lot of boxes to mark too, you know."

"Oh, don't be a scrooge. Traveling with Brezhnev, you can get whatever you want, and as much as you want."

After a short, fierce battle for the marker, Victor left with it, having vaguely promised something in return.

His target was a large bakery on the ground floor of a massive off-white building not far from Paveletskaya Metro station. Two ostentatious pilasters on either side of the dingy entrance bore witness to earlier pretensions of grandeur. The rain was heavy, relentless, and very cold. Victor really could have used an umbrella on his quarter-mile walk from the bus stop. The near-freezing temperature didn't help. As he slogged toward the bakery, he assessed the situation. There was no way for him to be alone on the busy sidewalk here, not even for a second. And only children write on walls, posts, and pilasters; too many people understand that there is only one reason for an adult to do that—to post a signal for another intelligence officer.

I wonder if anyone's ever done research on the technique of posting a mark in public unobtrusively. I really hate "secure means of communications." Hey, calm down. Here's the right pilaster. Wait, do they mean "right" as you face the building, or "right" as you face the street? I hate "secure means of communications."

Victor slowed his walk, looking around in eager anticipation of a meeting, as if truly relishing the bracing weather. He stopped near what he hoped was the "right" pilaster. He continued to peer out over the heads of the passersby, looking out for his approaching date. He leaned back against the pilaster. As if the cold, steady rain weren't enough, icy water from a clogged gutter poured down his back, just between the upturned collar of his coat and the back of his head. *I'd like to know why they pay the goddamned maintenance people. These miserable gutters haven't been touched in years.* Still appearing to search optimistically for his date, Victor uncapped the marker and brought it out of his coat pocket.

He casually put his right arm behind his back, exploring just how high he'd be able to reach to leave an easily visible mark. *Five feet is way too high. The most I can manage is about four. To hell with it, so Misha has to get his butt down some to see it.* He began to draw his "V" mark, pushing the fat marker into the wall as hard as he could. He attempted to reinforce both lines of the "V" several times, to make sure. *At best I look like a poet lost in creative reverie. More like an idiot daydreaming. Smile.* He looked around. No one was paying any attention to him, preoccupied as they were with the heavy rain. Except for a very old lady, who glanced at Victor, shook her head, and clucked in sympathy as she passed him on her way into the bakery. *She thinks I'm crazy. Come to think of it, she's got a point. There, done.*

Victor dropped his arm and put his hand back in his pocket. He started to move off slowly, still looking around for his date, then gradually accelerated into a confident stride down the street. *I must have a gallon of that damn drain water inside my shirt. I'll probably drip all the way home.* He looked back at the bakery one more time for his errant date. *My God, I've just drawn a memorial for myself! It'll be there for ages.* His "V" was at least an inch thick—a fat black slash easily visible a mile away.

Victor was thinking about where to dispose of the marker as he hurried home to a hot shower.

Keeping his emotions in check was very difficult. Especially those concerning his parents. Realizing that his father would have to withstand most of the burden of a KGB investigation, he decided against giving him even a hint of what was about to happen. It was a decision based on his father's own principle: You have a chance only if you genuinely don't know.

It was a slightly different story with his mother. As long as his father was around, she'd probably not attract too much scrutiny.

Victor's birthday a week before their departure was a good opportunity for them to see their relatives without any retrospective suspicion on the part of the future investigators. Both Olga and Victor had known that it would be an enormously difficult emotional situation. During the party they tried to avoid each other's eyes—both were struggling to keep their emotions under control.

After his birthday party, Victor took a quick moment alone with his mother as he walked them to a taxi. He took her arm and said, "Mama, I want you to be sure about one thing. Don't ever count me dead until you've actually seen my body and you're sure it's mine."

Five-alarm fire. She looked up at him. "Victor, what are you saying?"

"Oh, nothing. Just in case. And please, you must never mention what I've just said to anyone."

"Not even to Father?" The taxi arrived, and the others began to converge.

"No one else. You'll understand later. Nobody—promise?"

"Yes." She was understandably upset. Victor was sure she assumed they'd discuss it later. Good. He wouldn't give her that chance, though. It would be too painful for them both. He took one last look at his parents. He'd probably never see them again.

Checking for a signal is much more dangerous than making one. If surveillance notices a KIO setting one, it means serious trouble. The KGB has been known to maintain stationary surveillance near a signal for weeks, watching the eyes of all passersby to see who really pays attention to a seemingly meaningless mark. All suspects are followed and investigated. Victor took special precautions. After work he and Olga went to a store near Dobryninskaya Metro. Half an hour was enough. They then took a trolley car that would take them to another station, passing the lamppost marked with the signal indicating a "green light." The trolley was crowded, so Victor found a place to stand in the back. Olga stood near the window, with her back to it, facing Victor. He was perfectly positioned. Shielded by Olga, and facing her and, of course, the window, he could see everything outside without anyone's being able to observe him watching for the signal. The trolley ran straight down the middle of Vavilova. All along the sidewalk on the right, barely twenty feet away, every single one of the tall, reinforced concrete lampposts was clearly visible through the trolley's window.

Bardina. *It's coming up soon. Watch for the fifth lamppost.* Victor leaned toward Olga, watching closely for his lamppost.

The trolley slowed to a crawl in a portion of the street that was under construction. *What the hell's going on?* The asphalt had been torn up, and a new trench was being dug. Every single lamppost was gone! There was nothing left to mark the signal on. *I hate "secure means of communications."*

Later, when they'd gotten out of the trolley, Victor explained to Olga what had happened. To his surprise, she laughed. "Now I understand why your jaw dropped in the trolley." She grew serious. "So, what do you make of it?"

"I think it's a bit too extreme even for the KGB to tear up the whole damn street if they see a KIO putting up a signal. So, my relatively educated conclusion is that we've just experienced bad luck in its purest form. A week ago I drove by and that street was perfectly normal."

"What do we do now?"

"We go. I think at this point it would be more dangerous for us to wait than to try. We'll assume it's a green light and proceed as planned. If it turns out to be a no-go, we'll just use our return tickets as a fallback and try again later." Victor sounded more confident than he felt. He'd have much preferred launching the operation with the blessing of an unambiguous go-ahead.

CHAPTER

12

THE TRAIN LEAVES AT 20:30.

17:30. Victor was sitting at his desk, checking through his diary. The diary was filled with his usual assortment of appointments, deadlines, and things to do. He appeared to be booked solid for the next two weeks, a little more sporadically scheduled after that, with just deadlines. *Looks normal. Good.*

He'd taken care not to finish up tasks during the last few days, so there'd be no impression of his having tied up loose ends. *Business as usual.* He walked over and opened his safe. The usual stack of documents, nothing extraordinarily sensitive. He'd fed that stuff back gradually to the Secretariat over the last two weeks. Left in the safe, highly sensitive documents could trigger extra lines of investigation by someone trying to link his disappearance with those issues. These extra lines could, by chance, lead to his real footprints. He went back to his desk.

"So, Michael, any great plans for the weekend?"

"Not really. But I do have a party tonight, so I've got to leave at the bell." On Fridays, the bell meant 17:45, and one of Michael's virtues was his remarkable consistency: every Friday he was out the door to the minute—if he hadn't managed to slip away earlier.

"How about you, Victor?"

"As a matter of fact, this is a weekend I'm really looking forward to. Remember I told you I bumped into an old buddy of mine the other day? Someone I haven't seen for ages?"

"Yes. Who is he, anyway?"

"Oh, just a friend—really funny guy. We met back when I was a student on vacation. He has a child my daughter's age, and he's invited the three of us to his dacha for the weekend. He's a lot of fun. Never met his wife, though."

"They've promised rain, you know. So you may be out of luck."

They say that if it's raining when you leave, it means good luck for the trip. "Maybe the bad weather will be over by tomorrow. Anyhow, I can't cancel our plans. He was so excited to see me."

"Good luck, then." Michael eyed the clock on the wall. "Oh God, I've got to run. 'Bye."

Me too. " 'Bye, Michael."

As Michael shot through the door, teeth-first, the phone rang.

"Sheymov."

"Victor, where's your report on New York?"

Damn. Boss. This could be a real problem. Strange, he doesn't usually stay late on Fridays. "I haven't finished it yet. Sorry."

"Could you—at least once in a while—get your reports to me on time?"

Think fast. He doesn't stay late on Fridays. "If you need it tonight, it'll take me a couple of hours. When are you leaving, Alexey Leontyevich?"

"That won't do. I've got to leave in twenty minutes." A pause. "OK, you go ahead and finish it tonight, then bring it to me first thing Monday morning."

"Will do. If I can't finish it tonight, I'll do it on Sunday."

"OK. Just make sure it's on my desk before nine. 'Bye."

"Good-bye, Alexey Leontyevich." *Damn! Now the alarm will be triggered at nine sharp on Monday. Three hours' less lead time. On the other hand, it could've been a lot worse. Close call.*

Victor closed his safe, secured both locks, and affixed his seal. He sat down at his desk and looked around the office—its dull furniture and empty painted walls. Lenin's portrait stared at him. *Bastard.* He felt the familiar rush of starting-line adrenaline—an energized lightness coursing through his body. He looked at the clock. *17:55.* He was already ten minutes late. *The train leaves at 20:30. Go.* Victor deliberately avoided his usual route out of Dom 2. He wanted to make sure he didn't accidentally bump into Boss. He raced to the Metro station and pushed his way into a car jammed with the usual rush-hour crush of bodies. He assaulted the bus with the same determination.

18:45. Victor rang his apartment doorbell. Olga was waiting.

"Are you ready?"

"Of course."

Victor quickly changed his clothes. Five minutes later all three of them were sitting silently together on the couch in the living room. It was a custom few Russians would skip before a long trip or an important journey. Theirs would be both. Victor broke the silence. "All right, my beautiful ladies, let's go." Victor and Olga both kissed Elena.

The door clicked softly shut behind them.

Once in the street, they looked for a taxi in the pouring rain, almost completely hidden under two umbrellas. Victor and Olga were both wearing black raincoats, which nicely concealed the fact that they both looked a bit heavier than usual. Elena was in a very feminine bright yellow coat with a matching beret. The large gym bags they were carrying were brightly colored, one red and white, the other blue and white.

Victor hadn't ordered a taxi by phone. Aside from the fact that the service was unreliable, it would also be a touch too obtrusive for the forthcoming investigation. *They'll find our cab driver anyway, but let them work for it and be satisfied with the results.* Besides, it was useful to spend a few minutes in front of the building and let some neighbors returning from work notice how the three Sheymovs were dressed. To make sure the investigators would be looking for differently dressed people.

A taxi appeared within five minutes, just as Victor had expected. As they piled in Victor said, "Varshavskaya, please." Olga turned for a last look at the apartment building. Victor did not. *19:00.*

Varshavskaya was the perfect place to vanish. An underpass from the street led to both a Metro station and a train station. Southbound trains headed for the countryside—a fifty-mile stretch of dachas, many of them far from the railroad, and served by local buses. Northbound trains went to one of Moscow's principal railroad stations, and on through to a number of other major stations.

In addition, Varshavskaya was where one of the main highways to the south began, so there were always a lot of people being picked up by their friends and relatives in cars just near the entrance to the Metro station. It was Victor's plan for the investigators to trace them to Varshavskaya and hit a dead end right there.

The cab ride to Varshavskaya took twenty minutes. When they got out of the cab, Victor stalled by digging around for something in one of the bags on the sidewalk. He knew that on a Friday evening at rush hour the taxi wouldn't be vacant for more than a moment, even in good weather. When the taxi had safely departed with its next fare, the three walked slowly toward the entrance of the station. *Now the cabby won't have an earthly idea of the direction we took.*

Once underground, Olga and Victor fiddled with their umbrellas, marking time as they waited for a couple of buses to disgorge passengers simultaneously. They didn't have to wait long and soon found themselves in the middle of a heavy stream of people. They stayed with the crowd of commuters heading for the Metro. Victor knew that even if they were tracked going into the Metro, there'd still be a lot of uncertainty as to where they'd go next.

Their position on the train was not left to chance. They worked their way to the rear of the first car. The brightly colored bags went one on top of the other in the corner, and the three Sheymovs stood shielding them. *19:30.*

A twenty-minute ride brought them to Ploschad Sverdlova. This was one of the older Metro stations, with marble walls and bronze statues. There were benches all along the train platform, tucked into comfortably deep bays. The station also happened to be the major hub for the lines in the center of Moscow. They hung back a bit when getting off the train, and in a few seconds most of the crowd had streamed along to the platform exit closest to the center of the train. They slowed down some more and went over to a bench, unbuttoning their coats. Olga undid Elena's for her. There was nothing unusual about a couple with a small child taking a moment to adjust themselves. Luckily, the bench was vacant. Victor unzipped both gym bags. In thirty seconds the platform was completely empty. *Two minutes between trains.*

"Now." They took off their coats. Quickly two other bags—one black, one grey, quietly bought for this occasion the day before—were pulled from the brightly colored ones. The old ones were then tucked away into the new bags, along with their raincoats. Less than thirty seconds. Their practice sessions had paid off.

The next crowd of passengers began to flow into the platform, spreading from the central entrance out to the ends of the train. Now there was a woman in a nondescript ocher jacket, a man in a red windbreaker, and a little boy in a short green jacket—three ordinary people who'd apparently just missed the last train and were now patiently waiting on the platform where the first car would stop. *19:55.* They got on the train and continued along the same line as before.

20:07. Belarusskaya Metro station, with the train station above it of the same name. Final metamorphosis. Similar platform, similar bench. They melded into the crowd leaving the next train. Now Olga was dressed in a baggy dull-brown sweater that completely concealed her figure. Her hair was down and loose, covering her forehead almost down to her eyes. Victor was in a dull-grey pullover and a cap. Anyone seeing Elena's grey cap and grey jacket from a distance would have taken her for a boy. The trio was easily the most nondescript group in the crowd.

Out of the Metro station, but still in the underground tunnel, they stopped at a crowded popular meeting place. *20:11.* It was only a seven-minute walk to their train, which would depart in nineteen minutes. They had to kill between five and seven minutes. If they arrived on the platform early, they'd come face-to-face with a lot of other passengers. However, by five minutes before the scheduled departure, most of the passengers would have claimed their seats and would be preoccupied with getting settled for the journey. The train would most likely be late, but showing up late was also risky. Their tickets could be resold after the station bell had rung—standard operating procedure because of the usual scarcity of tickets. Victor wanted to take no chances in the station. *This place is full of police—some uniformed and some not—and these guys have professional memories.*

Olga knelt down by Elena: "Darling, do you remember the game we're playing?"

"Yes, Mama. We're playing that I'm a boy and my name's Alesha. But, Mama, why do you think all these people are silly and think I'm a boy? I'm a girl, and they should know that."

Victor was wondering how to come to the rescue, but Olga was quicker. "No, darling, they're not silly at all. That's the point of the game, remember? You're dressed like a boy to see if you can fool everyone on our trip. You lose if anyone guesses you're a girl, see? Whether or not you win depends on how well you play the game. If you talk about dolls and other things that little girls like, of course they'll know you're a girl. But if you don't talk too much and you carry yourself like a big tough boy, they'll never guess, and you'll win!"

"But I don't like dolls."

"That'll make it easier for you. Think of the boys in your kindergarten, then act just like them."

Elena shook her head. "They talk too much. And they fight. I have nobody to fight here."

The discussion about boys' behavioral patterns took up most of their walk to the train. It ended as they boarded, with Elena still only half-convinced.

They went along the very narrow corridor of the car to their compartment in the middle. Victor immediately closed the sliding door.

Two minutes to departure. Now it was Victor's turn for fancy footwork. A porter entered their compartment without knocking. That was to be expected. These guys ruled supreme in their cars, and behaved accordingly, doing pretty much what they wanted. *Keep a low profile. They remember.*

Olga shielded Elena, saying, "Alesha, please drink this. You must, if you want to feel better."

Victor, wearing a cap and glasses, quickly ushered the porter back into the corridor, and in a thick Ukrainian accent asked, "I gave you the tickets, didn't I?"

"Sure, but you folks are taking up the whole compartment, and there are only three of you. I have to put somebody in with you. There are a lot of people out there who couldn't get tickets." Victor knew exactly what the guy was up to. It was a standard practice, although hardly legitimate. The major portion of a porter's income came from extracurricular activities, like selling extra spaces and pocketing the money himself.

"Look, our eldest son got real sick at the last moment—some kind of awful flu. We had to leave him with my folks. I think our youngest son is coming down with it now. I'd be much obliged if we could just be left alone." With these words Victor handed him some money, half the price of a ticket. More than that would be excessive—and be remembered.

The porter hesitated, shaking his head. "But you've already paid for that ticket. If I sell it, I could get you some money back."

Victor wanted to settle the dispute as quickly and quietly as possible. "Look, I've got two sick kids, and my wife is jumpy. I don't need any fights just now."

The man put the money in his pocket. "OK, but I'll tell you something, if I had to pay someone every time my wife was jumpy, I'd have been panhandling long ago. Let me know if you need anything."

"Thanks. I'll come later to get some tea."

Victor returned to the compartment and locked the door. "It's all right."

"How did you manage to handle him? Those guys are so nasty!"

Victor chuckled. "It seems he discovered we belong to the same organization."

"What?"

"The brotherhood of oppressed husbands."

20:35. Finally, the train moved, only five minutes behind schedule.

* * *

Surprisingly, perhaps because she was tired by the adventure so far, Elena fell asleep almost immediately. For the first hour Victor and Olga looked out the window in silence, watching as the familiar Moscow scenery dwindled into the rainy dusk. When the accelerating train flew by the tiny station that was the stop for Victor's parents' dacha, they finally looked at each other. As they thought about everything they were leaving behind— friends, family, everything—Victor could see his own sadness and nostalgia reflected in Olga's soft, dark eyes.

She broke the silence and pulled them both back into the present: "You think we're OK so far?"

"Yes, I'm positive. Our little detours would have driven anyone tailing us crazy; they would have shown themselves. I saw nothing." *Unless, of course, the KGB has known about this all along, has us under blanket coverage, and is only waiting to see if they can make a really big stink. No, surely not. If that were the case, they'd never have let me answer all the Americans' questions.*

"I hope so." Olga looked at Victor pensively. "Now we're in God's hands. No matter what happens, Victor, I want you to know that I don't regret anything."

"I know. Neither do I."

They fell silent again. Then Olga said, "I spoke to my mother on the phone yesterday. It was so difficult. I don't know how I managed to keep my voice as cheerful as usual. There were tears in my throat the whole time. I started to cry as I hung up, having just promised to see her next week."

Victor saw that Olga was very close to tears.

"Darling, I'm afraid that's the price we have to pay for our convictions. It's not we who are to blame, it's the communist system." After a pause he continued gently, "Olga, we can't afford to become emotional now. The danger's not over yet, not by a long shot." *Easy to say.*

"Sorry. I'll be OK in a minute."

"Let me fetch some tea."

Victor left to find the porter. Soon he returned with four thin glasses in metal holders. They were filled with a steaming semitransparent liquid that could hardly be called tea. It was customary on trains to add baking soda when brewing vats of tea because apparently the soda increased the amount of color extracted from tea leaves. The end product, however, was a strange-colored potion with a baking-soda aftertaste. At least it was hot. None of them could eat, so the food they'd brought with them was untouched.

As they slowly sipped the potion, Victor tried to shift Olga back into combat mode by going over the details of their operation. "Let's review what we've done so far. Did you mention this trip to anybody?" *At least we don't have to worry about eavesdropping here. Trains are much too noisy for an easy fix. Besides, if they're covering us that closely now, we're already dead and just don't know it yet.*

"Just one neighbor. I told her we were going to the dacha of an old friend of yours."

"Good. One's plenty—let them work. Did she ask where it was?"

"Yes. I just said I wasn't sure but didn't think it was too far. She wasn't curious, and was more concerned and sympathetic about the rotten weather."

"How did you leave things in the apartment?"

"Strictly as usual. The refrigerator's pretty full. There are a few unwashed dishes in the sink. I even set some laundry to soak in the washing machine. I've left stuff soaking over a weekend before. It's normal."

"You didn't take anything extra, did you?"

"No, just the things we put together last night. Only the kind of stuff people take on a weekend trip. Except three rolls of film with family album photos. Oh, I paid the bill for Elena's summer camp last week."

"All right, I think we're in good shape. Now let's run through what's going to happen tomorrow. I still haven't decided whether we should stay on this train all the way to Uzhgorod or get off one stop earlier at Mukachevo and take a local train the rest of the way instead."

"I'm afraid that's your department."

"I know, but it's a tough call. Uzhgorod is in the border zone. On the one hand the Border Guards will every now and then raid trains like this one. They ask everyone for full identification and want to know exactly where you're going and who you'll be staying with. That'll blow up everything I've been lining up so carefully. Also, our being here would be registered, and good-bye to any hope that they'd count us dead. Besides, if the crossing is aborted for this time, we have to come up with an explanation for the trip. Of course, we could come up with a cover story, but it would be disastrous if one of them got paranoid and tried to verify it. End of game. But on the other hand, if we get off at an earlier stop and take a local train, we'll expose our faces to a lot more people. Also, even though it's less likely, we cannot discount the possibility of a raid by the Border Guards there either. On top of that, those local trains are much less reliable, and we might be late. That would mean we'd cross the border in the afternoon instead of at the understaffed lunch hour, which isn't the best thing to do."

Olga shrugged. "Victor, I'm afraid I can't help you here. . . . Wait, it'll be Saturday—that means more packed local trains will be running in the morning. Wouldn't a local train make more sense, then?"

"Yes, you're right. The possibility of a Border Guard raid on a local train on Saturday morning is nil, and it'll be easy for us to 'disappear' in a crowded train. That's it, then—we'll catch a local at Mukachevo."

After going over the details for another hour, Victor insisted that they try and get as much sleep as possible. *Tomorrow's too important to be tired— and who knows when we'll sleep again. Or where.*

Victor lay quietly on his berth. It was impossible to fall asleep. He knew that Olga wasn't sleeping either. Elena, however, was fast asleep—the untroubled slumber of a child. Nothing was going to wake her. Victor tried to block out the thought that this could be their last twelve hours together.

In the course of these recent events, Victor had now worked against the First CD, Intelligence; the Second CD, Counterintelligence; the Seventh Directorate, Surveillance; and the 12th Department, Eavesdropping. Now he was facing yet another KGB enemy, the Border Guards.

The Soviet border. Thousands of miles of it—over land, sea, and mountains—all equally well fortified. To call it a formidable obstacle would be a gross understatement. At least two rows of barbed wire, *zastava* or stations every few miles, machine-gun towers, a harrowed strip of land at least a hundred yards wide, then another strip heavily booby-trapped with flare mines, heavy round-the-clock patrols on foot with dogs, by car, or on horseback—endless echelons of all that stuff, starting more than twenty miles inside and growing denser and denser toward the border. Countless informants in local villages on both sides of the border. Victor felt relieved and lucky that none of that would be his concern at the time.

Crossing the border by car, one has to go through one or two preliminary checkpoints before getting to the main checkpoint, where a very thorough check is performed on all documents—for people as well as for cars and luggage. Dogs are led around the cars and the luggage. The dogs are trained to distinguish between Soviets and foreigners. One little suspicion—just one human hunch of a dog's dislike of something—and all luggage is searched, taken apart down to small pieces of cloth. Cars are disassembled, or rather split virtually into molecules.

It's going to be hard enough as it is. But with even perfect preparations, just one tip to the KGB, something like "Someone's going to cross the border this week," would be enough to get us all dead. For real.

Dogs are fed at lunch time, without deviation. Discipline. That should help us.

Around dawn he fell into a heavy, restless doze, the options and possible complications of the coming day running relentlessly through his mind. So far, since his initial visit to the American embassy in Warsaw, it had been a very smooth ride. But his experience had taught him to be suspicious when things seemed to be going too well. *Don't forget Murphy's Law.* Particularly when dealing with the KGB. With them it was all or nothing—either a smooth ride or a total failure, with virtually no middle ground.

Mukachevo, the last stop before their destination, was about thirty miles from Uzhgorod. The border zone officially began just beyond the small town. However, formal zone regulations were not enforced here—partly because of the distance to the border, partly because Uzhgorod itself was not a typical border point—it was a large town right on the border. But the main reason the zone here was not typical was that this was the border between the U.S.S.R. and Czechoslovakia—a Warsaw Pact country—and, therefore, was a little less heavily defended than were the borders shared with unfriendly countries. Most of the traffic to and from Western Europe crossed the Soviet border at Chop, a border town ten miles to the south. Consequently, the bulk of the border traffic at Uzhgorod consisted of local business and visitors between Czechoslovakia and the U.S.S.R. Nonetheless, one couldn't relax completely. Uniformed Border Guards were a common sight.

10:05. They pulled into Mukachevo right on schedule. The porter opened the car door and returned to his compartment for the duration of the five-minute stop. He had much to do before the train arrived at its final destination. With their few pieces of luggage, the trio quickly slipped off the train and into the station. Victor glanced at the clock. *10:10. Our driver makes his first one-minute stop at 11:30. If necessary, further stops every half-hour at alternating places. The next local train for Uzhgorod leaves in ten minutes and takes fifty minutes—maybe an hour. The Moscow train makes it in just twenty minutes. That's another good thing about this choice—we'd have had almost an hour to kill when we got there. I don't like the idea of shining our faces in Uzhgorod at all. Twenty minutes is risky enough.*

Victor bought the tickets, and they got on the local train. As they'd predicted, it was fairly crowded, but Olga managed to get a seat and held Elena on her lap. Victor stood nearby. *10:40.* Minutes dragging like days. *The driver should be going through his countersurveillance procedure. Hopefully, he's got black.*

Victor looked at Olga. *She's very tense.* He leaned to her and whispered in her ear, "There's still a chance we'll be going back tonight. We never did get the signal. Remember those stupid missing lampposts?"

Olga responded with a smile.

10:50. Victor touched Olga's leg with his knee. She looked up. He nodded slightly toward Elena.

Olga took the small dark bottle out of her pocket and said, "Medicine time, darling."

Elena's response was louder than Victor would have liked. "Why? I'm not sick. Besides, I'm a tough boy." She was certainly still playing their game—her way.

It took two minutes to negotiate a compromise—medicine taken in exchange for an extra half-hour up before bed that night.

Victor looked at Elena gravely. *My God, if you knew the danger I'm putting you through, my little darling. Some day, you'll judge me for yourself.* Dangerous territory. *Stop it! Concentrate.*

11:05. The train stopped. *Get out of the station. Too many Militia, too many security people.* Staying in the middle of the crowd that had poured off the train, they proceeded outside.

11:12. There were a couple of vacant benches in the square in front of the station. They took one of them.

Victor had visited Uzhgorod three years earlier, on a car trip from Prague. That time he'd crossed the border with all due official ceremony, salutes and all. In the evening, he and his party had dined with the head of the local KGB station and his top staff. After spending the night, they'd returned. *What if I were to bump into any of those people now? That would be the purest form of bad luck.*

11:18. The medication was working—Elena was dozing off fast, leaning against Olga.

Olga turned to Victor. "Why don't I carry both bags? Then it would be easier for you to carry her."

"No, I'm OK, don't worry. Just remember to open the car door for me first, and don't forget to close the trunk."

11:22. "Let's go."

Olga gave Victor a long look. She kissed the sleeping Elena, lifted her, and placed her gently in the crook of Victor's left arm. He nodded, and they picked up the bags and started walking. They crossed the square and proceeded along the right sidewalk.

After they'd gone about a block Victor said, "I never knew children grew so fast. She was much lighter two days ago."

Olga smiled. "Just make sure it isn't you getting older."

Two blocks from the station square. Now turn right. They turned into a smaller, quieter street.

They walked a block and a half. Victor said, "Time?" He couldn't see his watch.

"Exactly one minute to go."

"Slow down a bit."

As they turned right again, Victor glanced back. Nobody. *Good.*

Then he saw the light grey Volga standing at the curb thirty feet ahead of them. *Damn. The trunk's open—I can't check the license plate. Too late.*

He hissed to Olga, "Go!" Instantly, she went straight to the back door on the right side of the car and opened it. At the same time, Victor dumped his bag into the open trunk. Olga took a step back to let Victor into the back of the car, Elena still in his arms. Then Olga moved around to the trunk and dumped her bag on top of Victor's. She closed the trunk, closed the back door, and jumped into the front seat. The car started moving even before the front door was shut. It accelerated and immediately made a left turn.

As Victor was getting into the car, still holding Elena with his left arm, he grasped the back of the seat with his right hand, pulled and lifted it, swinging it forward toward himself. The whole seat pivoted at the floor line until it was standing up, leaning forward. Then Victor pulled the base of the seat's back up and slipped Elena into the space behind. He then quickly arranged himself on the floor next to her. *Practice makes perfect. Head toward the driver's side.* He lay face up and maneuvered the sleeping Elena onto the cushion of his right arm, with her head on his right shoulder. Both parts of the seat were shells, without springs or structure. Only the plastic material of the seat, reinforced with steel wires underneath, kept the shape of the seat. With his left hand he pulled the back of the seat down above them. It clicked into place. Now his head was squeezed between the back of the seat and the front wall of the trunk. He couldn't see anything. Extending his left hand, he finally managed to catch hold of the upright seat and pull it down into place. It clicked too. Only then did he allow himself the luxury of a long, deep breath.

The next thing he heard was a man's voice speaking Russian with a Polish accent. "Not bad, under forty seconds. Welcome."

Victor and Olga both said: "Thank you, hello."

"Peter, how are you doing under there?" As far as the driver was concerned, Victor was "Peter," and Olga was "Nina."

"Fine, I guess. I'm glad they were smart enough to cut out a good portion of the frame of the trunk wall. Otherwise, we might be in trouble."

"Everything's first class in this company."

I wonder what their coach class is like. Victor was really squeezed.

Olga: "How's she doing?"

"Sleeping like a baby."

Victor could feel the car making a number of turns. *Countersurveillance clearing again? But that doesn't make much sense—too late for that now.* As if the driver had read Victor's thoughts, he announced, "We have to kill some time. We took a peek at the checkpoint today—it's not too crowded. We don't want to be there before noon. A sergeant who's a buddy of mine will be on duty at lunchtime."

"Voitek, how do you pay him?"

The driver chuckled. "A few dollars now and then, American cigarettes, *Playboy,* some other crap. I'm just a small-time operator."

Voitek was just what he said he was—a small-time Polish smuggler. *But I know you're a big-time spy.* He worked the triple junction of the Polish, Ukrainian, and Czechoslovakian borders, sometimes wandering into Hungary. A cheerful, likable guy, he'd cultivated good connections in each place, and consequently was able to slip through the border checkpoints easily. *No system is impregnable, that is, if you're smart, patient, and work hard at it.* Voitek wasn't making a killing at his cover enterprise, but he wasn't doing badly either. The fact that he owned his own Volga was proof of his modest success. In fact, the Volga he was driving on this trip looked the same as his but was specially modified for the occasion.

Despite the cleverly concealed air vents—narrow gaps along the edges of the hiding space—Victor and Elena's "first-class" compartment was rapidly becoming hot. In addition, both were dressed far too warmly for the occasion. *It's the details.* The close proximity of the exhaust pipe didn't help any. Anticipating the problem of Elena's growing restive at the worst possible time, Victor opted for the lesser of two evils.

"Hey, cargo to bridge: it's getting real hot down here. I'm afraid if we don't cross pretty soon, she's going to wake up."

Victor liked Voitek's calm response: "All right then, let's go. This way we'll be at the checkpoint several minutes past noon." About thirty minutes earlier than planned. Victor felt the car accelerate.

Then he heard Voitek ask Olga, "Nina, are you sure you've got your cover story straight?"

"Of course." She was his girlfriend, born in Russia, now living with him in Warsaw. This was the first time she'd accompanied him on a trip.

"Do you speak any Polish? It shouldn't be necessary, but just in case."

"No, but I speak a little Ukrainian."

"Good. Pure Russian sticks out around here. I have your passport. Don't go to the booth with me, but don't stay in the car either. Get out, stretch your legs a little, but stay close to the car. Leave your door wide open."

"OK."

Suddenly, the car bounced violently up and down—obviously Voitek had hit a sizable pothole going at a pretty good clip. Elena's head smacked hard against the roof of their cave. The way they were folded in, there was nothing Victor could have done to protect her. He was both horrified and angry. Elena groaned as if she were going to wake up. All Victor could do was to put his left hand on her forehead and try to soothe her back to sleep. She groaned again, but more quietly, and subsided.

"Jesus, Voitek, that wasn't great down here. I could have crushed her."

"Sorry, Peter, my fault."

Olga's voice: "Is she OK?"

"I think so. She's fallen asleep again, but not as soundly."

Voitek: "Quiet. We're approaching the first checkpoint." He turned on the tape player.

Good idea, and Billy Joel's a great choice. Hopefully, it'll cover if Elena screams. But Victor's approval was premature. Unfortunately, Voitek liked his music loud and didn't realize that the car's acoustics amplified the sound in the hidden compartment. The music was deafening. *Elena's bound to wake up. There's nothing I can do. He wouldn't be able to hear me. I can't even cover Elena's ears.*

The car stopped. Then it started again. *Must have been another car in front of us.* The car stopped again.

"Your papers, please." *Border Guard.* "Destination?"

"Prague. Then back to Warsaw."

"Proceed."

The car started moving, slowly. Mercifully, the music stopped. "We're OK, so far. Two minutes to the main checkpoint."

"Voitek, the music's way too loud—it's going to wake her. Make it half as loud next time, OK?"

"Sure. Are you still OK down there?"

"So far, so good."

Soon the car stopped again. Then it was stop-and-go for some time. Victor's position was not exactly relaxing. A cramp in his right leg that had started earlier was intensifying. He clenched his teeth. *Relax. This part will only last a few minutes. Dammit! Feels like eternity. Concentrate on something else.*

What's the main danger now? Elena waking up. Anything else? Sneezing. They say the World War I pilots developed the best technique to stop a sneeze. Those guys had real incentive, too. Those planes were so unreliable that one good sneeze could be deadly— could throw the plane into a tailspin. Whether or not that part's true, the technique does seem to work: rub both sides of the root of your nose with two fingers. The problem is, I couldn't do that now for either of us, even if I needed to. Do people sneeze in their sleep? Damn this cramp! I know how to get rid of it, but there's no way I can stretch my leg out.

He heard Billy Joel come on again, more quietly this time. The car stopped again, and this time Victor heard one of the doors open. He felt the car rock slightly and heard the door close. *Voitek.* Several seconds later he heard a door open again, and again the car rocked. This time, however, the door wasn't shut. *Olga. I wonder how she's doing?*

A loud voice just to the right of the car: "So, you're still sneaking around, are you? Open the trunk." *A Border Guard.*

"Open it." The sound of the trunk's being opened. A short pause, then a loud, "All right, close it." Victor winced at the slam. Guard's voice, quiet again: "You old bastard, you must be doing real well—a tape player in your car, the latest tapes, a pretty new girlfriend. Say, you know Billy Joel's my girlfriend's favorite. Why don't you just give me a little present, she'd love it."

"Sure, I'll bring it over next time."

"Next time, next time. Why don't you buy it for yourself next time and give this one to me?"

"Sure, no problem." Abruptly, Billy Joel's voice ceased. Victor knew there was plenty of noise outside, but for a moment all he was aware of was the dead silence. Instinctively, he held his breath. Then gradually he began to hear other sounds: another car pulling away, other voices. The next two minutes felt like the longest of his life.

Finally, the car rocked again, and he heard two doors click shut. Then the sound of the engine's starting up, which to his ears was the best music in the world. The car started rolling.

"Stay quiet." *Voitek.*

Several seconds later, one more stop.

"Papers, please." Slovak voice. *A Slovak border guard.*

"Destination?"

"Prague. Then back to Warsaw."

"Proceed."

The car pulled away, steadily picking up speed.

"Bingo! We're in the clear. How're you doing down there?"

"Fine. We're just soaking wet. She's going to wake up very soon."

Somehow, the next ten minutes were easier.

"You can come out now, but you still have to keep your head down."

Victor pushed the seat up and gratefully took a big gulp of fresh air. Both Olga and Voitek were all smiles. Victor eased Elena out, and Olga grabbed her and started kissing her. In the fresh air, Elena started breathing easier and drifted off into a more stable sleep. Sitting on the backseat floor, Victor could finally take care of his cramp.

After a smooth twenty-minute ride on the E-50 highway, they turned into a small picnic area near a beautiful lake. Victor peeked out as the car stopped thirty feet from the only other car parked in the area—a burgundy Mercedes with German license plates. He saw two people waiting: a tall woman in her late twenties, and a short, trim man with a pipe, in his late fifties. Victor stepped out of the Volga and looked at the man. There was something about the way he carried himself as he approached their car. *Must be a chief of some sort, jumped in personally at the end of a spectacular operation.*

Victor smiled, took a few steps toward the approaching man and extended his hand. To Victor's intense surprise the man looked right though him, brushed past him, and went straight to Voitek, who was getting out of the car. *What's going on?* Victor was so astonished that his hand was still extended. Without turning to watch, Victor heard the man address Voitek in English. Although the tone was friendly, the voice had a distinct edge to it. It belonged to someone accustomed to command.

Victor had heard rumors about the CIA's obsession with control. *My God, those rumors must be true!* The theory, one of the most ridiculous in intelligence, had been dreamed up by some psychologist many years before, and had been immediately dismissed after being laughed at by every intelligence service worth a damn. The rumor was that the CIA set firm and total control above everything else, including common sense, and stipulated that control must be established right from the very beginning, and never relinquished thereafter.

I can't believe they could be that dumb. It's clear to any stupid sheep that this kind of obsession is a recipe for disaster. But if the rumors are true, then why haven't they tried this technique on me before? Misha was probably too smart for that.

Olga hadn't moved away from the car—Elena was still sleeping inside. Victor slowly turned and walked over to her. One look at Victor's face was all Olga needed to understand that there was a problem, and that Victor needed her to play along.

He was seething. *You want to play hardball? Sure, any time. I'll show you a little piece of reality.*

With his back turned to the others, Victor started telling Olga some funny stories in Russian. Olga played along, laughing right on cue. Her eyes did not leave his, and it appeared that the two of them were completely oblivious to anything else around them. Victor sensed someone behind him. He ignored the presence and continued with his story, and Olga continued to laugh. A moment later, there was a chuckle from behind. Neither Victor nor Olga acknowledged it.

Several more seconds passed. "Excuse me!" in heavily accented Russian. Victor started another story.

"Excuse me!" Somebody tapped Victor's shoulder.

"Will you excuse me, darling?" As he turned slowly, Victor's whole being communicated barely concealed irritation, and his subtext was crystal clear: "I was talking to a lady, you jerk. Didn't you notice that?" The chief was standing about two feet away, his pipe clenched tightly between protruding teeth.

"Hello," said the man as he extended his hand.

As if examining a lab specimen, Victor looked at the man's forehead, then allowed his eyes to travel slowly down, stopping at the man's brown shoes. Only then did he speak. "Who are you?"

The man was startled. At a loss for any better reaction, he said, "My name is Bob, I . . ."

Victor stepped slightly to the right, brushed past Bob, and walked toward his companion, who was standing ten feet away.

"Hello, I'm Peter. How are you?"

The woman, obviously Bob's assistant, had watched the entire scene and didn't seem to know what to do. Timidly, she extended her hand. "Hello, I'm Laura." Her Russian was impeccable.

Victor smiled. "Beautiful place, beautiful weather, isn't it? I hope you had a good trip."

"Yes, thank you."

"Let me introduce you to my wife."

Victor led her over to Olga. Bob had to move out of the way to let Victor and Laura pass. "Laura, this is Nina, Nina, this is Laura."

The women exchanged pleasantries.

Elena woke up, and the crisis subsided. Olga and Laura immediately went to attend to her, leaving Victor and the still-stunned Bob alone.

Victor pretended to look around at the view, studiously ignoring Bob. The CIA officer could take it no longer.

"Look, I'm sorry. I was rude. Tension, you know."

Bullcrap, the tension was back there, on the other side of the border. This part of the

operation is a vacation by comparison. Your rudeness was just part of your stupid insti-
tutional policy—and it's going to get you into trouble down the road. "I see."

"Let me have a word with you."

"Sure."

"Look, I apologize. This is no time to quarrel. Let's leave it behind us."

"OK, I wasn't a choirboy, either."

Bob chuckled. "You've got guts, I'll say that. With some it might work,
but not with your type."

"If I didn't, I wouldn't be here. Let's just forget about it."

"Yeah. OK. Look Peter, we've got to get going. We've got clothing for
all of you in the car—two bags. You have to change everything. Leave all
your stuff with Voitek; he'll give it to our backup."

"All right. Where's the other car?"

"A few miles down the road. Do you want all three of you to go in one
car?"

"Yes."

"OK. Let's move."

Victor and Olga walked over to the Mercedes to pick up their new
bags. "Victor, what happened? You were so mad."

"He tried to bully me, so I had to deal with it. I can't afford to be bul-
lied now. See, I'm not going over there just to pick up a bonus and retire.
I'm going to America to work, to fight against Communism. Whenever
you come into a new group, you have to establish yourself. And that
means you can't duck a fight, which you might otherwise do. Or you'll be
pushed around by everyone. Only when you're strong and well established in a group can you afford to duck a fight being forced on you. But
don't worry, it's over. I don't think he's a bad guy. Just a victim of their
doctrine. What's Laura like?"

"She's a nice girl, very tactful."

Olga took Elena behind some bushes on one side to change, and Victor went behind some others. Five minutes later they rejoined their drivers, who were chatting near the Volga. The new clothing had been perfectly chosen. Laura's hand was obvious. Everything was comfortable for
a long trip, just right for the weather, and fit well.

Their old clothing was packed up and put into the Volga. Victor and
Olga approached Voitek. *This is the guy who's really got a lot of guts. I hope
someday I can pay him back.* "Voitek, I don't know how to express my gratitude. Thank you. I consider myself indebted to you."

Voitek smiled. "Oh, it's nothing, Peter. Good luck to all three of you
guys. Have a good trip, and have a good life." He glanced at his watch.

"And now I really must be off."

Victor and Olga watched the departing Volga, the car and the driver they'd remember for the rest of their lives.

After the Volga was gone, all five of them quickly got into the Mercedes. They turned right onto the E-50 heading west and soon came upon another Mercedes with a couple inside, parked at a small rest area. They pulled over and stopped next to it. Laura got out and quickly slipped into the backseat of the other car. Both cars then pulled back onto the highway, Bob following a hundred yards behind.

"All right, make yourselves comfortable. We'll be in here for a while." Bob's mood was improving. "Here are your new passports and cover stories. Study them carefully now, just in case." He handed them each an envelope, and Olga gave him an envelope with her old documents.

For ten minutes Olga and Victor studied the papers.

Bob interrupted the silence. "Olga, there are two boxes in the backseat over there, with plenty of food. Would you play hostess?"

Olga? Oh, yes. Smart. Otherwise, Elena would start asking questions.

"With pleasure. I was just about to say that I was starving. Anyone else hungry?"

"Yes!" was the unanimous answer.

Showing a more human side of himself, Bob said apologetically, "I didn't eat much today either." He chuckled. "Nervous, I guess."

Everyone's afraid to express a victorious mood. No one wants to scare the luck away. Good.

After a wonderful lunch, obviously Laura's achievement, the general mood lifted even further. The beautiful weather and the gorgeous scenery of the Slovakian mountains made the ride most enjoyable.

Victor was studying the map when Bob started the discussion.

"From here, we have a few options to choose from. In Germany, we'd have the choice of taking a military plane or a commercial airline. In Austria we can only go commercially. What do you think, Victor?"

He's apologizing again, trying to make it look like he's giving me a choice. "I think commercial is better. Military flights are monitored, so a link could be picked up."

"That's exactly what we thought. So that's settled, then? Commercial out of Austria?"

"I think so. What's the sense in going to Germany? The border control there is much tougher."

"I agree. Have you been in Czechoslovakia before?"

"Yes, about three years ago, on a TDY."

"So, you know the borders here?"

Victor nodded.

Bob continued, "Then, in your opinion, where would be the best point to cross?"

He's really laying it on thick, but I'll play along. "Bratislava's closer, but the KGB is very active there. They do pretty much whatever they want. So, I'd vote for Cheske Budejovitse, unless you know something I don't."

"Great minds think alike. We felt the same way. So, that's where we'll head."

Victor smiled. *What crap. You'd already decided that long ago. The other "options" are strictly for backup, and a military plane would only be used in an emergency. At least you're smart.* He started feeling better toward Bob. The first disastrous impression was slowly dissolving.

"Bob, where's our backup car?"

"Two-three miles back. They'll stay out of sight. We'd only see them if we stop, and even then, there'd be no contact, just signals."

Good, they seem to know what they're doing.

It was three in the afternoon when they made their first pit stop. Laura came over from the other car to relieve Bob at the wheel. Bob went to the second car to rest in the backseat. Then they were under way again.

They maintained a steady speed, taking care not to go too fast. The last thing they wanted was an encounter with the police. By dusk the scenery had become less dramatic, and fatigue was clearly taking its toll on all of them. Their pit stops were brief—only five to seven minutes, just enough for gas, a trip to the bathroom, and a change of drivers. Victor's offer to drive was predictably rejected: "You're precious cargo; let's keep it that way. But thanks for the offer anyway."

Several times they doubled back along small roads, the backup car watching their tail. Each loop cost them twenty to thirty minutes. By ten o'clock Bob was getting tense.

"Victor, we're running a bit late, so we have to decide what to do before the next pit stop—about a half hour from now."

"All right, what are the options?"

"We can't drive all night. Between two and four in the morning there are virtually no cars out on the road, so the chance of being stopped by a patrol is too high. As a matter of fact, I wouldn't go much past one o'clock. What do you think about camping out, Victor?"

"I'd rather not improvise in an area we don't know too well."

"One of the people in the second car says he knows a couple of good spots, but I agree with you. I don't like the idea of camping out either."

"How far is your safe house?"

"About four hours away, so it's kind of tight."

"What if we went a little faster? As I recall, the road ahead is a bit better, we're almost out of the mountainous terrain. I think we could make it by one thirty. Should be all right."

"Yeah. Let's discuss it with the others at the pit stop."

At the gas station it was decided they'd speed up a notch and go for the safe house. At one thirty the lead car slowed down, approaching a small exit. With nobody visible behind them, Laura, still at the wheel, quickly flashed the headlights. The lead car turned sharply and took the exit. Laura followed, accelerating, to get them out of sight of the highway as fast as possible. Both cars switched to their parking lights and stopped. A few minutes later they saw a single car pass on the highway—their backup. Victor looked at Laura quizzically. She responded, "They'll double back from the next exit." Two more minutes passed. Nobody else went by.

Both cars pulled away. Two or three miles later, without breaking speed, the lead car suddenly turned into a driveway that was completely hidden by high trees. Laura followed. As they came around a sharp curve in the driveway, they saw the lead car standing with its lights out. Abruptly, Laura stopped the car and turned off the lights without shutting off the engine. They sat that way quietly for five minutes to make sure that no one was following. Their eyes got used to the darkness.

The lead car started rolling very slowly, still without lights—even its brake lights weren't operating, switched off by a special switch. The half-moon barely provided enough light to see the twisting driveway. Laura followed slowly. After crossing a wooden bridge over a tiny creek, they saw a small farmhouse with a large barn standing beside it. Both cars rolled into the barn. Two more cars were already there, a Volvo and an Opel. It was just before two in the morning.

After a quick supper Bob took Victor aside and unfolded the map. "There are two crossing points near Cheske Budejovitse. We plan to cross the border here, at Wullowitz, approaching from the northwest, instead of from the east, avoiding a direct route to Vienna, and going to Linz instead. Then we'll go due east to Vienna."

Victor nodded.

"We have to get out of here at dawn. Tomorrow's Sunday. The border crossing opens at eight. The morning traffic is heaviest between nine and ten. We should be there just about that time."

The people from the Volvo and the Opel went outside to keep watch. Everyone else tried to catch a couple of hours of sleep.

At dawn they switched cars. Laura, Olga, Victor, and Elena rode in the Volvo, and the others were in the Opel. At their last stop before the border with Austria, about twenty miles short of Cheske Budejovitse, Bob took the wheel of the Volvo.

They pulled up to the checkpoint at nine forty. There were a couple of dozen cars and a few trucks moving steadily through. As they fell into the line for the checkpoint, the cars had changed places, and now the Volvo was directly in front of the Opel. Slightly more than a half hour later, everyone got out of the cars. Victor, first of the group in line, handed in his and Olga's Western passports. Although Victor spoke only a few words of Czech, but he figured most people appreciate it when a foreigner makes the effort to speak their language—with the notable exception of the French. He smiled at the border guard and said in his best, broken Czech, "Nothing to declare."

Just then, the driver of the Opel, their new backup and obviously an annoying type, leaned in over Victor's shoulder from behind and loudly interrupted: "Somebody just told me all crystal purchased in Czechoslovakia must be declared. I'm sure he's wrong. Can you verify that, officer?"

The Czech officer, clearly not happy with the unceremonious intervention, politely said, "I'll deal with that question when your turn comes."

"Oh, no. I've already spent a long time in this line. And then you'd send me back again? I know all your tricks."

Now I'm the good guy for a change. Victor looked back at the interloper and in a voice that conveyed politely concealed annoyance, tried to hold his own. "I'm sorry, but it's still my turn."

The officer shot Victor a look that said, "See the crap I have to deal with all the time?"

The loud voice continued to demand attention. The officer's patience was wearing thin. Abruptly, he stamped Victor and Olga's passports, quickly dealt with Bob's, and then, smiling with malevolent anticipation, turned to deal with the driver of the Opel.

After a short stop on the Austrian side, the Volvo pulled out and got under way. Bob glanced in the rearview mirror and chuckled. "I bet our folks'll be there for a long time. I wouldn't be surprised if they got strip searched, just for good measure."

Victor laughed: "That trick's as old as the world itself, but it works every time. But I think we were in pretty good shape even without it."

"I agree, but a little extra precaution didn't hurt. We're in the clear now, congratulations. To all of us."

Everyone was happy, but too tired to fully appreciate the moment. Even as they all smiled broadly, Victor said, "It's great, and I know the main part is behind us, but I'd still rather postpone the congratulations till Washington."

Bob laughed: "Superstitious? You may be right. The KGB is very strong here. I even heard a rumor that they train the students of the KGB school in Vienna."

"No rumor. It's true."

They found their party at a shopping center in Linz. Half an hour later the Opel pulled in. They switched cars again. Now Bob and the Sheymovs were riding in a BMW with diplomatic license plates, and a second car followed.

In three hours they arrived at a safe house close to Vienna. Everyone was dreaming of a long, hot shower and a lot of sleep.

Early the next morning Olga and Victor were enjoying the garden of the safe house.

"Victor, it all went so smoothly and easily that I almost feel like we've just been out for a long ride, and all our old fears are fading away."

"Of course. That's a sign of a true world-class intelligence operation. A perfect operation always looks like one smooth ride. Outsiders cannot possibly comprehend the complexity of such an operation, how much effort and time was put in, and how many people it takes to make it happen. Just one letup by just one of those people could translate into a disaster. That's why out of the dozens of intelligence services in the world only a handful, but as a practical matter, just two, can more or less reliably perform such an operation."

"'More or less reliably' means, I guess, that even in this case the risk is great?"

"Absolutely. Lady Luck is very capricious. Take just one out of countless possibilities: if somebody lost control of their car and rammed into us in Czechoslovakia. As we were foreigners, the local counterintelligence would've gotten involved right away. Our documents and our cover stories, no matter how good they were, would've been uncovered in a matter of a couple of hours. Or if they simply happened to stop and detain us, looking for somebody else. Remember that stupid drop off by the Mercedes in Moscow?"

At that moment Laura came out with Elena, both ready to go.

Both the short ride to Schwechat airport and the long flight to New York were uneventful. During the journey, Victor began to like Bob more. He was obviously an intelligent and well-traveled man.

The approach to New York was a disappointment. The weather robbed them of the chance to see the Statue of Liberty or the Manhattan skyline. Victor was surprised and touched when he heard Bob almost apologizing for it.

"Don't worry, you've provided us with plenty of opportunities to see it later. I'd rather have this disappointment than any other slipup earlier."

Bob just smiled in return. When the Boeing 747 landed at Kennedy airport, their group was first off the plane. Victor turned to Bob, "Now, at last, it's time for congratulations. And gratitude. My deepest thanks to everyone involved. And thank you."

"Victor, it's only our job."

They followed the corridor from the gate to the terminal and were led to an office.

The reception ceremony in that room was brief, consisting of a short speech given by an official in charge of the arrival arrangements: "Ladies and gentlemen, we have just successfully concluded an operation that is not only of extreme importance to our country, but is also unique. This is the first time in history that a person in such a sensitive position has come over to our side. And it is the first time in history that a KGB officer has ever been successfully exfiltrated from within the Soviet Union—not to mention that that included his family as well. Congratulations to all of us."

All arrival formalities were quickly dispensed with, and in no time they were guided outside through a side door. To Victor's surprise, they were surrounded by bodyguards.

"Bob, what are they afraid of here?"

"Nothing, it's just a precaution."

They walked to a small twin-engine plane with the engines running. The six of them and two of the bodyguards boarded it. *The bodyguards look so friendly. So different from their KGB counterparts.*

Elena seemed to be uncomfortable with the air pressure in the small plane. She fidgeted for a bit and then, apparently remembering why they'd taken the trip, suddenly asked, "Daddy, why did your friend build his dacha so far from Moscow? Grandpa's dacha is much closer."

"Well, I guess he couldn't find a plot of land any closer."

Elena sighed: "Poor thing. This is way too far for a weekend visit."

Everyone who understood Russian burst into laughter.

Olga quietly leaned over to Victor: "We made it. I'm so grateful to all these people."

"So am I. A brilliant operation, thoroughly professional." He hesitated thoughtfully. "I wonder about the guy responsible for it. Not the people at the top, but the one who really designed this operation, who then fought it through the political and bureaucratic red tape, and finally assured its perfect execution. I owe him for more than my life."

"I'm sure you'll have a chance to meet him."

An hour later, the plane landed in Washington. They were met by a motorcade, which delivered them two hours later to a large safe house in the countryside. They were told, "This will be your home for a while."

Their long journey was over. Their new life had begun. Now Victor could afford emotions again. Finally, he would have his chance to start scoring blows against the Communist Party and the KGB. He was more determined than ever to fulfill his goal—to inflict the maximum possible damage to the ultimately evil system.

Appendix

A List of the KGB Units Pertinent to the Material in this Book

A full description of the KGB's structure, functions, and interrelationships would probably take several volumes and is unlikely to be written by any one person. The following is a simplified version of the organization's structure pertinent to the events described in this book.

The KGB was comprised of several major divisions that were independent of one another but closely tied operationally. These divisions were:

—The First Chief Directorate, responsible for intelligence gathering all over the world, as well as for influencing world events in favor of the Soviet Union by every imaginable subversive method. It was also responsible for preventing defections abroad.

—The Second Chief Directorate, responsible for counterintelligence, intelligence gathering within the Soviet Union, recruiting foreigners on Soviet territory for espionage, and recruiting Soviet citizens as informers.

—The Third Directorate, responsible for military counterintelligence and for ensuring the "ideological fitness" or loyalty of the military to the Communist Party. In fact, all the field operations of this Directorate were woven into the fabric of the Soviet military. Every military unit had a representative of the Third Directorate who was subordinate to the KGB, not the military.

—The Fourth Directorate, responsible for the maintenance of the nuclear-war bunkers for high-level government officials.

—The Fifth Directorate, responsible for suppressing ideological dissent, running the Soviet Orthodox Church, and laying the groundwork for the First Chief Directorate's subversive promotion of favorable opinion about the country's position and policy.

—The Seventh Directorate, responsible for the surveillance of foreigners and Soviet citizens within the Soviet Union.

—The Eighth Chief Directorate, responsible for the regulation and security of all Soviet cipher communications, the operation of all KGB cipher communications, and, up to the mid-seventies, the interception of communications all over the world. A more elaborate description of this Directorate is given below.

—The Ninth Directorate, responsible for providing bodyguards for Party and government officials.

—The Fifteenth Directorate, responsible for the physical security of the Party's and government's most important buildings.

—The Sixteenth Directorate, formerly a part of the Eighth Chief Directorate, responsible for eavesdropping on foreign communications all over the world.

—The Border Guards Chief Directorate, responsible for sealing off and securing the country's entire border.

—The Government Communications Directorate, responsible for the government's and the Party Central Committee's telephone communications.

—The Technical Operational Support Directorate, responsible for technical support not covered by specialized units.

—The Household Directorate, responsible for supplying the KGB with everything from tanks and aircraft to pencils and sandwiches.

There were also some independent units smaller than a Chief Directorate or a Directorate and directly subordinate to the leadership of the KGB, such as the Twelfth Department, which was responsible for eavesdropping on the telephone calls of high-level Soviet government officials and some foreign diplomats inside the country.

The formal structure of the KGB was pyramidal, so Chief Directorates were comprised of Directorates, which were themselves made up of Departments. The Departments had Sections, and the Sections were comprised of Groups. The number designations were confusing, even to KGB insiders. This was deliberate, and was intended to protect the organization from minor leaks about the KGB's operations. A classic example was the common mixing up of the Sixteenth Directorate of the KGB, involved in "Sigint" (signal intelligence) operations, with the Sixteenth Department of the First Chief Directorate, strictly a "Humint" (human intelligence) unit, responsible for running so-called "especially valuable agents," a substantial number of whom were foreign cipher clerks. Both were called "the Sixteenth" in the jargon. When somebody referred to "the Sixteenth," only those who really knew the organization would understand which unit was intended. And even most officers in the First Chief Directorate did not.

To help the reader more easily understand the terminology used in this book, the formal structure of the Eighth Chief Directorate follows:

—Directorate A was responsible for providing all the cipher communications of the KGB and the leadership of the country, as well as training its officers, guaranteeing the overall security (including technical, operational, and personnel) of the cipher communications of the KGB, and supervising the development and installation of new cipher equipment.

—Directorate B was responsible for the production of all the cipher keys for the country's communications.

—Directorate C was responsible for the technical security of the country's cipher communications and for supervising the development of new equipment.

Going further down the pyramid of Directorate A of the Eighth CD, there was:

—The First Department, responsible for the cipher communications of the KGB with its stations abroad, except for communications with the Illegals (Soviet spies working abroad under the cover of foreign nationals).

—The Second Department, responsible for the cipher communications of the KGB inside the country.

—The Third Department, described below.

—The Fourth Department, responsible for the maintenance of the nuclear wartime cipher communications for high-level government officials. This Department worked closely with the KGB's Fourth Directorate.

In addition to the Departments, there were three Sections, which reported directly to the Directorate Chief. They were responsible for communications with all the KGB Illegals, for the communications of the top government officials on visits abroad, and for the supplies of the Directorate.

The structure of the Third Department was as follows:

—The First Section, responsible for training the Directorate officers.

—The Second Section, responsible for supervising the development of new cipher equipment.

—The Third Section, responsible for the overall security of KGB cipher communications, new installations abroad, and relevant personnel traveling abroad.

About the Author

Victor Sheymov was born in Moscow on May 9, 1946, to a well-educated family. Both his parents were World War II veterans. His father, a military scientist, was one of the founders of the Soviet ICBM program; his mother was a respected physician. Sheymov attended the elite Bauman Institute, or Moscow State Technical University, where the future executives of the Soviet military-industrial complex received the most rigorous six-year training in technology and management. Sheymov graduated in 1969 and went on to a top-secret scientific research institute at the Ministry of Defense, whose mission was the development of a Soviet Star Wars program—some fifteen years before the U.S. decided to embark on its own SDI program. There, Sheymov was part of a team working on guidance systems for satellite weapons.

Sheymov left the institute in 1971 to join the KGB. He was assigned to the supersecret Eighth Chief Directorate, which at the time was in charge of the KGB's global communications and eavesdropping systems. His specialty was cipher-communications security, and he worked in an inner tower of Moscow Center at Dzerzhinsky Square, then the headquarters of the KGB.

The KGB is highly compartmentalized, but Sheymov, picked as a future leader, was carefully trained in every major aspect of KGB operations. By 1976 he had become the Eighth Chief Directorate's ace troubleshooter. In 1978 he was promoted to major, having moved up four ranks in just five years. He was given broad responsibilities in a major upgrade of KGB cipher-communications security.

His unique access gave Sheymov a perspective on the methods and purposes of the KGB that cumulatively led to his disillusionment, not only with the KGB, but with the Soviet state and the ideology of Communism. He resolved to escape, and to inflict the greatest possible damage on the KGB and its master, the Communist Party.

In 1980, after establishing a contact with the CIA, Victor and his wife, Olga, and their five-year-old daughter were exfiltrated from Moscow. The KGB were even persuaded that they were dead. For his contribution to the national security of the United States, Sheymov was awarded the CIA's highest medal.

Now a U.S. citizen with an MBA from a major American university, Victor Sheymov is a business consultant, and writes articles for a variety of publications. His wife, Olga, having received her second degree in the United States, pursues her career as an artist.

The **Naval Institute Press** is the book-publishing arm of the U.S. Naval Institute, a private, nonprofit society for sea service professionals and others who share an interest in naval and maritime affairs. Established in 1873 at the U.S. Naval Academy in Annapolis, Maryland, where its offices remain, today the Naval Institute has more than 100,000 members worldwide.

Members of the Naval Institute receive the influential monthly magazine *Proceedings* and discounts on fine nautical prints, ship and aircraft photos, and subscriptions to the quarterly *Naval History* magazine. They also have access to the transcripts of the Institute's Oral History Program and get discounted admission to any of the Institute-sponsored seminars offered around the country.

The Naval Institute's book-publishing program, begun in 1898 with basic guides to naval practices, has broadened its scope in recent years to include books of more general interest. Now the Naval Institute Press publishes more than sixty titles each year, ranging from how-to books on boating and navigation to battle histories, biographies, ship and aircraft guides, and novels. Institute members receive discounts on the Press's nearly 400 books in print.

Full-time students are eligible for special half-price membership rates. Life memberships are also available.

For a free catalog describing Naval Institute Press books currently available, and for further information about U.S. Naval Institute membership, please write to:

Membership & Communications Department
U.S. Naval Institute
118 Maryland Avenue
Annapolis, Maryland 21402-5035

Or call, toll-free, (800) 233-USNI.

THE NAVAL INSTITUTE PRESS

TOWER OF SECRETS
A Real Life Spy Thriller

Designed by Karen L. White

Set in Monotype Baskerville on a Macintosh IIci
and output by BG Composition
Baltimore, Maryland

Printed on 50-lb. Domtar Perfection antique
and bound in Holliston Crown Linen
by the Maple-Vail Book Manufacturing Group
York, Pennsylvania